Lecture Notes in Computer Science

Edited by G. Goos, J. Hartmanis, and J. van Le

Lecture Notes in Computer Science

Springer
Berlin
Heidelberg
New York
Barcelona
Hong Kong
London
Milan
Paris
Singapore
Tokyo

Roland Backhouse   José Nuno Oliveira (Eds.)

Mathematics of Program Construction

5th International Conference, MPC 2000
Ponte de Lima, Portugal, July 3-5, 2000
Proceedings

 Springer

Series Editors

Gerhard Goos, Karlsruhe University, Germany
Juris Hartmanis, Cornell University, NY, USA
Jan van Leeuwen, Utrecht University, The Netherlands

Volume Editors

Roland Backhouse
University of Nottingham
School of Computer Science and Information Technology
Jubilee Campus, Nottingham NG8 1BB, UK
E-mail: rcb@cs.nott.ac.uk

José Nuno Oliveira
Universidade do Minho, Departamento de Informática
Campus de Gualtar, 4700-320 Braga, Portugal
E-mail: jno@di.uminho.pt

Cataloging-in-Publication Data applied for

Die Deutsche Bibliothek - CIP-Einheitsaufnahme

Mathematics of program construction : 5th international conference ;
proceedings / MPC 2000, Ponte de Lima, Portugal, July 3 - 5, 2000.
Roland Backhouse ; José Nuno Oliveira (ed.). - Berlin ; Heidelberg ;
New York ; Barcelona ; Hong Kong ; London ; Milan ; Paris ; Singapore ;
Tokyo : Springer, 2000
  (Lecture notes in computer science ; Vol. 1837)
  ISBN 3-540-67727-5

CR Subject Classification (1998): D.1-2, F.2-4, G.2

ISSN 0302-9743
ISBN 3-540-67727-5 Springer-Verlag Berlin Heidelberg New York

Springer is a company in the BertelsmannSpringer publishing group.
© Springer-Verlag Berlin Heidelberg 2000

Typesetting: Camera-ready by author, data conversion by Da-TeX Gerd Blumenstein
Printed on acid-free paper   SPIN: 10722010   06/3142 – 5 4 3 2 1 0

Preface

This volume contains the proceedings of MPC 2000, the fifth international conference on Mathematics of Program Construction. This series of conferences aims to promote the development of mathematical principles and techniques that are demonstrably useful and usable in the process of constructing computer programs (whether implemented in hardware or software). The focus is on techniques that combine precision with concision, enabling programs to be constructed by formal calculation. Within this theme, the scope of the series is very diverse, including programming methodology, program specification and transformation, programming paradigms, programming calculi, and programming language semantics.

The quality of the papers submitted to the conference was in general very high. However, the number of submissions has decreased compared to the previous conferences in the series. Each paper was refereed by at least five and often more committee members. In order to maintain the high standards of the conference the committee took a stringent view on quality; this has meant that, in some cases, a paper was rejected even though there was a basis for a good conference or journal paper but the submitted paper did not meet the committee's required standards. In a few cases a good paper was rejected on the grounds that it did not fit within the scope of the conference.

In addition to the 12 papers selected for presentation by the program committee, this volume contains the extended abstracts of three invited talks: *Integrating Programming, Properties, and Validation*, by Mark Jones (Oregon Graduate Institute, USA); *Regular Expressions Revisited: a Coinductive Approach to Streams, Automata, and Power Series*, by Jan Rutten (CWI, The Netherlands), and *Formal Methods and Dependability*, by Cliff Jones (University of Newcastle, UK).

The conference took place in Ponte de Lima, Portugal and was organized by the Informatics Department of Minho University, Braga, Portugal. The previous four conferences were held in 1989 at Twente, The Netherlands, in 1992 at Oxford, United Kingdom, in 1995 at Kloster Irsee, Germany, and in 1998 at Marstrand near Göteborg in Sweden. The proceedings of these conferences were published as LNCS 375, 669, 947, and 1422, respectively.

Four international events were co-located with the conference: the second workshop on *Constructive Methods for Parallel Programming*, the second workshop on *Generic Programming*, the workshop on *Subtyping and Dependent Types in Programming*, and the third workshop on *Attribute Grammars and their Applications*. We thank the organizers of these events for their interest in sharing the atmosphere of the conference.

April 2000

Roland Backhouse
José Nuno Oliveira

Acknowledgements

We are very grateful to the members of the program committee and their referees for their care and diligence in reviewing the submitted papers. We are also grateful to the local organization and the sponsoring institutions.

Program Committee

Roland Backhouse (co-chair, UK)
Richard Bird (UK)
Eerke Boiten (UK)
Dave Carrington (Australia)
Jules Desharnais (Canada)
José Fiadeiro (Portugal)
Jeremy Gibbons (UK)
Lindsay Groves (New Zealand)
Zhenjiang Hu (Japan)
John Hughes (Sweden)
Johan Jeuring (The Netherlands)
Burghard von Karger (Germany)
Dick Kieburtz (USA)

Carlos Delgado Kloos (Spain)
K. Rustan M. Leino (USA)
Christian Lengauer (Germany)
Lambert Meertens (The Netherlands)
Sigurd Meldal (Norway)
Eugenio Moggi (Italy)
Bernhard Moeller (Germany)
Oege de Moor (UK)
Dave Naumann (USA)
José N. Oliveira (co-chair, Portugal)
Kaisa Sere (Finland)
Mark Utting (New Zealand)
Phil Wadler (USA)

Organizing Committee

Pedro Rangel Henriques
Luís Soares Barbosa

José Bernardo Barros
Carla Oliveira

Sponsoring Institutions

The generous support of the following companies and institutions is gratefully acknowledged:

Universidade do Minho, Braga
Câmara Municipal, Ponte de Lima
Fundação para a Ciência e a Tecnologia (FAC Program), Portugal
Adega Cooperativa, Ponte de Lima
Andersen Consulting, Lisbon
Enabler, Porto
Pahldata, Lisbon
SIBS - Sociedade Interbancária de Serviços, Lisbon
Sidereus Ltd, Porto
TURIHAB - Solares de Portugal, Ponte de Lima

External Referees

All submitted papers were reviewed by members of the program committee and a number of external referees, who produced extensive review reports and without whose work the conference would lose its quality standards. To the best of our knowledge the list below is accurate. We apologize for any omissions or inaccuracies.

Scott Aaronson
Mikhail Auguston
Nuno Barreiro
Peter T. Breuer
Sharon Curtis
John Derrick
Thorsten Ehm
Colin Fidge
Marc Frappier
Daniel Fridlender
Sergei Gorlatch
Ian Hayes
Lorenz Huelsbergen
Graham Hutton

Patrik Jansson
Linas Laibinis
Antónia Lopes
A.K. McIver
Ray Nickson
Isabel Nunes
Peter C. Ölveczky
Dusko Pavlovic
John Reynolds
Markus Roggenbach
Mauno Rönkkö
Jeff Sanders
Bernhard Schätz
Tim Sheard

Mark Shields
Ganesh Sittampalam
Graeme Smith
Mike Spivey
Richard St-Denis
Ketil Stoelen
Elena Troubitsyna
Axel Wabenhorst
Michal Walicki
David Walker
Heike Wehrheim
Michel Wermelinger
Jim Woodcock

Table of Contents

Integrating Programming, Properties, and Validation

Mark P. Jones

Department of Computer Science and Engineering
Oregon Graduate Institute of Science and Technology
Beaverton, Oregon, USA
mpj@cse.ogi.edu

Current program development environments provide excellent support for many desirable aspects of modern software applications such as performance and interoperability, but almost no support for features that could directly enhance correctness and reliability. In this talk, I will describe the first steps that we are making in a project to develop a new kind of program development environment. Our goal is to produce a tool that actively supports and encourages its users in thinking about, stating, and validating key properties of software as an integral part of the programming process.

The environment that we are designing will allow programmers to assert properties of program elements as part of their source code, capturing intuitions and insights about its behavior at the time it is written. These property assertions will also provide an opportunity to give more precise interfaces to software components and libraries. Even by themselves, assertions can provide valuable documentation, and can be type checked to ensure a base level of consistency with executable portions of the program. Critically, however, our environment will allow property assertions to be annotated with "certificates" that provide evidence of validity. By adopting a generic interface, many different forms of certificate will be supported, offering a wide range of validation options—from low-cost instrumentation and automated testing, to machine-assisted proof and formal methods. Individual properties and certificates may pass through several points on this spectrum as development progresses, and as higher levels of assurance are required. To complete the environment, a suite of "property management" tools will provide users with facilities to browse or report on the status of properties and associated certificates within a program, and to explore different validation strategies.

We plan to evaluate our system by applying it to some real-world, security related problems, and we hope to demonstrate that it can contribute to the development of more robust and dependable software applications. For example, a tighter integration between programming and validation should provide the mechanisms that we need to move towards a model for accountability in software, and away from the ubiquitous "as is" warranties that we see today. More specifically, this could allow vendors to provide and sell software on the strength of firm *guarantees* about its behavior, and allow users to identify the responsible parties when a software system fails.

R. Backhouse and J. N. Oliveira (Eds.): MPC 2000, LNCS 1837, pp. 1–1, 2000.

Polytypic Values Possess Polykinded Types

Ralf Hinze

Institut für Informatik III, Universität Bonn
Römerstraße 164, 53117 Bonn, Germany
ralf@informatik.uni-bonn.de
http://www.informatik.uni-bonn.de/~ralf/

Abstract. A polytypic value is one that is defined by induction on the structure of types. In Haskell types are assigned so-called kinds that distinguish between manifest types like the type of integers and functions on types like the list type constructor. Previous approaches to polytypic programming were restricted in that they only allowed to parameterize values by types of one fixed kind. In this paper we show how to define values that are indexed by types of arbitrary kinds. It turns out that these polytypic values possess types that are indexed by kinds. We present several examples that demonstrate that the additional flexibility is useful in practice. One paradigmatic example is the mapping function, which describes the functorial action on arrows. A single polytypic definition yields mapping functions for datatypes of arbitrary kinds including first- and higher-order functors. Polytypic values enjoy polytypic properties. Using kind-indexed logical relations we prove among other things that the polytypic mapping function satisfies suitable generalizations of the functorial laws.

1 Introduction

It is widely accepted that type systems are indispensable for building large and reliable software systems. Types provide machine checkable documentation and are often helpful in finding programming errors at an early stage. Polymorphism complements type security by flexibility. Polymorphic type systems like the Hindley-Milner system [21] allow the definition of functions that behave uniformly over all types. However, even polymorphic type systems are sometimes less flexible that one would wish. For instance, it is not possible to define a polymorphic equality function that works for all types—the parametricity theorem [29] implies that a function of type $\forall a.a \rightarrow a \rightarrow Bool$ must necessarily be constant. As a consequence, the programmer is forced to program a separate equality function for each type from scratch.

Polytypic programming [3,2] addresses this problem. Actually, equality serves as a standard example of a polytypic function that can be defined by induction on the structure of types. In a previous paper [8] the author has shown that polytypic functions are uniquely defined by giving cases for primitive types, the unit type, sums, and products. Given this information a tailor-made equality function can be automatically generated for each user-defined type.

R. Backhouse and J. N. Oliveira (Eds.): MPC 2000, LNCS 1837, pp. 2–27, 2000.

Another useful polytypic function is the so-called mapping function. The mapping function of a unary type constructor F applies a given function to each element of type a in a given structure of type F a—we tacitly assume that F does not include function types. Unlike equality the mapping function is indexed by a type constructor, that is, by a function on types. Now, mapping functions can be defined for type constructors of arbitrary arity. In the general case the mapping function takes n functions and applies the i-th function to each element of type a_i in a given structure of type F $a_1 \ldots a_n$. Alas, current approaches to polytypic programming [11,8] do not allow to define these mapping functions at one stroke. The reason is simply that the mapping functions have different types for different arities.

This observation suggests a natural extension of polytypic programming: it should be possible to assign a type to a polytypic value that depends on the arity of the type-index. Actually, we are more ambitious in that we consider not only first-order but also higher-order type constructors. A type constructor is said to be higher-order if it operates on type constructors rather than on types. To distinguish between types, first-order and higher-order type constructors, they are often assigned so-called kinds [17], which can be seen as the 'types of types'. Using the notion of kind we can state the central idea of this paper as follows: polytypic values possess types that are defined by induction on the structure of kinds. It turns out that the implementation of this idea is much simpler than one would expect.

The rest of this paper is organized as follows. Section 2 illustrates the approach using the example of mapping functions. Section 3 introduces the language of kinds and types, which is based on the simply typed lambda calculus. Section 4 explains how to define polytypic values and polykinded types and Section 5 shows how to specialize a polytypic value to concrete instances of datatypes. Section 6 presents several examples of polytypic functions with polykinded types, which demonstrate that the extension is useful in practice. Polytypic values enjoy polytypic properties. Section 7 shows how to express polytypic laws using kind-indexed logical relations. Among other things, we show that the polytypic mapping function satisfies suitable generalizations of the functorial laws. Finally, Section 8 reviews related work and Section 9 concludes.

2   A Worked-Out Example: Mapping Functions

This section illustrates the central idea by means of a worked-out example: mapping functions. For concreteness, the code will be given in the functional programming language Haskell 98 [25]. Throughout, we use Haskell as an abbreviation for Haskell 98. Before tackling the polytypic mapping function let us first take a look at different datatypes and associated monotypic mapping functions. As an aside, note that the combination of a type constructor and its mapping function is often referred to as a functor.

As a first, rather simple example consider the list datatype.

$$\textbf{data } \textit{List } a = \textit{Nil} \mid \textit{Cons } a \text{ } (\textit{List } a)$$

Actually, *List* is not a type but a unary type constructor. In Haskell the 'type' of a type constructor is specified by the kind system. For instance, *List* has kind $\star \rightarrow \star$. The '$\star$' kind represents manifest types like *Int* or *Bool*. The kind $\kappa_1 \rightarrow \kappa_2$ represents type constructors that map type constructors of kind κ_1 to those of kind κ_2. The mapping function for *List* is given by

$$
\begin{aligned}
&mapList &&:: \forall a_1\, a_2.(a_1 \rightarrow a_2) \rightarrow (List\ a_1 \rightarrow List\ a_2)\\
&mapList\ mapa\ Nil &&= Nil\\
&mapList\ mapa\ (Cons\ v\ vs) &&= Cons\ (mapa\ v)\ (mapList\ mapa\ vs)\ .
\end{aligned}
$$

The mapping function takes a function and applies it to each element of a given list. It is perhaps unusual to call the argument function *mapa*. The reason for this choice will become clear as we go along. For the moment it suffices to bear in mind that the definition of *mapList* rigidly follows the structure of the datatype.

The *List* type constructor is an example of a so-called regular or uniform type. Briefly, a regular type is one that can be defined as the least fixpoint of a functor. Interestingly, Haskell's type system is expressive enough to rephrase *List* using an explicit fixpoint operator [19]. We will repeat this construction in the following as it provides us with interesting examples of datatypes and associated mapping functions. First, we define the so-called base or pattern functor of *List*.

$$\textbf{data}\ ListF\ a\ b = NilF \mid ConsF\ a\ b$$

The type *ListF* has kind $\star \rightarrow (\star \rightarrow \star)$, which shows that binary type constructors are curried in Haskell. The following definition introduces a fixpoint operator on the type level (**newtype** is a variant of **data** introducing a new type that is isomorphic to the type on the right-hand side).

$$\textbf{newtype}\ Fix\ f = In\ (f\ (Fix\ f))$$

The kind of *Fix* is $(\star \rightarrow \star) \rightarrow \star$, a so-called second-order kind. The order of a kind is given by $order(\star) = 0$ and $order(\kappa_1 \rightarrow \kappa_2) = max\{1 + order(\kappa_1), order(\kappa_2)\}$. It remains to define *List* as a fixpoint of its base functor (**type** defines a type synonym).

$$\textbf{type}\ List'\ a = Fix\ (ListF\ a)$$

Now, how can we define the mapping function for lists thus defined? For a start, we define the mapping function for the base functor.

$$
\begin{aligned}
&mapListF &&:: \forall a_1\, a_2.(a_1 \rightarrow a_2) \rightarrow \forall b_1\, b_2.(b_1 \rightarrow b_2)\\
& && \rightarrow (ListF\ a_1\ b_1 \rightarrow ListF\ a_2\ b_2)\\
&mapListF\ mapa\ mapb\ NilF = NilF\\
&mapListF\ mapa\ mapb\ (ConsF\ v\ w)\\
& \qquad\qquad = ConsF\ (mapa\ v)\ (mapb\ w)
\end{aligned}
$$

Since the base functor has two type arguments, its mapping function takes two functions, *mapa* and *mapb*, and applies them to values of type a_1 and b_1, respectively. Even more interesting is the mapping function for *Fix*

$$mapFix \quad\quad :: \forall f_1\, f_2.(\forall a_1\, a_2.(a_1 \to a_2) \to (f_1\, a_1 \to f_2\, a_2))$$
$$\to (Fix\, f_1 \to Fix\, f_2)$$
$$mapFix\; mapf\; (In\; v) = In\; (mapf\; (mapFix\; mapf)\; v)\ ,$$

which takes a polymorphic function as argument. In other words, *mapFix* has a so-called rank-2 type signature [16]. Though not in the current language definition, rank-2 type signatures are supported by recent versions of the Glasgow Haskell Compiler GHC [28] and the Haskell interpreter Hugs [15]. The argument function, *mapf*, has a more general type than one would probably expect: it takes a function of type $a_1 \to a_2$ to a function of type $f_1\, a_1 \to f_2\, a_2$. By contrast, the mapping function for *List* (which also has kind $\star \to \star$) takes $a_1 \to a_2$ to *List* $a_1 \to$ *List* a_2. The definition below demonstrates that the extra generality is vital.

$$mapList' \quad\quad :: \forall a_1\, a_2.(a_1 \to a_2) \to (List'\, a_1 \to List'\, a_2)$$
$$mapList'\; mapa = mapFix\; (mapListF\; mapa)$$

The argument of *mapFix* has type $\forall b_1\, b_2.(b_1 \to b_2) \to (ListF\, a_1\, b_1 \to ListF\, a_2\, b_2)$, that is, f_1 is instantiated to *ListF* a_1 and f_2 to *ListF* a_2.

The list datatype is commonly used to represent sequences of elements. An alternative data structure, which supports logarithmic access, is C. Okasaki's type of binary random-access lists [24].

data *Fork a* = *Fork a a*
data *Sequ a* = *Empty* | *Zero (Sequ (Fork a))* | *One a (Sequ (Fork a))*

Since the type argument is changed in the recursive calls, *Sequ* is an example of a so-called nested or non-regular datatype [4]. Though the type recursion is nested, the definition of the mapping function is entirely straightforward.

$$mapFork \quad\quad\quad\quad :: \forall a_1\, a_2.(a_1 \to a_2) \to (Fork\, a_1 \to Fork\, a_2)$$
$$mapFork\; mapa\; (Fork\; v_1\; v_2) = Fork\; (mapa\; v_1)\; (mapa\; v_2)$$

$$mapSequ \quad\quad\quad\quad\quad :: \forall a_1\, a_2.(a_1 \to a_2) \to (Sequ\, a_1 \to Sequ\, a_2)$$
$$mapSequ\; mapa\; Empty \quad = Empty$$
$$mapSequ\; mapa\; (Zero\; vs) \;\; = Zero\; (mapSequ\; (mapFork\; mapa)\; vs)$$
$$mapSequ\; mapa\; (One\; v\; vs) = One\; (mapa\; v)\; (mapSequ\; (mapFork\; mapa)\; vs)$$

Note that *mapSequ* requires polymorphic recursion [23]: the recursive calls have type $\forall a_1\, a_2.(Fork\, a_1 \to Fork\, a_2) \to (Sequ\, (Fork\, a_1) \to Sequ\, (Fork\, a_2))$, which is a substitution instance of the declared type. Haskell allows polymorphic recursion only if an explicit type signature is provided.

Since *Sequ* is a nested type, it cannot be expressed as a fixpoint of a functor. However, it can be rephrased as a fixpoint of a higher-order functor [4]. Again, we will carry out the construction to generate examples of higher-order kinded datatypes. The higher-order base functor associated with *Sequ* is

data *SequF s a* = *EmptyF* | *ZeroF (s (Fork a))* | *OneF a (s (Fork a))* .

Since $Sequ$ has kind $\star \to \star$, its base functor has kind $(\star \to \star) \to (\star \to \star)$. The fixpoint operator for functors of this kind is given by

$$\textbf{newtype } HFix\ h\ a = HIn\ (h\ (HFix\ h)\ a)\ .$$

Since the fixpoint operator takes a second-order kinded type as argument, it has a third-order kind: $((\star \to \star) \to (\star \to \star)) \to (\star \to \star)$. Finally, we can define $Sequ$ as the least fixpoint of $SequF$.

$$\textbf{type } Sequ' = HFix\ SequF$$

As a last stress test let us define a mapping function for $Sequ'$. As before we begin by defining mapping functions for the component types.

$$mapSequF :: \forall s_1\ s_2.(\forall b_1\ b_2.(b_1 \to b_2) \to (s_1\ b_1 \to s_2\ b_2))$$
$$\to \forall a_1\ a_2.(a_1 \to a_2) \to (SequF\ s_1\ a_1 \to SequF\ s_2\ a_2)$$
$$mapSequF\ maps\ mapa\ EmptyF$$
$$= EmptyF$$
$$mapSequF\ maps\ mapa\ (ZeroF\ vs)$$
$$= ZeroF\ (maps\ (mapFork\ mapa)\ vs)$$
$$mapSequF\ maps\ mapa\ (OneF\ v\ vs)$$
$$= OneF\ (mapa\ v)\ (maps\ (mapFork\ mapa)\ vs)$$

This example indicates why argument $maps$ of kind $\star \to \star$ must be polymorphic: both calls of $maps$ are instances of the declared type. In general, the argument mapping function may be applied to many different types. Admittedly, the type signature of $mapSequF$ looks quite puzzling. However, we will see in a moment that it is fully determined by $SequF$'s kind. Even more daunting is the signature of $mapHFix$, which has rank 3. Unfortunately, no current Haskell implementation supports rank-3 type signatures. Hence, the following code cannot be executed.

$$mapHFix :: \forall h_1\ h_2.(\forall f_1\ f_2.(\forall c_1\ c_2.(c_1 \to c_2) \to (f_1\ c_1 \to f_2\ c_2))$$
$$\to \forall b_1\ b_2.(b_1 \to b_2) \to (h_1\ f_1\ b_1 \to h_2\ f_2\ b_2))$$
$$\to \forall a_1\ a_2.(a_1 \to a_2) \to (HFix\ h_1\ a_1 \to HFix\ h_2\ a_2)$$
$$mapHFix\ maph\ mapa\ (HIn\ v)$$
$$= HIn\ (maph\ (mapHFix\ maph)\ mapa\ v)$$

Finally, applying $mapHFix$ to $mapSequF$ we obtain the desired function.

$$mapSequ' :: \forall a_1\ a_2.(a_1 \to a_2) \to (Sequ'\ a_1 \to Sequ'\ a_2)$$
$$mapSequ' = mapHFix\ mapSequF$$

Now, let us define a polytypic version of map. The monotypic instances above already indicate that the type of the mapping function depends on the kind of the type index. In fact, the type of map can be defined by induction on the structure of kinds. A note on notation: we will write type and kind indices in angle brackets. Hence, $map\langle t :: \kappa \rangle$ denotes the application of the polytypic map to the type t of kind κ. We use essentially the same syntax both for polytypic values and for polykinded types. However, they are easily distinguished by their 'types', where the 'type' of kinds is given by the superkind '$\square$' ('$\star$' and '$\square$' are sometimes called sorts).

What is the type of *map* if the type-index has kind $\star$? For a manifest type, say, t, the mapping function $map\langle t :: \star\rangle$ equals the identity function. Hence, its type is $t \to t$. In general, the mapping function $map\langle t :: \kappa\rangle$ has type $Map\langle\kappa\rangle\ t\ t$, where $Map\langle\kappa\rangle$ is defined as follows.

$$
\begin{aligned}
Map\langle\kappa :: \square\rangle & \quad :: \kappa \to \kappa \to \star \\
Map\langle\star\rangle\ t_1\ t_2 & \quad = t_1 \to t_2 \\
Map\langle\kappa_1 \to \kappa_2\rangle\ t_1\ t_2 & = \forall x_1\ x_2 . Map\langle\kappa_1\rangle\ x_1\ x_2 \to Map\langle\kappa_2\rangle\ (t_1\ x_1)\ (t_2\ x_2)
\end{aligned}
$$

The first line of the definition is the so-called kind signature, which makes precise that $Map\langle\kappa :: \square\rangle$ maps two types of kind κ to a manifest type. In the base case $Map\langle\star\rangle\ t_1\ t_2$ equals the type of a conversion function. The inductive case has a very characteristic form, which we will encounter time and again. It specifies that a 'conversion function' between the type constructors t_1 and t_2 is a function that maps a conversion function between x_1 and x_2 to a conversion function between $t_1\ x_1$ and $t_2\ x_2$, for all possible instances of x_1 and x_2. Roughly speaking, $Map\langle\kappa_1 \to \kappa_2\rangle\ t_1\ t_2$ is the type of a 'conversion function'-transformer. It is not hard to see that the type signatures we have encountered before are instances of this scheme.

How can we define the polytypic mapping function itself? It turns out that the technique described in [8] carries over to the polykinded case, that is, to define a polytypic value it suffices to give cases for primitive types, the unit type '1', sums '+', and products '$\times$'. To be able to give polytypic definitions in a pointwise style, we treat 1, '+', and '$\times$' as if they were given by the following datatype declarations.

$$
\begin{aligned}
\textbf{data } 1 \quad &= () \\
\textbf{data } a + b &= Inl\ a \mid Inr\ b \\
\textbf{data } a \times b &= (a, b)
\end{aligned}
$$

Assuming that we have only one primitive type, Int, the polytypic mapping function is given by

$$
\begin{aligned}
map\langle t :: \kappa\rangle & \quad :: Map\langle\kappa\rangle\ t\ t \\
map\langle 1\rangle\ () & \quad = () \\
map\langle Int\rangle\ i & \quad = i \\
map\langle +\rangle\ mapa\ mapb\ (Inl\ v) & = Inl\ (mapa\ v) \\
map\langle +\rangle\ mapa\ mapb\ (Inr\ w) & = Inr\ (mapb\ w) \\
map\langle\times\rangle\ mapa\ mapb\ (v, w) & = (mapa\ v, mapb\ w)\ .
\end{aligned}
$$

This straightforward definition contains all the ingredients needed to derive *maps* for arbitrary datatypes of arbitrary kinds. And, in fact, all the definitions we have seen before were automatically generated using a prototype implementation of the polytypic programming extension described in the subsequent sections. Finally, note that we can define *map* even more succinctly if we use a point-free style—as usual, the *map*s on sums and products are denoted $(+)$ and $(\times)$.

$$
\begin{aligned}
map\langle 1\rangle &= id \\
map\langle Int\rangle &= id \\
map\langle +\rangle\ mapa\ mapb &= mapa + mapb \\
map\langle \times\rangle\ mapa\ mapb &= mapa \times mapb
\end{aligned}
$$

3   The Simply Typed Lambda Calculus as a Type Language

This section introduces kinds and types. The type system is essentially that of Haskell [25] smoothing away some of its irregularities. Haskell offers one basic construct for defining new types: datatype declarations. In general, a **data** declaration has the following form.

data $D\ x_1\ \ldots\ x_\kappa = Q_1\ t_{11}\ \ldots\ t_{1m_1}\ |\ \cdots\ |\ Q_n\ t_{n1}\ \ldots\ t_{nm_n}$

This constructs combines no less than four different features: type abstraction, type recursion, n-ary sums, and n-ary products. The types on the right-hand side are built from type constants (that is, primitive type constructors), type variables, and type application. Thus, Haskell's type system essentially corresponds to the simply typed lambda calculus with kinds playing the rôle of types. This motivates the following definitions.

Definition 1. *Kind terms are formed according to the following grammar.*

$$K ::=\ \star\ |\ (K \to K)$$

Type terms are built from type constants and type variables using type application and type abstraction. We annotate type constants and type variables with their kinds, that is, a type variable is a pair consisting of a name and a kind. If (s, κ) is a type constant or a type variable, we define $kind\ (s, \kappa) = \kappa$.

Definition 2. *Given a set of kinded type constants $C \subseteq \Sigma^* \times K$ and a set of kinded type variables $X \subseteq \Sigma^* \times K$ type pseudo-terms are formed according to*

$$T ::= C\ |\ X\ |\ (T\ T)\ |\ (\Lambda X.T)\ |\ \mu_K\ |\ \forall_K\ .$$

The choice of C is more or less arbitrary; we only require C to include functional types. For concreteness, we use

$$C = \{\,1 :: \star, Int :: \star, (+) :: \star \to \star \to \star, (\times) :: \star \to \star \to \star, (\to) :: \star \to \star \to \star\,\}\ .$$

The set of pseudo-terms includes a family of fixpoint operators indexed by kind: $\mu_\star$ corresponds to *Fix* and $\mu_{\star\to\star}$ to *HFix*. Usually, we write $\mu x.t$ for $\mu_\kappa(\Lambda x.t)$ and similarly for the universal quantifier $\forall_\kappa$.

Definition 3. *The set of legal type terms of kind κ, notation $T(\kappa)$, is defined by $T(\kappa) = \{ t \in T \mid \vdash t :: \kappa \}$ where $\vdash t :: \kappa$ means that the statement $t :: \kappa$ is derivable using the rules depicted in Fig. 1. The set of monomorphic type terms of kind κ, denoted $T^{\circ}(\kappa)$, is the subset of $T(\kappa)$ of terms not containing occurrences of $\forall$.*

$$\frac{}{c :: kind\ c}\ (\text{T-CONST}) \qquad \frac{}{x :: kind\ x}\ (\text{T-VAR})$$

$$\frac{t_1 :: (\kappa_1 \rightarrow \kappa_2) \qquad t_2 :: \kappa_1}{(t_1\ t_2) :: \kappa_2}\ (\text{T-}\rightarrow\text{-ELIM}) \qquad \frac{t :: \kappa}{(\Lambda x.t) :: (kind\ x \rightarrow \kappa)}\ (\text{T-}\rightarrow\text{-INTRO})$$

$$\frac{}{\mu_\kappa :: (\kappa \rightarrow \kappa) \rightarrow \kappa}\ (\text{T-FIX}) \qquad \frac{}{\forall_\kappa :: (\kappa \rightarrow \star) \rightarrow \star}\ (\text{T-ALL})$$

Fig. 1. Kind rules

It is worth noting that since type constants and type variables are annotated with their kinds, we do not require a typing environment. Furthermore, note that the type arguments of polytypic values will be restricted to monomorphic types, see Section 5.

Given this type language we can easily translate datatype declarations into type terms. For instance, the type T defined by the schematic **data** declaration above is modelled by (we tacitly assume that the kinds of the type variables have been inferred)

$$\mu D.\Lambda x_1 \ldots x_\kappa.(t_{11} \times \cdots \times t_{1m_1}) + \cdots + (t_{n1} \times \cdots \times t_{nm_n})\ ,$$

where $t_1 \times \cdots \times t_0 = 1$. For simplicity, n-ary sums are reduced to binary sums and n-ary products to binary products.

In Section 5 we require the following conversion rules for type terms.

Definition 4. *The convertibility relation on type terms, denoted '$\leftrightarrow$', is given by the following axioms*

$$(\Lambda x.t)\ u \leftrightarrow t\ [x := u] \qquad\qquad (\beta)$$

$$\mu t \leftrightarrow t\ (\mu t) \qquad\qquad (\mu)$$

plus rules for reflexivity, symmetry, transitivity, and congruence.

4   Defining Polytypic Values

The definition of a polytypic value consists of two parts: a type signature, which typically involves a polykinded type, and a set of equations, one for each type constant. Likewise, the definition of a polykinded type consists of two parts: a kind signature and one equation for kind $\star$. Interestingly, the equation for functional kinds need not be explicitly specified. It is inevitable because of the way type constructors of kind $\kappa_1 \rightarrow \kappa_2$ are specialized. We will return to this point in the following section. In general, a polykinded type definition has the following schematic form.

$$
\begin{aligned}
&Poly\langle \kappa :: \Box \rangle && :: \kappa \rightarrow \cdots \rightarrow \kappa \rightarrow \star \\
&Poly\langle \star \rangle\ t_1\ \ldots\ t_n && = \ldots \\
&Poly\langle \kappa_1 \rightarrow \kappa_2 \rangle\ t_1\ \ldots\ t_n = \forall x_1\ \ldots\ x_n.Poly\langle \kappa_1 \rangle\ x_1\ \ldots\ x_n \\
&&& \rightarrow Poly\langle \kappa_2 \rangle\ (t_1\ x_1)\ \ldots\ (t_n\ x_n)
\end{aligned}
$$

The kind signature makes precise that the kind-indexed type $Poly\langle \kappa :: \Box \rangle$ maps n types of kind κ to a manifest type (for $Map\langle \kappa :: \Box \rangle$ we had $n = 2$). The polytypic programmer merely has to fill out the right-hand side of the first equation.

Given the polykinded type a polytypic value definition takes on the following schematic form.

$$
\begin{aligned}
&poly\langle t :: \kappa \rangle && :: Poly\langle \kappa \rangle\ t\ \ldots\ t \\
&poly\langle 1 \rangle && = \ldots \\
&poly\langle Int \rangle && = \ldots \\
&poly\langle + \rangle\ polya\ polyb && = \ldots \\
&poly\langle \times \rangle\ polya\ polyb && = \ldots \\
&poly\langle \rightarrow \rangle\ polya\ polyb && = \ldots
\end{aligned}
$$

Again, the polytypic programmer has to fill out the right-hand sides. To be well-typed, the $poly\langle c :: \kappa \rangle$ instances must have type $Poly\langle \kappa \rangle\ c\ \ldots\ c$ as stated in the type signature. We do not require, however, that an equation is provided for every type constant c in C. In case an equation for c is missing, we tacitly add $poly\langle c \rangle = undefined$. For instance, map is not defined for functional types. In fact, none of the examples in this paper can be sensibly defined for the function space constructor (a polytypic function that can be defined for functional types is the embedding-projection map, see [9]).

5   Specializing Polytypic Values

This section is concerned with the specialization of polytypic values to concrete instances of datatypes. We have seen in Section 2 that the structure of each instance of $map\langle t \rangle$ rigidly follows the structure of t. Perhaps surprisingly, the intimate correspondence between the type and the value level holds not only for map but for all polytypic values. In fact, the process of specialization can be seen as an interpretation of the simply typed lambda calculus. The polytypic programmer specifies the interpretation of type constants. Given this information the meaning of a type term—that is, the specialization of a polytypic value— is fixed: type application is interpreted by value application, type abstraction by value abstraction, and type recursion by value recursion. Consequently, the extension of $poly$ to arbitrary type terms is given by (we will refine this definition below)

$$poly\langle x \rangle \quad = poly_x$$
$$poly\langle t_1\ t_2 \rangle = (poly\langle t_1 \rangle)\ (poly\langle t_2 \rangle)$$
$$poly\langle \Lambda x.t \rangle = \lambda poly_x.poly\langle t \rangle$$
$$poly\langle \mu_\kappa \rangle \quad = fix\ .$$

Note that we allow only monomorphic types as type arguments. This restriction is, however, quite mild. Haskell, for instance, does not allow universal quantifiers in **data** declarations. For the translation we use a simple variable naming convention, which obviates the need for an explicit environment. We agree upon that $poly\langle x \rangle$ is mapped to the variable $poly_x$. We often write $poly_x$ by concatenating the name of the polytypic value and the name of the type variable as in *mapa*. Of course, to avoid name capture we assume that $poly_x$ is distinct from variables introduced by the polytypic programmer.

The definition of *poly* makes precise that the specialization for a type constructor is a function. This explains why $Poly\langle \kappa_1 \to \kappa_2 \rangle\ t_1\ \ldots\ t_n$ must necessarily be a functional type. In the rest of this section we show that $poly\langle t \rangle$ is indeed well-typed. To this end we must first fix the target language we are compiling polytypic values to. Since we require first-class polymorphism, we will use a variant of the polymorphic lambda calculus [6], $F\omega$, augmented by a polymorphic fixpoint operator. A similar language is also used as the internal language of the Glasgow Haskell Compiler [26].

Similar to the type language we annotate value constants and variables with their types. If (s, t) is a constant or a variable, we define *type* $(s, t) = t$. Note that the type of a constant must be closed.

Definition 5. *Given a set of typed constants $P \subseteq \Sigma^* \times T(\star)$ and a set of typed variables $V \subseteq \Sigma^* \times T(\star)$ pseudo-terms are formed according to*

$$E ::= P \mid V \mid (E\ E) \mid (\lambda V.E) \mid (E\ T) \mid (\lambda X.E) \mid fix\ .$$

Here, $e\ t$ denotes universal application and $\lambda x.e$ denotes universal abstraction. Note that we use the same syntax for value abstraction $\lambda v.e$ (here v is a value variable) and universal abstraction $\lambda x.e$ (here x is a type variable). The set of value constants P should include enough suitable functions to enable defining the $poly\langle c \rangle$ instances for each of the type constants c in C.

Definition 6. *The set of legal terms of type t, notation $E(t)$, is defined by $E(t) = \{ e \in E \mid \vdash e :: t \}$ where $\vdash e :: t$ means that the statement $e :: t$ is derivable using the rules depicted in Fig. 2.*

The type signature of a polytypic value determines the type for closed type indices. However, since the specialization is defined by induction on the structure of type terms, we must also explicate the type for type indices that contain free type variables. To motivate the necessary amendments let us take a look at an example first. Consider specializing *map* for the type *Matrix* given by

$$\frac{}{p :: type\ p}\ (\text{CONST}) \qquad \frac{}{v :: type\ v}\ (\text{VAR})$$

$$\frac{e_1 :: (t_1 \to t_2) \qquad e_2 :: t_1}{(e_1\ e_2) :: t_2}\ (\to\text{-ELIM}) \qquad \frac{e :: t}{(\lambda v.e) :: (type\ v \to t)}\ (\to\text{-INTRO})$$

$$\frac{e :: (\forall x.t) \qquad u :: kind\ x}{(e\ u) :: t\ [x := u]}\ (\forall\text{-ELIM}) \qquad \frac{e :: t \qquad x\ \text{not free in the type}}{(\lambda x.e) :: (\forall x.t)\quad \text{of a free variable of } e}\ (\forall\text{-INTRO})$$

$$\frac{}{fix :: \forall a.(a \to a) \to a}\ (\text{FIX})$$

$$\frac{e :: t \qquad t \leftrightarrow u}{e :: u}\ (\text{CONV})$$

Fig. 2. Typing rules

$\Lambda a.List\ (List\ a)$. The fully typed definition of $mapMatrix$ is

$$mapMatrix :: \forall a_1\ a_2.(a_1 \to a_2) \to (Matrix\ a_1 \to Matrix\ a_2)$$
$$mapMatrix = \lambda a_1\ a_2.\lambda mapa :: a_1 \to a_2.mapList\ (List\ a_1)\ (List\ a_2)$$
$$(mapList\ a_1\ a_2\ mapa)\ .$$

First of all, the type of $mapMatrix$ determines the type of $mapa$, which is $Map\langle\star\rangle\ a_1\ a_2 = a_1 \to a_2$. Now, $Matrix$ contains the type term $List\ a$, in which a occurs free. The corresponding mapping function is $mapList\ a_1\ a_2\ mapa$, which has type $List\ a_1 \to List\ a_2$. In general, $poly\langle t :: \kappa\rangle$ has type $Poly\langle\kappa\rangle\ (t)_1 \ \ldots\ (t)_n$ where $(t)_i$ denotes the type term t, in which every free type variable x has been replaced by x_i. To make this work we lay down that the value variable $poly_x$ has type $Poly\langle kind\ x\rangle\ x_1\ \ldots\ x_n$ and that the x_i are fresh type variables associated with x. Given these prerequisites the fully typed extension of $poly$ is defined by

$$poly\langle t :: \kappa\rangle :: Poly\langle\kappa\rangle\ (t)_1\ \ldots\ (t)_n$$
$$poly\langle x\rangle\ = poly_x$$
$$poly\langle t_1\ t_2\rangle = (poly\langle t_1\rangle)\ (t_2)_1\ \ldots\ (t_2)_n\ (poly\langle t_2\rangle)$$
$$poly\langle\Lambda x.t\rangle = \lambda x_1\ \ldots\ x_n.\lambda poly_x.poly\langle t\rangle$$
$$poly\langle\mu_\kappa\rangle\ = \lambda x_1\ \ldots\ x_n.\lambda poly_x.fix\ (Poly\langle\kappa\rangle\ (\mu x_1)\ \ldots\ (\mu x_n))$$
$$(poly_x\ (\mu x_1)\ \ldots\ (\mu x_n))\ .$$

Theorem 1. *If* $poly\langle c\rangle \in E(Poly\langle kind\ c\rangle\ c\ \ldots\ c)$ *for all type constants* $c \in C$, *then* $poly\langle u\rangle \in E(Poly\langle\kappa\rangle\ (u)_1\ \ldots\ (u)_n)$ *for all type terms* $u \in T^\circ(\kappa)$.

Proof. We use induction on the derivation of $u :: \kappa$. We content ourselves with one illustrative case.

Case $u = \mu_\kappa$: Note that $kind\ x_i = kind\ x = \kappa \to \kappa$ (the kinds of the type variables do not appear explicitly in the definition of $poly$). By convention, we have $poly_x :: Poly\langle\kappa \to \kappa\rangle\ x_1\ \ldots\ x_n$. Consequently,

$$poly_x\ (\mu x_1)\ \ldots\ (\mu x_n)$$
$$:: Poly\langle\kappa\rangle\ (\mu x_1)\ \ldots\ (\mu x_n) \to Poly\langle\kappa\rangle\ (x_1\ (\mu x_1))\ \ldots\ (x_n\ (\mu x_n))$$

and since $\mu t \leftrightarrow t\,(\mu t)$ and $\mathit{fix} :: \forall a.(a \to a) \to a$ we obtain

$$\lambda x_1 \;\ldots\; x_n.\lambda \mathit{poly}_x.\mathit{fix}\,(\mathit{Poly}\langle\kappa\rangle\,(\mu x_1)\;\ldots\;(\mu x_n))\,(\mathit{poly}_x\,(\mu x_1)\;\ldots\;(\mu x_n))$$
$$:: \forall x_1 \;\ldots\; x_n.\mathit{Poly}\langle\kappa \to \kappa\rangle\,x_1\;\ldots\;x_n \to \mathit{Poly}\langle\kappa\rangle\,(\mu x_1)\;\ldots\;(\mu x_n)$$

as desired.   □

Let us conclude the section by noting a trivial consequence of the specialization. Since the structure of types is reflected on the value level, we have $\mathit{poly}\langle\Lambda a.f\,(g\,a)\rangle = \lambda \mathit{poly}_a.\mathit{poly}\langle f\rangle\,((\mathit{poly}\langle g\rangle)\,\mathit{poly}_a)$. Writing composition as usual this implies, in particular, that $\mathit{map}\langle f \cdot g\rangle = \mathit{map}\langle f\rangle \cdot \mathit{map}\langle g\rangle$. Perhaps surprisingly, this relationship holds for all polytypic values, not only for mapping functions. A similar observation is that $\mathit{poly}\langle\Lambda a.a\rangle = \lambda \mathit{poly}_a.\mathit{poly}_a$ for all polytypic values. Abbreviating $\Lambda a.a$ by Id we have, in particular, that $\mathit{map}\langle\mathit{Id}\rangle = \mathit{id}$. As an aside, note that these polytypic identities are not to be confused with the familiar functorial laws $\mathit{map}\langle f\rangle\,\mathit{id} = \mathit{id}$ and $\mathit{map}\langle f\rangle\,(\varphi \cdot \psi) = \mathit{map}\langle f\rangle\,\varphi \cdot \mathit{map}\langle f\rangle\,\psi$ (see Section 7.1), which are base-level identities.

6 Examples

6.1 Polytypic Equality

The equality function equal serves as a typical example of a polytypic value. The polykinded equality type is fairly straightforward: for a manifest type $\mathit{equal}\langle t\rangle$ has type $t \to t \to \mathit{Bool}$, which determines the following definition.

$$
\begin{aligned}
&\mathit{Equal}\langle\kappa :: \square\rangle &&:: \kappa \to \star \\
&\mathit{Equal}\langle\star\rangle\,t &&= t \to t \to \mathit{Bool} \\
&\mathit{Equal}\langle\kappa_1 \to \kappa_2\rangle\,t &&= \forall x.\mathit{Equal}\langle\kappa_1\rangle\,x \to \mathit{Equal}\langle\kappa_2\rangle\,(t\,x)
\end{aligned}
$$

For ease of reference we will always list the equation for functional kinds even though it is fully determined by the theory. Assuming that a suitable equality function for Int is available, the polytypic equality function can be defined as follows (for reasons of readability we use a Haskell-like notation rather than $F\omega$).

$$
\begin{aligned}
&\mathit{equal}\langle t :: \kappa\rangle &&:: \mathit{Equal}\langle\kappa\rangle\,t \\
&\mathit{equal}\langle 1\rangle\,()\,() &&= \mathit{True} \\
&\mathit{equal}\langle\mathit{Int}\rangle\,i\,j &&= \mathit{equalInt}\,i\,j \\
&\mathit{equal}\langle +\rangle\,\mathit{equala}\,\mathit{equalb}\,(\mathit{Inl}\,v_1)\,(\mathit{Inl}\,v_2) &&= \mathit{equala}\,v_1\,v_2 \\
&\mathit{equal}\langle +\rangle\,\mathit{equala}\,\mathit{equalb}\,(\mathit{Inl}\,v_1)\,(\mathit{Inr}\,w_2) &&= \mathit{False} \\
&\mathit{equal}\langle +\rangle\,\mathit{equala}\,\mathit{equalb}\,(\mathit{Inr}\,w_1)\,(\mathit{Inl}\,v_2) &&= \mathit{False} \\
&\mathit{equal}\langle +\rangle\,\mathit{equala}\,\mathit{equalb}\,(\mathit{Inr}\,w_1)\,(\mathit{Inr}\,w_2) &&= \mathit{equalb}\,w_1\,w_2 \\
&\mathit{equal}\langle \times\rangle\,\mathit{equala}\,\mathit{equalb}\,(v_1, w_1)\,(v_2, w_2) &&= \mathit{equala}\,v_1\,v_2 \wedge \mathit{equalb}\,w_1\,w_2
\end{aligned}
$$

Now, since equal has a kind-indexed type we can also specialize it for, say, unary type constructors.

$$\mathit{equal}\langle f :: \star \to \star\rangle :: \forall x.(x \to x \to \mathit{Bool}) \to (f\,x \to f\,x \to \mathit{Bool})$$

This gives us an extra degree of flexibility: $equal\langle f \rangle$ op v w checks whether corresponding elements in v and w are related by op. Of course, op need not be an equality operator. PolyLib [12] defines an analogous function but with a more general type:

$$pequal\langle f :: \star \to \star \rangle :: \forall x_1\ x_2.(x_1 \to x_2 \to Bool) \to (f\ x_1 \to f\ x_2 \to Bool)\ .$$

Here, the element types need not be identical. And, in fact, $equal\langle t :: \kappa \rangle$ can be assigned the more general type $PEqual\langle \kappa \rangle\ t\ t$ given by

$$
\begin{aligned}
PEqual\langle \kappa :: \Box \rangle & :: \kappa \to \kappa \to \star \\
PEqual\langle \star \rangle\ t_1\ t_2 & = t_1 \to t_2 \to Bool \\
PEqual\langle \kappa_1 \to \kappa_2 \rangle\ t_1\ t_2 & = \forall x_1\ x_2.PEqual\langle \kappa_1 \rangle\ x_1\ x_2 \to PEqual\langle \kappa_2 \rangle\ (t_1\ x_1)\ (t_2\ x_2)\ ,
\end{aligned}
$$

which gives us an even greater degree of flexibility.

6.2   Mapping and Zipping Functions

In Section 2 we have seen how to define mapping functions for types of arbitrary kinds. Interestingly, the polytypic map subsumes so-called higher-order maps. A higher-order functor operates on a functor category, which has as objects functors and as arrows natural transformations. In Haskell we can model natural transformations by polymorphic functions.

$$\textbf{type}\ f_1 \stackrel{.}{\to} f_2 = \forall a.f_1\ a \to f_2\ a$$

A natural transformation between functors F_1 and F_2 is a polymorphic function of type $F_1 \stackrel{.}{\to} F_2$. A higher-order functor H then consists of a type constructor of kind $(\star \to \star) \to (\star \to \star)$, such as $SequF$, and an associated mapping function of type $(f_1 \stackrel{.}{\to} f_2) \to (H\ f_1 \stackrel{.}{\to} H\ f_2)$. Now, the polytypic map gives us a function of type

$$
\begin{aligned}
map\langle H \rangle :: \forall f_1\ f_2.(\forall b_1\ b_2.(b_1 \to b_2) \to (f_1\ b_1 \to f_2\ b_2)) \\
\to (\forall a_1\ a_2.(a_1 \to a_2) \to (H\ f_1\ a_1 \to H\ f_2\ a_2))\ .
\end{aligned}
$$

Given a natural transformation α of type $f_1 \stackrel{.}{\to} f_2$ there are basically two alternatives for constructing a function of type $\forall b_1\ b_2.(b_1 \to b_2) \to (f_1\ b_1 \to f_2\ b_2)$: $\lambda m.\alpha \cdot map\langle f_1 \rangle\ m$ or $\lambda m.map\langle f_2 \rangle\ m \cdot \alpha$. The naturality of α, however, implies that both alternatives are equal. Consequently, the higher-order map is given by

$$
\begin{aligned}
hmap\langle h :: (\star \to \star) \to (\star \to \star) \rangle & :: \forall f_1\ f_2.(f_1 \stackrel{.}{\to} f_2) \to (h\ f_1 \stackrel{.}{\to} h\ f_2) \\
hmap\langle h \rangle\ (\alpha :: f_1 \stackrel{.}{\to} f_2) & = map\langle h \rangle\ (\lambda m.\alpha \cdot map\langle f_1 \rangle\ m)\ id\ .
\end{aligned}
$$

Using definitions similar to the one in Section 2 we can also implement embedding-projection maps [9] of type $MapE\langle \star \rangle\ t_1\ t_2 = (t_1 \to t_2, t_2 \to t_1)$, monadic maps [5,20] of type $MapM\langle \star \rangle\ t_1\ t_2 = t_1 \to M\ t_2$ for some monad M, and arrow maps [13] of type $MapA\langle \star \rangle\ t_1\ t_2 = t_1 \rightsquigarrow t_2$ for some arrow type $(\rightsquigarrow)$.

Closely related to mapping functions are zipping functions. A binary zipping function takes two structures of the same shape and combines them into a single structure. For instance, the list *zip* takes a function of type $a_1 \to a_2 \to a_3$, two lists of type *List* a_1 and *List* a_2 and applies the function to corresponding elements producing a list of type *List* a_3. The type of the polytypic *zip* is essentially a three parameter variant of *Map*.

$$Zip\langle \kappa :: \Box \rangle \qquad\qquad :: \kappa \to \kappa \to \kappa \to \star$$
$$Zip\langle \star \rangle \; t_1 \, t_2 \, t_3 \qquad = t_1 \to t_2 \to t_3$$
$$Zip\langle \kappa_1 \to \kappa_2 \rangle \, t_1 \, t_2 \, t_3 = \forall x_1 x_2 x_3 . Zip\langle \kappa_1 \rangle x_1 x_2 x_3 \to Zip\langle \kappa_2 \rangle (t_1 x_1)(t_2 x_2)(t_3 x_3)$$

The definition of *zip* is similar to that of *equal*.

$$zip\langle t :: \kappa \rangle \qquad\qquad\qquad\qquad :: Zip\langle \kappa \rangle \; t \; t \; t$$
$$zip\langle 1 \rangle \; () \; () \qquad\qquad\qquad\qquad = ()$$
$$zip\langle Int \rangle \; i \; j \qquad\qquad\qquad\qquad = \textbf{if } equalInt \; i \; j \textbf{ then } i \textbf{ else } undefined$$
$$zip\langle + \rangle \; zipa \; zipb \; (Inl \; v_1) \; (Inl \; v_2) \;\; = Inl \; (zipa \; v_1 \; v_2)$$
$$zip\langle + \rangle \; zipa \; zipb \; (Inl \; v_1) \; (Inr \; w_2) = undefined$$
$$zip\langle + \rangle \; zipa \; zipb \; (Inr \; w_1) \; (Inl \; v_2) = undefined$$
$$zip\langle + \rangle \; zipa \; zipb \; (Inr \; w_1) \; (Inr \; w_2) = Inr \; (zipb \; w_1 \; w_2)$$
$$zip\langle \times \rangle \; zipa \; zipb \; (v_1, w_1) \; (v_2, w_2) \;\; = (zipa \; v_1 \; v_2, zipb \; w_1 \; w_2)$$

Note that the result of *zip* is a partial structure if the two arguments have not the same shape. Alternatively, one can define a zipping function of type $Zip\langle \star \rangle \; t_1 \, t_2 \, t_3 = t_1 \to t_2 \to Maybe \; t_3$, which uses the exception monad *Maybe* to signal incompatibility of the argument structures, see [7].

6.3   Reductions

A reduction or a crush [18] is a polytypic function that collapses a structure of values of type x into a single value of type x. This section explains how to define reductions that work for all types of all kinds. To illustrate the main idea let us start with three motivating examples. The first one is a function that counts the number of values of type *Int* within a given structure of some type.

$$Count\langle \kappa :: \Box \rangle \qquad\qquad\qquad :: \kappa \to \star$$
$$Count\langle \star \rangle \; t \qquad\qquad\qquad\qquad = t \to Int$$
$$Count\langle \kappa_1 \to \kappa_2 \rangle \; t \qquad\qquad = \forall x . Count\langle \kappa_1 \rangle \; x \to Count\langle \kappa_2 \rangle \; (t \; x)$$

$$count\langle t :: \kappa \rangle \qquad\qquad\qquad\qquad :: Count\langle \kappa \rangle \; t$$
$$count\langle 1 \rangle \; () \qquad\qquad\qquad\qquad = 0$$
$$count\langle Int \rangle \; i \qquad\qquad\qquad\qquad = 1$$
$$count\langle + \rangle \; counta \; countb \; (Inl \; v) \;\; = counta \; v$$
$$count\langle + \rangle \; counta \; countb \; (Inr \; w) = countb \; w$$
$$count\langle \times \rangle \; counta \; countb \; (v, w) \;\; = counta \; v + countb \; w$$

Next, let us consider a slight variation: the function $size\langle t\rangle$ defined below is identical to $count\langle t\rangle$ except for $t = Int$, in which case $size$ also returns 0.

$$
\begin{aligned}
size\langle t :: \kappa\rangle && &:: Count\langle \kappa\rangle\ t \\
size\langle 1\rangle\ () && &= 0 \\
size\langle Int\rangle\ i && &= 0 \\
size\langle +\rangle\ sizea\ sizeb\ (Inl\ v) && &= sizea\ v \\
size\langle +\rangle\ sizea\ sizeb\ (Inr\ w) && &= sizeb\ w \\
size\langle \times\rangle\ sizea\ sizeb\ (v, w) && &= sizea\ v + sizeb\ w
\end{aligned}
$$

It is not hard to see that $size\langle t\rangle\ v$ returns 0 for all types t of kind $\star$ (provided v is finite and fully defined). So one might be led to conclude that $size$ is not a very useful function. This conclusion is, however, too rash since $size$ can also be parameterized by type constructors. For instance, for unary type constructors $size$ has type

$$
size\langle f :: \star \to \star\rangle :: \forall x.(x \to Int) \to (f\ x \to Int)
$$

Now, if we pass the identity function to $size$, we obtain a function that sums up a structure of integers. Another viable choice is $const\ 1$; this yields a function of type $\forall x.f\ x \to Int$ that counts the number of values of type x in a given structure of type $f\ x$.

$$
\begin{aligned}
fsum\langle f :: \star \to \star\rangle &:: f\ Int \to Int \\
fsum\langle f\rangle &= size\langle f\rangle\ id \\[4pt]
fsize\langle f :: \star \to \star\rangle &:: \forall x.f\ x \to Int \\
fsize\langle f\rangle &= size\langle f\rangle\ (const\ 1)
\end{aligned}
$$

Using a similar approach we can also flatten a structure into a list of elements. The type of the polytypic flattening function

$$
\begin{aligned}
Flatten_z\langle \kappa :: \square\rangle &:: \kappa \to \star \\
Flatten_z\langle \star\rangle\ t &= t \to List\ z \\
Flatten_z\langle \kappa_1 \to \kappa_2\rangle\ t &= \forall x.Flatten_z\langle \kappa_1\rangle\ x \to Flatten_z\langle \kappa_2\rangle\ (t\ x)
\end{aligned}
$$

makes use of a simple extension: $Flatten_z\langle \kappa\rangle$ takes an additional type parameter, z, that is passed unchanged to the base case. One can safely think of z as a type parameter that is global to the definition. The code for $flatten$ is similar to the code for $size$.

$$
\begin{aligned}
flatten\langle t :: \kappa\rangle && &:: \forall z.Flatten_z\langle \kappa\rangle\ t \\
flatten\langle 1\rangle\ () && &= Nil \\
flatten\langle Int\rangle\ i && &= Nil \\
flatten\langle +\rangle\ flattena\ flattenb\ (Inl\ v) && &= flattena\ v \\
flatten\langle +\rangle\ flattena\ flattenb\ (Inr\ w) && &= flattenb\ w \\
flatten\langle \times\rangle\ flattena\ flattenb\ (v, w) && &= flattena\ v \mathbin{+\!\!+} flattenb\ w
\end{aligned}
$$

$$
\begin{array}{ll}
fsum\langle f :: \star \to \star \rangle & :: f\ Int \to Int \\
fsum\langle f \rangle & = reduce\langle f \rangle\ 0\ (+)\ id \\
fsize\langle f :: \star \to \star \rangle & :: \forall x.f\ x \to Int \\
fsize\langle f \rangle & = reduce\langle f \rangle\ 0\ (+)\ (const\ 1) \\
fand\langle f :: \star \to \star \rangle & :: f\ Bool \to Bool \\
fand\langle f \rangle & = reduce\langle f \rangle\ True\ (\wedge)\ id \\
fall\langle f :: \star \to \star \rangle & :: \forall x.(x \to Bool) \to (f\ x \to Bool) \\
fall\langle f \rangle\ p & = reduce\langle f \rangle\ True\ (\wedge)\ p \\
fflatten\langle f :: \star \to \star \rangle & :: \forall x.f\ x \to List\ x \\
fflatten\langle f \rangle & = reduce\langle f \rangle\ Nil\ (+\!\!+)\ wrap \\
gflatten\langle g :: \star \to \star \to \star \rangle & :: \forall x\ y.g\ x\ y \to List\ (x + y) \\
gflatten\langle g \rangle & = reduce\langle g \rangle\ Nil\ (+\!\!+)\ (wrap \cdot Inl)\ (wrap \cdot Inr)
\end{array}
$$

Fig. 3. Examples of reductions

As before, *flatten* is pointless for types but useful for type constructors.

$$
\begin{array}{ll}
fflatten\langle f :: \star \to \star \rangle & :: \forall a.f\ a \to List\ a \\
fflatten\langle f \rangle & = flatten\langle f \rangle\ wrap\ \textbf{where}\ wrap\ v = Cons\ v\ Nil
\end{array}
$$

The definitions of *size* and *flatten* exhibit a common pattern: the elements of a base type are replaced by a constant (0 and *Nil*, respectively) and the pair constructor is replaced by a binary operator ((+) and (+$\!$+), respectively). The polytypic function *reduce* abstracts away from these particularities.

$$
\begin{array}{ll}
Red_z\langle \kappa :: \square \rangle & :: \kappa \to \star \\
Red_z\langle \star \rangle\ t & = t \to z \\
Red_z\langle \kappa_1 \to \kappa_2 \rangle\ t & = \forall x.Red_z\langle \kappa_1 \rangle\ x \to Red_z\langle \kappa_2 \rangle\ (t\ x) \\
reduce\langle t :: \kappa \rangle & :: \forall z.z \to (z \to z \to z) \to Red_z\langle \kappa \rangle\ t \\
reduce\langle t \rangle\ e\ (\oplus) & = red\langle t \rangle \\
\quad \textbf{where} & \\
\quad red\langle 1 \rangle\ () & = e \\
\quad red\langle Int \rangle\ i & = e \\
\quad red\langle + \rangle\ reda\ redb\ (Inl\ v) & = reda\ v \\
\quad red\langle + \rangle\ reda\ redb\ (Inr\ w) & = redb\ w \\
\quad red\langle \times \rangle\ reda\ redb\ (v, w) & = reda\ v \oplus redb\ w
\end{array}
$$

Note that we can define *red* even more succinctly using a point-free style.

$$
\begin{array}{ll}
red\langle 1 \rangle & = const\ e \\
red\langle Int \rangle & = const\ e \\
red\langle + \rangle\ reda\ redb & = reda\ \triangledown\ redb \\
red\langle \times \rangle\ reda\ redb & = uncurry\ (\oplus) \cdot (reda \times redb)
\end{array}
$$

Here, (∇) is the so-called junction operator [2]. The type of $reduce\langle f \rangle$ where f is a unary type constructor is quite general.

$$reduce\langle f :: \star \to \star \rangle :: \forall z.z \to (z \to z \to z) \to (\forall x.(x \to z) \to (f \; x \to z))$$

Fig. 3 lists some typical applications of $reduce\langle f \rangle$ and $reduce\langle g \rangle$ where g is a binary type constructor.

7   Properties of Polytypic Values

This section investigates another important aspect of polytypism: polytypic reasoning. The section is structured as follows. Section 7.1 shows how to generalize the functorial laws to datatypes of arbitrary kinds and explains how to prove these generalizations correct. In Section 7.2 we develop a general framework for conducting polytypic proofs. This framework is then illustrated in Section 7.3 by several examples.

7.1   Functorial Laws

To classify as a functor the mapping function of a unary type constructor must satisfy the so-called functorial laws:

$$\begin{aligned} map\langle f \rangle \; id \quad &= id \\ map\langle f \rangle \; (\varphi \cdot \psi) &= map\langle f \rangle \; \varphi \cdot map\langle f \rangle \; \psi \;, \end{aligned}$$

that is, $map\langle f \rangle$ preserves identity and composition. If the type constructor is binary, the functor laws take the form

$$\begin{aligned} map\langle g \rangle \; id \; id \quad &= id \\ map\langle g \rangle \; (\varphi_1 \cdot \psi_1) \; (\varphi_2 \cdot \psi_2) &= map\langle g \rangle \; \varphi_1 \; \varphi_2 \cdot map\langle g \rangle \; \psi_1 \; \psi_2 \;. \end{aligned}$$

How can we generalize these laws to datatypes of arbitrary kinds? Since $map\langle t \rangle$ has a kind-indexed type, it is reasonable to expect that the functorial properties are indexed by kinds, as well. So, what form do the laws take if the type index is a manifest type, say, t? In this case $map\langle t \rangle$ does not preserve identity; it *is* the identity.

$$\begin{aligned} map\langle t \rangle &= id \\ map\langle t \rangle &= map\langle t \rangle \cdot map\langle t \rangle \end{aligned}$$

The pendant of the second law states that $map\langle t \rangle$ is idempotent (which is a simple consequence of the first law). Given this base case the generalization to arbitrary kinds is within reach. The polytypic version of the first functorial law states that $map\langle t \rangle \in \mathcal{I}\langle \kappa \rangle$ for all types $t \in T^\circ(\kappa)$, where $\mathcal{I}\langle \kappa \rangle$ is given by

$$\begin{aligned} \varphi \in \mathcal{I}\langle \star \rangle \quad &\equiv \varphi = id \\ \varphi \in \mathcal{I}\langle \kappa_1 \to \kappa_2 \rangle &\equiv \forall v \, \text{\tiny\textbf{.}} \, v \in \mathcal{I}\langle \kappa_1 \rangle \supset \varphi \; v \in \mathcal{I}\langle \kappa_2 \rangle \;. \end{aligned}$$

The relation $\mathcal{I}$ strongly resembles a so-called unary logical relation [22]. The second clause of the definition is characteristic for logical relations; it guarantees that the relation is closed under type application and type abstraction. We will call $\mathcal{I}$ and its colleagues polytypic logical relations (or simply logical relations) for want of a better name. Section 7.2 details the differences between polytypic and 'classical' logical relations.

Similarly, the polytypic version of the second functorial law expresses that $(map\langle t\rangle, map\langle t\rangle, map\langle t\rangle) \in \mathcal{C}\langle\kappa\rangle$ for all types $t \in T^\circ(\kappa)$, where $\mathcal{C}\langle\kappa\rangle$ is given by

$$(\varphi_1, \varphi_2, \varphi_3) \in \mathcal{C}\langle\star\rangle \qquad \equiv \varphi_1 \cdot \varphi_2 = \varphi_3$$
$$(\varphi_1, \varphi_2, \varphi_3) \in \mathcal{C}\langle\kappa_1 \to \kappa_2\rangle \equiv \forall v_1\ v_2\ v_3 \blacksquare (v_1, v_2, v_3) \in \mathcal{C}\langle\kappa_1\rangle$$
$$\supset (\varphi_1\ v_1, \varphi_2\ v_2, \varphi_3\ v_3) \in \mathcal{C}\langle\kappa_2\rangle \ .$$

Note again the characteristic form of the second clause. It expresses that functions are related if related arguments are taken to related results. It is not hard to see that the monotypic functorial laws are instances of these polytypic laws.

Turning to the proof of the polytypic laws we must show (1) that $map\langle c\rangle \in \mathcal{I}\langle kind\ c\rangle$ and $(map\langle c\rangle, map\langle c\rangle, map\langle c\rangle) \in \mathcal{C}\langle kind\ c\rangle$ for all type constants $c \in C$ and (2) that $fix \in \mathcal{I}\langle\kappa\rangle$ and $(fix, fix, fix) \in \mathcal{C}\langle\kappa\rangle$ for all $\kappa \in K$. The first part follows directly from the functorial laws of $(+)$ and $(\times)$. The second part is more delicate. The usual approach is to impose two further conditions on logical relations: they must be pointed and chain-complete[1]—we tacitly assume that we are working in a domain-theoretical setting. Then one can invoke fixpoint induction to show that fixpoint operators are logically related. Now, $\mathcal{C}$ satisfies these requirements; $\mathcal{I}$, however, does not since it fails to be pointed (clearly, $\bot = id$ does not hold in general).

Let us take a closer look at the reason for this failure. To this end consider the type $Tree = \mu TreeF$ with $TreeF = \Lambda a.1 + a \times a$. The associated mapping function is $mapTree = fix\ mapTreeF$ with $mapTreeF = \lambda mapa.id + mapa \times mapa$. Now, it is fairly obvious that we cannot prove $mapTree = id$ with the machinery developed so far. In a sense, the problem is that equality is only 'weakly typed': we must prove $\varphi\ v = v$ for all $v :: Tree$. Clearly, the approximations of $mapTree$, $mapTreeF^i \bot$, do not satisfy this strong condition. However, $mapTreeF^i \bot\ v = v$ holds for all elements $v :: TreeF^i\ 0$. Here, 0 is the 'empty' type, which contains $\bot$ as the single element. In other words, approximations on the value level and approximations on the type level should go hand in hand. This can be accomplished by parameterizing logical relations with the types involved: $\varphi \in \mathcal{I}\langle\star\rangle\ t \equiv \varphi = id :: t \to t$. Given this modification it is not hard to show that $\mathcal{I}\langle\star\rangle$ is pointed, that is, $\bot \in \mathcal{I}\langle\star\rangle\ 0$. We can then invoke a polytypic version of Scott and de Bakker's fixpoint induction to conclude that $fix \in \mathcal{I}\langle\kappa\rangle\ \mu$ for all $\kappa \in K$. Polytypic fixpoint induction can be stated as the following inference rule:

$$\frac{\bot \in P\langle 0\rangle \qquad \forall x \blacksquare \forall v \blacksquare v \in P\langle x\rangle \supset \varphi\ v \in P\langle t\ x\rangle}{fix\ \varphi \in P\langle\mu t\rangle} \text{(FP-INDUCTION)} ,$$

[1] A relation $\mathcal{R}$ is pointed if $\bot \in \mathcal{R}$; it is chain-complete if $S \subseteq \mathcal{R} \supset \bigsqcup S \in \mathcal{R}$ for every chain S.

where P is a type-indexed chain-complete predicate. Here, chain-completeness means that whenever $\varphi^i \perp \in P\langle t^i\, 0\rangle$ for all $i \in \mathbb{N}$ then $fix\, \varphi \in P\langle \mu t\rangle$.

7.2   Polytypic Logical Relations

Logical relations were originally developed for the study of typed lambda calculi. The interested reader is referred to J. Mitchell's textbook [22] for a comprehensive treatment of logical relations. The basic idea is as follows. Say, we are given two models of the simply typed lambda calculus. Then the Basic Lemma of logical relations establishes that the meaning of a term in one model is logically related to its meaning in the other model (provided the meanings of the constants are logically related).

We have discussed in Section 5 that the specialization of a polytypic value can be seen as an interpretation of the simply typed lambda calculus. Actually, the interpretation is a two-stage process: the specialization maps a type term to a value term, which is then interpreted in some fixed domain-theoretic model. Note that we require domain-theoretic models in order to cope with (type) recursion. The only additional requirement is that the model must satisfy the polytypic fixpoint induction rule.

Models based on universal domains such as $P\omega$ are suitable for this purpose, see [1,22]. These models allow to interpret types as certain elements (closures or finitary projections) of the universal domain, so that type recursion can be interpreted by the (untyped) least fixpoint operator operator. Then the polytypic fixpoint induction rule is just a two-argument version of the ordinary fixpoint induction rule.

There are basically two differences to the 'classical' notion of logical relation. (1) We do not relate elements in two different models but different elements (obtained via the specialization) in the same model, that is, for some fixed model the meaning of $poly_1\langle t\rangle$ is logically related to the meaning of $poly_2\langle t\rangle$. (2) The type of $poly_1\langle t\rangle$ and $poly_2\langle t\rangle$ and consequently the type of their meanings depends on the type-index t. For that reason polytypic logical relations are parameterized by types (respectively, by the meaning of types). We have motivated this extension at some length in the previous section.

Now, for presenting the Basic Lemma we will use a 'semantic version' of $poly$, where the meaning of $poly\langle c\rangle$ is an element in some domain.

$$
\begin{aligned}
poly\langle x\rangle\, \eta &= \eta\, x \\
poly\langle t_1\, t_2\rangle\, \eta &= (poly\langle t_1\rangle\, \eta)\, (poly\langle t_2\rangle\, \eta) \\
poly\langle \Lambda x.t\rangle\, \eta &= \lambda v.poly\langle t\rangle\, (\eta(x := v)) \\
poly\langle \mu_\kappa\rangle\, \eta &= fix
\end{aligned}
$$

Here, η is an environment that maps type variables to values, and $\eta(x := v)$ is syntax for extending the environment η by the binding $x := v$. It is understood that the constructions on the right-hand side denote semantic values, for instance, $\lambda v.poly\langle t\rangle\, (\eta(x := v))$ denotes a function mapping v to $poly\langle t\rangle\, (\eta(x := v))$. For closed type terms we write $poly\langle t\rangle$ instead of $poly\langle t\rangle\, \eta$.

In presenting logical relations we will restrict ourselves to the binary case. The extension to the n-ary case is, however, entirely straightforward.

Definition 7. *A binary logical relation $\mathcal{R}$ over $\mathcal{D}_1$ and $\mathcal{D}_2$, where $\mathcal{D}_1$ and $\mathcal{D}_2$ are kind-indexed types, is a kind-indexed relation such that*

1. $\mathcal{R}\langle\kappa\rangle\ t_1\ \ldots\ t_n \subseteq \mathcal{D}_1\langle\kappa\rangle\ t_1\ \ldots\ t_n \times \mathcal{D}_2\langle\kappa\rangle\ t_1\ \ldots\ t_n$,
2. $(\varphi_1, \varphi_2) \in \mathcal{R}\langle\kappa_1 \to \kappa_2\rangle\ t_1\ \ldots\ t_n$
   $\equiv \forall x_1\ \ldots\ x_n \,.\, \forall v_1\ v_2 \,.\, (v_1, v_2) \in \mathcal{R}\langle\kappa_1\rangle\ x_1\ \ldots\ x_n$
   $\qquad\qquad \supset (\varphi_1\ v_1, \varphi_2\ v_2) \in \mathcal{R}\langle\kappa_2\rangle\ (t_1\ x_1)\ \ldots\ (t_n\ x_n)$,
3. *$\mathcal{R}$ is pointed,*
4. *$\mathcal{R}$ is chain-complete.*

Usually, a logical relation will be defined for the base case $\star$; the second clause of the definition then shows how to extend the relation to functional kinds. The third and the fourth condition ensure that a logical relation relates fixpoint operators. It is generally easy to prove that a relation is pointed: note that $\mathcal{R}\langle\kappa_1 \to \kappa_2\rangle$ is pointed if $\mathcal{R}\langle\kappa_2\rangle$ is pointed; hence it suffices to show that $\mathcal{R}\langle\star\rangle$ is pointed. Similarly, $\mathcal{R}\langle\kappa_1 \to \kappa_2\rangle$ is chain-complete if $\mathcal{R}\langle\kappa_1\rangle$ and $\mathcal{R}\langle\kappa_2\rangle$ are chain-complete; $\mathcal{R}\langle\star\rangle$ is chain-complete if it takes the form of an equation.

Lemma 1 (Basic Lemma). *Let $\mathcal{R}$ be a logical relation over $Poly_1$ and $Poly_2$ and let $poly_1\langle t\rangle :: Poly_1\langle\kappa\rangle\ t\ \ldots\ t$ and $poly_2\langle t\rangle :: Poly_2\langle\kappa\rangle\ t\ \ldots\ t$ be such that*

$$(poly_1\langle c\rangle, poly_2\langle c\rangle) \in \mathcal{R}\langle kind\ c\rangle\ c\ \ldots\ c$$

for every type constant $c \in C$. If η_1 and η_2 are environments and $\theta_1, \ldots, \theta_n$ are type substitutions such that $(\eta_1\ x, \eta_2\ x) \in \mathcal{R}\langle kind\ x\rangle\ (x\theta_1)\ \ldots\ (x\theta_n)$ for every type variable $x \in \mathrm{free}(t)$, then

$$(poly_1\langle t\rangle\ \eta_1, poly_2\langle t\rangle\ \eta_2) \in \mathcal{R}\langle\kappa\rangle\ (t\theta_1)\ \ldots\ (t\theta_n)$$

for every type term $t \in T^\circ(\kappa)$.

Proof. We use induction on the derivation of $u :: \kappa$.
Case $u = c$: the statement holds trivially since $\mathcal{R}$ relates constants.
Case $u = x$: the statement holds since η_1 and η_2 are related.
Case $u = t_1\ t_2$: by the induction hypothesis, we have

$(poly_1\langle t_1\rangle\ \eta_1, poly_2\langle t_1\rangle\ \eta_2) \in \mathcal{R}\langle\kappa_1 \to \kappa_2\rangle\ (t_1\theta_1)\ \ldots\ (t_1\theta_n)$
$\equiv \forall x_1\ \ldots\ x_n \,.\, \forall v_1\ v_2 \,.$
$\qquad (v_1, v_2) \in \mathcal{R}\langle\kappa_1\rangle\ x_1\ \ldots\ x_n$
$\qquad \supset ((poly_1\langle t_1\rangle\ \eta_1)\ v_1, (poly_2\langle t_1\rangle\ \eta_2)\ v_2) \in \mathcal{R}\langle\kappa_2\rangle\ ((t_1\theta_1)\ x_1)\ \ldots\ ((t_1\theta_n)\ x_n)$

and

$$(poly_1\langle t_2\rangle\ \eta_1, poly_2\langle t_2\rangle\ \eta_2) \in \mathcal{R}\langle\kappa_1\rangle\ (t_2\theta_1)\ \ldots\ (t_2\theta_n)\ ,$$

which implies $(poly_1\langle t_1\ t_2\rangle\ \eta_1, poly_2\langle t_1\ t_2\rangle\ \eta_2) \in \mathcal{R}\langle\kappa_2\rangle\ ((t_1\ t_2)\theta_1)\ \dots\ ((t_1\ t_2)\theta_n)$.

Case $u = \Lambda x.t$: we have to show that

$$(poly_1\langle\Lambda x.t\rangle\ \eta_1, poly_2\langle\Lambda x.t\rangle\ \eta_2) \in \mathcal{R}\langle kind\ x \to \kappa\rangle\ ((\Lambda x.t)\theta_1)\ \dots\ ((\Lambda x.t)\theta_n)$$
$$\equiv \forall x_1\ \dots\ x_n \blacksquare \forall v_1\ v_2 \blacksquare$$
$$(v_1, v_2) \in \mathcal{R}\langle kind\ x\rangle\ x_1\ \dots\ x_n$$
$$\supset ((poly_1\langle\Lambda x.t\rangle\ \eta_1)\ v_1, (poly_2\langle\Lambda x.t\rangle\ \eta_2)\ v_2)$$
$$\in \mathcal{R}\langle\kappa\rangle\ (((\Lambda x.t)\theta_1)\ x_1)\ \dots\ (((\Lambda x.t)\theta_n)\ x_n)\ .$$

Assume that $(v_1, v_2) \in \mathcal{R}\langle kind\ x\rangle\ x_1\ \dots\ x_n$. Since the modified environments $\eta_1(x := v_1)$ and $\eta_2(x := v_2)$ are related, we can invoke the induction hypothesis to obtain

$$(poly_1\langle t\rangle\ (\eta_1(x := v_1)), poly_2\langle t\rangle\ (\eta_2(x := v_2)))$$
$$\in \mathcal{R}\langle\kappa\rangle\ (t(\theta_1(x := x_1)))\ \dots\ (t(\theta_n(x := x_n)))\ .$$

Now, since $((\Lambda x.t)\theta_i)\ x_i = t(\theta_i(x := x_i))$, the statement follows.

Case $u = \mu_\kappa$: we have to show that

$$(fix, fix) \in \mathcal{R}\langle(\kappa \to \kappa) \to \kappa\rangle\ \mu\ \dots\ \mu$$
$$\equiv \forall x_1\ \dots\ x_n \blacksquare \forall\varphi_1\ \varphi_2 \blacksquare (\varphi_1, \varphi_2) \in \mathcal{R}\langle\kappa \to \kappa\rangle\ x_1\ \dots\ x_n$$
$$\supset (fix\ \varphi_1, fix\ \varphi_2) \in \mathcal{R}\langle\kappa\rangle\ (\mu x_1)\ \dots\ (\mu x_n)\ .$$

Assume that φ_1 and φ_2 are related. By definition of logical relations, we have

$$(\varphi_1, \varphi_2) \in \mathcal{R}\langle\kappa \to \kappa\rangle\ x_1\ \dots\ x_n$$
$$\equiv \forall y_1\ \dots\ y_n \blacksquare \forall v_1\ v_2 \blacksquare$$
$$(v_1, v_2) \in \mathcal{R}\langle\kappa\rangle\ y_1\ \dots\ y_n$$
$$\supset (\varphi_1\ v_1, \varphi_2\ v_2) \in \mathcal{R}\langle\kappa\rangle\ (x_1\ y_1)\ \dots\ (x_n\ y_n)\ .$$

Since $\mathcal{R}$ is pointed, we furthermore have $(\bot, \bot) \in \mathcal{R}\langle\kappa\rangle\ 0\ \dots\ 0$. The polytypic fixpoint induction rule then implies $(fix\ \varphi_1, fix\ \varphi_2) \in \mathcal{R}\langle\kappa\rangle\ (\mu x_1)\ \dots\ (\mu x_n)$. $\square$

7.3   Examples

Mapping Functions The functorial laws are captured by the logical relations $\mathcal{I}$ and $\mathcal{C}$, which we have discussed at length in Section 7.1.

$$\mathcal{I}\langle\star\rangle\ t \qquad\qquad \subseteq t \to t$$
$$\varphi \in \mathcal{I}\langle\star\rangle\ t \qquad\qquad \equiv \varphi = id :: t \to t$$
$$\mathcal{C}\langle\star\rangle\ t_1\ t_2\ t_3 \qquad\qquad \subseteq (t_2 \to t_3) \times (t_1 \to t_2) \times (t_1 \to t_3)$$
$$(\varphi_1, \varphi_2, \varphi_3) \in \mathcal{C}\langle\star\rangle\ t_1\ t_2\ t_3 \equiv \varphi_1 \cdot \varphi_2 = \varphi_3 :: t_1 \to t_3$$

It is not hard to see that both $\mathcal{I}$ and $\mathcal{C}$ are pointed and chain-complete. Since $map\langle c\rangle \in \mathcal{I}\langle kind\ c\rangle\ c$ and $(map\langle c\rangle, map\langle c\rangle, map\langle c\rangle) \in \mathcal{C}\langle kind\ c\rangle\ c\ c\ c$ for all type constants $c \in C$, the Basic Lemma implies $map\langle t\rangle \in \mathcal{I}\langle\kappa\rangle\ t$ and $(map\langle t\rangle, map\langle t\rangle, map\langle t\rangle) \in \mathcal{C}\langle\kappa\rangle\ t\ t\ t$ for all closed type terms $t \in T^\circ(\kappa)$.

Reductions Using a minor variant of $\mathcal{C}$ we can also relate reductions and mapping functions.

$$\mathcal{C}_z \langle \star \rangle \; t_1 \; t_2 \qquad\qquad \subseteq (t_2 \to z) \times (t_1 \to t_2) \times (t_1 \to z)$$
$$(\varphi_1, \varphi_2, \varphi_3) \in \mathcal{C}_z \langle \star \rangle \; t_1 \; t_2 \equiv \varphi_1 \cdot \varphi_2 = \varphi_3 :: t_1 \to z$$

Here, z is some fixed type that is passed unchanged to the base case. Now, given an element $e :: z$ and an operation $(\oplus) :: z \to z \to z$, we have

$$(reduce \langle t \rangle \; e \; (\oplus), map \langle t \rangle, reduce \langle t \rangle \; e \; (\oplus)) \in \mathcal{C}_z \langle \kappa \rangle \; t \; t \; .$$

An immediate consequence of this property is

$$reduce \langle f \rangle \; e \; (\oplus) \; \varphi \cdot map \langle f \rangle \; \psi = reduce \langle f \rangle \; e \; (\oplus) \; (\varphi \cdot \psi) \; ,$$

which shows how to fuse a reduction with a map. Now, in order to prove the polytypic property we merely have to verify that the statement holds for every type constant $c \in C$. Using the point-free definitions of map and red this amounts to showing that

$$\begin{aligned}
const \; e \cdot id &= const \; e \\
(\varphi_1 \bigtriangledown \varphi_2) \cdot (\psi_1 + \psi_2) &= (\varphi_1 \cdot \psi_1) \bigtriangledown (\varphi_2 \cdot \psi_2) \\
uncurry \; (\oplus) \cdot (\varphi_1 \times \varphi_2) \cdot (\psi_1 \times \psi_2) &= uncurry \; (\oplus) \cdot ((\varphi_1 \cdot \psi_1) \times (\varphi_2 \cdot \psi_2)) \; .
\end{aligned}$$

All three conditions hold.

Previous approaches to polytypic programming [11,7] required the programmer to specify the action of a polytypic function for the composition of two type constructors: for instance, for $fsize$ the polytypic programmer had to supply the equation $fsize \langle f_1 \cdot f_2 \rangle = fsum \langle f_1 \rangle \cdot map \langle f_1 \rangle \; (fsize \langle f_2 \rangle)$. Interestingly, using $reduce$-map fusion this equation can be derived from the definitions of $fsize$ and $fsum$ given in Fig. 3.

$$
\begin{aligned}
&fsize \langle f_1 \cdot f_2 \rangle \\
={}& \quad \{ \text{ definition } fsize \} \\
&reduce \langle f_1 \cdot f_2 \rangle \; 0 \; (+) \; (const \; 1) \\
={}& \quad \{ \; poly \langle f_1 \cdot f_2 \rangle = poly \langle f_1 \rangle \cdot poly \langle f_2 \rangle \; \} \\
&reduce \langle f_1 \rangle \; 0 \; (+) \; (reduce \langle f_2 \rangle \; 0 \; (+) \; (const \; 1)) \\
={}& \quad \{ \text{ definition } fsize \} \\
&reduce \langle f_1 \rangle \; 0 \; (+) \; (fsize \langle f_2 \rangle) \\
={}& \quad \{ \; reduce\text{-}map \text{ fusion } \} \\
&reduce \langle f_1 \rangle \; 0 \; (+) \; id \cdot map \langle f_1 \rangle \; (fsize \langle f_2 \rangle) \\
={}& \quad \{ \text{ definition } fsum \} \\
&fsum \langle f_1 \rangle \cdot map \langle f_1 \rangle \; (fsize \langle f_2 \rangle)
\end{aligned}
$$

As a final example let us generalize the fusion law for reductions given by L. Meertens in [18]. To this end we use the logical relation $\mathcal{F}$ defined by

$$\mathcal{F}_{z_1,z_2}\langle \star \rangle \, t \qquad\qquad \subseteq (t \to z_1) \times (t \to z_2)$$
$$(\varphi_1, \varphi_2) \in \mathcal{F}_{z_1,z_2}\langle \star \rangle \, t \equiv h \cdot \varphi_1 = \varphi_2 :: t \to z_2 \ ,$$

where z_1 and z_2 are fixed types and $h :: z_1 \to z_2$ is a fixed function. The polytypic fusion law, which gives conditions for fusing the function h with a reduction, then takes the following form (to ensure that $\mathcal{F}$ is pointed h must be strict)

$$h \perp = \perp$$
$$\cap \ h \ n = e$$
$$\cap \ h \ (v \oplus w) = h \ v \otimes h \ w$$
$$\supset (reduce\langle t \rangle \ n \ (\oplus), reduce\langle t \rangle \ e \ (\otimes)) \in \mathcal{F}_{z_1,z_2}\langle \kappa \rangle \, t \ .$$

We can apply this law, for instance, to prove that $length \cdot fflatten\langle f \rangle = fsize\langle f \rangle$.

8   Related Work

The idea to assign polykinded types to polytypic values is, to the best of the author's knowledge, original. Previous approaches to polytypic programming [11,8] were restricted in that they only allowed to parameterize values by types of one fixed kind. Three notable exceptions are Functorial ML (FML) [14], the work of F. Ruehr [27], and the work of P. Hoogendijk and R. Backhouse [10]. FML allows to quantify over functor arities in type schemes (since FML handles only regular, first-order functors, kinds can be simplified to arities). However, no formal account of this feature is given and the informal description makes use of an infinitary typing rule. Furthermore, the polytypic definitions based on this extension are rather unwieldy from a notational point of view. F. Ruehr also restricts type indices to types of one fixed kind. Additional flexibility is, however, gained through the use of a more expressive kind language, which incorporates kind variables. This extension is used to define a higher-order map indexed by types of kind $(\alpha \to \star) \to \star$, where α is a kind variable. Clearly, this mapping function is subsumed by the polytypic map given in Section 2. Whether kind polymorphism has other benefits remains to be seen. Finally, definitions of polytypic values that are indexed by relators of different arities can be found in the work of P. Hoogendijk and R. Backhouse on commuting datatypes [10].

The results in this paper improve upon my earlier work on polytypic programming [8] in the following respects. As remarked above the previous work considered only polytypic values indexed by types of one fixed kind. Furthermore, the approach could only handle type indices of second-order kind or less and type constants (that is, primitive type constructors) were restricted to first-order kind or kind $\star$. Using polykinded types all these restrictions can be dropped.

9   Conclusion

Haskell possesses a rich type system, which essentially corresponds to the simply typed lambda calculus (with kinds playing the rôle of types). This type system presents a challenge for polytypism: how can we define polytypic values and how can we assign types to these values? This paper offers satisfactory answers to both questions. It turns out that polytypic values possess polykinded types, that is, types that are defined by induction on the structure of kinds. Interestingly, to define a polykinded type it suffices to specify the image of the base kind; likewise, to define a polytypic value it suffices to specify the images of type constants. Everything else comes for free. In fact, the specialization of a polytypic value can be regarded as an interpretation of the simply typed lambda calculus. This renders it possible to adapt one of the main tools for studying typed lambda calculi, logical relations, to polytypic reasoning. To prove a polytypic property it suffices to prove the assertion for type constants. Everything else is taken care of automatically. We have applied this framework to show among other things that the polytypic *map* satisfies polytypic versions of the two functorial laws.

Acknowledgements

I would like to thank Johan Jeuring for stimulating discussions on polytypic programming and for his suggestion to rewrite Section 7. Thanks are furthermore due to Fritz Ruehr for his helpful comments on an earlier draft of this paper. Finally, I am grateful to the five anonymous referees, who went over and above the call of duty, providing numerous constructive comments for the revision of this paper.

References

1. Roberto Amadio, Kim B. Bruce, and Giuseppe Longo. The finitary projection model for second order lambda calculus and solutions to higher order domain equations. In *Proceedings of the Symposium on Logic in Computer Science, Cambridge, Massachusetts*, pages 122–130. IEEE Computer Society, June 1986. 20
2. Roland Backhouse, Patrik Jansson, Johan Jeuring, and Lambert Meertens. Generic Programming — An Introduction —. In S. Doaitse Swierstra, Pedro R. Henriques, and Jose N. Oliveira, editors, *3rd International Summer School on Advanced Functional Programming, Braga, Portugal*, volume 1608 of *Lecture Notes in Computer Science*, pages 28–115, Berlin, 1999. Springer-Verlag. 2, 18
3. Richard Bird, Oege de Moor, and Paul Hoogendijk. Generic functional programming with types and relations. *Journal of Functional Programming*, 6(1):1–28, January 1996. 2
4. Richard Bird and Lambert Meertens. Nested datatypes. In J. Jeuring, editor, *Fourth International Conference on Mathematics of Program Construction, MPC'98, Marstrand, Sweden*, volume 1422 of *Lecture Notes in Computer Science*, pages 52–67. Springer-Verlag, June 1998. 5
5. M. M. Fokkinga. Monadic maps and folds for arbitrary datatypes. Technical Report Memoranda Informatica 94-28, University of Twente, June 1994. 14

6. Jean-Yves Girard. *Interprétation fonctionelle et élimination des coupures dans l'arithmétique d'ordre supérieur.* PhD thesis, Université Paris VII, 1972. 11

7. Ralf Hinze. Polytypic functions over nested datatypes. *Discrete Mathematics and Theoretical Computer Science*, 3(4):159–180, September 1999. 15, 23

8. Ralf Hinze. A new approach to generic functional programming. In Thomas W. Reps, editor, *Proceedings of the 27th Annual ACM SIGPLAN-SIGACT Symposium on Principles of Programming Languages, Boston, Massachusetts, January 19-21*, pages 119–132, January 2000. 2, 3, 7, 24

9. Ralf Hinze. Polytypic programming with ease, January 2000. In submission. 10, 14

10. Paul Hoogendijk and Roland Backhouse. When do datatypes commute? In Eugenio Moggi and Giuseppe Rosolini, editors, *Proceedings of the 7th International Conference on Category Theory and Computer Science (Santa Margherita Ligure, Italy, September 4-6)*, volume 1290 of *Lecture Notes in Computer Science*, pages 242–260. Springer-Verlag, 1997. 24

11. Patrik Jansson and Johan Jeuring. PolyP—a polytypic programming language extension. In *Conference Record 24th ACM SIGPLAN-SIGACT Symposium on Principles of Programming Languages, POPL'97, Paris, France*, pages 470–482. ACM-Press, January 1997. 3, 23, 24

12. Patrik Jansson and Johan Jeuring. PolyLib—A library of polytypic functions. In Roland Backhouse and Tim Sheard, editors, *Informal Proceedings Workshop on Generic Programming, WGP'98, Marstrand, Sweden*. Department of Computing Science, Chalmers University of Technology and Göteborg University, June 1998. 14

13. Patrik Jansson and Johan Jeuring. Calculating polytypic data conversion programs, 1999. In submission. 14

14. C. B. Jay, G. Bellè, and E. Moggi. Functorial ML. *Journal of Functional Programming*, 8(6):573–619, November 1998. 24

15. M. P. Jones and J. C. Peterson. *Hugs 98 User Manual*, May 1999. Available from http://www.haskell.org/hugs. 5

16. Daniel Leivant. Polymorphic type inference. In *Proc. 10th Symposium on Principles of Programming Languages*, 1983. 5

17. Nancy Jean McCracken. *An Investigation of a Programming Language with a Polymorphic Type Structure.* PhD thesis, Syracuse University, June 1979. 3

18. Lambert Meertens. Calculate polytypically! In H. Kuchen and S.D. Swierstra, editors, *Proceedings 8th International Symposium on Programming Languages: Implementations, Logics, and Programs, PLILP'96, Aachen, Germany*, volume 1140 of *Lecture Notes in Computer Science*, pages 1–16. Springer-Verlag, September 1996. 15, 24

19. Erik Meijer and Graham Hutton. Bananas in space: Extending fold and unfold to exponential types. In *Conference Record 7th ACM SIGPLAN/SIGARCH and IFIP WG 2.8 International Conference on Functional Programming Languages and Computer Architecture, FPCA'95, La Jolla, San Diego, CA, USA*, pages 324–333. ACM-Press, June 1995. 4

20. Erik Meijer and Johan Jeuring. Merging monads and folds for functional programming. In J. Jeuring and E. Meijer, editors, *1st International Spring School on Advanced Functional Programming Techniques, Båstad, Sweden*, volume 925 of *Lecture Notes in Computer Science*, pages 228–266. Springer-Verlag, Berlin, 1995. 14

21. Robin Milner. A theory of type polymorphism in programming. *Journal of Computer and System Sciences*, 17(3):348–375, 1978. 2

22. John C. Mitchell. *Foundations for Programming Languages*. The MIT Press, Cambridge, MA, 1996. 19, 20

23. Alan Mycroft. Polymorphic type schemes and recursive definitions. In M. Paul and B. Robinet, editors, *Proceedings of the International Symposium on Programming, 6th Colloquium, Toulouse, France*, volume 167 of *Lecture Notes in Computer Science*, pages 217–228, 1984. 5

24. Chris Okasaki. *Purely Functional Data Structures*. Cambridge University Press, 1998. 5

25. Simon Peyton Jones and John Hughes, editors. *Haskell 98 — A Non-strict, Purely Functional Language*, February 1999. Available from http://www.haskell.org/-definition/. 3, 8

26. Simon L. Peyton Jones. Compiling Haskell by program transformation: A report from the trenches. In Hanne Riis Nielson, editor, *Programming Languages and Systems—ESOP'96, 6th European Symposium on Programming, Linköping, Sweden, 22–24 April*, volume 1058 of *Lecture Notes in Computer Science*, pages 18–44. Springer-Verlag, 1996. 11

27. Karl Fritz Ruehr. *Analytical and Structural Polymorphism Expressed using Patterns over Types*. PhD thesis, University of Michigan, 1992. 24

28. The GHC Team. *The Glasgow Haskell Compiler User's Guide, Version 4.04*, September 1999. Available from http://www.haskell.org/ghc/documentation.html. 5

29. Philip Wadler. Theorems for free! In *The Fourth International Conference on Functional Programming Languages and Computer Architecture (FPCA'89), London, UK*, pages 347–359. Addison-Wesley Publishing Company, September 1989. 2

The Zip Calculus[*]

Mark Tullsen

Department of Computer Science
Yale University
New Haven CT 06520-8285
tullsen@cs.yale.edu

Abstract. Many have recognized the need for genericity in programming and program transformation. Genericity over data types has been achieved with polymorphism. Genericity over type constructors, often called polytypism, is an area of active research. This paper proposes that another kind of genericity is needed: genericity over the length of tuples. Untyped languages allow for such genericity but typed languages do not (except for languages allowing dependent types). The contribution of this paper is to present the "zip calculus," a typed lambda calculus that provides genericity over the length of tuples and yet does not require the full generality of dependent types.

1 Introduction

The key to writing robust software is abstraction, but genericity is often needed to use abstraction: to write a generic sort routine, genericity over types is needed (i.e., polymorphism); to write a generic fold (or catamorphism, a function inductively defined over an inductive data structure), genericity over *type constructors* (e.g., List and Tree where List a and Tree a are types) is needed—this is often called polytypism.

In program transformation the need for genericity is amplified. For example, in a monomorphic language, one cannot write a polymorphic sort but must write sortInt, sortFloat, and etc. One will have laws about sortInt and sortFloat instead of just one law about a generic sort; also one must transform sortInt and sortFloat separately, even if the program derivation can be "cut-and-pasted". So, the ability to write a generic function, sort, reduces not only program size, but also the number of laws and the length of program derivations.

Consequently, the program transformation community—notably the Bird-Meertens Formalism (or Squiggol) community [3,12,13]—has been working to make programs more generic: not just polymorphic, but polytypic [8,9,10,11]. However, the genericity provided by polymorphism and polytypism is still not adequate to achieve certain abstractions; another form of genericity is often needed—genericity over the length of tuples. This paper shows the usefulness of "n-tuples" (tuples whose lengths are unknown) and proposes a method to extend a programming language with n-tuples.

---

[*] This research was supported in part by NSF under Grant Number CCR-9706747.

R. Backhouse and J. N. Oliveira (Eds.): MPC 2000, LNCS 1837, pp. 28–44, 2000.
© Springer-Verlag Berlin Heidelberg 2000

Section 2 gives examples of the usefulness of n-tuples. Section 3 describes a typed lambda calculus, "the zip calculus", which gives genericity over n-tuples. Section 4 returns to the examples and shows what programs, laws, and program derivations look like using the zip calculus; other applications are also presented, including how to generalize catamorphisms to mutually recursive data types. Finally, section 5 discusses some limitations and compares this work to related work.

2   Why Are N-Tuples Needed?

An n-tuple is a tuple whose length is unknown. This section presents the usefulness of n-tuples: just like polymorphism and polytypism, n-tuples result in more general programs (2.1), more general laws about those programs (2.2), and more general program derivations (2.3).

2.1   More General Programs

The following functions are defined in the Haskell [6] Prelude and Libraries

```
zip  :: ([a],[b])→[(a,b)]
zip3 :: ([a],[b],[c])→[(a,b,c)]
...
zip7 :: ([a],[b],[c],[d],[e],[f],[g])→[(a,b,c,d,e,f,g)]
```

which combine lists element-wise.[1] Also, there are the family of functions unzip, unzip3, ... and the family of functions zipWith, zipWith3, ... To write the zip3, ..., zip7 functions is not hard but tedious. It is clearly desirable to abstract over these and write one generic zip, one generic zipWith, and one generic unzip.

2.2   More General Laws

Note the free theorem [18] for zip:

```
map(cross(f,g)) o zip  =  zip o cross(map f,map g)
where
cross (f,g) (x,y) = (f x,g y)
```

(Note that "o" is used for function composition; "map f" applies f to each element of a list.) The comparable theorem for zip3 is

```
map(cross3(f,g,h)) o zip3 = zip3 o cross3(map f,map g,map h)
where
cross3 (f,g,h) (x,y,z) = (f x, g y, h z)
```

---

[1] Actually, it is their curried counterparts which are defined, but the uncurried version is used here for illustrative purposes.

To generate these laws is not hard but tedious and error-prone. To formulate this *family* of laws yet another family of functions is needed: `cross`, `cross3`, `cross4`, ... And note the following laws for 2-tuples and 3-tuples[2]

```
(fst x, snd x) = x
(fst3 x, snd3 x, thd3 x) = x
```

for which one needs *another* set of families of functions: `fst`, `fst3`, `fst4`, ... and `snd`, `snd3`, `snd4`, ... One would wish to generalize over these *families* of laws. Having fewer and more generic laws is very desirable in a program transformation system: one has fewer laws to learn, fewer laws to search, and more robust program derivations (i.e., program derivations are more likely to remain valid when applied to a modified input program).

2.3   More General Program Derivations

It is common to have program derivations of the following form:

>   `fst e`   *Prove the case for the*
> `= ...`   *"fst" of the tuple.*
> `= e1`
>
> Similarly, `snd e = e2`   *Wave hands.*
>
> Thus,   *Make a conclusion about*
>   `e = (fst e,snd e) = (e1,e2)`   *the tuple as a whole.*

When arguing informally, this works well and of course scales easily to 3-tuples and up. However, in a practical program transformation system this "similarly" step must be done without "hand waving" and hopefully without duplicating the derivation. One way to do this is to express the above law in some meta-language or meta-logic where one could say something like $\forall n.\forall i < n.P(\#i)$ (using ML syntax for projections where $\#1 = $ `fst`, $\#2 = $ `snd`).

However, a meta-language is now needed to express program laws. A simpler approach to transformation, the schematic approach [7], avoids the use of a meta-language: program laws are of the form "$e_1 = e_2 \Leftarrow e_3 = e_4$" ($e_1, e_2, e_3, e_4$ are programs in the language, all free variables are implicitly universally quantified, and the premise is optional); program derivations are developed by successively applying program laws: the law is instantiated, the premise is satisfied, then the conclusion is used to replace equals for equals. However, using this approach for the above derivation requires one to generate nearly identical derivations for the `fst` and `snd` cases. Is it possible to avoid this duplication of derivations? Note that, in general, the form of (`e1,e2`) is (`C[fst]`,`C[snd]`)[3] (or can be

---

[2] Ignoring the complication that these laws are not valid in Haskell, which has lifted tuples; these same laws are valid in the Zip Calculus which has unlifted tuples.

[3] Where `C[e]` represents a program context `C[]` with its holes filled by expression e.

transformed into such a form). So, one would like to merge the two similar derivations

```
fst e = ... = C[fst]
snd e = ... = C[snd]
```

into a single derivation

```
#i e  = ... = C[#i]
```

However, this still does not work because the "i" in #i must be a constant and cannot be a variable or expression (in order for the program to be type-able). But if "i" could be a variable, then simple equational reasoning can be used—as in the schematic approach—without the need to add a meta-language. The zip calculus allows one to do this.

3   The Zip Calculus

The zip calculus is a typed lambda calculus extended with n-tuples and sums. In particular, it starts as F_ω—though in the form of a Pure Type System (PTS) [2,15]. To this is added a construct for n-tuples and then n-sums are added (very simply using n-tuples). As the syntax of terms and types was becoming very close (because tuples exist at the type level), the choice of a PTS seemed natural: in a PTS, terms, types, and kinds are all written in the same syntax. Also, the generality of a PTS makes for fewer typing rules. However, the generality of a PTS can make a type system harder to understand: it is difficult to know what is a valid term, type, and kind without understanding the type checking rules.

3.1   Syntax and Semantics

The syntax of the terms of the zip calculus is in Fig. 1. The pseudo syntactic classes i, d, and t are used to provide intuition for what is enforced by the type system (but not by the syntax). The first five terms in Fig. 1 correspond to F_ω, encoded as a PTS (although one needs to see the typing rules in the following section to get the full story). In a PTS, terms and types are merged into a single syntax. The correspondence between F_ω in the standard formulation and as a PTS is as follows:

standard	PTS		
$\lambda x{:}\alpha.\, e$	$\lambda x{:}\alpha.\, e$		value abstraction
$\Lambda\alpha.e$	$\lambda\alpha{:}\star.\, e$		type abstraction
$\alpha \to \beta$	$\Pi v{:}\alpha.\, \beta$	(v not free in β)	function type
$\forall\alpha.B$	$\Pi\alpha{:}\star.\, B$		quantification

So, lambda abstractions are used both for value abstractions and type abstractions; Π terms are used for the function type and quantification; $\star$ represents the type of types. (For a more leisurely introduction to Pure Type Systems, see [15].)

$$
\begin{array}{lll}
e & ::= v & \text{variables} \\
  & \mid \lambda v{:}t.\,e & \text{abstraction} \\
  & \mid e_1 e_2 & \text{application} \\
  & \mid \Pi v{:}t_1.\,t_2 & \text{type of abstractions} \\
  & \mid \star & \text{type of types} \\[4pt]
  & \mid \langle e_1, e_2, ...\rangle & \text{tuple} \\
  & \mid m_n & \text{projection } (1 \le m \le n) \\
  & \mid n\mathsf{d} & \text{dimension } (1 \le n) \\
  & \mid \mathrm{D} & \text{type of dimensions} \\[4pt]
  & \mid +_d t & \text{sum type} \\
  & \mid \mathit{In}_d & \text{constructors for } +_d \\
  & \mid \mathsf{case}_d & \text{destructor for } +_d \\
\end{array}
$$

$$
\begin{array}{lll}
i & ::= e & \text{projections (of type } n\mathsf{d}) \\
d & ::= e & \text{dimensions (of type D)} \\
t & ::= e & \text{types and kinds (of type } \star \text{ or } \square) \\
\end{array}
$$

$$
m, n ::= \{\text{natural numbers}\}
$$

Fig. 1. Syntax

To this base are added the following: (1) Tuples which are no longer restricted to the term level but also exist at the type level. (2) Projection constants (m_n - get the m-th element of an n-tuple), their types ($n\mathsf{d}$ - dimensions, where $m_n{:}n\mathsf{d}$; "d" here is the literal character), and "D" the type of these $n\mathsf{d}$ ("D" has a role analogous to $\star$). And (3) n-sums made via n-tuples: for n-sums ($+_{n\mathsf{d}}\langle t_1, ..., t_n\rangle$) the constructor family, $\mathit{In}_{n\mathsf{d}}$, is an n-tuple of constructors and the destructor $\mathsf{case}_{n\mathsf{d}}$ takes an n-tuple of functions.

Since one can write tuples of types, one must distinguish between $\langle t_1, t_2\rangle$ (a tuple of types, having kind $\Pi_-{:}2\mathsf{d} \to \star$)[4] and $\times_{2\mathsf{d}}\langle t_1, t_2\rangle$ (a type, i.e., something with kind $\star$).

A 3-tuple such as $\langle e_1, e_2, e_3\rangle$ is a function whose range is the set $\{1_3, 2_3, 3_3\}$ (the projections with type $3\mathsf{d}$). To get the second element of a 3-tuple, one applies the 2_3 projection to it; thus "$\langle e_1, e_2, e_3\rangle\,2_3$" reduces to e_2. The type of the tuple is a "dependent type" (a Π term): for instance, $\langle e_1, e_2, e_3\rangle$ has type "$\Pi i : 3\mathsf{d}\,.\,\langle E_1, E_2, E_3\rangle\,i$" where $e_i : E_i$. Genericity over tuple length is achieved because we can write functions such as "$\lambda d : D.\lambda i : d.e$" in which d can be any dimension (1d,2d,...). Although tuples are functions, the following syntactic sugar is used to syntactically distinguish tuple functions from standard functions:

---

[4] The variable "_" is used for unused variables.

Reduction Rules:

$$(\lambda v{:}t.e_1)\,e_2 = e_1\{e_2/v\} \quad (\beta\ \text{reduce})$$
$$\langle e_1,...,e_n\rangle\,i_n = e_i \quad (\times\ \text{reduce})$$
$$\text{case}_d\,e\,(In_d.i\ e') = e.i\ e' \quad (+\ \text{reduce})$$

Eta laws:

$$\lambda v{:}a.\,e\,v = e \quad \text{if } e :: \Pi a{:}A.b,\ v \notin \text{fv}(e) \quad (\Pi\ \text{eta})$$
$$\langle e\,1_n,...,e\,n_n\rangle = e \quad \text{if } e :: \Pi i{:}nd.\,A \quad (\times\ \text{eta})$$
$$\text{case}_d\,In_d\,e = e \quad \text{if } e :: +_d A \quad (+\ \text{eta})$$

Instantiation:

$$h \circ \text{case}_d\,f = \text{case}_d\,\langle^{i:d}\,h \circ f.i\rangle \qquad \text{if } h \text{ strict} \quad (\text{inst})$$
$$C[\text{case}_d\,\langle^{i:d}\lambda v{:}t.\,e\rangle\,x] = \text{case}_d\,\langle^{i:d}\lambda v{:}t.\,C[e]\rangle\,x \quad \text{if } C[] \text{ strict} \quad (\text{inst})$$

Fig. 2. Laws

$$\langle^{i:d}\ e\rangle \equiv \lambda i{:}d.\ e$$
$$e.i \equiv e\ i$$
$$\times_d t \equiv \Pi i{:}d.t\ i$$

Also, in what follows, $a \to b$ is used as syntactic sugar for $\Pi_{-}{:}a.\,b$; in this case, a Π type corresponds to a normal function.

The semantics is given operationally: the three reduction rules of Fig. 2 are applied left to right with a leftmost outermost reduction strategy. Translating the (β reduce) and (Π eta) laws into the above syntactic sugar gives these laws:

$$\langle^{i:d}e\rangle.j = e\{j/i\} \qquad\qquad (\text{n-tuple reduce})$$
$$\langle^{i:d}e.i\rangle = e \qquad \text{if } e :: \times_d A,\ i \notin \text{fv}(e) \qquad (\text{n-tuple eta})$$

To give some intuition regarding the semantics of n-tuples, note this equivalence:

$$\langle^{i:2d}\ \langle f,g\rangle.i\ \langle x,y\rangle.i\rangle$$

= {× eta}

$$\langle\langle^{i:2d}\ \langle f,g\rangle.i\ \langle x,y\rangle.i\rangle.1_2,$$
$$\langle^{i:2d}\ \langle f,g\rangle.i\ \langle x,y\rangle.i\rangle.2_2\rangle$$

= {*n-tuple reduce*, twice}

$$\langle\langle f,g\rangle.1_2\ \langle x,y\rangle.1_2,$$
$$\langle f,g\rangle.2_2\ \langle x,y\rangle.2_2\rangle$$

= {× *reduce*, four times}

$$\langle f\ x,\ g\ y\rangle$$

The tuples $\langle f,g\rangle$ and $\langle x,y\rangle$ are "zipped" together, thus the name "zip calculus."

$$\frac{\Gamma \vdash a : A, \quad \Gamma \vdash B : s, \quad A =_\beta B}{\Gamma \vdash a : B} \ \text{(conv)} \qquad\qquad \frac{c : s \in \mathcal{A}}{\vdash c : s} \ \text{(axiom)}$$

$$\frac{\Gamma \vdash A : s}{\Gamma, x : A \vdash x : A} \ \text{(var)} \qquad\qquad \frac{\Gamma \vdash b : B \quad \Gamma \vdash A : s}{\Gamma, x : A \vdash b : B} \ \text{(weak)}$$

$$\frac{\Gamma \vdash f : (\Pi x : A.B), \quad \Gamma \vdash a : A}{\Gamma \vdash f\, a : B\{a/x\}} \ \text{(app)} \qquad \frac{\Gamma, x : A \vdash b : B, \quad \Gamma \vdash (\Pi x : A.B) : t}{\Gamma \vdash (\lambda x : A.b) : (\Pi x : A.B)} \ \text{(lam)}$$

$$\frac{\Gamma \vdash A : s, \quad \Gamma, x : A \vdash B : t, \quad (s,t,u) \in \mathcal{R}}{\Gamma \vdash (\Pi x : A.B) : u} \ \text{(pi)}$$

Fig. 3. Type Judgments for a Pure Type System

$$\frac{\forall j \in \{1..n\}. \ \Gamma \vdash a_j : A_j, \quad \Gamma \vdash (\Pi i : nd. \langle A_1, \dots, A_n \rangle\, i) : t}{\Gamma \vdash \langle a_1, \dots, a_n \rangle \ : \ \Pi i : nd. \langle A_1, \dots, A_n \rangle\, i} \ \text{(tuple)}$$

Fig. 4. Additional Type Judgments for the Zip Calculus

3.2 The Type System

The terms of a PTS consist of the first four terms of Fig. 1 (variables, lambda abstractions, applications, and Π terms) plus a set of constants, $\mathcal{C}$. The specification of a PTS is given by a triple $(\mathcal{S}, \mathcal{A}, \mathcal{R})$ where $\mathcal{S}$ is a subset of $\mathcal{C}$ called the sorts, $\mathcal{A}$ is a set of axioms of the form "$c : s$" where $c \in \mathcal{C}$, $s \in \mathcal{S}$, and $\mathcal{R}$ is a set of rules of the form $(s1, s2, s3)$ where $s1, s2, s3 \in \mathcal{S}$. The typing judgments for a PTS are as in Fig. 3. In a PTS, the definition of $=_\beta$ in the judgment (conv) is beta-equivalence (alpha-equivalent terms are identified).

In the zip calculus, the set of sorts is $\mathcal{S} = \{1\mathrm{d}, 2\mathrm{d}, \dots\} \cup \{\star, \square, D\}$, the set of constants is $\mathcal{C} = \mathcal{S} \cup \{m_n | 1 \le m \le n\}$, and the axioms $\mathcal{A}$ and rules $\mathcal{R}$ are as follows:

$\mathcal{A}$ axioms	$\mathcal{R}$ rules	
$\star : \square$	$(\star, \star, \star)$	$\lambda v_e : t . e$
$m_n : nd$	$(\square, \star, \star)$	$\lambda v_t : T . e$
$nd : D$	$(\square, \square, \square)$	$\lambda v_t : T . t$
$D : \square$	$(D, D, \star)$	$\lambda v_i : d . i$
	$(D, \star, \star)$	$\lambda v_i : d . e$
	$(D, \square, \square)$	$\lambda v_i : d . t$

The $\mathcal{R}$ rules, used in the (pi) rule, indicate what lambda abstractions are allowed (which is the same as saying which Π terms are well-typed). Here there are six $\mathcal{R}$ rules which correspond to the six allowed forms of lambda abstraction. The expression to the right of each rule is an intuitive representation of the type of lambda abstraction which the rule represents (e - terms, t - types, T - kinds, i - projections, d - dimensions, v_x - variable in class x). For instance, the $(D, D, \star)$ rule means that lambda abstractions are allowed of form $\lambda v_i : d . i$ where $d : D$ (i.e., d is a dimension such as 3d) and thus v_i represents a projection such as 2_3

$$\frac{\Gamma \vdash f :\!\twoheadrightarrow (\Pi x : A.B), \quad \Gamma \vdash a : A', \ A =_\beta A'}{\Gamma \vdash f\,a : B\{a/x\}} \ (\text{app})$$

$$\frac{x : A \in \Gamma}{\Gamma \vdash x : A} \ (\text{var})$$

$$\frac{\Gamma, x : A \vdash b : B, \quad \Gamma \vdash (\Pi x : A.B) : t}{\Gamma \vdash (\lambda x : A.b) : (\Pi x : A.B)} \ (\text{lam})$$

$$\frac{c : s \in \mathcal{A}}{\vdash c : s} \ (\text{axiom})$$

$$\frac{\Gamma \vdash A :\!\twoheadrightarrow s, \quad \Gamma, x : A \vdash B :\!\twoheadrightarrow t, \quad (s,t,u) \in \mathcal{R}}{\Gamma \vdash (\Pi x : A.B) : u} \ (\text{pi})$$

$$\frac{\Gamma \vdash a : A, \quad A \twoheadrightarrow_\beta B}{\Gamma \vdash a :\!\twoheadrightarrow B} \ (\text{red})$$

Fig. 5. Syntax Directed Type Judgments for a Functional PTS

$$\frac{\forall j \in \{1..n\}. \ \Gamma \vdash a_j :\!\twoheadrightarrow A_j, \quad \Gamma \vdash (\Pi i : nd. \langle A_1, \ldots, A_n \rangle\, i) : t}{\Gamma \vdash \langle a_1, ..., a_n \rangle \ : \ \Pi i : nd. \langle A_1, \ldots, A_n \rangle\, i} \ (\text{tuple1})$$

$$\frac{\forall j \in \{1..n\}. \ \Gamma \vdash a_j :\!\twoheadrightarrow A}{\Gamma \vdash \langle a_1, ..., a_n \rangle \ : \ \Pi\_ : nd. A} \ (\text{tuple2})$$

$$\frac{\Gamma \vdash f :\!\twoheadrightarrow C, \quad \Gamma \vdash a :\!\twoheadrightarrow A, \ C =_\eta \Pi x : A.B}{\Gamma \vdash f\,a : B\{a/x\}} \ (\text{app}')$$

$$\frac{\Gamma \vdash a : A, \quad A \twoheadrightarrow_{\beta\delta} B}{\Gamma \vdash a :\!\twoheadrightarrow B} \ (\text{red}')$$

Fig. 6. Syntax Directed Type Judgments for the Zip Calculus

and the body i must have type D, and the type of the type of this whole lambda expression is $\star$.

In the zip calculus there is an additional term, $\langle e_1, e_2, ... \rangle$, which cannot be treated as a constant in a PTS (ignoring sums for the moment). The addition of this term requires two extensions to the PTS: one, an additional typing judgment (Fig. 4) and two, the $=_\beta$ relation in the (conv) judgment must be extended to include not just (β reduce) but also ($\times$ reduce) and ($\times$ eta).

To get generic sums, one needs only add $+$ as a constant and the following two primitives

```
In   :: ΠI:D. Πa:×ᵢ⟨-:ᴵ ⋆⟩.      ×ᵢ⟨ⁱ:ᴵ a.i→+ᵢ a⟩
case :: ΠI:D. Πa:×ᵢ⟨-:ᴵ ⋆⟩. Πb:⋆. ×ᵢ⟨ⁱ:ᴵ a.i→b⟩ → (+ᵢ a→b)
```

where In is a generic injection function: e.g., for the sum $+_{2d}\langle a, b \rangle$ the two injection functions are "(In 2d $\langle a, b \rangle$).1_2" and "(In 2d $\langle a, b \rangle$).2_2".

3.3 Type Checking

There are numerous properties, such as subject reduction, which are true of Pure Type Systems in general [2]. There are also known type checking algorithms for certain subclasses of PTSs. Although the zip calculus is not a PTS, it is hoped that most results for PTSs will carry over to the "almost PTS" zip calculus.

A PTS is functional when the relations $\mathcal{A}$ and $\mathcal{R}$ are functions ($c : s_1 \in \mathcal{A}$ and $c : s_2 \in \mathcal{A}$ imply $s_1 = s_2$; $(s, t, u_1) \in \mathcal{R}$ and $(s, t, u_2) \in \mathcal{R}$ imply $u_1 = u_2$). In the zip calculus, $\mathcal{A}$ and $\mathcal{R}$ are functions. If a PTS is functional there is an efficient type-checking algorithm as given in Fig. 5 (cf. [15] and [17]), where the type judgments of Fig. 3 have been restructured to make them syntax-directed. The judgment (red) defines the relation "$\Gamma \vdash x :\twoheadrightarrow X$" and $\twoheadrightarrow_\beta$ is beta-reduction.

This algorithm can be modified as in Fig. 6. The rules (tuple1) and (tuple2) replace (tuple) from Fig. 4. The rules (app') and (red') replace the (app) and (red) judgments of Fig. 5. Here $\twoheadrightarrow_{\beta\delta}$ is $\twoheadrightarrow_\beta$ extended with ($\times$ reduce) and $=_\eta$ is equality up to ($\times$ eta) convertibility. The reason for the change of (app) is because f may evaluate to

$$\langle \Pi x : a_1.b_1, ..., \Pi x : a_n.b_n \rangle.i$$

and application should be valid when, for instance, this is equivalent to a type of the form

$$\Pi x : (\langle a_1, ..., a_n \rangle.i) . \langle b_1, ..., b_n \rangle.i$$

A proof of the soundness and completeness of this algorithm should be similar to that in [17].

4   Examples

This section provides several examples of the usefulness of the zip calculus. Writing programs in an explicitly typed calculus can be onerous; to alleviate this, some syntactic shortcuts are often used in the following: the "$:t$" is dropped in lambdas and in the n-tuple syntactic sugar; m is put for the projection m_n; the dimension d is dropped from $\times_d$; and, when applying dimensions and types, "f_{d,t_1,t_2}" is put for "$f\,d\,t_1\,t_2$". Also, $f\,x = e$ is syntactic sugar for $f = \lambda x.e$. The following conventions are used for variables: t, a, b, c, A, B, C for types (terms of type $\star$); i, j, k, l for projections (terms of type $n\mathsf{d}$); and d, I, J, K, L for dimension variables (terms of type D).

4.1   More General Programs

An uncurried `zip3` is as follows in Haskell:

```
zip3 :: ([a],[b],[c]) → [(a,b,c)]
zip3 (a:as,b:bs,c:cs) = (a,b,c) : zip3 (as,bs,cs)
zip3 _            = []
```

If Haskell had n-tuples, one could write a generic `zip` as follows:

```
zip :: ×⟨ⁱ [a.i]⟩ → [×a]
zip   ⟨ⁱ x.i:xs.i⟩ = x : zip xs
zip   _          = []
```

Note that patterns are extended with n-tuples. Unfortunately, this function cannot be written in the zip calculus (extended with recursive data types and a fix point operator) unless a primitive such as `seqTupleMaybe` is added:

```
seqTupleMaybe :: ×⟨ⁱ a.i → Maybe b.i⟩ → ×a → Maybe(×b)
```

However, once this primitive is added, one can define n-tuple patterns in terms of this primitive. (Using `seqTupleMaybe` we can translate patterns out of the language similarly to that done in [16].) Section 5.1 returns to this problem of functions that must be primitives.

4.2 More General Laws

The parametricity theorem for an uncurried zip3

```
map(cross3 ⟨f,g,h⟩) o zip3 = zip3 o cross3 ⟨map f,map g,map h⟩
where
cross3 ⟨f,g,h⟩ ⟨x,y,z⟩ = ⟨f x, g y, h z⟩
```

can be generalized in the zip calculus to this:

```
map(crossd f) o zip = zip o crossd ⟨i:d map f.i⟩
where
crossd f x = ⟨i:d f.i x.i⟩
```

And this law

$$\langle x.1_3,\ x.2_3,\ x.3_3 \rangle = x$$

can be generalized to the (n-tuple eta) law:

$$\langle^{i:d} x.i \rangle = x$$

4.3 More General Derivations

The original motivation for the zip calculus was to create a language adapted to program transformation. This section shows how the zip calculus can simplify program transformation.

A formal derivation of the program derivation sketched in section 2.3 would consist of three sub-derivations

$$e.1_2 = \ldots = C[1_2] \qquad\qquad \text{(lemma-1)}$$

$$e.2_2 = \ldots = C[2_2] \qquad\qquad \text{(lemma-2)}$$

```
    e
=                                    {× eta}
    ⟨e.1₂, e.2₂⟩
=                                    {lemma-1, lemma-2}
    ⟨C[1₂],C[2₂]⟩
```

in which the first two (lemma-1, lemma-2) are virtually identical. Using n-tuples these two sub-derivations can be merged into a single derivation (lemma-n), giving this derivation:

```
e.i = ... = C[i]                        (lemma-n)

   e
=                                       {n-tuple eta}
   ⟨ⁱ e.i ⟩
=                                       {lemma-n}
   ⟨ⁱ C[i] ⟩
```

So, without using a meta-language, we have a derivation that is both shorter and more generic. Another example is the derivation of a law, called Abides:

```
case ⟨λx.⟨a1,b1⟩ , λy.⟨a2,b2⟩⟩ x
                  =
⟨case ⟨λx.a1,λy.a2⟩ x , case ⟨λx.b1,λy.b2⟩ x⟩
```

Its derivation is

```
  case ⟨λx.⟨a1,b1⟩ , λy.⟨a2,b2⟩⟩ x
=                                       {× eta}
  ⟨(case ⟨λx.⟨a1,b1⟩ , λy.⟨a2,b2⟩⟩ x).1 ,
   (case ⟨λx.⟨a1,b1⟩ , λy.⟨a2,b2⟩⟩ x).2 ⟩
=                                       {inst, twice}
  ⟨(case ⟨λx.⟨a1,b1⟩.1, λy.⟨a2,b2⟩.1⟩ x) ,
   (case ⟨λx.⟨a1,b1⟩.2, λy.⟨a2,b2⟩.2⟩ x) ⟩
=                                       {× reduce, four times}
  ⟨case ⟨λx.a1, λy.a2⟩ x ,
   case ⟨λx.b1, λy.b2⟩ x ⟩
```

Here is a generic version of Abides

```
  case ⟨ⁱ λy.⟨ʲ m.i.j y⟩⟩ x = ⟨ʲ case ⟨ⁱ λy. m.i.j y⟩ x⟩
```

and its derivation is

```
    case ⟨ⁱ λy.⟨ʲ m.i.j y⟩⟩ x
=                                       {n-tuple eta}
  ⟨ʲ (case ⟨ⁱ λy.⟨ʲ m.i.j y⟩⟩ x).j⟩
=                                       {inst}
  ⟨ʲ  case ⟨ⁱ λy.⟨ʲ m.i.j y⟩.j⟩ x⟩
=                                       {n-tuple reduce}
  ⟨ʲ  case ⟨ⁱ λy.  m.i.j y   ⟩ x⟩
```

which corresponds directly to the non-generic derivation above. Note that instantiation is only applied once (not twice) and reduction once (not four times), and this law is generic over sums of any length and products of any length.

4.4   Nested N-Tuples

Typical informal notations for representing n-tuples are ambiguous: e.g., one writes $f \overline{x}$ for the "vector" $\langle f x_1, ..., f x_n \rangle$ but now $g(f \overline{x})$ could signify either $\langle g(f x_1), ..., g(f x_n) \rangle$ or $g \langle f x_1, ..., f x_n \rangle$. These notations do not extend to nested n-tuples. In the zip calculus one can easily manipulate nested n-tuples ("matrices"). For example, the application of a function to every element of a three-dimensional matrix is coded as follows (note that $\langle^{-d}x\rangle$ is a tuple of identical elements):

$$\text{map3Dmatrix}_{I,J,K,a,b}$$
$$:: \; (a \to b) \to \times \langle^{-:I} \times \langle^{-:J} \times \langle^{-:K} a\rangle\rangle\rangle \to \times \langle^{-:I} \times \langle^{-:J} \times \langle^{-:K} b\rangle\rangle\rangle$$
$$\text{map3Dmatrix}_{I,J,K,a,b}$$
$$= \lambda f.\lambda m. \langle^{i:I} \langle^{j:J} \langle^{k:K} f \; m.i.j.k\rangle\rangle\rangle$$

In the definition of map3Dmatrix, the expression $\langle^{i:I} \langle^{j:J} \langle^{k:K} f \; m.i.j.k\rangle\rangle\rangle$ is a 3-dimensional matrix where "f m.i.j.k" is the value of the ".i.j.k"-th element, which here is "f" applied to the corresponding value of the original matrix "m.i.j.k". Matrix transposition is straightforward:

$$\text{transpose}_{I,J,a} \; :: \; \times \langle^{i:I} \times \langle^{j:J} a.i.j\rangle\rangle \to \times \langle^{j:J} \times \langle^{i:I} a.i.j\rangle\rangle$$
$$\text{transpose}_{I,J,a} = \lambda x. \langle^{j:J} \langle^{i:I} x.i.j\rangle\rangle$$

The transpose is done by "reversing" the subscripts of x. Note that the type variable "a" above is a *matrix* of types and, for any n, transpose could be applied to a tuple of n-tuples. An application of transpose would be reduced as follows:

$$(\text{transpose}_{3d,2d,a}\langle\langle x1,x2\rangle,\langle y1,y2\rangle,\langle z1,z2\rangle\rangle).2.3$$
$$\to \; \langle^{j} \langle^{i} \langle\langle x1,x2\rangle,\langle y1,y2\rangle,\langle z1,z2\rangle\rangle.i.j\rangle\rangle.2.3$$
$$\to \quad \langle^{i} \langle\langle x1,x2\rangle,\langle y1,y2\rangle,\langle z1,z2\rangle\rangle.i.2\rangle \;\; .3$$
$$\to \qquad \langle\langle x1,x2\rangle,\langle y1,y2\rangle,\langle z1,z2\rangle\rangle.3.2$$
$$\to \qquad \langle z1,z2\rangle.2$$
$$\to \qquad z2$$

Note the various ways one can transform a two dimensional matrix:

$\langle^{i} \langle^{j} m.i.j\rangle\rangle$	m itself
$\langle^{j} \langle^{i} m.i.j\rangle\rangle$	the transpose of m
$\langle^{i} \langle^{j} f \; m.i.j\rangle\rangle$	f applied to each element of m
$\langle^{i} f \langle^{j} m.i.j\rangle\rangle$	f applied to each "row" of m
$\langle^{j} f \langle^{i} m.i.j\rangle\rangle$	f applied to each "column" of m

Clearly this notation extends to matrices of higher dimensions. Some laws about the transpose function are as follows:

$$m.i.j = (\text{transpose}_{I,J,a} m).j.i$$
$$m = \text{transpose}_{J,I,b}(\text{transpose}_{I,J,a} m)$$

Here is a proof of the latter (a proof of the former is part of the derivation):

$\text{transpose}_{J,I,b}(\text{transpose}_{I,J,a}\; m)$

$$
\begin{aligned}
&= \langle^{1} \langle^{k} \langle^{j} \langle^{i} m.i.j\rangle\rangle.k.1\rangle\rangle && \{\textit{unfold transpose, twice}\} \\
&= \langle^{1} \langle^{k}\;\; \langle^{i} m.i.k\rangle\; .1\;\;\rangle\rangle && \{\textit{n-tuple reduce}\} \\
&= \langle^{1} \langle^{k}\qquad m.1.k\qquad\rangle\rangle && \{\textit{n-tuple reduce}\} \\
&= \langle^{1}\qquad\quad m.1 \qquad\quad\rangle && \{\textit{n-tuple eta}\} \\
&= \qquad\qquad m && \{\textit{n-tuple eta}\}
\end{aligned}
$$

4.5   Generic Catamorphisms

It was obvious that Haskell's `zip` family of functions could benefit from n-tuples; but interestingly, catamorphisms [10,11,13] can also benefit from n-tuples, giving catamorphisms over mutually recursive data structures.

First, a fix point operator for terms, `fix`, and a fix point operator at the type level, μ, must be added to the calculus. Normally, the kind of μ is $(\star \to \star) \to \star$ (i.e., it takes a functor of kind $\star \to \star$ and returns a type), but here the kind of μ_d is $(\times\langle^{\div d}\star\rangle \to \times\langle^{\div d}\star\rangle) \to \times\langle^{\div d}\star\rangle$, i.e., it takes a functor transforming d-tuples of types and returns a d-tuple of types. (In the following, the subscript of μ is dropped when clear from the context.) The primitives `in` and `out` now work on tuples of functions. Note how their types have been extended:

$$
\begin{aligned}
&\text{in}_{F} && :: F(\mu F) \to \mu F && \text{original} \\
&\text{in}_{I,F} && :: \times\langle^{i:I} (F(\mu F)).i \to (\mu F).i\rangle && \text{n-tuple}
\end{aligned}
$$

$$
\begin{aligned}
&\text{out}_{F} && :: \mu F \to F(\mu F) && \text{original} \\
&\text{out}_{I,F} && :: \times\langle^{i:I} (\mu F).i \to (F(\mu F)).i\rangle && \text{n-tuple}
\end{aligned}
$$

From these a more generic `cata` can be defined:

$$
\begin{aligned}
&\text{cata}_{F,a} && :: (F\; a \to a) \to (\mu F \to a) && \text{original} \\
&\text{cata}_{I,F,a} && :: \times\langle^{i:I} (F\; a).i \to a.i\rangle \to \times\langle^{i:I} (\mu F).i \to a.i\rangle && \text{n-tuple}
\end{aligned}
$$

$$
\begin{aligned}
&\text{cata}_{F,a} && \phi = \text{fix } \lambda f. \phi \circ (F\; f) \circ \text{out}_{F} && \text{original} \\
&\text{cata}_{I,F,a} && \phi = \text{fix } \lambda f.\langle^{i:I} \phi.i \circ (F\; f).i \circ (\text{out}_{I,F}).i\rangle && \text{n-tuple}
\end{aligned}
$$

(Of course, since the definition of `cata` is polytypic in the first place, this assumes that there is some form of polytypism—note the application of the functor F to a term.) So, $\text{cata}_{nd,F,a}$ takes and returns an n-tuple of functions. All laws (such as cata-fusion) can now be generalized. Also, the standard functor laws for a functor F of kind $\star \to \star$

$$
\begin{aligned}
\text{id} &= F\; \text{id} \\
F\; f \circ F\; g &= F\; (f \circ g)
\end{aligned}
$$

can be generalized to functors of kind $\times\langle^{\div I}\star\rangle \to \times\langle^{\div J}\star\rangle$:

$$\langle -\!:^{J}\ \mathtt{id}\rangle = F\ \langle -\!:^{I}\ \mathtt{id}\rangle$$
$$\langle j\!:^{J}\ (F\ \mathtt{f}).j\ \circ\ (F\ \mathtt{g}).j\rangle = F\ \langle i\!:^{I}\ \mathtt{f}.i\ \circ\ \mathtt{g}.i\ \rangle$$

The original cata and functor laws can be derived from these by instantiating the n-tuples to 1-tuples and then making use of the isomorphism $\times\langle a\rangle \approx a$ (the bijections being $\lambda x.\,x.1_1$ and $\lambda x.\langle x\rangle$).

5 Conclusion

5.1 Limitations

The zip calculus does not give polytypism (nor does polytypism give n-tuples); these are orthogonal language extensions:

- Polytypism: generalizes `zipList`, `zipMaybe`, `zipTree`, ...
- N-tuples: generalizes `zip`, `zip3`, `zip4`, ...

An n-tuple is similar to a heterogeneous array (or heterogenous finite list); but although one can map over n-tuples, zip n-tuples together, and transpose nested n-tuples, one *cannot induct* over n-tuples. So, n-tuples are clearly limited in what they can express. As a result, one cannot define the following functions in the zip calculus:

```
tupleToListd       :: ×⟨-:d a⟩ → list a
seqTupleL,seqTupleR :: Monad m => ×⟨i a.i→m b.i⟩ → ×a→m(×b)
```

However, if we provide `seqTupleL` and `seqTupleR` as primitives,

- Each of these families of Haskell functions can be generalized to one generic function: `zip...`, `zipWith...`, `unzip...`, and `liftM1...`
- The function `seqTupleMaybe` from section 4.1 can be defined.
- Several of Haskell's list functions could also be defined for n-tuples: `zip`, `zip3`, ..., `zipWith`, `zipWith3`, ..., `unzip`, `unzip3`, ..., `map`, `sequence`, `mapM`, `transpose`, `mapAccumL`, `mapAccumR`. (These functions all act "uniformly" on lists—they act on lists without permuting the elements or changing their length.)

Other functions cannot even be given a type in the zip calculus. For instance, there is the `curry` family of functions

```
curry2 :: (a->b->c)    -> (a,b)->c
curry3 :: (a->b->c->d) -> (a,b,c)->d
...
```

but there is no way to give a type to a generic `curry`. Extending the zip calculus to type this generic `curry` is an area for future research.

5.2   Relation to Other Work

Polytypic programming [10,11,13] has similar goals to this work (e.g., PolyP [8] and Functorial ML [9]). However, as just noted, the genericity of polytypism and n-tuples appear orthogonal. As seen in section 4.5, with *both* polytypism and n-tuples some very generic programs and laws can be written.

Two approaches that achieve the same genericity as n-tuples are the following: First, one can forgo typed languages and use an untyped language to achieve this level of genericity: e.g., in Lisp a list can be used as an n-tuple. Second, a language with dependent types [1] could encode n-tuples (and much more); though the disadvantages are that type checking is undecidable (not to mention the lack of type inference) and the types are more complex. However, the zip calculus can be viewed as a way to add dependent types to a typed language in a restricted way.

It would be a simple and obvious extension to allow for finite sets other than the naturals as projections, e.g., one could have strings as projections and finite sets of strings as dimensions. Currently, projections have their dimension embedded (e.g., the projection "1_3" has dimension (or type) "3d"); to allow for projections that are "polymorphic" over dimensions (e.g., projection 1 could be applied to a tuple of any size) would take the zip calculus into the realm of extensible records [4,14,19]. N-tuples and extensible records seem to be orthogonal issues, though further investigation is required.

Related also is Hoogendijk's thesis [5] in which he develops a notation for n-tuple valued functors for program calculation; his notation is variable free, categorical, and heavily overloaded.

5.3   Summary

Implementation has not been addressed. One method is to simply inline all n-tuples, although this could lead to code explosion and does not support separate compilation. Another method is to implement n-tuples as functions (as they are just another form of function); just as there is a range of implementation techniques for polymorphic functions, there are analogous choices for implementing functions generic over dimensions.

Future work is (1) to give a formal proof of various properties of the zip calculus, such as subject reduction, (2) to extend the zip calculus to be polytypic, (3) to increase the expressiveness of the zip calculus (so `seqTupleL`, `seqTupleR`, and `tupleToList` can be defined in the language and `curry` could be given a type), and (4) to implement a type inference algorithm for the zip calculus.

I hope to have shown that the genericity provided by n-tuples is useful in a programming language and particularly useful in program transformation. Although there are other solutions, the calculus presented here is a simple solution to getting n-tuples in a typed language. One notable benefit of n-tuples in a transformation system is that they allow one to do many program transformations by simple equational reasoning which otherwise would require a meta-language.

Acknowledgements

I would like to thank Valery Trifonov for many helpful discussions and the anonymous referees for many useful suggestions.

References

1. Lennart Augustsson. Cayenne — a language with dependent types. In *Proceedings of the ACM SIGPLAN International Conference on Functional Programming (ICFP '98)*, volume 34(1) of *ACM SIGPLAN Notices*, pages 239–250. ACM, June 1999. 42
2. H. P. Barendregt. Lambda calculi with types. In S. Abramsky, D. M. Gabbay, and T. S. E. Maibaum, editors, *Handbook of Logic in Computer Science*. Oxford University Press, Oxford, 1992. 31, 35
3. Richard Bird and Oege de Moor. *Algebra of Programming*. Prentice Hall, 1997. 28
4. Benedict R. Gaster and Mark P. Jones. A polymorphic type system for extensible records and variants. Technical report NOTTCS-TR-96-3, University of Nottingham, Languages and Programming Group, Department of Computer Science, Nottingham NG7 2RD, UK, November 1996. 42
5. Paul Ferenc Hoogendijk. *A Generic Theory of Datatypes*. PhD thesis, Dept. of Math. and Computing Science, Eindhoven Univ. of Technology, 1997. 42
6. P. Hudak, S. P. Jones, and P. Wadler. Report on the programming language Haskell. *SIGPLAN Notices*, 27(5), May 1992. 29
7. Gérard Huet and Bernard Lang. Proving and applying program transformations expressed with second order patterns. *Acta Informatica*, 11:31–55, 1978. 30
8. P. Jansson and J. Jeuring. PolyP - a polytypic programming language extension. In *POPL '97: The 24th ACM SIGPLAN-SIGACT Symposium on Principles of Programming Languages*, pages 470–482. ACM Press, 1997. 28, 42
9. C. B. Jay, G. Bellè, and E. Moggi. Functorial ML. *Journal of Functional Programming*, 8(6):573–619, 1998. 28, 42
10. G. R. Malcolm. Data structures and program transformation. *Science of Computer Programming*, 14:255–279, 1990. 28, 40, 42
11. Grant Malcolm. *Algebraic Data Types and Program Transformation*. PhD thesis, University of Groningen, 1990. 28, 40, 42
12. L. Meertens. Algorithmics - towards programming as a mathematical activity. In J. W. de Bakker, E. M. Hazewinkel, and J. K. Lenstra, editors, *Proceedings of the CWI Symposium on Mathematics and Computer Science*, pages 289–334. North-Holland, 1986. CWI Monographs, volume 1. 28
13. Erik Meijer, Maarten Fokkinga, and Ross Paterson. Functional programming with bananas, lenses, envelopes and barbed wire. In John Hughes, editor, *Functional Programming Languages and Computer Architecture*, pages 124–144. Springer Verlag, June 1991. LNCS 523. 28, 40, 42
14. Atsushi Ohori. A polymorphic record calculus and its compilation. *ACM Transactions on Programming Languages and Systems*, 17(6):844–895, November 1995. 42
15. Simon Peyton Jones and Erik Meijer. Henk: a typed intermediate language. In *Proc. 1997 ACM SIGPLAN Workshop on Types in Compilation (TIC'97)*, Amsterdam, The Netherlands, June 1997. 31, 36

16. Mark Tullsen. First class patterns. In E. Pontelli and V. Santos Costa, editors, *Second International Workshop on Practical Aspects of Declarative Languages (PADL'00)*, volume 1753 of *Lecture Notes in Computer Science*, pages 1–15. Springer-Verlag, January 2000. 37

17. L. S. Van Benthem Jutting, J. McKinna, and R. Pollack. Checking algorithms for pure type systems. *Lecture Notes in Computer Science*, 806:19–61, 1994. 36

18. P. Wadler. Theorems for free! In *Functional Programming Languages and Computer Architecture*. Springer Verlag, 1989. 29

19. M. Wand. Complete type inference for simple objects. In *Proc. IEEE Symp. on Logic in Computer Science*, pages 37–44, 1987. Corrigendum in *Proc. IEEE Symp. on Logic in Computer Science*, page 132, 1988. 42

Separation and Reduction

Ernie Cohen

Telcordia Technologies
ernie@research.telcordia.com

Abstract. We present some new theorems that equate an iteration to a sequential composition of stronger iterations, and use these theorems to simplify and generalize a number of known techniques for pretending atomicity in concurrent programs.

1 Introduction

One way to simplify the analysis of a concurrent program is to pretend that certain complex operations execute atomically. For example, one can sometimes pretend that messages are received as soon as they are sent, or that servers respond immediately to requests. *Reduction* theorems provide formal justification for such pretenses; they typically depend on commutativity arguments to convert an arbitrary execution to an equivalent one in which complex operations run without interruption.

Proofs of reduction theorems (as well as many other theorems in concurrency control) can be simplified by applying general-purpose *separation* theorems that equate an iteration to a sequential composition of stronger iterations. Separation theorems have received little attention, partly because the obvious theorems are not strong enough for serious applications, and partly because they are awkward to state and prove in formalisms that do not support sequential composition of nondeterministically terminating iterations. Nevertheless, the use of separation has allowed us to consistently generalize and simplify existing reduction techniques; the new reduction theorems

- work in arbitrary contexts (e.g., allowing control to start or end inside of a critical section),
- have weaker hypotheses, (e.g., allowing environment actions to move control in and out of critical sections),
- apply to both terminating and nonterminating executions, and
- have shorter, simpler proofs.

2 Omega Algebra

An *omega algebra* is an algebraic structure over the operators (in order of increasing precedence) 0 (nullary), 1 (nullary), + (binary infix), · (binary infix,

R. Backhouse and J. N. Oliveira (Eds.): MPC 2000, LNCS 1837, pp. 45–59, 2000.

usually written as simple juxtaposition), $\star$ (binary infix, same precedence as $\cdot$), * (unary suffix), and $^{\omega}$ (unary suffix), satisfying the following axioms[1]:

$$(x + y) + z = x + (y + z) \qquad\qquad x \leq y \Leftrightarrow x + y = y$$
$$x + y = y + x$$
$$x + x = x \qquad\qquad\qquad x^{*} = 1 + x + x^{*}\, x^{*}$$
$$0 + x = x \qquad\qquad x\, y \leq x \Rightarrow x\, y^{*} = x \qquad (*\ \mathrm{ind})$$
$$x\,(y\, z) = (x\, y)\, z \qquad\qquad x\, y \leq y \Rightarrow x^{*}\, y = y \qquad (*\ \mathrm{ind})$$
$$0\, x = x\, 0 = 0$$
$$1\, x = x\, 1 = x \qquad\qquad\qquad x \star y = x^{\omega} + x^{*}\, y$$
$$x\,(y + z) = x\, y + x\, z \qquad\qquad x^{\omega} = x\, x^{\omega}$$
$$(x + y)\, z = x\, z + y\, z \qquad x \leq y\, x + z \Rightarrow x \leq y \star z \qquad (\star\ \mathrm{ind})$$

(In parsing formulas, $\cdot$ and $\star$ associate to the right; e.g., $u\, v \star x \star y$ parses to $(u \cdot (v^{\omega} + v^{*} \cdot (x^{\omega} + x^{*} \cdot y)))$. In proofs, we use the hint "(dist)" to indicate application of the distributivity laws, and the hint " (hyp)" to indicate the use of hypotheses.)

These axioms are sound and complete for the usual equational theory of omega-regular expressions. (Completeness holds only for *standard* terms, where the first arguments to $\cdot$, $^{\omega}$, and $\star$ are regular.) Thus, we make free use, without proof, of familiar equations from the theory of (omega-)regular languages (e.g., $x^{*}\, x^{*} = x^{*}$).

It is easy to see that the axioms not mentioning $^{\omega}$ or $\star$ are closed under duality, where the dual of a formula is obtained by reversing the arguments to $\cdot$. Moreover, it can be shown that the remaining axioms are a conservative extension, so the dual of any theorem not mentioning $^{\omega}$ or $\star$ is also a theorem. In hints, we indicate the use of the dual of a theorem by priming the hint (as in (10)').

Many of our theorems treat $*$ iteration and $\star$ iteration in a uniform way; to facilitate these, the symbol $\circ$ (binary infix, right associative, same precedence as $\cdot$ and $\star$) ranges over the functions $\star$ and $(\lambda x, y : x^{*}\, y)$. For example the equation $x \circ x \circ y = x \circ y$ abbreviates the conjunction $x^{*}\, x^{*}\, y = x^{*}\, y \ \wedge \ x \star x \star y = x \star y$. Several theorems of this type are used in our proofs:

$$x \circ y = y + x\, x \circ y \qquad\qquad (1)$$
$$x^{*}\, x \circ y = x \circ y \qquad\qquad (2)$$
$$x \star x \circ y = x \star y \qquad\qquad (3)$$
$$(x + y) \circ z = (y^{*}\, x) \circ y \circ z \qquad\qquad (4)$$
$$(x + y) \circ z = y \circ z + y^{*}\, x\, (x + y) \circ z \qquad\qquad (5)$$
$$x \circ y \circ z \leq (x + y) \circ z \qquad\qquad (6)$$
$$x \circ x \circ y = x \circ y \qquad\qquad (7)$$
$$x \circ y = x^{*}\, y + x \circ 0 \qquad\qquad (8)$$

---

[1] The axioms not mentioning ω are equivalent to Kozen's axioms for Kleene algebra[5], plus the three axioms for omega terms.

y is a *complement* of x iff $x\ y\ =\ 0$ and $x + y\ =\ 1$. It is easy to show that complements (when they exist) are unique and that complementation is an involution; a *predicate* is an element of the algebra with a complement. In this paper, p, q, and Q range over predicates, with complements $\bar{p}$, $\bar{q}$, and $\bar{Q}$. It is easy to show that the predicates form a Boolean algebra, with $+$ as disjunction, $\cdot$ as conjunction, 0 as *false*, 1 as *true*, complementation as negation, and $\leq$ as implication. Common properties of Boolean algebras (e.g., $p\ q = q\ p$) are used silently in proofs, as is the fact

$$x\ p\ y = 0 \implies x\ y = x\ \bar{p}\ y$$

Unlike previous axiomatizations of omega-regular languages, the omega algebra axioms support several interesting programming models, where (intuitively) 0 is magic, 1 is skip, $+$ is chaotic nondeterministic choice, $\cdot$ is sequential composition, $\leq$ is refinement, x^* is executed by executing x any finite number of times, and x^ω is executed by executing x an infinite number of times. (This correspondence holds only for standard terms.) The results of this paper are largely motivated by the *relational model*, where terms denote binary relations over a state space, 0 is the empty relation, 1 is the identity relation, $\cdot$ is relational composition, $+$ is union, $*$ is reflexive-transitive closure, $\leq$ is subset, and x^ω relates an input state s to an output state if there is an infinite sequence of states starting with s, with consecutive states related by x. (Thus, x^ω relates an input state to either all states or none, and $x^\omega = 0$ iff x is well-founded.) Predicates are identified with the set of states in their domain (i.e., the states from which they can be executed). In examples, we use the relational model exclusively; however, our theorems are equally applicable to trace-based models, where actions can have permanent effects (like output) that cannot be erased by later divergence.

In using omega algebra to reason about a program, we usually work with two terms, one describing the finite executions of the program, the other describing the infinite executions. However, when working with flat iterations (as we do here), we can merge these terms into a single term using $\circ$ and a continuation variable. For example, to say that the program that executes x for a while is equivalent to the program that executes y for a while, we write the equation $x \circ z = y \circ z$; the instantiation $\circ =^*$, $z = 1$ (i.e., $x^* = y^*$) says that the two programs have the same finite executions, and the instantiation $\circ = \star$, $z = 0$ (i.e., $x^\omega = y^\omega$) says that the two programs have the same infinite executions. Whenever possible, we prefer to work directly with $\circ$ equations, taking care of both finite and infinite executions with a single proof.

3   Iteration

A standard theorem in program verification says that a predicate preserved by the body of a loop is preserved by the loop. The *iteration theorem*, below, generalizes the loop invariance theorem by (1) generalizing the invariant (x) from predicates to arbitrary terms; (2) allowing the loop body (y) to be transformed (into z) by the passage of the invariant[2]; and (3) allowing for exceptional cases (w) where the invariant is not preserved:

$$x\,y \le z\,x + w \implies x\,y \circ u \le z \circ (x\,u + w\,y \circ u) \tag{9}$$

We prove the $*$ and $\star$ cases separately. Here's the $*$ part:

$$
\begin{array}{lll}
x\,y^*\,u & \le & \{x\,y^* \le z^*\,(x + w\,y^*)\ \text{(below)}\} \\
z^*\,(x + w\,y^*)\,u & = & \{\text{(dist)} \qquad\qquad\qquad\qquad\ \} \\
z^*\,(x\,u + w\,y^*\,u) & &
\end{array}
$$

$$
\begin{array}{lll}
x\,y^* & \le & \{x \le z^*\,(x + w\,y^*) \qquad\qquad\ \} \\
z^*\,(x + w\,y^*)\,y^* & = & \{\text{(proof below); (}* \text{ ind)} \quad\ \} \\
z^*\,(x + w\,y^*) & &
\end{array}
$$

$$
\begin{array}{lll}
z^*\,(x + w\,y^*)\,y & = & \{\text{(dist)} \qquad\qquad\qquad\qquad\qquad\ \} \\
z^*\,x\,y + z^*\,w\,y^*\,y & \le & \{x\,y \le z\,x + w\ \text{(hyp)} \qquad\qquad\ \} \\
z^*\,(z\,x + w) + z^*\,w\,y^*\,y & \le & \{\text{(dist); } z^*\,z \le z^*; \ y^*\,y \le y^*\ \} \\
z^*\,x + z^*\,w + z^*\,w\,y^* & \le & \{w \le w\,y^*; \text{ (dist)} \qquad\qquad\ \} \\
z^*\,(x + w\,y^*) & &
\end{array}
$$

And here's the $\star$ part:

$$
\begin{array}{lll}
x\,y \star u & = & \{y \star u = u + y\,y \star u\ (1)\} \\
x\,(u + y\,y \star u) & = & \{\text{(dist)} \qquad\qquad\qquad\qquad\ \} \\
x\,u + x\,y\,y \star u & \le & \{x\,y \le z\,x + w\ \text{(hyp)} \quad\ \} \\
x\,u + (z\,x + w)\,y \star u & = & \{\text{(dist)} \qquad\qquad\qquad\qquad\ \} \\
z\,(x\,y \star u) + (x\,u + w\,y \star u) & &
\end{array}
$$

so $x\,y \star u \le z \star (x\,u + w\,y \star u)$ by ($\star$ ind)

□

The separation theorems of the next section are often used in tandem with the following "loop elimination" lemmas that remove extraneous iterations:

$$x\,y = 0 \implies x\,y \circ z = x\,z \tag{10}$$

$$
\begin{array}{lll}
x\,y \circ z & \le & \{x\,y = 0\ \text{(hyp), so } x\,y \le 0\,x; \text{ (iter)}\} \\
0 \circ x\,z & = & \{0 \circ u = u \qquad\qquad\qquad\qquad\qquad\ \} \\
x\,z & &
\end{array}
$$

□

---

[2] This allows the iteration theorem to subsume forward data refinement and simulation (and backward refinement and simulation for finite executions).

$$x\, y = 0 \implies x \circ y = y + x \circ 0 \tag{11}$$

$$
\begin{array}{lll}
x \circ y & = & \{\, 8 \qquad\qquad\qquad\quad \} \\
x^* \, y + x \circ 0 & = & \{x\, y = 0 \ \text{(hyp)}; \ (10)'\} \\
y + x \circ 0 &&
\end{array}
$$

□

4   Separation

In this section, we prove some general theorems for rewriting an iteration to a sequential composition of stronger iterations. They typically have the form

$$\ldots \implies (x + y) \circ z = x \circ y \circ z$$

(In proofs, we show only $(x + y) \circ z \le x \circ y \circ z$; the reverse inequality follows from 6.) We call these "separation theorems" because they allow a heterogeneous iteration of x's and y's to be partitioned into separate x and y iterations. In a programming context, we can think of x and y as transition relations; the conclusion says that running x and y concurrently for a while has the same effect as running x for a while and then running y for a while.

$$y\, x \le x\, y^* \implies (x + y) \circ z = x \circ y \circ z \tag{12}$$

$$
\begin{array}{lll}
(x + y) \circ z & \le & \{1 \le y^*; \ (x + y) \circ z = (y^* \, x) \circ y \circ z \ (4)\} \\
y^* \, (y^* \, x) \circ y \circ z & \le & \{y^* \, (y^* \, x) \le x\, y^* \ \text{(below)}; \ \text{(iter)} \qquad\} \\
x \circ y^* \, y \circ z & = & \{y^* \, y \circ z = y \circ z \ (2) \qquad\qquad\qquad \} \\
x \circ y \circ z &&
\end{array}
$$

$$
\begin{array}{lll}
y^* \, y^* \, x & = & \{y^* \, y^* = y^* \qquad\qquad\qquad\qquad\qquad \} \\
y^* \, x & \le & \{y\, x \le x\, y^* \ \text{(hyp)}; \ \text{(iter)}' \qquad\quad\ \} \\
x \, (y^*)^* & = & \{(y^*)^* = y^* \qquad\qquad\qquad\qquad\quad\ \ \} \\
x\, y^* &&
\end{array}
$$

□

The hypotheses of 12 can be weakened in several ways. The first two variations are based on the following lemma:

$$y\, x \le x\, (x + y)^* \implies (x + y) \circ z \le x \star y \circ z \tag{13}$$

$$
\begin{array}{lll}
(x + y) \circ z & = & \{\, 5 \qquad\qquad\qquad\qquad\qquad\qquad\quad \} \\
y \circ z + y^* \, x \, (x + y) \circ z & \le & \{y\, x \le x\, (x + y)^* \ \text{(hyp)}; \ \text{(iter)}'\} \\
y \circ z + x\, ((x + y)^*)^* \, (x + y) \circ z & = & \{(u^*)^* = u^*; \ u^* \, u \circ z = u \circ z \quad \} \\
(2) && \\
y \circ z + x\, (x + y) \circ z &&
\end{array}
$$

so $(x + y) \circ z \le x \star y \circ z$ by $(\star \ \text{ind})$

□

Two separation theorems follow immediately from 13. For $\star$ separation, we can strengthen the conclusion to an equality, and we can obtain a * separation theorem by eliminating infinite executions of x:

$$y\,x \le x\,(x+y)^* \implies (x+y)\star z = x \star y \star z \tag{14}$$

$$x^\omega = 0 \,\wedge\, y\,x \le x\,(x+y)^* \implies (x+y)^* = x^*\,y^* \tag{15}$$

The hypothesis $x^\omega = 0$ of 15 cannot be eliminated. For example, if $x = \{\langle 0,1\rangle, \langle 1,2\rangle, \langle 2,2\rangle\}$ and $y = \{\langle 1,0\rangle, \langle 2,0\rangle\}$, then $y\,x = \{\langle 1,1\rangle, \langle 2,1\rangle\} \le x\,y\,x$, and $\langle 2,1\rangle \in y\,x$, but $\langle 2,1\rangle \notin x^*\,y^*$.

In the special case of * separation, 12 can be strengthened as follows:

$$y\,x \le (x+1)\,y^* \implies (x+y)^* = x^*\,y^* \tag{16}$$

$$
\begin{aligned}
(x+y)^* &\le &\{u^* = (u+1)^* &\quad\} \\
((x+1)+y)^* &= &\{y\,(x+1) \le (x+1)\,y^* \text{ (below); separation (12)}\} \\
(x+1)^*\,y^* &= &\{(x+1)^* = x^* &\quad\} \\
x^*\,y^*
\end{aligned}
$$

$$
\begin{aligned}
y\,(x+1) &= &\{(\text{dist}) &\quad\} \\
y\,x + y &\le &\{y\,x \le (x+1)\,y^* \text{ (hyp)}; y \le (x+1)\,y^* &\quad\} \\
(x+1)\,y^*
\end{aligned}
$$

$\square$

The hypothesis of 16 cannot be weakened to $y\,x \le x^*\,y^*$. For example, if $y = \{\langle 0,1\rangle, \langle 1,2\rangle\}$ and $x = \{\langle 1,2\rangle, \langle 2,3\rangle\}$, then $y\,x = \{\langle 0,2\rangle, \langle 1,3\rangle\} \le x^*\,y^*$, and $\langle 0,3\rangle \in (x+y)^*$ but $\langle 0,3\rangle \notin x^*\,y^*$. Note also that the hypothesis of 16 do not work for $\star$ iteration; for example, in a two-state relational model, if $x = \{\langle 0,1\rangle\}$ and $y = \{\langle 1,0\rangle\}$, then $(x+y)\star 0 = \{\langle 0,0\rangle, \langle 0,1\rangle, \langle 1,0\rangle, \langle 1,1\rangle\}$ but $x\star y\star 0 = \{\}$.

Combining 14 and the dual of 16 gives another theorem that works for both iterators:

$$y\,x \le x\,x^*\,(1+y) \implies (x+y)\circ z = x \circ y \circ z \tag{17}$$

$$
\begin{aligned}
\textit{true} &\implies &\{y\,x \le x\,x^*\,(1+y) \text{ (hyp)} &\quad\} \\
y\,x \le x\,x^*\,(1+y) &\implies &\{x\,x^* \le x^* &\quad\} \\
y\,x \le x^*\,(1+y) &\implies &\{(16)' \text{ with } x,y := y,x &\quad\} \\
(x+y)^*\,z = x^*\,y^*\,z &\implies &\{y\,x \le x\,(x+y)^* \text{ (hyp)}; (14)\} \\
(x+y)\circ z = x \circ y \circ z
\end{aligned}
$$

$\square$

Finally, more complex separation theorems are possible. For example:

$$y\,x \le (x+z)\,y^* \ \wedge \ z\,x = 0 \implies (x+y+z) \circ u = x \circ (y+z) \circ u \qquad (18)$$

$$
\begin{array}{lll}
(x+y+z) \circ u & \le & \{z \le y^*\,z & \} \\
(x+y^*\,z+y) \circ u & = & \{y\,(x+y^*\,z) \le (x+y^*\,z)\,y^* \ \text{(below)}; \ (12)\} \\
(x+y^*\,z) \circ y \circ u & = & \{z\,x = 0 \ \text{(hyp)}; \ \text{so} \ (y^*\,z)\,x = 0; \ (12) & \} \\
x \circ (y^*\,z) \circ y \circ u & = & \{(y^*\,z) \circ y \circ u = (y+z) \circ u \ (4) & \} \\
x \circ (y+z) \circ u
\end{array}
$$

$$
\begin{array}{lll}
y\,(x+y^*\,z) & = & \{(\text{dist}) & \} \\
y\,x + y\,y^*\,z & \le & \{y\,x \le (x+z)\,y^* \ \text{(hyp)} & \} \\
(x+z)\,y^* + y\,y^*\,z & \le & \{z \le y^*\,z; \ y\,y^*\,z \le y^*\,z\,y^*; \ (\text{dist}) & \} \\
(x+y^*\,z)\,y^*
\end{array}
$$

$\square$

5   Reduction

The separation theorems of the last section can be viewed as special cases of theorems of the form

$$\ldots \implies (x+y) \circ z = (p\,x + q\,y) \circ (\bar{p}\,x + \bar{q}\,y) \circ z$$

where $p = 1$ and $q = 0$. In this section, we prove several such theorems, where the seperands are obtained by prefixing or postfixing summands of the original iterand with predicates.

One way to interpret a theorem of the form above is as follows; other interpretations are given later in the section. Let x and y be programs with critical sections, let p mean that y is in a critical section and let q mean that x is in a critical section. The conclusion says that every concurrent execution of x and y is equivalent to one that executes in two phases: in the first phase, x executes only when y is in a critical section (and vice versa), and in the second phase, x executes only when y is not in a critical section (and vice versa). If the execution starts in a $\bar{p}\,\bar{q}$ state (i.e., one where neither program is in its critical section), the first phase vanishes (thanks to loop elimination) and we have a corollary of the form

$$\ldots \implies \bar{p}\,\bar{q}\,(x+y) \circ z = \bar{p}\,\bar{q}\,(\bar{p}\,x + \bar{q}\,y) \circ z$$

which says that we can pretend that critical sections are not interrupted. This amounts to pretending that critical sections are executed atomically.

5.1   Fair Progress Reduction

Consider a finite class of workers x_i, each of whom, at any time, are classified as "fast" (p_i) or "slow" $(\bar{p}_i)$. The classification system can depend on the particular worker, so one worker might be classified as slow if anybody is waiting for him, while another might be classified as slow unless he's waiting for somebody else.

The only restriction we place on the classification is that if it is possible to execute a fast worker x_i followed by a slow worker x_j, then (1) x_j must already be classified as slow, and (2) the same effect can be obtained by executing x_j and then x_i.

The following theorem says that, under these conditions, any execution of the system is equivalent to one that executes in two phases, where only slow workers execute in the first phase and only fast workers execute in the second phase:

$$(\forall i : p_i \, x_i \, \overline{p_j} \, x_j \le \overline{p_j} \, x_j \, x_i) \implies (+i : x_i) \circ y = (+i : \overline{p_i} \, x_i) \circ (+i : p_i \, x_i) \circ y \quad (19)$$

Let $u = (+i : \overline{p_i} \, x_i)$, and let $v = (+i : p_i \, x_i)$; then $(+i : x_i) = u + v$, and

$$
\begin{array}{lcl}
v \, u & = & \{\text{(dist)} \ \} \\
(+i : p_i \, x_i \, (+j : \overline{p_j} \, x_j)) & = & \{\text{(dist)} \ \} \\
(+i, j : p_i \, x_i \, \overline{p_j} \, x_j) & \le & \{\text{(hyp)} \ \} \\
(+i, j : \overline{p_j} \, x_j \, x_i) & = & \{\text{(dist)} \ \} \\
(+j : \overline{p_j} \, x_j) \, (+i : x_i) & = & \{\text{def } u, v\} \\
u \, (u + v) & \le & \{ \qquad \} \\
u \, u^* \, (1 + v) & &
\end{array}
$$

$$\text{so } (u + v) \circ y = u \circ v \circ y \text{ by } 17$$

$\square$

For example, let the workers be connected by unbounded FIFO queues (at least one between every pair of distinct workers); at each step, a worker can receive any number of messages (but at most one from any queue) and send any number of messages. (As in all of our examples using queues, we assume that the only operations on queues are blocking send and receive operations.) Let p_i mean that every outgoing queue of x_i is longer than every incoming queue of x_i. The hypotheses of the theorem are then satisfied, because (1) at most one worker is fast at any time, and (2) if a worker is fast, all of his outgoing queues are nonempty, so $p_i \, x_i \, \overline{p_j} \, x_j \le x_j \, x_i$ (since the data manipulated by the x_j action is not modified by the x_i action).

An important special case is where there are exactly two workers, with a single FIFO queue (initially empty) in each direction, and at each step a worker either sends a single message or receives a single message. Then, in the first phase, the two queue lengths never differ by more than one, and so the phase can be parsed as a sequence of "macro steps", each with one step for each worker. For many protocols, only a finite number of states are reachable in the first phase; since only one worker gets to execute in the second phase, a number of interesting properties (maximum queue length, freedom from deadlock, etc.) are decidable for such protocols; see [4].

5.2   One-Way Reduction

A special case of fair progress reduction occurs when one of the workers (y below) is always slow:

$$p\,x\,\overline{p} = 0 \;\wedge\; p\,x\,y \leq y\,x \;\Longrightarrow\; (x+y)\circ z = (\overline{p}\,x+y)\circ(p\,x)\circ z \qquad (20)$$

(19), where i ranges over $\{0, 1\}$, $x_0 := x$, $x_1 := y$, $p_0 := p$, $p_1 := 0$.

□

For example, let y be (the transition relation of) a program with critical sections, where p means that control is inside a critical section. The hypotheses say that x cannot move control out of the critical section, and that, from inside the critical section, x actions commute to the right past y actions. The conclusion says that any execution is equivalent to one that executes in two phases: during the first phase, x does not execute when control is in a critical section of y (i.e., critical sections execute atomically), and during the second phase, x executes exclusively, with control remaining in the critical section.

One-way reduction can be applied in many pipelining situations. For example, let x and y be programs that communicate via FIFO queues, and let p hold when every queue from x to y is nonempty. The hypotheses of 20 say that (1) x cannot empty a queue from x to y (i.e., messages cannot be unsent), and (2) if every queue from x to y is nonempty, then the result of performing an x step followed by a y step can be obtained by performing a y step first[3]. The conclusion says that we can pretend that execution proceeds in two phases; in the first phase, x executes only when one of his queues to y is empty, and in the second phase, only x gets to execute. In the special case where there is only one queue from x to y, the first phase condition says, in effect, that messages from x are received as soon as they are sent.

One shortcoming of fair progress reduction is that the $\star$ part of the theorem can't be dualized. On the other hand, we can prove the dual of 20 as follows:

$$\overline{p}\,x\,p = 0 \;\wedge\; y\,x\,p \leq x\,y \;\Longrightarrow\; (x+y)\circ z = (x\,p)\circ(y+x\,\overline{p})\circ z \qquad (21)$$

(18) with $x := x\,p$, $y := y + x\,\overline{p}$, $z := x\,\overline{p}$, $u := z$, justified as follows:

$$
\begin{array}{lll}
(y + x\,\overline{p})\,(x\,p) & = & \{(\text{dist}) \hspace{4.5cm}\} \\
y\,x\,p + x\,\overline{p}\,x\,p & = & \{\overline{p}\,x\,p = 0 \ (\text{hyp}) \hspace{3cm}\} \\
y\,x\,p & \leq & \{y\,x\,p \leq x\,y \ (\text{hyp}) \hspace{3cm}\} \\
x\,y & \leq & \{x = x\,p + x\,\overline{p};\ y \leq y + x\,\overline{p}\} \\
(x\,p + x\,\overline{p})\,(y + x\,\overline{p}) & & \\[2mm]
(x\,\overline{p})\,(x\,p) & = & \{\overline{p}\,x\,p = 0 \ (\text{hyp}) \hspace{3cm}\} \\
0 & &
\end{array}
$$

□

---

[3] This holds only if queues from y to x are unbounded, and y receives at most one message per queue per step.

In contexts where control starts and ends outside of the critical section, we can eliminate the extra x iterations with loop elimination:

$$\overline{p}\, x\, p = 0 \ \wedge\ y\, x\, p \leq x\, y \implies \overline{p}\,(x + y) \circ z = \overline{p}\,(y + x\,\overline{p}) \circ z \tag{22}$$

$$p\, x\, \overline{p} = 0 \ \wedge\ p\, x\, y \leq y\, x \implies (x + y) \circ \overline{p} = (\overline{p}\, x + y) \circ (\overline{p} + (p\, x) \circ 0) \tag{23}$$

5.3   Two-Phased Reduction

Two-phased reductions combine 20 and 21. For this section and the next, we assume the following hypotheses:

$$q\, y\, p = 0$$
$$\overline{p}\, x\, p = 0$$
$$q\, x\, \overline{q} = 0$$
$$y\, x\, p \leq x\, y$$
$$q\, x\, y \leq y\, x$$

These hypotheses can be read as follows. Think of the critical sections of y as operating in two phases, where p (resp. q) means control is in the first (resp. second) phase. The first hypothesis says that control cannot pass directly from the second phase to the first phase without first leaving the critical section (this defines what we mean by a "two-phased" critical section). The next two hypotheses say that x cannot move control into the first phase or out of the second. The last two hypotheses say that x actions left-commute out of the first phase and right-commute out of the second phase. (Note that there are no constraints on an action that moves control from the first phase to the second phase.) The conclusion says that we can pretend that execution consists of a sequence of first phase x actions, followed by a phase where the critical section executes atomically, followed by a sequence of second phase x actions:

$$(x + y) \circ z = (x\, p) \circ (y + \overline{q}\, x\, \overline{p}) \circ (q\, x) \circ z \tag{24}$$

$(x + y) \circ z$	$\leq$	$\{\ 20 \hspace{4cm} \}$
$(x\, p) \circ (y + x\,\overline{p}) \circ z$	$\leq$	$\{q\,(x\,\overline{p})\, y \leq y\,(x\,\overline{p})$ (below); (21)$\}$
$(x\, p) \circ (y + \overline{q}\, x\, \overline{p}) \circ (q\, x) \circ z$		

$q\,(x\,\overline{p})\, y$	$\leq$	$\{q\, x\, \overline{q} = 0$ (hyp) $\hspace{1.5cm}\}$
$q\, x\, q\, y$	$\leq$	$\{q\, y\, p = 0$ (hyp) $\hspace{1.7cm}\}$
$q\, x\, y\, \overline{p}$	$\leq$	$\{q\, x\, y \leq y\, x$ (hyp) $\hspace{1.3cm}\}$
$y\, x\, \overline{p}$		

□

Again, by assuming control begins/ends outside of the critical section, we can eliminate the extra x iterations; for example,

$$\overline{p}\,(x + y) \circ \overline{q} = \overline{p}\,(\overline{q}\, x\, \overline{p} + y) \circ (\overline{q} + (q\, x) \circ 0) \tag{25}$$

Two-phased reduction is usually applied to pretend the atomicity of an operation that gathers information/resources, possibly executes some global atomic action, and then releases information/resources. Here are some examples of such operations (ignoring the subtleties of each case):

- a fragment of a sequential program that contains at most one access to a shared variable (the so-called single-assignment rule);
- a database transaction that that never obtains a lock after releasing a lock [9];
- a sequence of semaphore p operations followed by a sequence of semaphore v operations [8];
- a fragment of a distributed program that receives messages, performs a local action, and then sends messages [6].

5.4   Lamport and Schneider's Reduction Theorem

In traditional program reasoning, the concern is program properties rather than program refinement; to apply reduction in this context, we need a way to turn properties of the "reduced" program (where critical sections execute atomically) into properties of the unreduced program. One way to do this is to restrict attention to states where control is outside the critical sections. For example, under the hypotheses of two-phased reduction, if Q always holds in the reduced program, then $p + q + Q$ always holds in the unreduced program (i.e., Q holds whenever control is outside the critical section). The early reduction theorems of Lipton [8] and Doeppner[3] had this structure. However, sometimes we want to show that Q holds in all states, even when control is inside the critical section.

A theorem of this kind was proposed by Lamport and Schneider [7]. In order to generalize their theorem to handle total correctness (with slightly stronger hypotheses), we write some of the hypotheses using $\circ$ iteration, with the understanding that the same interpretation of $\circ$ (* or $\star$) is to be used for the hypotheses and theorem 26 below. Their hypotheses, suitably generalized, are as follows (in addition to the other hypotheses of section 5.3):

$$I = I\,\overline{p}$$
$$I\,(y + \overline{q}\,x\,\overline{p}) \circ \overline{p}\,\overline{q}\,\overline{Q} = 0$$
$$\overline{p}\,Q\,(y\,p)^*\,\overline{Q} = 0$$
$$\overline{Q}\,(q\,y)^*\,\overline{q}\,Q = 0$$
$$\overline{Q}\,1^\omega \le \overline{Q}\,(q\,y)^*\,\overline{q}\,1^\omega$$
$$(q\,x) \circ 0 = 0$$

These hypotheses can be read as follows:

- the initialization code I leaves control outside of the first phase;
- Q always holds in the reduced program whenever control is outside of the critical section; for $\circ = \star$, we also assume that the reduced program terminates;

- it is impossible to start outside the first phase and run first-phase actions so as to falsify Q;
- it is impossible to run second-phase actions, ending outside the second phase, so as to truthify Q; and
- from any state where control is in the second phase and Q is *false*, it is possible to execute second phase actions so as to bring control outside of the second phase[4]
- For $\circ = \star$, x cannot execute forever with control in the second phase. (If $\circ =^*$, the formula is trivially satisfied.)

The following theorem says that Q always holds in the unreduced program (and if $\circ =^\omega$, the program terminates):

$$I\,(y+x)^*\,\overline{Q} = 0 \qquad (26)$$

Define $L = (y + \overline{q}\,x\,\overline{p})$; then

$$
\begin{array}{lll}
I\,(y+x) \circ \overline{Q} & \leq & \{1 \leq 1^\omega & \} \\
I\,(y+x) \circ \overline{Q}\,1^\omega & = & \{\overline{Q}\,1^\omega = \overline{Q}\,(q\,y)^*\,\overline{q}\,1^\omega \text{ (hyp)} & \} \\
I\,(y+x) \circ \overline{Q}\,(q\,y)^*\,\overline{q}\,1^\omega & \leq & \{\overline{Q}\,(q\,y)^*\,\overline{q}\,Q = 0 \text{ (hyp)}; \; \overline{Q} \leq 1 & \} \\
I\,(y+x) \circ (q\,y)^*\,\overline{q}\,\overline{Q}\,1^\omega & \leq & \{q\,y \leq y + x; \; u \circ u^*\,v = u \circ v & \} \\
I\,(y+x) \circ \overline{q}\,\overline{Q}\,1^\omega & = & \{I = I\,\overline{p} \text{ (hyp)}; \; (25) & \} \\
I\,\overline{p}\,L \circ (\overline{q}\,\overline{Q}\,1^\omega + (q\,x) \circ 0) & = & \{(q\,x) \circ 0 = 0 \text{ (hyp)} & \} \\
I\,\overline{p}\,L \circ \overline{q}\,\overline{Q}\,1^\omega & \leq & \{\overline{p}\,u \circ v \leq u \circ \overline{p}\,(u\,p) \circ v \text{ (below)} & \} \\
I\,L \circ \overline{p}\,(L\,p) \circ \overline{q}\,\overline{Q}\,1^\omega & \leq & \{L\,p = y\,p & \} \\
I\,L \circ \overline{p}\,(y\,p) \circ \overline{q}\,\overline{Q}\,1^\omega & \leq & \{I\,L \circ (y\,p) \circ 0 \leq I\,L \circ 0 = 0 \text{ (hyp)}\} \\
I\,L \circ \overline{p}\,(y\,p)^*\,\overline{q}\,\overline{Q}\,1^\omega & \leq & \{\overline{p}\,Q\,(y\,p)^*\,\overline{Q} = 0 \text{ (hyp)} & \} \\
I\,L \circ \overline{p}\,\overline{Q}\,(y\,p)^*\,\overline{q}\,\overline{Q}\,1^\omega & \leq & \{(y\,p)\,\overline{q} \leq y\,p \leq \overline{q}\,y \text{ (hyp)}; (\text{iter})' & \} \\
I\,L \circ \overline{p}\,\overline{Q}\,\overline{q}\,y^*\,\overline{Q}\,1^\omega & \leq & \{I\,L \circ \overline{p}\,\overline{q}\,\overline{Q} = 0 \text{ (hyp)} & \} \\
0 & & &
\end{array}
$$

$$
\begin{array}{lll}
\overline{p}\,u \circ v & \leq & \{u \leq u\,u^*\,\overline{p} + u\,p & \} \\
\overline{p}\,(u\,u^*\,\overline{p} + u\,p) \circ v & \leq & \{(u\,p)\,(u\,u^*\,\overline{p}) \leq (u\,u^*\,\overline{p})\,1; \; (12) & \} \\
\overline{p}\,(u\,u^*\,\overline{p}) \circ (u\,p) \circ v & \leq & \{\overline{p}\,(u\,u^*\,\overline{p}) \leq (u\,u^*)\,\overline{p}; \; (\text{iter}) & \} \\
(u\,u^*) \circ \overline{p}\,(u\,p) \circ v & = & \{(u\,u^*) \circ w = u \circ w & \} \\
u \circ \overline{p}\,(u\,p) \circ v & & &
\end{array}
$$

$\square$

5.5   Back's Theorem

Back[1, 2] proposed a reduction theorem for total correctness. Instead of breaking critical sections of y into phases, his theorem partitions the environment action x

---

[4] There are two ways to talk about possibility (i.e., relational totality) in omega algebras. The one used here is that x is total on a domain p iff $p\,x\,1^\omega = p\,1^\omega$ (i.e. all effects of x can be later obliterated). This works fine for the relational model, and fits in well with proof checking mechanisms. An alternative, which works for other programming models, is that x is total on p iff, for every y, $y\,p\,x = 0 \implies y\,p = 0$.

into two components, r and l; inside a critical section, r (resp. l) actions can always be pushed to the right (resp. left). Suitably generalized, his theorem uses the following hypotheses:

$$r\,p\,y \leq y\,r$$
$$y\,p\,l \leq l\,y$$
$$r\,p\,l \leq l\,r$$
$$p\,r\,\overline{p} = 0$$
$$\overline{p}\,l\,p = 0$$

The first three conditions say that, inside of the critical section, r actions commute to the right of l and y actions, and l actions commute to the left of r and y actions. The last two conditions say that r (resp. l) cannot move control out of (resp. in to) the critical section. The theorem says that we can pretend (in the main phase) that critical sections execute atomically:

$$(y + r + l) \circ z = (p\,l) \circ (y + \overline{p}\,l + r\,\overline{p}) \circ (r\,p) \circ z \qquad (27)$$

$$
\begin{array}{lll}
(y + r + l) \circ z & = & \{l = p\,l + \overline{p}\,l \qquad\qquad\qquad\quad\} \\
(p\,l + y + r + \overline{p}\,l) \circ z & = & \{\ 18 \text{ with } x := p\,l,\ y := y + r,\} \\
& & \{z := \overline{p}\,l,\ \text{proofs (a),(b) below}\} \\
(p\,l) \circ (y + r + \overline{p}\,l) \circ z & = & \{r = r\,p + r\,\overline{p} \qquad\qquad\qquad\ \} \\
(p\,l) \circ (y + r\,\overline{p} + \overline{p}\,l + r\,p) \circ z & = & \{\text{proof (c) below, (17)} \qquad\qquad\ \} \\
(p\,l) \circ (y + r\,\overline{p} + \overline{p}\,l) \circ (r\,p) \circ z
\end{array}
$$

$$
\begin{array}{lll}
\text{(a):} \\
(y + r + \overline{p}\,l)\,(p\,l) & = & \{(\text{dist}) \qquad\qquad\qquad\qquad\qquad\quad\} \\
y\,p\,l + r\,p\,l + \overline{p}\,l\,p\,l & = & \{\overline{p}\,l\,p = 0\ (\text{hyp}) \qquad\qquad\qquad\quad\} \\
y\,p\,l + r\,p\,l & = & \{y\,p\,l \leq l\,y,\ \ r\,p\,l \leq l\,r\ (\text{hyp})\} \\
l\,y + l\,r & \leq & \{l = p\,l + \overline{p}\,l;\ (\text{dist}) \qquad\qquad\quad\} \\
(p\,l + \overline{p}\,l)\,(y + r)
\end{array}
$$

$$
\begin{array}{lll}
\text{(b):} \\
(\overline{p}\,l)\,(p\,l) & = & \{\overline{p}\,l\,p = 0\ (\text{hyp}) \qquad\qquad\qquad\quad\} \\
0
\end{array}
$$

$$
\begin{array}{lll}
\text{(c):} \\
(r\,p)\,(y + r\,\overline{p} + \overline{p}\,l) & = & \{(\text{dist}) \qquad\qquad\qquad\qquad\qquad\quad\} \\
r\,p\,y + r\,p\,r\,\overline{p} + r\,p\,\overline{p}\,l & = & \{p\,r\,\overline{p} = 0\ (\text{hyp});\ p\,\overline{p} = 0 \quad\} \\
r\,p\,y & \leq & \{r\,p\,y \leq y\,r\ (\text{hyp}) \qquad\qquad\qquad\} \\
y\,r & \leq & \{r = r\,p + r\,\overline{p} \qquad\qquad\qquad\quad\} \\
(y + r\,\overline{p} + \overline{p}\,l)\,((r\,p) + (y + r\,\overline{p} + \overline{p}\,l))
\end{array}
$$

$\square$

Again, assuming that $r\,p$ actions terminate (i.e., r actions cannot leave control inside the critical section forever), we obtain a simpler reduction theorem by loop elimination:

$$(r\ p) \circ 0 = 0 \implies \bar{p}\ (y + r + l) \circ \bar{p} = \bar{p}\ (y + \bar{p}\ l + r\ \bar{p}) \circ \bar{p} \qquad (28)$$

A typical application of Back's theorem is the following asynchronous snapshot algorithm. Let y be a program whose critical section actions record values of some subset of the program variables, and let p mean that not all of these variables are recorded. (The critical section is entered by discarding all recorded values). Let r (resp. l) be a sum of transitions that read and write variables in an arbitrary way, where each of these transitions can execute only if all (resp. none) of the variables it accesses are recorded. The hypotheses of Back's theorem then hold (r and l do not change the set of recorded variables, and so don't move control in or out of the critical section; each summand of r commutes with each summand of l because they must access disjoint sets of variables, etc.). Thus, we can pretend that the entire state is recorded without interruption.

6   Conclusion

In summary, separation theorems are powerful tools for reasoning about concurrency control. Our experience with reduction resulted in theorems that were uniformly simpler, more powerful, and easier to prove than the originals. These theorems also show the advantages of working with simple iteration constructs (as opposed to the usual **do** or **while** loops), and of retaining sequential composition as a first-class operator.

Acknowledgments

Members of IFIP WG2.3, particularly J. R. Rao and Jay Misra, provided useful feedback on earlier versions of this work. The anonymous referees also provided a number of helpful suggestions.

References

1. R. J. R. Back. Refining atomicity in parallel algorithms. In *Parallel Architectures and Languards Europe*. Springer-Verlag, 1989.
2. R. J. R. Back and J. von Wright. Reasoning algebraically about loops. *Acta Informatica*, 36(4), 1999.
3. T. Doeppner. Parallel program correctness through refinement. In *ACM Symposium on Principles of Programming Languages*, 1977.
4. M. G. Gouda and Y. T. Yu. Protocol validation by maximal progress state exploration. Technical Report CS-TR-211, The University of Texas at Austin, 1982.
5. D. Kozen. A completeness theorem for Kleene algebra and the calculus of regular events. *Information and Computation*, 110(2):366–390, 1994.
6. L. Lamport. A theorem on atomicity in distributed algorithms. *Distributed COmputing*, 4:59–68, 1990.

7. L. Lamport and F. B. Schneider. Pretending atomicity. Technical Report Research Report 44, Compaq System Research Center, 1989.
8. R. J. Lipton. Reduction: A method of proving properties of parallel programs. *Communications of the ACM*, 18(12):717–721, 1975.
9. C. Papadimitriou. *The Theory of Database Concurrency Control*. Computer Science Press, 1986.

Reasoning about Non-terminating Loops Using Deadline Commands

Ian Hayes

School of Computer Science and Electrical Engineering,
The University of Queensland, Brisbane, 4072, Australia.
ianh@csee.uq.edu.au

Abstract. It is common for a real-time process to consist of a nonterminating loop monitoring an input and controlling an output. Hence a real-time program development method needs to support nonterminating loops. Earlier work on real-time program development has produced a real-time refinement calculus that makes use of a novel deadline command which allows timing constraints to be embedded in real-time programs. The addition of the deadline command to the real-time programming language gives the significant advantage of providing a real-time programming language that is machine independent. This allows a more abstract approach to the program development process.

In this paper we add possibly nonterminating loops to the refinement calculus. First we examine the semantics of possibly nonterminating loops, and use them to reason directly about a simple example. Then we develop simpler refinement rules that make use of a loop invariant.

1 Introduction

Our overall goal is to provide a method for the formal development of real-time programs. One problem with real-time programs is that the timing characteristics of a program are not known until it is compiled for a particular machine, whereas we would prefer a machine independent program development method. The approach we have taken is to extend a real-time programming language with a *deadline* command [2] that allows timing constraints to be incorporated into a real-time program. The result is a machine-independent real-time programming language. This allows a more abstract approach to the program development process. Of course the compiled version of the program needs to be checked to make sure that it meets all the deadlines specified in the extended language when the program is run on a particular machine. We consider such checking to be part of an extended compilation phase for the program, rather than part of the program development phase. Unfortunately, there is the possibility that the compiled code may not meet all the deadlines. In this case the program is not suitable and either we need to redevelop (parts of) the program, or alternatively find a faster machine or a compiler that generates better code.

To date we have developed a sequential real-time refinement calculus [6,7] that can be viewed as an extension [5] of the standard sequential refinement

R. Backhouse and J. N. Oliveira (Eds.): MPC 2000, LNCS 1837, pp. 60–79, 2000.
© Springer-Verlag Berlin Heidelberg 2000

calculus [15]. The rules we have previously used for introducing loops only consider terminating loops [7], and include a novel rule that uses a timing deadline (rather than a loop variant) to show termination [8]. However, real-time control applications can require that a relationship is maintained between inputs and outputs over all time (not just between the initial value of variables and the final value of variables). Hence we need to be able to develop loops that may not terminate. In this paper we examine the problem of incorporating nonterminating loops into our refinement calculus, and develop both a direct method using the loop semantics, as well as a method closer to the usual loop invariant approach.

1.1 Related Work

We concentrate our comparison with related work on approaches that develop real-time programs from abstract specifications. The two approaches we consider are Scholefield's Temporal Agent Model (TAM) [16,17], and Hooman's assertional specification and verification of real-time programs [12].

All the methods introduce some form of time variable that allows reference to the start and finish times of commands, and that can be used to specify timing constraints and relationships. The two main features that distinguish our work are the addition of the deadline command, and the use of timed traces for inputs, outputs and local variables.

TAM provides a real-time refinement calculus. If we compare the sequential aspects of TAM with our approach, the main difference is in the treatment of deadlines. In TAM, deadlines are specified as a constraint on the execution time allowed for a command. This restricts deadlines to the command structure of the TAM language. In comparison, we express deadlines via a separate **deadline** command. This allows more flexibility in specifying timing constraints. In addition to being able to specify constraints that match the structure of the language, one can also specify constraints on execution paths that cross the boundaries of language constructs, e.g., a path that begins before an alternation command and ends within one branch of the alternation, or a path from a point within the body of a loop back around to a point within the body of the loop on its next iteration.

A consequence of the TAM approach to deadlines is that it is necessary to specify a constant representing the evaluation time for all guards of an alternation, even though in practice the guard evaluation time is different for different branches of an alternation. In our approach there is no need for such a constant: guard evaluation is just considered to be part of the execution time of each path on which the guard appears. The real constraints are the overall constraint on each path. There is no necessity to have an additional, more restrictive, constraint on the guard evaluation.

Another difference is in the treatment of inputs and outputs. TAM provides shunts for communication between processes and for communication with the environment. Our approach treats inputs and outputs as traces over time. One of the main application areas we see for our work is in the specification and refinement of systems with continuous variables, such as the level of water in a mine shaft [13]. The level of water in the mine shaft is a continuous real-valued function of time (it is a *timed trace*). A program monitoring the water level will sample the timed trace, but in order to provide an abstract specification of the operation of the program it is necessary to refer to such timed traces. Within this paper we define a simple **read** command, that samples an input, but because we use timed traces, more complex input commands, such as an analog-to-digital conversion, can be handled within the same framework.

Hooman's work [12] on assertional specification and verification extends the use of traditional Hoare logic triples to real-time systems. The real-time interface of the program with the environment can be specified using primitives denoting the timing of observable events. The interpretation of triples has been adapted to require the postcondition to hold for terminating and non-terminating computations in order to handle non-terminating loops.

Each of the atomic commands in Hooman's language has an associated constant representing its execution time, and compound commands, such as **if-then-else**, have constants representing such things as the time to evaluate the guard. For example, Hooman [12, page 126] introduces a constant, T_a, representing the execution time of an assignment command. An obvious problem is that not all assignments take the same amount of time, but further, given a single assignment command, its execution time may vary greatly (due to the effects of pipelines or caches) depending upon the preceding commands in the path. Timing constraints on program components must be broken down into timing constraints on the individual commands. The overall approach is similar to that used in TAM and suffers in the same ways in comparison to the use of a **deadline** command to specify timing constraints on paths.

The seemingly small addition of the **deadline** command in our work has had a significant impact on the whole development method, and importantly, has allowed developments to treat real-time constraints in a more realistic and practical manner than in the other approaches.

- During the refinement process, **deadline** commands can be used to separate out timing constraints, leaving behind a requirement to be met that does not explicitly contain timing constraints. The standard refinement calculus can be used to develop such components.
- The timing constraints are on execution paths through the program and are not necessarily constrained to the phrase structure of the programming language. This allows more realistic timing constraints to be devised.
- A timing constraint is on a whole execution path rather than each command in the path, and hence is less restrictive in terms of allowable implementations.

Section 2 outlines the real-time refinement calculus and specifies a simple alarm detection example. Section 3 defines a possibly nonterminating loop construct and applies the semantics directly to the alarm example. Section 4 develops refinement laws for introducing possibly nonterminating loops; the laws make use of loop invariants to simplify the reasoning.

2   Real-Time Refinement Calculus

We model time by nonnegative real numbers:

$$Time \mathrel{\widehat=} \{r : \mathbf{real} \mid 0 \le r < \infty\} \;,$$

where real numbers include infinity and allow operations such as comparisons with infinity. The real-time refinement calculus makes use of a special real-valued variable, τ, for the current time. To allow for nonterminating programs, we allow τ to take on the value infinity (∞).

$$Time_\infty \mathrel{\widehat=} Time \cup \{\infty\}$$

In real-time programs we distinguish three kinds of variables:

- inputs, which are under the control of the environment of the program,
- outputs, which are under the control of the program, and
- local variables, which are under the control of the program, but unlike outputs are not externally visible.

All variables are modelled as total functions from $Time$ to the declared type of the variable. We use the term *program variables* to refer to those variables under the control of the program, i.e., outputs and local variables. Note that it is not meaningful to talk about the value of a variable at time infinity. Only the (special) current time variable, τ, may take on the value infinity. We sometimes need to refer to the set of all variables in scope. We call this ρ, and the subset containing just the program variables (outputs and local variables, but not inputs) we call $\hat\rho$.

The semantics of the specification command follows an approach similar to that of Utting and Fidge [18]. In this paper we represent the semantics of a command by a predicate in a form similar to that of Hehner [10,9]. The predicate relates the start time of a command, τ_0, to its finish time, τ, (which may be infinity) and constrains the traces of the variables over time [18]. All our commands insist that time does not go backwards: $\tau_0 \le \tau$.

The meaning function $\mathcal{M}$ takes the variables in scope, ρ, and a command C and returns the corresponding predicate, $\mathcal{M}_\rho(C)$. As for Hehner, refinement of commands is defined as reverse implication:

$$C \sqsubseteq D \mathrel{\widehat=} \mathcal{M}_\rho(C) \Longleftarrow \mathcal{M}_\rho(D) \;,$$

where the reverse implication holds for all possible values of the variables, including τ_0 and τ.

Aside: earlier semantics [18,7] was based on predicate transformers rather than predicates. In that semantics a nonterminating loop is equivalent to **abort**, as in Dijkstra's calculus [1]. Hence that semantics is not suitable for this paper.

2.1   Real-Time Specification Command

We define a possibly nonterminating real-time *specification command* with a syntax similar to that of Morgan [15]:

$$\infty x\colon [P,\quad Q]\ ,$$

where x is a vector of variables called the *frame*, P is the assumption made by the specification, and Q is its effect. The '∞' at the beginning is just part of the syntax; it indicates that the command might not terminate.

P is assumed to hold at the start time of the command. Although variables are modelled as functions of time, we allow the assumption to refer to variables without using an explicit time index, with the understanding that these stand for the values of the variables at the start time, τ_0. For a predicate, P, we use the notation $P @ s$ to stand for P with all free occurrences of τ replaced by s, and all unindexed occurrences of a variable, v, replaced by $v(s)$.

The effect Q is a relation between the start time τ_0 and the finish time τ, as well as a constraint on the program variable traces. We use the notation $Q@(s, t)$ to stand for the predicate Q with all free occurrences of τ_0 and τ replaced by s and t, respectively, and all unindexed occurrences of a variable, v, replaced by $v(t)$, and all occurrences of initial variables, v_0, replaced by $v(s)$.

The frame, x, of a specification command lists those program variables that may be modified by the command. All other program variables in scope, i.e., in $\hat{\rho}$ but not x, are defined to be stable for the duration of the command. The predicate $stable(v, S)$ states that the variable v has the same value over all the times in the set S:

$$stable(v, S) \mathrel{\hat{=}} S \neq \{\} \Rightarrow (\exists\, x \bullet v(\!(S)\!) = \{x\})\ ,$$

where $v(\!(S)\!)$ is the image of the set S through the function v. We allow the first argument of stable to be a vector of variables, in which case all variables in the vector are stable. The notation $[s \ldots t]$ stands for the closed interval of times from s to t, and $(s \ldots t)$ stands for the open interval. We also allow half-open and half-closed intervals. The notation $\hat{\rho} \setminus x$ stands for the set of program variables ($\hat{\rho}$) minus the set of variables in x.

Definition 1 (real-time specification). *Given variables, ρ, a frame, x, contained in $\hat{\rho}$, a predicate, P, involving τ and the variables in ρ, and a predicate, Q, involving τ_0, τ, variables in ρ, and initial variables (zero-subscripted variables) corresponding to those in ρ, the meaning of a possibly nonterminating real-time specification command is defined by the following.*

$$\mathcal{M}_\rho\left(\infty x\colon [P,\quad Q]\right) \mathrel{\hat{=}} \tau_0 \leq \tau \,\wedge$$
$$(\tau_0 < \infty \wedge P @ \tau_0 \Rightarrow Q @ (\tau_0, \tau) \wedge stable(\hat{\rho} \setminus x, [\tau_0 \ldots \tau]))$$

Note that if assumption P does not hold initially the command still guarantees that time does not go backwards. Because the time variable may take on the value infinity, the above specification command allows nontermination. Note that if $\tau = \infty$ the predicate Q may not depend on the value of variables at time τ, because variables are only defined over $Time$, and not $Time_\infty$.

As abbreviations, if the assumption, P, is omitted, then it is taken to be $true$, and if the frame is empty the ':' is omitted.

All of the executable commands (Sect. 2.2) in our language only constrain the values of the program variables over the time interval over which they execute. Typically the effect of a specification command only constrains the values of variables over the execution interval of the command: $\lbrace\!\lbrace\tau_0 \dots \tau\,\rbrack$. However, we do not put any such restriction in the definition of a specification command because, although the effect may constrain the value of variables before τ_0 or after τ, the assumption of the specification may be strong enough to allow the effect to be replaced by one that only constrains the variables over the execution interval of the command. Such 'replacement' steps are part of the refinement process. For example, if the effect constrains the value of the variables before τ_0, then in order for the specification to be implementable, the assumption should have at least as strong a constraint on the variables before τ_0, in which case the effect can be replaced by one that does not constrain the variables before τ_0. It is also possible for the effect to constrain the value of the variables after τ. For example, for a central heater controller, the effect of a specification may require the temperature to be above some lower limit $mintemp$ for some time interval after τ. This is implementable provided the assumption of the specification implies that the rate of change of the temperature over time is limited. The specification can be implemented by ensuring the temperature is above $mintemp$ by a large enough margin to ensure the temperature remains over $mintemp$ over the required interval assuming the maximum rate of fall of the temperature.

2.2   Real-Time Commands

Other real-time commands can be defined in terms of equivalent specification commands. Here we define: a terminating (no '∞' prefix) specification command, $x\colon [P, \quad Q]$; an assumption, $\{P\}$; the null command, **skip**, that does nothing and takes no time; a command, **idle**, that does nothing but may take time; an absolute delay command; a multiple assignment; a command, **read**, to sample a value from an external input; the deadline command; the most nondeterministic command, **chaos**; and the best of all (but unimplementable) command, **magic**. External outputs may be modified using assignments. The expressions used in the commands are assumed to be idle-stable, that is, their value does not change over time provided all the program variables are stable.

Definition 2 (idle-stable). *Given variables, ρ, an expression E is* idle-stable *provided*

$$\tau_0 \leq \tau \wedge stable(\hat{\rho}, \lbrack\tau_0 \dots \tau\,\rbrack) \Rightarrow E \,@\, \tau_0 = E \,@\, \tau \ .$$

In practice this usually means that an idle-stable expression cannot refer to the special time variable, τ, or to the value of external inputs.

Definition 3. *Given an idle-stable, time-valued expression D; a vector of program variables, **x**; a vector of idle-stable expressions, **E**, of the same length as **x** and assignment compatible with **x**; a program variable, v; and an input i that is assignment compatible with v, the real-time commands are defined as follows.*

$$\boldsymbol{x}\colon [P, \quad Q] \;\widehat{=}\; \infty\boldsymbol{x}\colon [P, \quad Q \wedge \tau < \infty]$$
$$\{P\} \;\widehat{=}\; [P, \quad \tau = \tau_0]$$
$$\textbf{skip} \;\widehat{=}\; [\tau_0 = \tau]$$
$$\textbf{idle} \;\widehat{=}\; [\tau_0 \leq \tau]$$
$$\textbf{delay until } D \;\widehat{=}\; [D \leq \tau]$$
$$\boldsymbol{x} := \boldsymbol{E} \;\widehat{=}\; \boldsymbol{x}\colon [\boldsymbol{x} \,@\, \tau = \boldsymbol{E} \,@\, \tau_0]$$
$$v : \textbf{read}(i) \;\widehat{=}\; v\colon [v \,@\, \tau \in i(\lceil \tau_0 \dots \tau \rceil)]$$
$$\textbf{deadline } D \;\widehat{=}\; [\tau_0 = \tau \leq D]$$
$$\textbf{chaos} \;\widehat{=}\; \{false\}$$
$$\textbf{magic} \;\widehat{=}\; [false]$$

The **deadline** command is novel. It takes no time and guarantees to complete by the given deadline. It is not possible to implement a deadline command by generating code. Instead we need to check that the code generated for a program that contains a deadline command will always reach the deadline command by its deadline [4]. We discuss this further with the example below.

The meaning of **chaos** is the predicate $\tau_0 \leq \tau$. It only guarantees that time increases and nothing more, not even stability of any program variable. The meaning of **magic** is $\tau_0 \leq \tau \wedge \tau_0 = \infty$. If it begins execution at a time other than infinity this reduces to *false* and hence it refines any other command. Given the definition of a specification command (and hence all the other commands), if a specification begins at time infinity its meaning is $\tau_0 \leq \tau$. Hence all commands are refined by **magic** in this case also.

2.3   Detecting an Alarm Signal

We consider a very simple example of possibly nonterminating behaviour to illustrate our approach. There is a Boolean *alarm* signal that indicates a fault has occurred.

input *alarm* : *Boolean*

The input *alarm* is modelled as a function from *Time* to its type, *Boolean*. Hence we can use expressions like $alarm(t)$, where t is of type time, to determine the value of *alarm* at time t.

We assume that, if the alarm is raised, it stays raised for at least $2p$ time units, where p is a constant. As this is a global assumption that is independent of the current time, we state it once and may assume it at any point in the program development. The notation *alarm* **over** $\lceil b \dots e \rceil$ stands for $\forall t : \lceil b \dots e \rceil \bullet alarm(t)$.

$$\left\{ \begin{array}{l} \forall t : Time \bullet alarm(t) \Rightarrow \\ \quad (\exists b, e : Time \bullet 2p \leq e - b \wedge t \in \lceil b \dots e \rceil \wedge \\ \quad alarm \textbf{ over } \lceil b \dots e \rceil \end{array} \right\} \tag{1}$$

The problem is to detect an *alarm* signal and terminate. If the alarm never occurs the program will not terminate. Because the concern of this paper is in developing nonterminating loops, we give the specification of just the loop, and assume appropriate initialisation has already taken place. The loop samples the value of the alarm with a sample period of p. It makes use of two local variables: the Boolean-valued variable al is used to hold the sample of the alarm on each iteration, and the time-valued variable s maintains the start time of the sampling period. (The type of s is the time type provided by the target language; that type is a subset of *Time*.) We assume al is initialised to false, and s is initialised to a time close to the start time of the program. There are two possible outcomes of executing the program: either the alarm is raised and the program terminates, or the alarm is never raised and the program never terminates. The notation *alarm* **in** $\lfloor s - p \dots \tau \rfloor$ stands for $\exists\, t : \lfloor s - p \dots \tau \rfloor \bullet alarm(t)$.

$$
\infty s, al: \left[\begin{array}{c} s - p \leq \tau \leq s \,\wedge \\ \neg\, al \end{array} \, , \begin{array}{c} (\tau < \infty \wedge al \,\wedge \\ alarm \textbf{ in } \lfloor s - p \dots \tau \rfloor \,\wedge \\ (\neg\, alarm) \textbf{ over } \lfloor s_0 + p \dots s - 2p \rfloor) \\ \vee \\ (\tau = \infty \wedge (\neg\, alarm) \textbf{ over } \lfloor s_0 + p \dots \infty \rfloor) \end{array} \right] \quad (2)
$$

The alarm detection example can be refined to a loop that samples the alarm once every p seconds (see Fig. 1). We give the code for the implementation first in order to explain the commands available in the real-time programming language, and so that the reader is aware of the final form of the program.

$$
\begin{aligned}
&\{s - p \leq \tau \leq s \wedge \neg\, al\}\,; \\
&\textbf{do}\,\neg\, al \rightarrow \\
&\qquad \textbf{delay until } s; \\
&\qquad al : \textbf{read}(alarm); \\
&\qquad \textbf{deadline } s + p; \\
&\qquad s := s + p \\
&\textbf{od}
\end{aligned} \quad (3)
$$

On each iteration the loop body delays until the start of the sample period, s; samples the value of the alarm using a read command; must reach the deadline by the end of the period, $s + p$; and increments s by the length of the period, p, to get the start of the next sample interval. If the value of the alarm when it was read was true, the loop terminates. The above loop guarantees that in any interval of length $2p$ the alarm is sampled at least once. The length is $2p$ rather than p because one sample may occur at the very start of its sample period and the next sample may occur at the very end of the next sample period, $2p$ time units later.

In reasoning about the timing behaviour of the above real-time program we do not need to separately consider the execution times of the guard evaluation, delay, read, assignment and loop iteration. Instead we reason about the time taken for execution paths ending in deadlines. In this case there are two paths to consider. The first enters the loop and reaches the deadline for the first time.

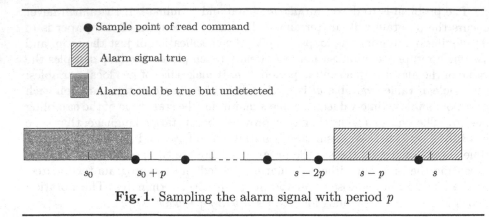

Fig. 1. Sampling the alarm signal with period p

This path starts before time s and must finish by $s + p$. Hence it has an execution time constraint of p. The second path starts at the deadline command, executes the assignment, loops back to the guard evaluation, delays and then reads the alarm; it has a time constraint of p as well. In calculating the constraint for the second path, although the deadline expression $(s + p)$ at the start of the path is same as the deadline expression $(s + p)$ at the end of the path, in the meantime s has been incremented by p, and that leads to a difference of p in the actual deadline times.

Aside: If the loop is followed by a deadline command then there will be a third path starting at the deadline command within the loop, executing the assignment, branching back to evaluate the loop guard and exiting the loop; such a path is treated similarly to the other two.

Expressing timing constraints on execution paths is both simpler and more general than having constraints on individual commands and components of commands. In addition, on architectures with pipelines and caches one can get better (lower) worst-case execution time bounds on whole paths, rather than individual commands, because the paths give additional context information that can be used to determine better worst-case execution time bounds [14].

2.4   Sequential Composition

Because we allow nonterminating commands, we need to be careful with our definition of sequential composition. If the first command of the sequential composition does not terminate, then the effect of the sequential composition must be the same as the effect of the first command. Otherwise it is the combined effect of the execution of the first followed by the second. Here we provide a definition of sequential composition in terms of the effects of the two commands.

Definition 4 (sequential composition). *Given variables, ρ, and real-time commands, C and D, their sequential composition is defined by the following.*

$$\mathcal{M}_\rho\,(C;\,D) \mathrel{\hat{=}} \exists\,\tau' : Time_\infty \bullet \mathcal{M}_\rho\,(C)\,@\,(\tau_0, \tau') \wedge$$
$$(\tau' = \tau = \infty \vee \mathcal{M}_\rho\,(D)\,@\,(\tau', \tau))$$

3   Definition of a Real-Time Loop Command

A real-time loop is similar to a conventional sequential programming loop, except that we take into account timing properties. To give the reader an idea of the differences between a real-time loop and a standard loop, we give the characteristic recurrences of both. A standard loop,

$$SDO \mathrel{\hat{=}} \mathbf{do}\, B \to C \,\mathbf{od} \ ,$$

satisfies the recurrence

$$SDO = \mathbf{if}\, B \to C;\, SDO \,\|\, \neg\, B \to \mathbf{skip}\,\mathbf{fi} \ .$$

In the standard calculus, this can be rewritten in the following form,

$$SDO = ([B]\,;\, C;\, SDO \,\|\, [\neg\, B]) \ ,$$

in which guarded commands of the form $B \to S$ are rewritten in the equivalent form of a coercion followed by the command ($[B]\,;\, S$); the if-fi is replaced by a demonic choice ($\|$) because the guards are complementary; and $[\neg\, B]\,;\,$ **skip** is replaced by its equivalent, $[\neg\, B]$.

For the real-time loop command,

$$DO \mathrel{\hat{=}} \mathbf{do}\, B \to C \,\mathbf{od} \ ,$$

there must exist a strictly positive time d, such that the following recurrence holds.

$$DO = \|[\ \mathbf{con}\, v : Time \bullet \{v = \tau\}\,;\, [B]\,;\, C;\, \mathbf{delay\ until}\, v + d \ ]\|;\, DO$$
$$\| \ [\neg\, B]$$

The logical constant v captures the start time of a single iteration. The coercion $[B]$ allows the first alternative to be executed if the guard evaluates to true. Note that in the real-time case the guard evaluation may take time: the coercion, $[B]$, may take time and must terminate. The delay until (absolute) time $v + d$ at the end of an iteration ensures that each iteration of the loop takes a minimum time, d. This rules out Zeno-like behaviour in which, for example, each iteration takes half the time of the previous iteration. The value of d can be arbitrarily small (e.g., 1 attosecond), but it must be greater than zero. (A loop of the form **do** *true* $\to$ ... **od** typically has the minimum overhead; its implementation may take no time to evaluate the guard, but there will be a minimum time overhead for the branch back to the start of the loop.)

The Boolean expression B is assumed to be idle-stable. That is, its value does not change with just the passage of time if the program variables are stable. In practice this means B cannot refer to the current time variable, τ, or to external inputs (which may change over time). We assume the guard evaluation terminates, but we place no explicit upper bound on the time taken for guard evaluation, because guard expressions may be arbitrarily complex. For a particular application there will be a time bound on guard evaluation, but this is catered for by using explicit deadline commands within the body of the loop. There is no need for a separate upper bound on the guard evaluation time in the definition of the loop.

After completing the command, C, in the body of the loop, it iterates back to the guard evaluation. The delay until $v + d$ at the end of the iteration not only ensures the minimum execution time for each iteration, it also allows for the time taken for the loop to branch back to the guard evaluation, because there is no explicit upper limit on the termination time of a delay command.

The exit alternative of the loop, $[\neg B]$, allows for the time taken to evaluate the guard (to false) and exit the loop, including the case when the guard of the loop is false initially. We place no explicit time bounds on this command in the loop definition, but for a particular application the code following the loop may include deadline commands, which explicitly introduce a time constraint. There is no lower time bound on the exit alternative because the loop **do** *false* $\rightarrow$ ... **od** can be implemented by **skip**, which takes no time.

In order to define the behaviour of a loop, we introduce an abbreviation to stand for the effect of one iteration of the loop.

$$ITERATION \; \widehat{=}$$
$$\mathcal{M}_\rho \left([\![\; \mathbf{con} \; v : \; Time \; \bullet \; \{v = \tau\} \; ; \; [B] \; ; \; C; \; \mathbf{delay \; until} \; v + d \;]\!] \right)$$

If we expand out this definition using the meanings of the component commands we get the following equivalent predicate, in which τ_1 and τ_2 are the start and finish times, respectively, of the command C.

$$ITERATION \equiv B @ \tau_0 \wedge \tau_0 + d \leq \tau \wedge$$
$$(\exists \tau_1, \tau_2 : Time \; \bullet \; \tau_0 \leq \tau_1 \leq \tau_2 \leq \tau \wedge$$
$$stable(\hat{\rho}, [\tau_0 \; ... \; \tau_1] \cup [\tau_2 \; ... \; \tau]) \wedge \mathcal{M}_\rho (C) @ (\tau_1, \tau_2))$$

To define the behaviour of a loop we introduce a possibly infinite, increasing sequence of times, $t_0 \leq t_1 \leq \ldots$, such that t_j represents the start time of iteration j (starting the numbering from zero) and t_{j+1} represents the finish time of iteration j. For the iteration starting at t_j, t_j corresponds to τ_0 in the predicate *ITERATION*, and t_{j+1} corresponds to τ. We develop the behaviour of the loop via three cases.

Termination. If the loop terminates after i iterations, then the termination time of the whole loop is some time after t_i (but less than infinity), the loop guard is false on termination, and for all previous iterations, j, where

$0 \leq j < i$, an iteration was executed at time t_j and it terminated.

$TERM \ \widehat{=}$

$$\exists\, i : \mathsf{N} \bullet t_i \leq \tau < \infty \wedge \neg\, B @ \tau \wedge stable(\hat{\rho}, \lceil t_i \,...\, \tau \rceil) \wedge$$
$$(\forall j : \mathsf{N} \bullet j < i \Rightarrow (t_{j+1} < \infty \wedge ITERATION @ (t_j, t_{j+1}))) \quad (4)$$

In the above, t_i is the finish time of the last iteration, and the later time τ is the finish time of the whole loop. During the interval from t_i until τ, all the program variables are stable, and hence, because B is idle-stable, $\neg\, B$ at t_i is equivalent to $\neg\, B$ at τ. Note the case when i is zero, which corresponds to the loop guard being initially false.

Infinite iteration. If the loop body terminates on every iteration of the loop, but the loop guard never becomes false, then the loop iterates forever. In this case the 'termination' time, τ, is infinity and there is an infinite sequence of iterations of the loop, such that the loop guard is true at the beginning of each iteration, and the body is executed (and terminates) on each iteration.

$FOREVER \ \widehat{=}$

$$\tau = \infty \wedge (\forall j : \mathsf{N} \bullet t_{j+1} < \infty \wedge ITERATION @ (t_j, t_{j+1})) \quad (5)$$

Note that the definition of $ITERATION$ includes the guard being true at the start of the iteration.

Non-termination of the loop body. The final case is if the loop does not terminate because the body of the loop does not terminate. In this case there is a finite sequence of starting times of iterations, $t_0, t_1, \ldots, t_i$. The body is executed at all the times from t_0 up to t_i, but the last execution of C does not terminate. The last iteration begins execution at t_i, the guard evaluates to true, and the loop body, C, begins execution at some later time τ_1 and never terminates.

$BODY\_NONTERM \ \widehat{=}$

$$\exists\, i : \mathsf{N} \bullet B @ t_i \wedge$$
$$(\exists\, \tau_1 : Time \bullet t_i \leq \tau_1 \wedge stable(\hat{\rho}, \lceil t_i \,...\, \tau_1 \rceil) \wedge$$
$$\mathcal{M}_\rho (C) @ (\tau_1, \tau) \wedge \tau = \infty) \wedge$$
$$(\forall j : \mathsf{N} \bullet j < i \Rightarrow (t_{j+1} < \infty \wedge ITERATION @ (t_j, t_{j+1}))) \quad (6)$$

We can combine all the above into the following single definition.

Definition 5 (repetition). *Given an idle-stable Boolean expression, B, and a command, C, a real-time repetition command is defined by the following.*

$$\mathcal{M}_\rho (\mathbf{do}\, B \rightarrow C\, \mathbf{od}) \ \widehat{=}\ (\exists\, d : Time;\ t : \mathsf{N} \rightarrow Time \bullet 0 < d \wedge t_0 = \tau_0 \wedge$$
$$(TERM \vee FOREVER \vee BODY\_NONTERM))$$

Note that there is just one choice made for d, and that value is used for all iterations of the loop. That rules out, for example, successive iterations of a loop choosing progressively smaller values of d, and hence it rules out Zeno-like behaviour. A particular implementation of a loop will determine a suitable value of d. Our implementation-independent approach allows any value.

3.1   Alarm Example

We illustrate the use of the loop definition by showing that the loop for the alarm detection implements the specification. In order to do this it is sufficient to know that the effect of a single iteration of the loop (3):

$$\|[\ \mathbf{con}\ v : Time;\ \{v = \tau\}\,;\,[\neg\, al];$$
$$\qquad \mathbf{delay\ until}\ s;\ al : \mathbf{read}(alarm);\ \mathbf{deadline}\ s + p;\ s := s + p;$$
$$\qquad \mathbf{delay\ until}\ v + d\ ]\|\ ,$$

implies

$$\neg\, al(\tau_0) \wedge al(\tau) \in alarm(\![\,\mathsf{E}\,s(\tau_0)\ ...\ min\{\tau, s(\tau)\}\,]\!]) \wedge s(\tau) = s(\tau_0) + p\ .$$

For the loop body to be executed, the guard of the loop must be true at the start time of the loop; hence $\neg\, al(\tau_0)$. The initial delay guarantees that the time at which $alarm$ is read is after the initial value of s, $s(\tau_0)$, and the deadline ensures that the value is read before $s(\tau_0) + p$. In addition the value is read before the termination time of the iteration, τ. Together these give that the value is read before the minimum of τ and $s(\tau_0) + p$. The assignment, $s := s + p$, ensures $s(\tau) = s(\tau_0) + p$. Note that the loop body introduces stronger constraints due to the final delay command and that we could make more detailed assertions about the values of the program's variables during the execution of the body, but it is sufficient that the above is implied by the loop body.

Using the abbreviation conventions described in Sect. 2.1 this predicate can be written

$$\neg\, al_0 \wedge al \in alarm(\![\,\mathsf{E}\,s_0\ ...\ min\{\tau, s\}\,]\!]) \wedge s = s_0 + p\ , \tag{7}$$

where the zero-subscripted names stand for the values of the variables at the start of the execution of the body and the unsubscripted names stand for the values of the variables at the end of the execution of the body. The upper bound $min\{\tau, s\}$ is required because in reasoning about the loop, if the loop terminates after that iteration we need a bound of τ, and if the loop does not terminate after that iteration we need a bound of s.

To reason about the loop we consider the three cases examined earlier: termination, infinite iteration, and nontermination of the loop body. For the alarm example the loop body always terminates, so we can ignore the last case. The infinite iteration case is the more novel so we consider that next. To simplify the expressions we abbreviate expressions of the form $s(t_j)$ to s_j. From the infinite iteration case (5) and the body (7), we can deduce the following.

$$\tau = \infty \wedge$$
$$(\forall j : \mathbb{N} \bullet t_{j+1} < \infty \wedge \neg\, al_j \wedge$$
$$\qquad al_{j+1} \in alarm(\![\,\mathsf{E}\,s_j\ ...\ min\{t_{j+1}, s_{j+1}\}\,]\!]) \wedge s_{j+1} = s_j + p)$$
$$\Rightarrow \text{as } al_j \text{ is false for all } j;\ \mathsf{E}\,s_j\ ...\ min\{t_{j+1}, s_{j+1}\}\,] \subseteq \mathsf{E}\,s_j\ ...\ s_{j+1}]$$
$$\tau = \infty \wedge$$

$$(\forall j : \mathbf{N} \bullet t_{j+1} < \infty \wedge false \in alarm(\lceil s_j \dots s_{j+1} \rceil) \wedge s_{j+1} = s_j + p)$$
$\Rightarrow$ from the minimum alarm duration assumption (1)
$$\tau = \infty \wedge (\neg\, alarm)\ \mathbf{over}\ \lceil s_0 + p \dots \infty)$$

For the last step, recall that (1) states that whenever *alarm* is true, it is true for at least $2p$ time units. For any value of j greater than zero, one can deduce that there exist times f_{j-1}, f_j and f_{j+1}, such that *alarm* is false at each of these times and

$$s_j - p \leq f_{j-1} \leq s_j \leq f_j \leq s_j + p \leq f_{j+1} \leq s_j + 2p \ .$$

Because $f_j - f_{j-1} \leq 2p$ and *alarm* is false at both f_{j-1} and f_j, *alarm* must be false over the whole interval $\lceil f_{j-1} \dots f_j \rceil$. Similarly *alarm* must be false over the interval $\lceil f_j \dots f_{j+1} \rceil$. Combining these two results, *alarm* must be false over the interval $\lceil f_{j-1} \dots f_{j+1} \rceil$. Because this interval includes $\lceil s_j \dots s_{j+1} \rceil$, *alarm* must be false over this interval. Finally, because this holds for all values of j greater than zero, one can deduce that *alarm* is false over the interval $\lceil s_0 + p \dots \infty)$. The start of this interval is $s_0 + p$ because the first sample of *alarm* can be as late as $s_1 = s_0 + p$.

For the termination case (4), we can deduce the following.

$$\exists i : \mathbf{N} \bullet t_i \leq \tau < \infty \wedge al \wedge stable(al, \lceil t_i \dots \tau \rceil) \wedge stable(s, \lceil t_i \dots \tau \rceil) \wedge$$
$$(\forall j : \mathbf{N} \bullet j < i \Rightarrow$$
$$(t_{j+1} < \infty \wedge \neg\, al_j \wedge al_{j+1} \in alarm(\lceil s_j \dots min\{t_{j+1}, s_{j+1}\} \rceil) \wedge$$
$$s_{j+1} = s_j + p))$$
$\Rightarrow$ split out the last iteration ($j = i - 1$); al_j is false for all previous iterations
$$\exists i : \mathbf{N} \bullet t_i \leq \tau < \infty \wedge al \wedge stable(al, \lceil t_i \dots \tau \rceil) \wedge stable(s, \lceil t_i \dots \tau \rceil) \wedge$$
$$al_i \in alarm(\lceil s_{i-1} \dots t_i \rceil) \wedge s_i = s_{i-1} + p \wedge$$
$$(\forall j : \mathbf{N} \bullet j < i - 1 \Rightarrow$$
$$(t_{j+1} < \infty \wedge false \in alarm(\lceil s_j \dots s_{j+1} \rceil) \wedge s_{j+1} = s_j + p))$$
$\Rightarrow$ from the stability of al and s, $al = al_i$ and $s = s_i$; $t_i \leq \tau$
$$\exists i : \mathbf{N} \bullet t_i \leq \tau < \infty \wedge al \wedge alarm\ \mathbf{in}\ \lceil s - p \dots \tau \rceil \wedge s = s_{i-1} + p \wedge$$
$$(\forall j : \mathbf{N} \bullet j < i - 1 \Rightarrow$$
$$(t_{j+1} < \infty \wedge false \in alarm(\lceil s_j \dots s_{j+1} \rceil) \wedge s_{j+1} = s_j + p))$$
$\Rightarrow$ from the minimum alarm duration assumption (1)
$$\tau < \infty \wedge al \wedge alarm\ \mathbf{in}\ \lceil s - p \dots \tau \rceil \wedge (\neg\, alarm)\ \mathbf{over}\ \lceil s_0 + p \dots s - 2p \rceil$$

The reasoning for the last step is similar to the reasoning for the infinite iteration case, except that in this case the argument that *alarm* is false over the interval $\lceil s_j \dots s_{j+1} \rceil$ only applies for j such that $1 \leq j \leq i - 3$, and hence *alarm* is false over the interval $\lceil s_1 \dots s_{i-2} \rceil = \lceil s_0 + p \dots s_{i-1} - p \rceil = \lceil s_0 + p \dots s - 2p \rceil$.

Together the termination and infinite iteration cases give the desired overall effect of the original specification (2).

4   Loop Introduction Laws

The above reasoning was done using the semantics of the loop directly, and hence was somewhat complicated. We would like a simpler approach closer to the conventional *loop invariant* approach [3,11]. In that approach, an invariant is assumed to hold initially and must be maintained by every iteration of the loop. When the loop terminates, as well as the loop guard being false, the invariant holds in the final state. However, this approach runs into the problem that, for a nonterminating loop, there is no such final state.

To use a loop invariant to reason about a nonterminating loop, the strategy we use is similar to that of Hooman [12, page 129]. There is a sequence of points of time corresponding to the starts of execution of the loop body at which the invariant is true. If the body of the loop always terminates, then the sequence is infinite. In that case, for any time, t, after the start time of the loop, there is always some later time, t', at which both the invariant, I, and the loop guard, B, hold.

$$\tau = \infty \wedge (\forall\, t : \mathit{Time} \bullet (\exists\, t' : \mathit{Time} \bullet t \leq t' \wedge (B \wedge I) \,@\, t')) \qquad (8)$$

If we assume that I holds immediately before the loop starts, we would like to assume that both B and I hold at the start of the execution of the command, C, within the loop body. However, there is a period of time corresponding to the guard evaluation between the two points in the program. Because B is assumed to be idle-stable, it will still hold at the start of the execution of C. For the invariant, I, we need the condition that, if I holds before evaluation of the guard, it will still hold after the evaluation. This is equivalent to I being invariant over the execution of an **idle** command, and we refer to this property as I being *idle-invariant*.

Definition 6 (idle-invariant). *For an environment with variables ρ, a predicate P is* idle-invariant *provided*

$$\tau_0 \leq \tau \wedge \mathit{stable}(\hat{\rho}, [\tau_0 \ldots \tau]) \Rightarrow P \,@\, \tau_0 \Rightarrow P \,@\, \tau \;.$$

The conditions idle-stable and idle-invariant differ in that for the former the value does not change over the execution of an idle command, whereas for the latter, if the value holds before, then it holds after. The latter differs from the former in that for idle-invariant, if the predicate is false beforehand, then it may become true during the execution of the idle.

If the command, C, in the loop body maintains the invariant, then on termination of C, I holds, and because I is idle-invariant, it will still hold after the delay at the end of the loop body, and hence at the start of the next iteration, as required.

The assumption that I is idle-invariant places restrictions on how I can refer to the current time variable, τ, because τ increases on execution of an idle command, and on how I refers to external inputs, because these may change over the execution of an idle command. For example, predicates of the form

$D \leq \tau$, where D is an idle-stable expression, are idle-invariant, but predicates of the form $\tau \leq D$ are not.

If I can be expressed in a form that does not refer to the current time, τ, and all references to external inputs are explicitly indexed with expressions that are idle-stable, then I is idle-invariant. In practice, the link between the current time, τ, and the invariant, I, is made through a time-valued program variable that approximates τ, e.g., the variable s in the alarm detection program (3). We return to this link later, but first we consider the alarm example.

4.1   Alarm Example

The invariant of the alarm detection loop is that al represents the sample of the alarm in the most recent iteration (or it is the first iteration and al is false), and the alarm sample has been false on all previous iterations, and hence the alarm has been false over (at least) the interval $[u + p \ldots s - 2p]$, where u represents the initial value of s just before the loop begins execution. We need to introduce the extra logical constant u, because we use s_0 to stand for the initial value of s on each iteration; u and s_0 only correspond on the first iteration. A little care is required to ensure that the invariant holds initially. That corresponds to the situation in which $s = u$ and al is initially false.

$$I \mathrel{\hat{=}} (al \in alarm([s - p \ldots min\{\tau, s\}]) \vee (\neg\, al \wedge s = u)) \wedge \qquad (9)$$
$$(\neg\, alarm) \textbf{ over } [u + p \ldots s - 2p]$$

Note that I is idle-invariant because, if $al \in alarm(S)$ for a time interval S, then $al \in alarm(T)$ for any time interval T that includes S.

To show that I is maintained by the loop in the alarm example it is sufficient to show $I_0 \wedge (7) \Rightarrow I$, where I_0 is I with all occurrences of τ and variables in the frame replaced by their zero-subscripted forms.

$I_0 \wedge (7)$
$\equiv (al_0 \in alarm([s_0 - p \ldots min\{\tau_0, s_0\}]) \vee (\neg\, al_0 \wedge s_0 = u)) \wedge$
$\quad (\neg\, alarm) \textbf{ over } [u + p \ldots s_0 - 2p] \wedge$
$\quad \neg\, al_0 \wedge al \in alarm([s_0 \ldots min\{\tau, s\}]) \wedge s = s_0 + p$
$\Rightarrow$ as $\neg\, al_0$; $[s_0 - p \ldots min\{\tau_0, s_0\}] \subseteq [s_0 - p \ldots s_0]$; $s = s_0 + p$
$\quad (false \in alarm([s_0 - p \ldots s_0]) \vee s_0 = u) \wedge$
$\quad (\neg\, alarm) \textbf{ over } [u + p \ldots s_0 - 2p] \wedge$
$\quad al \in alarm([s - p \ldots min\{\tau, s\}]) \wedge s = s_0 + p$

If $s_0 = u$ then $[u + p \ldots s - 2p] = [u + p \ldots s_0 - p]$ is empty, and hence $(\neg\, alarm) \textbf{ over } [u + p \ldots s - 2p]$ holds. Otherwise, because

$$(\neg\, alarm) \textbf{ over } [u + p \ldots s_0 - 2p] \wedge (\neg\, alarm) \textbf{ in } [s_0 - p \ldots s_0]\ ,$$

from the minimum alarm duration property (1) one can deduce $(\neg\, alarm) \textbf{ over }$ $[u + p \ldots s_0 - p] = [u + p \ldots s - 2p]$. Hence we can deduce the following.

$\quad al \in alarm([s - p \ldots min\{\tau, s\}]) \wedge (\neg\, alarm) \textbf{ over } [u + p \ldots s - 2p]$
$\Rightarrow I$

On termination we know that both $\neg B$ and I hold. For the alarm example, B is '$\neg al$'. Hence, if the loop terminates, we can deduce the following.

$$\tau < \infty \wedge al \wedge (al \in alarm(\lceil s - p \dots min\{\tau, s\}\rceil) \vee (\neg al \wedge s = u)) \wedge$$
$$(\neg alarm) \textbf{ over } \lceil u + p \dots s - 2p\rceil$$
$$\Rightarrow \tau < \infty \wedge al \wedge alarm \textbf{ in } \lceil s - p \dots \tau\rceil \wedge (\neg alarm) \textbf{ over } \lceil u + p \dots s - 2p\rceil$$

If the loop never terminates, the loop body will be executed at an infinite number of progressively increasing times. Hence for any time, t, there exists a later time, t', at which the loop invariant and loop guard hold (8). For the alarm example this gives the following.

$$\tau = \infty \wedge (\forall t : Time \bullet (\exists t' : Time \bullet t \leq t' \wedge$$
$$(\neg al \wedge (al \in alarm(\lceil s - p \dots min\{\tau, s\}\rceil) \vee (\neg al \wedge s = u)) \wedge$$
$$(\neg alarm) \textbf{ over } \lceil u + p \dots s - 2p\rceil) @ t'))$$

The interesting clause for the nontermination case is the last one concerning $\neg alarm$. However, because s is not explicitly related to t', one cannot deduce the desired conclusion of the specification (2), i.e., $(\neg alarm) \textbf{ over } \lceil u + p \dots \infty\rceil$. If we examine the loop implementation (3), it is clear that at the start of execution of the loop body the time must be before $s + p$, because the deadline of $s + p$ later in the body of the loop could not be met otherwise. Hence we may add a deadline of $s + p$ at the beginning of the loop body, with no effect at all on its overall behaviour, because there is a later (more constraining) occurrence of exactly the same deadline. The loop becomes the following.

$$\{s = u \wedge s - p \leq \tau \leq s \wedge \neg al\};$$

do $\neg al \rightarrow$

 deadline $s + p$;

 delay until s;

 $al : \textbf{read}(alarm)$;

 deadline $s + p$;

 $s := s + p$

od

Hence for the infinite iteration case, one may now deduce that for any time, t, there exists a later time, t', at which the command, C, begins execution and hence at which both B and I hold. In addition, because of the added deadline, we have the additional information that $t' \leq s(t') + p \equiv (\tau \leq s + p) @ t'$.

$$\tau = \infty \wedge (\forall t : Time \bullet (\exists t' : Time \bullet$$
$$(\neg al \wedge (al \in alarm(\lceil s - p \dots min\{\tau, s\}\rceil) \vee (\neg al \wedge s = u)) \wedge$$
$$(\neg alarm) \textbf{ over } \lceil u + p \dots s - 2p\rceil \wedge t \leq \tau \leq s + p) @ t'))$$

Hence for any time, w, such that $u + p \leq w$, if we choose t such that $w + 3p \leq t$, then there exists a t' such that the invariant holds at t' and $w + 3p \leq t \leq t'$, but $t' \leq s + p$ and hence $w + 3p \leq s + p$, i.e., $w \leq s - 2p$, and hence from the invariant $(\neg \; alarm)$ **over** $[u + p \ldots w]$. Because this holds for any w, we can deduce the desired conclusion:

$$\tau = \infty \wedge (\neg \; alarm) \; \textbf{over} \; [u + p \ldots \infty) \; .$$

4.2   Refinement Laws

The reasoning used above can be used to derive the following refinement law for introducing a loop with a terminating body.

Law 7 (loop with terminating body). *Given an idle-stable, Boolean-valued expression, B; an idle-invariant predicate, I, not involving τ_0 or initial (zero-subscripted) variables; and an idle-stable, time-valued expression, D; then*

$$\infty x \colon [I, \quad (\tau < \infty \wedge \neg \, B \wedge I) \vee (\tau = \infty \wedge I_\infty)]$$
$$\sqsubseteq \; \textbf{do} \, B \rightarrow \textbf{deadline} \, D; \; x \colon [B \wedge I \wedge \tau \leq D, \quad I] \; \textbf{od} \; ,$$

where $I_\infty \; \widehat{=} \; (\forall \, t : Time \bullet (\exists \, t' : Time \bullet (B \wedge I \wedge t \leq \tau \leq D) @ \, t'))$.

Finally we would like a more general law that allows the development of a loop in which the loop body may not terminate. As before, if the loop body does terminate we require that it re-establishes the invariant, I, and hence if the loop terminates one can deduce $\tau < \infty \wedge \neg \, B \wedge I$, but if the loop body does not terminate then it must establish some other condition, R. In this case the whole loop establishes $\tau = \infty \wedge R$. If the loop does not terminate but the loop body always terminates, then as before we can deduce $\tau = \infty \wedge I_\infty$. This gives the following law.

Law 8 (loop with nonterminating body). *Given an idle-stable, Boolean-valued expression, B; an idle-invariant predicate, I, not involving τ_0 or initial (zero-subscripted) variables; an idle-stable, time-valued expression, D; and a predicate R not involving τ_0 or initial variables; then*

$$\infty x \colon [I, \quad (\tau < \infty \wedge \neg \, B \wedge I) \vee (\tau = \infty \wedge (I_\infty \vee R))]$$
$$\sqsubseteq \; \textbf{do} \, B \rightarrow \textbf{deadline} \, D;$$
$$\infty x \colon [B \wedge I \wedge \tau \leq D, \quad (\tau < \infty \wedge I) \vee (\tau = \infty \wedge R)]$$
$$\textbf{od} \; .$$

The predicates I and R may not refer to τ_0 or initial variables because I and R are used both in the specification, in which τ_0 is the start time of the whole loop, and in the body of the loop, in which τ_0 is the start time of an iteration. In order to refer to the start time of the whole loop within I or R it is necessary to introduce a fresh logical constant to stand for the start time (e.g., u in the alarm example).

Note that Law 7 (loop with terminating body) is a special case of Law 8 (loop with nonterminating body) with R the predicate *false*.

5   Conclusions

The primary advantage of the approach taken in this paper is that we develop code for a *machine-independent* real-time programming language, and hence do not need to consider the detailed execution times of language constructs as part of the development process. This is achieved through the simple mechanism of adding a deadline command to our programming language. The approach allows the real-time calculus to appear to be a straightforward extension of the standard refinement calculus [5]. Of course, the compilation process now has the added burden of checking that the deadlines are met [4].

This paper has successfully extended this approach to develop possibly non-terminating loops, as required for nonterminating control applications. For the semantics of the loop we considered three cases: a terminating loop, infinite iteration, and a nonterminating loop body. Although it is possible to reason about loops using the semantics directly (as in Sect. 3.1), as with the standard refinement calculus, it is advantageous to develop refinement laws that make use of loop invariants. The termination case is the same as the conventional refinement calculus, with the exception that it is simpler because one does not need to use a loop variant to prove that the loop terminates (because it may not).

The infinite iteration case is the most interesting to deal with. We use the fact that, if the loop body always terminates and the loop iterates for ever, then the invariant is true at an infinite number of progressively increasing times. However, in order to reason about loops in a machine-independent manner, we require that the loop invariant be idle-invariant, so that it holds over the executions of the guard evaluation and branch back phases of loop execution. This restricts the form of the invariant and blurs the link between the invariant and the current time variable, τ. To re-establish the link between the invariant and the time at which the invariant is true, a deadline command can be added to the start of the loop body. That leads to our final refinement laws for nonterminating loops.

Acknowledgements

This research was funded by Australian Research Council (ARC) Large Grant A49801500, *A Unified Formalism for Concurrent Real-time Software Development*. I would like to thank David Carrington, Colin Fidge, Stephen Grundon, Graeme Smith and Luke Wildman for feedback on earlier drafts of this paper, and Brendan Mahony and Mark Utting for fruitful discussions on the topic of this paper, and the members of IFIP Working Group 2.3 on Programming Methodology for feedback on this topic, especially Rick Hehner for his advice on how to simplify our approach.

References

1. Edsger W. Dijkstra. *A Discipline of Programming*. Prentice-Hall, 1976. 63
2. C. J. Fidge, I. J. Hayes, and G. Watson. The deadline command. *IEE Proceedings—Software*, 146(2):104–111, April 1999. 60

3. R. W. Floyd. Assigning meaning to programs. *Math. Aspects of Comput. Sci.*, 19:19–32, 1967. 74

4. S. Grundon, I. J. Hayes, and C. J. Fidge. Timing constraint analysis. In C. Mc-Donald, editor, *Computer Science '98: Proc. 21st Australasian Computer Science Conf. (ACSC'98), Perth, 4–6 Feb.*, pages 575–586. Springer-Verlag, 1998. 66, 78

5. I. J. Hayes. Separating timing and calculation in real-time refinement. In J. Grundy, M. Schwenke, and T. Vickers, editors, *International Refinement Workshop and Formal Methods Pacific 1998*, pages 1–16. Springer-Verlag, 1998. 60, 78

6. I. J. Hayes and M. Utting. Coercing real-time refinement: A transmitter. In D. J. Duke and A. S. Evans, editors, *BCS-FACS Northern Formal Methods Workshop (NFMW'96)*, Electronic Workshops in Computing. Springer Verlag, 1997. 60

7. I. J. Hayes and M. Utting. A sequential real-time refinement calculus. Technical Report UQ-SVRC-97-33, Software Verification Research Centre, The University of Queensland, URL http://svrc.it.uq.edu.au, 1997. 59 pages. 60, 61, 63

8. I. J. Hayes and M. Utting. Deadlines are termination. In D. Gries and W.-P. de Roever, editors, *IFIP TC2/WG2.2, 2.3 International Conference on Programming Concepts and Methods (PROCOMET'98)*, pages 186–204. Chapman and Hall, 1998. 61

9. E. C. R. Hehner. Termination is timing. In J.L.A. van de Snepscheut, editor, *Mathematics of Program Construction*, volume 375 of *Lecture Notes in Computer Science*, pages 36–47. Springer-Verlag, June 1989. 63

10. E. C. R. Hehner. *A Practical Theory of Programming*. Springer Verlag, 1993. 63

11. C. A. R. Hoare. An axiomatic approach to computer programming. *Comm. ACM*, 12:576–580, 583, 1969. 74

12. J. Hooman. Assertional specification and verification. In M. Joseph, editor, *Real-time Systems: Specification, Verification and Analysis*, chapter 5, pages 97–146. Prentice Hall, 1996. 61, 62, 74

13. M. Joseph, editor. *Real-time Systems: Specification, Verification and Analysis*. Prentice Hall, 1996. 62

14. Sung-Soo Lim, Young Hyun Bae, Gyu Tae Jang, Byung-Do Rhee, Sang Lyul Min, Chang Yun Park, Heonshik Shin, Kunsoo Park, Soo-Mook Moon, and Chong Sang Kim. An accurate worst case timing analysis for RISC processors. *IEEE Trans. on Software Eng.*, 21(7):593–604, July 1995. 68

15. C. C. Morgan. *Programming from Specifications*. Prentice Hall, second edition, 1994. 61, 64

16. D. J. Scholefield. *A Refinement Calculus for Real-Time Systems*. PhD thesis, Department of Computer Science, University of York, U.K., 1992. 61

17. D. J. Scholefield, H. Zedan, and He Jifeng. A specification-oriented semantics for the refinement of real-time systems. *Theoretical Computer Science*, 131:219–241, 1994. 61

18. M. Utting and C. J. Fidge. A real-time refinement calculus that changes only time. In He Jifeng, editor, *Proc. 7th BCS/FACS Refinement Workshop*, Electronic Workshops in Computing. Springer, July 1996. URL http://www.springer.co.uk/eWiC/Workshops/7RW.html. 63

Quantum Programming

J. W. Sanders and P. Zuliani

Programming Research Group,Oxford University Computing Laboratory,
Oxford, OX1 3QD, England
{jeff,pz}@comlab.ox.ac.uk

Abstract. In this paper a programming language, $qGCL$, is presented
for the expression of quantum algorithms. It contains the features required to program a 'universal' quantum computer (including initialisation and observation), has a formal semantics and body of laws, and
provides a refinement calculus supporting the verification and derivation of programs against their specifications. A representative selection
of quantum algorithms are expressed in the language and one of them is
derived from its specification.

1 Introduction

The purpose of this paper is to present a programming language, $qGCL$, for
quantum computation.

Quantum algorithms are usually described in pseudo code. For semantic support there are two models of quantum computation: quantum networks [8,2] and
quantum Turing machines [7]. The former provides a data-flow view and so is
relevant when considering implementation in terms of gates; whilst it expresses
modularisation well, it fails to express (demonic) nondeterminism or probability
(both features of quantum computation). The latter is appropriate for complexity analysis but as inappropriate for modularised description and reasoning
about correctness of quantum algorithms as standard Turing machines are for
that purpose for standard algorithms.

With $qGCL$ we introduce an extension of the guarded-command language to
express quantum algorithms. It contains both (demonic) nondeterminism and
probability. The former arises in the specification of several quantum algorithms
(and so in their derivations) and the latter is required in order to 'observe' a
quantum system. $qGCL$ has a rigorous semantics and body of laws as a result
of other work (on probabilistic semantics; see for example [23]) and so benefits
from an associated refinement calculus (exhibiting notions of program refinement, data refinement, containing high-level control structures and combining
specification constructs with code). Moreover it abstracts implementation concerns like the representation of assignments as unitary transformations and the
execution of those unitary transformations as gates.

After the invention of various efficient quantum algorithms there seems to
have been a period of consolidation in which frameworks have been sought to
relate those algorithms. The 'hidden subgroup problem' [25] has been seen as a

R. Backhouse and J. N. Oliveira (Eds.): MPC 2000, LNCS 1837, pp. 80–99, 2000.

conceptually unifying principle whilst 'multi-particle interference' [6] has been proposed as a unifying principle closer to implementation. More pragmatically, several simulations have been proposed [1,26,31] at various levels of applicability.

Not surprisingly we take the formal-methods or 'MPC' view that a derivation is worth a thousand simulations (or more!). Thus in an area containing subtle algorithms formal reasoning can be expected to come into its own. One approach would be to perform derivations of quantum program in a standard model and 'bolt on' reasoning to cover their probabilistic and quantum behaviour. A more elegant alternative would be a single formalism in which all aspects of a quantum program's functionality are reasoned about at once. It might be thought that such a formalism would be unwieldy. ¿From our experience with probabilistic semantics we have found that not to be the case; it has led us to the present proposal.

There have been at least two previous attempts to treat quantum computation from a programming-language perspective: Greg Baker's Q-GOL [1] and Bernhard Ömer's Quantum Computation Language, QCL [26]. The former provides a graphical tool for building and simulating quantum circuits using the gate formalism for quantum computation. It does not offer a concise programming language and is not able to implement and simulate all known quantum algorithms.

Ömer's QCL is a high-level architecture-independent programming language for quantum computers, with a syntax very like that of C and an interpreter powerful enough to implement and simulate all known quantum algorithms. It incorporates neither probabilism nor nondeterminism, has no notion of program refinement (and so no refinement calculus) and no semantics; furthermore only standard observation is allowed. QCL is appropriate for numerical simulation of quantum algorithms, whilst $qGCL$'s abstraction, rigorous semantics and associated refinement calculus seem to make it more suitable for program derivation, correctness proof and teaching.

Only experience will show whether $qGCL$ is pitched at the right level of abstraction. However to support that view we here express in it a representative selection of quantum algorithms and perform an exemplary, though simple, derivation.

2 Quantum Types

In this section we study, for use in quantum computation, a transformation q that converts a classical type to its quantum analogue. With but one simple exception, in section 6.5, quantum algorithms require application of q only to registers and so here we restrict ourselves to that case.

Let $\mathbb{B}$ denote the type $\{0, 1\}$ treated either as booleans or bits, as convenience dictates. For natural number n let $0 \mathbin{..} n$ denote the interval of natural numbers at least 0 but less than n

$$0 \mathbin{..} n \ \widehat{=}\ \{i \mid 0 \le i < n\}.$$

A (classical) register of size n is a vector of n booleans. The type of all registers of size n is thus defined to be the set of boolean-valued functions on $0 \mathinner{\ldotp\ldotp} n$

$$\mathbb{B}^n \; \widehat{=} \; 0 \mathinner{\ldotp\ldotp} n \longrightarrow \mathbb{B}.$$

Naturally we are interested in n at least 1 and identify $\mathbb{B}^1$ with $\mathbb{B}$.

The state of a classical system can be expressed using registers. ¿From quantum theory we learn [1] —for example from Young's double-slit experiment— that the state of a quantum system is modelled using 'phase' information associated with each standard state. We follow convention [13,27] and represent phase as a complex number of modulus at most 1. The probability of observing a state is then the modulus squared of its phase; and all probabilities sum to 1.

That leads to the following definition.

The quantum analogue of $\mathbb{B}^n$ is

$$q(\mathbb{B}^n) \; \widehat{=} \; \{\chi : \mathbb{B}^n \to \mathbb{C} \mid \sum_{x : \mathbb{B}^n} |\chi(x)|^2 = 1\}. \tag{1}$$

An element of $q(\mathbb{B})$ is called a *qubit* [28] and that of $q(\mathbb{B}^n)$ a *qureg*.

Classical state is embedded in its quantum analogue by the Dirac delta function

$$\delta : \mathbb{B}^n \longrightarrow q(\mathbb{B}^n)$$
$$\delta_x(y) \; = \; (y = x).$$

The range of δ, $\{\delta_x \mid x \in \mathbb{B}^n\}$, forms a *basis* for quantum states in this sense:

any qureg $\chi : q(\mathbb{B}^n)$ is a square-convex complex superposition of standard states

$$\chi = \sum_{x : \mathbb{B}^n} \chi(x)\delta_x, \qquad \sum_{x : \mathbb{B}^n} |\chi(x)|^2 = 1.$$

(In physics δ_x is denoted by the ket $|x\rangle$. Our choice of notation has been determined by audience background.)

The Hilbert space $\mathbb{B}^n \longrightarrow \mathbb{C}$ (with the structure making it isomorphic to $\mathbb{C}^{2^n}$) is called the *enveloping space* of $q(\mathbb{B}^n)$; it is the Hilbert space of lowest dimension containing $q(\mathbb{B}^n)$ as unit sphere. We shall see that, because the elements of the range of δ are pairwise orthogonal in the enveloping space, they are observably distinct with probability 1.

3   Tensor Products

In a standard programming language the state of a program having independent component program variables can be expressed, more for theoretical than practical convenience, as a single variable equal to the Cartesian product of the

---

[1] In the talk which this paper accompanies the relevant features of quantum theory will be introduced in a tutorial manner.

components. The quantum analogue is that quantum state is the tensor product of its independent state components (equation (2)). In describing algorithms we thus have a choice between using individual variables, combining them when required (for example by finalisation) using tensor product; and using a vector of variables but subjecting it to transformation by the tensor product of a particular function on a particular component with the identity function on the remaining components. To support both approaches we require the tensor product both of registers and of functions.

The tensor product of (standard) registers is defined

$$\otimes : \mathbb{B}^m \times \mathbb{B}^n \longrightarrow \mathbb{B}^{m+n}$$
$$(x \otimes y)(i) \ \hat{=} \ x(i \operatorname{div} n) \times y(i \operatorname{mod} n)$$

and readily shown to be surjective. That definition lifts, via δ and linearity, to quantum registers

$$\otimes : q(\mathbb{B}^m) \times q(\mathbb{B}^n) \longrightarrow q(\mathbb{B}^{m+n}) \, .$$

Well definedness (i.e. square-summability to 1) is immediate.

For sets E and F of quregs we write

$$E \otimes F \ \hat{=} \ \{ \chi \otimes \xi \mid \chi \in E \wedge \xi \in F \} \, .$$

Then the property of q alluded to above is the isomorphism

$$q(\mathbb{B}^m \times \mathbb{B}^n) \ \cong \ q(\mathbb{B}^m) \otimes q(\mathbb{B}^n) \, . \tag{2}$$

(Since both sides are finite-dimensional vector spaces the proof is a matter of counting dimension. The left-hand side evidently has basis

$$\{ (\delta_x, \delta_y) \mid x \in \mathbb{B}^m \wedge y \in \mathbb{B}^n \}$$

whilst a basis for the right-hand side consists of the equinumerous set

$$\{ \delta_x \otimes \delta_y \mid x \in \mathbb{B}^m \wedge y \in \mathbb{B}^n \} \, .)$$

Next tensor product of functions on registers is defined

$$\otimes : (\mathbb{B}^m \longrightarrow \mathbb{B}^m) \times (\mathbb{B}^n \longrightarrow \mathbb{B}^n) \longrightarrow (\mathbb{B}^{m+n} \longrightarrow \mathbb{B}^{m+n})$$
$$(A \otimes B)(x \otimes y) \ \hat{=} \ A(x) \otimes B(y) \, .$$

Finally $\otimes$ is extended by linearity to functions on quantum registers, for which we follow tradition and use the same symbol yet again

$$\otimes : q(\mathbb{B}^m \longrightarrow \mathbb{B}^m) \times q(\mathbb{B}^n \longrightarrow \mathbb{B}^n) \longrightarrow q(\mathbb{B}^{m+n} \longrightarrow \mathbb{B}^{m+n}) \, .$$

4   Probabilistic Language pGCL

In the next section we introduce an imperative quantum-programming language. But first, in this section, we recall Dijsktra's guarded-command language [11], GCL, extended to include probabilism [21,23] and called *pGCL*.

Syntax for the guarded-command language consists of all but the last of these constructs

var	variable declaration
skip	no op
abort	abortion
$x := e$	assignment
$P \, \mathbf{;} \, Q$	sequencing
if $[] \, b_i \longrightarrow S_i$ **fi**	conditional
do $[] \, b_i \longrightarrow S_i$ **od**	iteration
$P \sqcap Q$	(demonic) nondeterminism
$P \, {}_r\oplus \, Q$	probabilism.

Semantics can be given either in terms of predicate transformers [11] or binary relations [17]. In the former case each program is thought of as transforming a post-condition to the weakest precondition from which termination, in a state satisfying that postcondition, is guaranteed. In the latter case each program is thought of as transforming initial state to final state, with a virtual state encoding non-termination.

We require the language to be extended, as usual, to embrace procedure invocation; see for example [20].

pGCL denotes the guarded-command language extended to contain probabilism. Program $P \, {}_r\oplus \, Q$ equals P with probability r and Q with probability $1-r$. Its semantics has been given in two forms, following the semantic styles of GCL. The transformer semantics [22] extends pre- and post-conditions to pre- and post-*expectations*: real-valued random variables; the relational semantics [16] relates each initial state to a set of final distributions. In either case refinement $P \sqsubseteq Q$ means that Q is at least as deterministic as P. The two models are related by a Galois connection embedding the relational in the transformer [22]. There is a family of sound laws [16,23], including those for data refinement, so that the language *pGCL* is embedded in a refinement calculus. It is that feature which we exploit.

In *pGCL* (demonic) nondeterminism is expressed semantically as the combination of all possible probabilistic resolutions

$$P \sqcap Q = \sqcap\{P \, {}_r\oplus \, Q \mid 0 \le r \le 1\}. \tag{3}$$

Thus a (demonic) nondeterministic choice between two programs is refined by any probabilistic choice between them

$$\forall \, r : [0,1] \bullet P \sqcap Q \sqsubseteq P \, {}_r\oplus \, Q \qquad \text{(introduce probabilism)}.$$

Probabilism does not itself yield nondeterminism: if P and Q are deterministic (maximal with respect to the refinement order) then so is $P \mathbin{_r\oplus} Q$. Unfortunately for most authors in the area of quantum computation *nondeterminism* means probabilism. One of the important (and technically difficult) features of *pGCL* is its combination of (demonic) nondeterminism and probabilism; the result seems to provide just the right expressive power for the treatment of quantum algorithms. Indeed of the examples to follow, those of Grover, Shor and Deutsch-Jozsa all feature both (demonic) nondeterminism and probabilism.

If a set E of expressions contains more than one element then in the guarded-command language the assignment $x :\in E$ means the nondeterministic choice over all individual assignments of elements of E to x. In *pGCL* that choice is interpreted to occur with *uniform* probability.

As we need them we introduce two pieces of derived syntax concerning probabilism: one a prefix combinator (display (6) to follow); the other weakening exact probability r in probabilistic choice to the interval $[r, 1]$ (definition (9) to follow).

5   Quantum Language qGCL

A *quantum program* is a *pGCL* program invoking quantum procedures (described below); the resulting language is called *qGCL*. It is important for us that *qGCL*, being expressed in terms of *pGCL*, inherits its refinement calculus. That enables us to combine code and specifications (and, less of a problem, to benefit from the usual liberties in writing programs, like using as guard the predicate 'N times') since the result has a semantic denotation to which refinement applies.

There are three types of *quantum procedure*: *initialisation* (or state preparation) followed by *evolution* and finally *finalisation* (or observation or state reduction). We now explain each of those three terms.

5.1   Initialisation

Initialisation is a procedure which simply assigns to its qureg state the uniform square-convex combination of all standard states

$$\chi : q(\mathbb{B}^n)$$
$$In(\chi) \mathrel{\hat{=}} \chi := 2^{-n/2} \sum_{x:\mathbb{B}^n} \delta_x .$$

There χ is a result parameter.

Initialisation so defined is *feasible* in the sense that it is achievable in practice [8] by initialising the qureg to the classical state δ_0 (where $\mathbf{0}$ denotes the register identically false) and then subjecting that to evolution by the (unitary) Hadamard transform, defined as a tensor power:

$$H_n : q(\mathbb{B}^n) \longrightarrow q(\mathbb{B}^n) \tag{4}$$
$$H_1(\chi)(x) \mathrel{\hat{=}} 2^{-1/2}(\chi(0) + (-1)^x \chi(1))$$
$$H_{n+1} \mathrel{\hat{=}} H_n \otimes H_1$$

where exponentiation of bits is standard $(-1)^x = -1 \lhd x \rhd 1$.

5.2   Evolution

Evolution consists of iteration of unitary transformations on quantum state. (It is thought of, after initialisation, as achieving all superposed evolutions simultaneously, which provides much of the reason for quantum computation's efficiency.) Again, evolution is feasible: it may be implemented using universal quantum gates [3,9].

For example on $\mathbb{B}$, after initialisation, evolution by the Hadamard transformation H_1 results in $\chi = \delta_0$ (because H_1 is not only unitary but equal to its own conjugate transpose and so self-inverse). Thus our definition of initialisation does not exclude setting state to equal δ_0 (or any other standard state for that matter). That fact is used in procedure Q in Shor's algorithm (and similarly in Simon's algorithm, not considered here).

Later we use this important example of evolution: for function $f : \mathbb{B}^n \longrightarrow \mathbb{B}^n$ between registers, transformation T_f between the corresponding quregs is defined *pointwise* to invert χ about 0 if f holds and otherwise to leave it unchanged

$$T_f : q(\mathbb{B}^n) \longrightarrow q(\mathbb{B}^n)$$
$$(T_f \chi)(x) \;\hat{=}\; (-1)^{f(x)} \chi(x) \;=\; -\chi(x) \lhd f(x) \rhd \chi(x). \tag{5}$$

Evidently T_f is unitary.

More complicated evolutions appear in section 6.

5.3   Finalisation

Finalisation is a little more difficult to define largely because of the notation required. We motivate it by considering first the simple qubit case (later called 'diagonal').

Simple observation of a qubit $\chi = \chi(0)\delta_0 + \chi(1)\delta_1$ reduces it, by the principles of quantum theory, to the standard state δ_x with probability $|\chi(x)|^2$, for $x : \mathbb{B}$. Thus it might be expressed, using probabilistic assignment, as a procedure with result parameter χ

$$\chi : q(\mathbb{B})$$
$$(\chi := \delta_0) \;_{|\chi(0)|^2} \oplus\; (\chi := \delta_1).$$

We find it convenient, for more general forms of observation, to conform to standard practice and return not just the reduced state (the eigenvector of the matrix corresponding to the observation) but also the eigenvalue, in this case 0 or 1. At the same time we note that the probability $|\chi(0)|^2$ equals the inner product of the vector χ in enveloping space with its projection on the one-dimensional subspace $\mathbb{C}\,\delta_0$

$$\langle \chi, P_{\mathbb{C}\,\delta_0}(\chi) \rangle \;=\; \chi(0)\overline{\chi(0)} \;=\; |\chi(0)|^2$$

where angle brackets denote inner product, $P_E(\chi)$ denotes projection of χ onto subspace E and overline denotes complex conjugate. The procedure above then becomes

$x : \mathbb{B}, \ \chi : q(\mathbb{B})$

$(x, \chi := 0, \delta_0) \ _{\langle \chi, P_{c\,\delta_0}(\chi) \rangle} \oplus \ (x, \chi := 1, \delta_1)$.

In that case enveloping space $\mathbb{B} \longrightarrow \mathbb{C}$ is the direct sum of the orthogonal subspaces $\mathbb{C}\,\delta_x$ for $x : \mathbb{B}$.

We now extend that simple case from qubits to quregs and from the family of subspaces $\mathbb{C}\,\delta_x$ to a family of arbitrary pairwise orthogonal subspaces which span enveloping space. In order to do so it is convenient to use the following notation for the probabilistic combination of a list of more than two programs.

If $[\,(P_j, r_j) \mid 0 \le j < m\,]$ denotes a finite indexed family of (program, number) pairs with $\sum_{0 \le j < m} r_j = 1$, then the probabilistic choice in which P_j is chosen with probability r_j is written in prefix form

$$\oplus [\, P_j \, @ \, r_j \mid 0 \le j < m \,] \tag{6}$$

(whose advantage is to avoid the normalising factors required by nested infix form).

Let $\mathcal{V} = [\, V_j \mid 0 \le j < m \,]$ be an indexed family of pairwise orthogonal subspaces which together span enveloping space,

$$span\, [\, V_j \mid 0 \le j < m \,] = \mathbb{B}^n \longrightarrow \mathbb{C},$$

where $span\,E$ denotes the (complex) vector space generated by any subset E of enveloping space. Finalisation with respect to $\mathcal{V}$ is defined to consist of a procedure which reduces state to lie in one of the subspaces in $\mathcal{V}$, with probability determined as it was in the simple case above:

$i : 0 \,..\, m, \ \chi : q(\mathbb{B}^n)$

$Fin[\mathcal{V}]\,(i, \chi) \ \widehat{=} \ \oplus [\,(i, \chi :\in \{j\}, \ V_j) \, @ \, \langle \chi, P_{V_j}(\chi) \rangle \mid 0 \le j < m \,]$

wherein i is a result parameter determining the subspace to which state is reduced and χ is a value-result parameter giving that state. In most cases (and with good physical reason if the observation is not 'complete' —i.e. V_i is more than one-dimensional— χ is not used, in which case we simply suppress it. We include χ in the definition of finalisation, however, because one of the quantum algorithms requires it (the last example). That definition provides the law 'introduce finalisation'.

The simple form of finalisation introduced in the qubit case is sufficiently important to warrant its own notation. We write Δ for the indexed family of subspaces $[\mathbb{C}\,\delta_x \mid x \in \mathbb{B}^n]$. Then finalisation with respect to Δ is called *diagonal* finalisation and abbreviated

$x : \mathbb{B}^n$

$Fin[\Delta]\,(x)$.

Its definition reduces to

$$\oplus [\, x \, @ \, |\chi(x)|^2 \mid x \in \mathbb{B}^n \,]$$

and the suppressed value of χ is determined by that of x since $q(\mathbb{B}^n) \cap \mathbb{C}\,\delta_x$ is a singleton. When an output number $i : 0 \mathbin{..} 2^n$ is required, it is produced by applying to $x : \mathbb{B}^n$ the function which yields a number, $num(x)$, whose binary representation equals its argument

$$num : \mathbb{B}^n \longrightarrow 0 \mathbin{..} 2^n \tag{7}$$
$$num(x) \mathrel{\widehat{=}} \textstyle\sum_{j:0..n} x(j) 2^j \,.$$

The definition of finalisation accords with general principles of quantum theory (e.g. [13,18,27]), which permit *simultaneous* finalisation (or observation) — i.e. in either order with the same result— since the subspaces in $\mathcal{V}$ are orthogonal. Thus feasibility of that definition is assured by general principles and in particular by Jozsa's characterisation [19] of quantum-observable functions.

It is interesting to note that finalisation is no more restrictive than probabilistic choice. Indeed a simple trigonometric argument shows that $P \mathbin{_r\oplus} Q$ can be achieved by a quantum program which uses $\oplus$ only in the form defined by finalisation.

For examples of finalisation we proceed to the next section.

6   Example Programs

In this section we demonstrate the expressive power of $qGCL$ by casting in it a representative selection of quantum algorithms and their specifications. Although it is their efficiency which validates these algorithms, we are interested here in formalising functionality. With each algorithm we state the feature of $qGCL$ it illustrates.

6.1   Fair Coin

The first example is chosen to illustrate initialisation and diagonal finalisation without any evolution, and is included as a consistency check. It shows how the formalism is able to capture genuine probabilistic behaviour (i.e. not merely that of a finite automaton satisfying some fairness condition).

The example finds serious application in formalisation of the 'Mach-Zehnder interferometer' and, in particular, so-called 'interference-free measurement' [12]. In that setting the following program models a beam-splitter (a half-silvered mirror which either transmits or reflects incident photons with equal probability) and the Hadamard transform (4) is used for evolution.

The toss of a fair coin is modelled by specifying the result to be a uniformly-distributed boolean:

var $i : \mathbb{B} \bullet$

$i :\in \mathbb{B}$

A quantum implementation is

> $\mathbf{var}\, \chi : q(\mathbb{B}),\; i : \mathbb{B}\; \bullet$
> $\quad In\,(\chi)\, \fatsemi$
> $\quad Fin[\Delta]\,(i)$

which may be checked to satisfy its specification since the probability with which $i = 0$ is of course

$$|\chi(0)|^2 = (2^{-1/2})^2 = \tfrac{1}{2}\,.$$

A formal proof is immediate from the definitions of initialisation and finalisation.

6.2   Grover's Point Search

The previous program can be proved to meet its probabilistic specification. The next example provides a more typical quantum algorithm which achieves its naïve specification only to within a margin of error. This example thus shows how $pGCL$ (and hence $qGCL$) captures this important type of behaviour.

The point search problem is: given an array f of 2^n bits containing a single 1, locate it. A program which is correct on every execution is specified without any recourse to probability:

$$\mathbf{var}\, j : 0 \,..\, 2^n \; \bullet \qquad\qquad\qquad (8)$$
$$j := f^{-1}(1)\,.$$

A standard algorithm is at best $O(2^n)$ in both the worst and average cases. However Grover's quantum algorithm [14], although correct only to within a margin of error ε (dependent on the number of loop iterations), is $O(2^{n/2})$ in both those cases. It is conveniently specified by introducing some derived syntax: $P_{\geq r}\oplus Q$ equals P with probability at least r and otherwise equals Q. It is defined (cf. equation (3))

$$P_{\geq r}\oplus Q \;\hat{=}\; \sqcap\{P_{\,s}\oplus Q \mid r \leq s \leq 1\} \qquad\qquad (9)$$

which by a semantic convexity argument [23] simplifies to $(P_{\,r}\oplus Q)\sqcap P$.

The error-prone point-search problem is thus specified to behave, with probability at least ε, like the naïve behaviour (8) and otherwise to terminate with an arbitrary value for j

> $\mathbf{var}\, j : 0 \,..\, 2^n \; \bullet$
> $\quad (j := f^{-1}(1))\; _{\geq \varepsilon}\oplus\, (j \in 0 \,..\, 2^n)\,.$

Grover's implementation contains evolution expressed as a loop and uses the function num (see (7)).

var $\chi : q(\mathbb{B}^n)$, $i : \mathbb{B}^n$, $j : 0 \ldots 2^n$ •
$\quad In\,(\chi)\,\S$
$\quad$**do** N times $\longrightarrow$
$\quad\quad\quad \chi := T_f(\chi)\,\S$
$\quad\quad\quad \chi := M(\chi)$
$\quad$**od**$\,\S$
$\quad Fin[\Delta]\,(i)\,\S$
$\quad j := num(i)$

There transform T_f is defined by (5) and transform M inverts χ (pointwise) about its average

$$M : q(\mathbb{B}^n) \longrightarrow q(\mathbb{B}^n)$$
$$(M\chi)(x) \;\hat{=}\; 2\left[2^{-n}\sum_{y:\mathbb{B}^n} \chi(y)\right] - \chi(x)\,.$$

We are not here concerned with the choice of N which determines the number of iterations of the loop. The function $\varepsilon = \varepsilon(N)$ is investigated in [4] and its place in a semantic (expectation-transformer) proof of correctness is explored in [5].

6.3   Deutsch-Jozsa Classification

So far the specifications have been (demonically) deterministic (though probabilistic) and we have used only diagonal finalisation. The next example meets a nondeterministic specification, exhibits non-diagonal finalisation and requires no margin for error.

A truth function $f : \mathbb{B}^n \longrightarrow \mathbb{B}$ is *constant* iff it takes only a single value. It is *balanced* iff it takes values 0 and 1 equally often

$$\#f^{-1}(0) = \#f^{-1}(1)\,.$$

For use in the next section we note:

$$f \text{ is constant iff } \#f^{-1}(1) \in \{0, 2^n\}, \tag{10}$$
$$f \text{ is balanced iff } \#f^{-1}(1) = 2^{n-1},$$
$$\text{and } \#f^{-1}(1) = \textstyle\sum_{x:\mathbb{B}^n} f(x)\,.$$

Any constant truth function f is not balanced. So any truth function is either not balanced or not constant, usually both. The Deutsch-Jozsa classification problem is to decide, for a given truth function, which holds; if both hold then either answer is correct.

Letting the result be encoded by variable $i : \mathbb{B}$, the problem is specified

var $i : \mathbb{B}$ •
$\quad$**if** $\quad i \longrightarrow f$ not balanced
$\quad[]\; \neg i \longrightarrow f$ not constant
$\quad$**fi**

A standard algorithm for the Deutsch-Jozsa classification problem is at least $O(2^n)$ in the worst case and on average evaulates f thrice. DeutschandJozsa's quantum algorithm [10] contains just *one* evolution step using the transformation T_f defined by equation (5). It is expressed in our notation:

var $\chi : q(\mathbb{B}^n)$, $i : \mathbb{B}$ •
$\quad In\,(\chi)\,\natural$
$\quad \chi := T_f(\chi)\,\natural$
$\quad Fin[\mathcal{V}]\,(i)$

where finalisation is non-diagonal

$\quad \mathcal{V} \,\widehat{=}\, [\, V,\, V^{\perp}\,]$
$\quad V \,\widehat{=}\, \mathbb{C} \sum_{y:\mathbb{B}^n} \delta_y$
$\quad V^{\perp} \,\widehat{=}\,$ the orthogonal complement of V .

A derivation of that algorithm (and hence its correctness) is exhibited in the next section.

6.4   Shor's Factorisation Algorithm

Shor's quantum algorithms [29] for factorisation and for discrete logarithm are at once the most mathematically sophisticated and relatively efficient practical quantum algorithms known. We consider the former algorithm which, as has been widely advertised, makes factorisation feasible by achieving an average-case polynomial efficiency instead of the standard exponential. Although it demonstrates no new features of $qGCL$ we include it as the most important quantum algorithm to date.

The factorisation problem is: given a natural number $n > 1$ find a prime divisor d of n. It is thus naturally nondeterministic (as was Deutsch-Jozsa classification):

var $d : 1 .. (n{+}1)$ •
$\quad d$ is a prime divisor of n .

For natural numbers x and y, we write $x \sqcup y$ for their maximum and $gcd(x, y)$ for their greatest-common divisor. Shor's algorithm is

var $t : \mathbb{B}$, $a, d, p : 0 \mathbin{..} (n{+}1)$ •
  $t := 0$;
  do $\neg t \longrightarrow$
      $a :\in 2 \mathbin{..} n$;
      $d := gcd(a, n)$;
      if $d \neq 1 \longrightarrow t := 1$
      [] $d = 1 \longrightarrow Q(a, n; p)$;
               if p odd $\longrightarrow t := 1$
               [] p even $\longrightarrow$
                 $d := gcd(a^{p/2}{-}1, n) \sqcup gcd(a^{p/2}{+}1, n)$;
                 $t := (d \neq 1)$
               fi
      fi
  od

The quantum content lies in procedure Q. It is our first example to use quantum state after finalisation, though it does so for only standard purposes.

var $\chi : q(\mathbb{B}^m {\times} \mathbb{B}^m)$, $x : \mathbb{B}^{2m}$, $c : \mathbb{B}^m$ •
  $In (\chi)$;
  $\chi := (I_m \otimes H_m)(\chi)$;
  $\chi := E(\chi)$;
  $\chi := (F_m \otimes I_m)(\chi)$;
  $Fin[\Delta] (x, \chi)$;
  $c := P_m(\chi)$;
  $p :=$ post processing of c

where:

m satisfies $n^2 \leq 2^m \leq 2n^2$;

H_m denotes the Hadamard transform defined by equation (4);

unitary transformation $E : q(\mathbb{B}^m {\times} \mathbb{B}^m) \longrightarrow q(\mathbb{B}^m {\times} \mathbb{B}^m)$ is defined in terms of modular exponentiation

$$E(\chi)(x, y) \;\hat{=}\; (x, y \oplus num^{-1}(a^{num(x)} \bmod n)) ;$$

$F_m : q(\mathbb{B}^m) \longrightarrow q(\mathbb{B}^m)$ is the quantum Fourier transform (see [15], section 3.2.2);

diagonal finalisation has been extended to return also state χ ;

$P_m : \delta(\mathbb{B}^m {\times} \mathbb{B}^m) \longrightarrow \mathbb{B}^m$ denotes a kind of projection

$$P_m(\delta_x \otimes \delta_y) \;\hat{=}\; x ; \text{ and}$$

the post processing of c is standard, using continued fractions to find efficiently the unique p for which

$$| \ num(c)/2^m - d/p \ | \le 2^{-(m+1)}.$$

The first two lines of procedure Q are equivalent (see section 5.2) to

$$\chi := (H_m \otimes I_n)(\delta_0)$$

(where δ_0 denotes the qureg containing $m+n$ zeroes); however our insistence that quantum programs begin with a standard initialisation obliges us to take the longer version.

Simon's quantum algorithm for his masking problem [30] is similar in structure, from our current point of view, to Shor's factorisation algorithm.

6.5   Finite Automaton

The previous algorithm uses quantum state *after* finalisation for the purpose of (standard) post processing. However since finalisation was diagonal, the quantum state could have been inferred from the eigenvalue returned by finalisation. The next example uses non-diagonal finalisation and makes genuine use of quantum state after finalisation. It thus justifies our inclusion of state in finalisation.

Recall that (standard) finite automata, whether deterministic or not and one-way or two-way, accept just regular languages. For quantum finite automata enough is already known to demonstrate that the picture is quite different (see [15], chapter 4).

A *one-measurement one-way quantum finite automaton* employs finalisation after reading its input string and so is readily expressed in our notation. So instead we consider the *many-measurement* version which employs finalisation after reading each symbol on its input string. It turns out (Kondacs and Watrous; see, for example, [15] p. 159) that a many-measurement one-way quantum finite automaton accepts a proper subset of regular expressions. Here we give sufficient of the definition to permit its translation into our programming language.

For any set Σ, let Σ^* denote the set of all finite sequences of elements of Σ. Suppose that set $\mathcal{S} = \{S_a, S_r, S_n\}$ of subsets of Σ^* *partitions* Σ^*. A sequence $s : \Sigma^*$ is said to be *accepted* by $\mathcal{S}$ if $s \in S_a$, to be *rejected* by it if $s \in S_r$ and to *fail classification* if $s \in S_n$. Evaluation of that is specified:

> **var** $i : \{a, r, n\}$ •
> $s \in S_i$.

But here we are interested in computing whether a prefix of a given sequence is accepted or rejected, since that gives rise to an automaton which continues to use its quantum state after finalisation. Its specification thus extends the previous one. In it $t \le s$ means that sequence t is a prefix of sequence s.

> **var** $i : \{a, r, n\}$ •
> $$\begin{pmatrix} i = a \Rightarrow \exists t \le s \bullet t \in S_a \\ i = r \Rightarrow \exists t \le s \bullet t \in S_r \\ i = n \Rightarrow s \in S_n \end{pmatrix}$$

(A stronger specification might reflect the fact that computation proceeds from left to right and so ensure that sequence t there is smallest.)

A *many-measurement one-way quantum finite automaton* is designed to achieve such a computation with efficient quantum evolution. It has a finite set Q of states, with distinguished acceptance states Q_a and rejection states Q_r

$$Q_a \subseteq Q$$
$$Q_r \subseteq Q$$
$$Q_a \cap Q_r = \{\,\}.$$

Thus $Q_a \cup Q_r$ need not exhaust Q.

On input sequence $s = [\sigma_0, \ldots, \sigma_{n-1}] : \Sigma^*$ the automaton evolves successively under unitary transformations

$$U_{init}, U_{\sigma_0}, \ldots, U_{\sigma_{n-1}}$$

subject to finalisation after each. If a finalisation leaves the automaton in an acceptance state then computation terminates with output value $i = a$; if it leaves the automaton in a rejection state then computation terminates with output value $i = r$; but otherwise the automaton reiterates. If it has not accepted or rejected a prefix of the input sequence, it terminates when the entire sequence has been read, with value $i = n$.

We thus let quantum state belong to $q(Q)$, defined as was qureg state by (1). Initialisation over $q(Q)$ is defined as for registers; its feasibility is assured by solubility of the appropriate simultaneous equations describing a unitary transformation that yields a uniform image of δ_0. For finalisation we take

$$\mathcal{V} \cong [\, V_a, V_r, V_n \,]$$
$$V_a \cong span\,\{\delta_x \mid x \in Q_a\}$$
$$V_r \cong span\,\{\delta_x \mid x \in Q_r\}$$
$$V_n \cong (V_a \oplus V_r)^\perp.$$

A program for such an automaton is

```
var χ : q(Q), b : 𝔹 •
    In(χ) ⨾
    χ, b := U_init(χ), 0 ⨾
    do ¬(b ∨ s = []) →
        Fin[V] (i, χ) ⨾
        if i ∈ {a, r} → b := 1
        [] i ∉ {a, r} → χ, s := U_head(s)(χ), tail(s)
        fi
    od
```

That can be expressed only because we allow quantum state to be returned by finalisation.

7   Example Derivation

We conclude by outlining an algebraic derivation of the Deutsch-Jozsa classification algorithm. It is to be emphasised that derivations (or verifications) using the
refinement calculus (i.e. the laws concerning refinement between programs —see
for example [20]) are quite different in style from those phrased in terms of semantics (c.f. [5]). We are interested primarily in the shape of the derivation; and we
shall see that it is largely standard. This example demonstrates how the refinement calculus which $qGCL$ inherits from $pGCL$ permits 'homogeneous' reasoning
about the functionality of quantum algorithms, without recourse to arguments
outside the formalism (pertaining for example to probabilism or 'quantism').

The following derivation can be followed intuitively as well as rigorously; the
steps involved correspond largely to steps in an informal explanation of why
the algorithm works. At one point $\sqsubseteq$ is extended to mean also data refinement,
of which care must (in general) be taken in the probabilistic setting; but here
the refinement is unproblematic. Interesting features of the derivation are the
appearance of quantum state and of the three quantum procedures.

var $i : \mathbb{B}$ •
  if $i \longrightarrow f$ not balanced
  $[]$ $\neg i \longrightarrow f$ not constant
  fi

$\sqsubseteq$ (10) and standard reasoning

var $i : \mathbb{B},\ j : 0 \mathinner{.\,.} 2^n$ •
  $j := \sum_{x : \mathbb{B}^n} f(x)\,$ ⨾
  if $j \neq 2^{n-1}$ $\longrightarrow$ $i := 1$
  $[]$ $j \notin \{0, 2^n\}$ $\longrightarrow$ $i := 0$
  fi

$\sqsubseteq$ standard reasoning

var $i : \mathbb{B},\ j : 0 \mathinner{.\,.} 2^n$ •
  $j := \sum_{x : \mathbb{B}^n} f(x)\,$ ⨾
  if $j \in \{0, 2^n\}$ $\longrightarrow$ $i := 1$
  $[]$ $j = 2^{n-1}$ $\longrightarrow$ $i := 0$
  $[]$ $j \notin \{0, 2^{n-1}, 2^n\}$ $\longrightarrow$ $(i := 1) \sqcap (i := 0)$
  fi

$\sqsubseteq$ arithmetic and standard and probabilistic reasoning

var $i : \mathbb{B},\ j : 0 \mathinner{.\,.} 2^n$ •
  $j := \sum_{x : \mathbb{B}^n} f(x)\,$ ⨾
  if $j \in \{0, 2^{n-1}, 2^n\}$ $\longrightarrow$ $(i := 1)\,_{|1-j/2^{n-1}|}\!\oplus (i := 0)$
  $[]$ $j \notin \{0, 2^{n-1}, 2^n\}$ $\longrightarrow$ $(i := 1) \sqcap (i := 0)$
  fi

$\sqsubseteq$ injective data refinement $k = 1 - j/2^{n-1}$

var $i : \mathbb{B}, \; k : [-1, 1]$ •
$\quad k := 2^{-n} \sum_{x:\mathbb{B}^n} (-1)^{f(x)} \, \fatsemi$
$\quad$ **if** $k \in \{-1, 0, 1\} \;\longrightarrow\; (i := 1) \,_{|k|}\oplus (i := 0)$
$\quad$ [] $k \notin \{-1, 0, 1\} \;\longrightarrow\; (i := 1) \sqcap (i := 0)$
$\quad$ **fi**

$\sqsubseteq$ $\qquad\qquad\qquad\qquad\qquad\qquad\qquad\qquad\qquad\qquad$ 'introduce probabilism'

var $i : \mathbb{B}, \; k : [-1, 1]$ •
$\quad k := 2^{-n} \sum_{x:\mathbb{B}^n} (-1)^{f(x)} \, \fatsemi$
$\quad (i := 1) \,_{|k|}\oplus (i := 0)$

$\sqsubseteq$ $\qquad\qquad\qquad\qquad\qquad\qquad\qquad\qquad\qquad\qquad$ 'sequential composition'

var $i : \mathbb{B}, \; k : [-1, 1], \; \chi : q(\mathbb{B}^n)$ •
$\quad \chi = 2^{-n/2} \sum_{x:\mathbb{B}^n} (-1)^{f(x)} \delta_x \, \fatsemi$
$\quad k := 2^{-n/2} \sum_{x:\mathbb{B}^n} \chi(x) \, \fatsemi$
$\quad (i := 1) \,_{|k|}\oplus (i := 0)$

$\sqsubseteq$ $\qquad\qquad\qquad\qquad\qquad$ 'sequential composition' and definition of T_f

var $i : \mathbb{B}, \; k : [-1, 1], \; \chi : q(\mathbb{B}^n)$ •
$\quad \chi := 2^{-n/2} \sum_{x:\mathbb{B}^n} \delta_x \, \fatsemi$
$\quad \chi := T_f(\chi) \, \fatsemi$
$\quad k := 2^{-n/2} \sum_{x:\mathbb{B}^n} \chi(x) \, \fatsemi$
$\quad (i := 1) \,_{|k|}\oplus (i := 0)$

$\sqsubseteq$ $\qquad\quad$ definitions of In, Fin and diminish by $k = \langle \chi, 2^{-n/2} \sum_{x:\mathbb{B}^n} (-1)^{f(x)} \delta_x \rangle$

var $i : \mathbb{B}, \; \chi : q(\mathbb{B}^n)$ •
$\quad In(\chi) \, \fatsemi$
$\quad \chi := T_f(\chi) \, \fatsemi$
$\quad Fin[\mathcal{V}](i)$

with family $\mathcal{V} = [\, V, V^\perp \,]$, where $V = \mathbb{C} \sum_{y:\mathbb{B}^n} \delta_y$.

8   Conclusions

We have proposed a language, $qGCL$, for the expression of quantum algorithms and their derivations. It exhibits several features, many as a result of the work on $pGCL$:

1. expressivity: the language is sufficiently expressive to capture existing quantum algorithms

2. simplicity: the language seems to be as simple as possible (by law (3)) whilst containing (demonic) nondeterminism and probability (the latter either in a form restricted to 'observation' or for general use)

3. abstraction: the language contains control structures and data structures at the level of abstraction of today's imperative languages whilst abstracting implementation concerns (like the representation of a function f on the underlying standard types by its Lecerf-Bennett form on their quantum analogues)

4. calculation: the language has a formal semantics, sound laws and provides a refinement calculus supporting verification and derivation of quantum programs

5. the language provides a uniform treatment of 'observation'.

We conclude that it does seem possible to treat quantum programs in a refinement calculus with the same degree of elegance and rigour as standard algorithms. Starting from a specification in which standard and probabilistic (but not quantum) expressions appear it is possible to derive quantum algorithms by introducing algorithmic and quantum structure (in the guise of quantum state and the three quantum proceedures).

We have still to learn whether there are reuseable data refinements, or other derivation clichés, appropriate to the derivation of quantum programs. But abstraction from implementation concerns seems to make quantum algorithms easier to express, understand and reason about. Unmentioned here are more general properties of the functor q on types and work on the compilation of the programs expressed in $qGCL$ ([32]).

Acknowledgements

The authors are pleased to acknowledge the quantity and quality of refereeing which resulted in an improved paper. In particular one referee is responsible for pointing out [1,26].

References

1. Greg Baker. http://www.ics.mq.edu.au/~gregb/q-gol. 81, 97
2. Adriano Barenco et al. Elementary gates of quantum computation. *Physical Review A*, **52**(5):3457–3467, 1995. 80
3. Adriano Barenco. A universal two-bit gate for quantum computation. *Proc. R. Soc. Lond.* A, **449**:679–683, 1995. 86
4. Michel Boyer, Gilles Brassard, Peter Hoyer and Alain Tapp. Tight bounds on quantum searching. In *Fourth Workshop on Physics and Computation*, editors T. Toffoli, M. Biaford and J. Lean, pages 36–43. New England Complex System Institute, 1996. 90
5. Michael Butler and Pieter Hartel. Reasoning about Grover's quantum search algorithm using probabilistic wp. University of Southampton technical report DSSE-TR-98-10, 1998. 90, 95

6. R. Cleve, A. Ekert, C. Macchiavello and M. Mosca. Quantum algorithms revisited. *Proc. R. Soc. Lond.*, A. **454**:339–354, 1998. 81

7. D. Deutsch. Quantum theory, the Church-Turing principle and the universal quantum computer. *Proc. R. Soc. Lond.* A, **400**:97–117, 1985. 80

8. D. Deutsch. Quantum computational networks. *Proc. R. Soc. Lond.* A, **425**:73–90, 1989. 80, 85

9. David Deutsch, Adriano Barenco and Artur Ekert. Universality in quantum computation. *Proc. R. Soc. Lond.* A, **449**:669–677, 1995. 86

10. David Deutsch and Richard Jozsa. Rapid solution of problems by quantum computation. *Proc. R. Soc. Lond.* A, **439**:553–558, 1992. 91

11. E. W. Dijkstra. *A Discipline of Programming*. Prentice-Hall International, 1976. 84

12. Avshalom C. Elitzur and Lev Vaidman. Quantum mechanical interaction-free measurements. *Foundations of Physics*, **32**(7):987–997, 1993. 88

13. R. P. Feynman. *The Feynman Lectures on Physics*, volume 3. Addison-Wesley, 1964. 82, 88

14. Lov K. Grover. A fast quantum mechanical algorithm for database search. In *Proceedings of the 28th ACM STOC*, pages 212–219, 1996. 89

15. Jozef Gruska. *Quantum Computing*. McGraw-Hill International (UK), Advanced Topics in Computer Science, 1999. 92, 93

16. He Jifeng, K. Seidel and A. K. McIver. Probabilistic models for the guarded command language. *Science of Computer Programming*, **28**:171–192, 1997. 84

17. C. A. R. Hoare He Jifeng. The weakest prespecification, parts I and II. Fundamenta Informatica, IX, 51–84, 217–252, 1986. 84

18. Chris J. Isham. *Lectures on Quantum Theory*. Imperial College Press, 1995. 88

19. Richard Josza. Characterising classes of functions computable by quantum parallelism. *Proc. R. Soc. Lond.* A, **435**:563–574, 1991. 88

20. Carroll Morgan. *Programming from Specifications*, second edition. Prentice-Hall International, 1994. 84, 95

21. K. Seidel, C. C. Morgan and A. K. McIver. Probabilistic imperative programming: a rigorous approach. 1996. Available at
http//www.comlab.ox.ac.uk/oucl/research/areas/probs/bibliography.html.
84

22. Carroll Morgan, Annabelle McIver and Karen Seidel. Probabilistic predicate transformers. *TOPLAS*, **18**(3):325–353, 1996. 84

23. Carroll Morgan and Annabelle McIver. *pGCL*: formal reasoning for random algorithms. *South African Computer Journal*, **22**:14–27, 1999. 80, 84, 89, 98

24. Carroll Morgan and A. K. McIver. Demonic, angelic and unbounded probabilistic choices in sequential programs. To appear in *Acta Informatica*; see the site at [23].

25. Michele Mosca and Artur Ekert. The hidden subgroup problem and eigenvalue estimation on a quantum computer. In *Proceedings of the 1st NASA Internation Conference on Quantum Compuing and Quantum Communication*. LNCS 1509, Springer-Verlag, 1998. 80

26. Bernhard Ömer. http://tph.tuwien.ac.at/ oemer. 81, 97

27. Asher Peres. *Quantum Theory: Concepts and Methods*. Kluwer Academic Publishers, 1998. 82, 88

28. Benjamin Schumacher. Quantum coding. *Physical Review* A, **51**(4):2738–2747, 1995. 82

29. Peter W. Shor. Algorithms for quantum computation: discrete log and factoring. In *Proceedings of the 35th IEEE FOCS*, pages 124–134, 1994. 91

30. Daniel R. Simon. On the power of quantum computation. In *Proceedings of the 35th IEEE FOCS*, pages 116–123, 1994. 93

31. Colin P. Williams and Scott H. Clearwater. *Explorations in Quantum Computing.* Springer-Verlag, New York, 1998.   81

32. Paolo Zuliani. *DPhil Thesis.* Oxford University. In preparation.   97

Regular Expressions Revisited:
A Coinductive Approach to Streams, Automata, and Power Series

J.J.M.M. Rutten

CWI
P.O. Box 94079, 1090 GB Amsterdam, The Netherlands
janr@cwi.nl
http://www.cwi.nl/~janr

Abstract

Regular expressions are a standard means for denoting formal languages that are recognizable by finite automata. Much less familiar is the use of syntactic expressions for (formal) power series. Power series generalize languages by assigning to words multiplicities in any semiring (such as the reals) rather than just Booleans, and include as a special case the set of streams (infinite sequences). Here we shall define an extended set of regular expressions with multiplicities in an arbitrary semiring. The semantics of such expressions will be defined coinductively, allowing for the use of a syntactic coinductive proof principle. To each expression will be assigned a nondeterministic automaton with multiplicities, which usually is a rather efficient representation of the power series denoted by the expression. Much of the above will be illustrated for the special case of streams of real numbers; other examples include automata and languages (sets of words), and task-resource systems (using the max-plus semiring). The coinductive definitions mentioned above take the shape of what we have called behavioural differential equations, on the basis of which we develop, as a motivating example, a theory of streams in a calculus-like fashion.

Our perspective is essentially coalgebraic. More precisely, the set of all formal power series, including the set of languages and the set of streams as special instances, is a final coalgebra. This fact is the basis for both the coinduction definition and the coinduction proof principle.

For general background on coalgebra, see [1] and [2]. The proceedings of the recently established workshop series CMCS (Coalgebraic Methods in Computer Science), contained in Volumes 11, 19, and 33 of Elsevier's Electronic Notes in Theoretical Computer Science, give a good impression of many of the latest developments in coalgebraic studies. References related to the theory summarized above are [3], dealing with automata and languages, and [4], on formal power series. A technical report on behavioural differential equations is in preparation.

R. Backhouse and J. N. Oliveira (Eds.): MPC 2000, LNCS 1937, pp. 100–101, 2000.
© Springer-Verlag Berlin Heidelberg 2000

References

1. Bart Jacobs and Jan Rutten. A tutorial on (co)algebras and (co)induction. *Bulletin of the EATCS*, 62:222–259, 1997. Available at URL: www.cwi.nl/ janr. 100
2. J.J.M.M. Rutten. Universal coalgebra: a theory of systems. Report CS-R9652, CWI, 1996. Available at URL: www.cwi.nl. To appear in Theoretical Computer Science. 100
3. J.J.M.M. Rutten. Automata and coinduction (an exercise in coalgebra). Report SEN-R9803, CWI, 1998. Available at URL: www.cwi.nl. Also in the proceedings of CONCUR '98, LNCS 1466, 1998, pp. 194–218. 100
4. J.J.M.M. Rutten. Automata, power series, and coinduction: taking input derivatives seriously (extended abstract). Report SEN-R9901, CWI, 1999. Available at URL: www.cwi.nl. Also in the proceedings of ICALP '99, LNCS 1644, 1999, pp. 645–654. 100

Proving Pointer Programs in Hoare Logic

Richard Bornat

Department of Computer Science, Queen Mary and Westfield College, University of
London, LONDON E1 4NS, UK
richard@dcs.qmw.ac.uk http://www.dcs.qmw.ac.uk/~richard

Abstract. It is possible, but difficult, to reason in Hoare logic about programs
which address and modify data structures defined by pointers. The challenge is
to approach the simplicity of Hoare logic's treatment of variable assignment,
where substitution affects only relevant assertion formulæ. The axiom of
assignment to object components treats each component name as a pointer-
indexed array. This permits a formal treatment of inductively defined data
structures in the heap but tends to produce instances of modified component
mappings in arguments to inductively defined assertions. The major weapons
against these troublesome mappings are assertions which describe spatial
separation of data structures. Three example proofs are sketched.

1 Introduction

The power of the Floyd/Hoare treatment of imperative programs [8][11] lies in its use
of variable substitution to capture the semantics of assignment: simply, R_E^x, the result
of replacing every free occurrence of variable x in R by formula E, is the precondition
which guarantees that assignment $x := E$ will terminate in a state satisfying R.[1] At a
stroke difficult semantic questions that have to do with stores and states are converted
into simpler syntactic questions about first-order logical formulæ.

We encounter several difficulties when we attempt to use a similar approach to
deal with programs which manipulate and modify recursive data structures defined by
pointers. The first difficulty, whose solution has been known for some time, is
aliasing: distinct and very different pointer formulæ may refer to the same object. The
second difficulty is the treatment of assertions which include inductive formulæ
describing heap data structures. The final difficulty is the complexity of the proofs:
not only do we have to reason formally about sets, sequences, graphs and trees, we
have to make sure that the locality of assignment operations is reflected in the
treatment of assertions about the heap.

For all of these reasons, Hoare logic isn't widely used to verify pointer programs.
Yet most low-level and all object-oriented programs use heap pointers freely. If we
wish to prove properties of the kind of programs that actually get written and used, we
shall have to deal with pointer programs on a regular basis.

---

[1] I neglect definedness conditions throughout this paper.

R. Backhouse and J. N. Oliveira (Eds.): MPC 2000, LNCS 1837, pp. 102–126, 2000.

In one situation program verification is a practical necessity. The idea of 'proof-carrying code' (see, for example, Necula and Lee [22] and Appel and Felty [1]) is that programs should be distributed along with a proof of their properties, the proof to be checked by each user before the program is used. Machine checkers are simple, reliable and fast, so if appropriate proofs can be provided we won't have to spend ages reading the fine print before running our latest downloaded system extension.

Proof-carrying code is a long way off, but being able to deal effectively with pointer programs will take us a step along the way.

This paper is therefore about verifying the properties of programs. It is not about proof development, but it is not intended as a challenge to those who prefer program refinement to program verification. Once we can make reliable proofs about imperative pointer algorithms, surely the mechanisms developed to support proof can be used in aid of other activities.

1.1 Background

This paper was inspired by the work of Morris, who put forward in 1981 [21] axioms for assignment to object components, described a mechanism for dealing with inductively defined data structures and presented a semi-formal proof of the Schorr-Waite graph marking algorithm. Earlier still, Burstall presented in 1972 [6] a treatment of list-processing algorithms and pointed out the analogy between the treatment of array element and object components; his Distinct Non Repeating List Systems made possible succinct and convincing proofs of list and tree algorithms. Recently Reynolds [24] revisited Burstall's work, refining the treatment of spatial separation between objects and data structures in the heap and extending its range of application, but working with forward rather than backward reasoning.

Attempts have been made to apply Hoare logic to pointer programs by incorporating a model of the store, or part of the store, into the assertion logic. Luckham and Suzuki [19], Leino [18] and Bijlsma [3], for example, identify a subsection of the heap with each pointer type. Kowaltowski [16] includes the entire heap.

Other work recognises the analogy between array element and object component assignment but doesn't do so effectively: both Hoare and Wirth [13] and Gries and Levin [10], for example, give an axiom for object-component assignment which deals only with the simplest non-pointer cases and neglects entirely to deal with pointer aliasing.

Cousot [7] gives a brief survey of other work, most of which is semantic in character and does not address the practical concerns of program verification.

1.2 Notation

I write $\rightarrow, \wedge, \vee, \neg$ for logical implication, conjunction, disjunction and negation; $\hat{=}$ means equal by definition; @ is append (sequence concatenation); $\pitchfork$ is disjointness of sequences; $\in$ is sequence and/or set membership. E_F^x is the result of substituting formula F for every free occurrence of variable x in formula E. $A \oplus B \mapsto E$ is a mapping which is everywhere the same as A, except at B which it maps to E. I use $\Rightarrow_f$ to define f-linked sequence data structures from section 6 onwards.

2 The Problem of Aliasing

The Hoare logic treatment of assignment is sound when we are sure that distinct variable names refer to distinct storage locations; it can mislead if that assurance is lost. *Aliasing*, which occurs when distinct formulæ describe the same storage location, comes in at least the following range of flavours.

- *Parameter aliasing* is the best known and probably the most difficult to deal with. It arises during the execution of procedures and functions, when a call-by-reference parameter (a **var** parameter in Pascal [14], for example) stands for a storage location outside the procedure which is also nameable in another way from within the procedure.
- *Subscript aliasing* arises in languages which use arrays: $b[I]$ and $b[J]$ are the same storage location just when $I = J$ as integers.
- *Pointer aliasing*, analysed below, arises when an object (a node, a record) can be referred to indirectly via a pointer value.[1]
- *Overlap aliasing* occurs when storage locations can contain storage locations, as when an object is updatable by assignment, simultaneously updating all of its components, and those components are each separately updatable storage locations.
- *View aliasing* occurs when the same area of store can be addressed in different ways, as with Pascal variant records, C [15] union types, or C casting.

Aliasing is caused by identity or overlap of *lvalues* (addresses of objects in the store, see Strachey [26]), but both subscript and pointer aliasing can be dealt with by comparing *rvalues* (contents of storage locations). That makes them in principle tractable in the Floyd/Hoare tradition, which deals entirely with rvalues. Parameter, overlap and view aliasing are outside the scope of this paper.

2.1 Subscript Aliasing

Distinct formulæ indexing the same array will be equivalent as lvalues if the rvalues of their subscript expressions are equal. The Pascal program fragment

```
b[i]:=b[j]+1;
if b[i]=b[j] then writeln(output, "aliased!")
else writeln(output, "distinct")
```

---

[1] In languages such as C [15] which allow pointers to stack components, pointer aliasing is used to imitate parameter aliasing. The obvious implementation of call by reference depends on the use of pointers. Pointer aliasing and parameter aliasing are, therefore, closely related. But at source language level they are distinct phenomena.

will print aliased! when i=j, or distinct when i<>j.

Following McCarthy and Painter [20] and Hoare and Wirth [13], there's a well-known solution to subscript aliasing. Even though, in every practical implementation of a programming language, an array is a collection of separately addressable storage locations, it can be treated as if it was a single variable containing a mapping from indices to rvalues. The instruction $b[I]:=E$ is considered to assign a new mapping $b \oplus I \mapsto E$ to b, and therefore $R^b_{b \oplus I \mapsto E}$ is the precondition that the assignment $b[I]:=E$ will terminate in a state satisfying R. Array element access is resolved by comparing indices, so that $(b \oplus I \mapsto E)[J] = (\text{if } I = J \text{ then } E \text{ else } b[J] \text{ fi})$.

This interpretation of array element assignment is a complete solution to the problem of subscript aliasing, though it must be used carefully with concurrent assignments in case there are aliases in the set of assigned locations. It resolves the problem entirely by the *rvalue* comparison $I = J$ in the reduction rule, even though aliasing is between *lvalues* $b[I]$ and $b[J]$.

2.2   Pointer Aliasing

In practice a computer memory is a giant array, and memory addresses – the primitive mechanism underlying lvalues and pointers – are its indices. Whenever two distinct occurrences of pointer values are equal, we have pointer aliasing.

Consider, for example, the problem (part of the in-place list-reversal example below) of moving an element from the head of one *tl*-linked list r to the head of a similar list p, using assignment to heap object components. If we write it as a sequence of non-concurrent assignments[1] we must use an auxiliary variable q and a sequence of at least four instructions, one of which alters a pointer in the heap. This is one solution:

$$q:=r; r:=r.tl; q.tl:=p; p:=q$$

At every intermediate stage of execution of this program there is more than one way to refer to particular objects in the store. After the first assignment, q and r are the same pointer; after the second, $q.tl$ and r; after the third, $q.tl$ and p; after the last, p and q. If the p and r lists aren't disjoint collections of objects, still more aliasing may be produced.

It's tempting to treat the heap as a pointer-indexed array of component-indexed objects, perhaps subdividing it by object type into sub-arrays (see, for example, Luckham and Suzuki [19] and Leino [18]). But in practice this has proved awkward to deal with. First, it means there has to be a translation between object-component formulæ in the program on the one hand and array-indexing formulæ in assertions on the other. Second, it forces us towards 'global reasoning': every object component assignment seems to affect every assertion which has to do with the heap. By contrast the Floyd-Hoare treatment of assignment to a variable concentrates attention on assertions that involve that variable, leaving others untouched, making steps of 'local reasoning' whose restriction to particular formulæ matches the locality of assignment

---

[1] I do not consider concurrent assignment in this paper.

to a single variable. Third, our assertions about the content of the heap usually need to be expressed inductively, using auxiliary definitions which can easily hide aliases.

Even though these difficulties might in principle be overcome, it feels like the wrong thing to do: we don't program with a memory array in mind but rather in terms of distinct variables, arrays, objects and components, and our reasoning should as far as possible operate at the same level as our thinking.

3 The Treatment of Subscript Aliasing

In [21] Morris introduced an assignment rule for assignment to components of heap objects which generalised Burstall's treatment [6] of hd/tl structures. He gave a treatment of inductively defined data structures using the notion of paths between objects, and presented a proof of the Schorr-Waite graph-marking algorithm [25] which seems far closer to a proof of the original than other published treatments [9][28].

3.1 Morris's Treatment

Morris treats a language which is like Java [2] in that it has pointer-aliasing but no parameter-aliasing, and no whole-object assignment. Program (stack) variables like x, y, p, q can hold pointers to objects in the heap. Objects (in the heap) have components indexed by names like e, f, g, h and are referred to using dot-suffix notation, for example $p.e.e.f$.

Because there is no whole-object assignment, aliasing is only of components of objects. Because there is no arithmetic on component names we know immediately, when e and f are distinct component names and no matter what the values of A and B, that $A.e$ can't be the same lvalue as $B.f$. Similarly, we know that $A.e$ and $B.e$ will be the same lvalue just when the rvalues A and B are equal.[1] Lvalue-aliasing of object components can therefore be detected by identity of component name and rvalue comparison of pointers.

These insights made it possible to define a rule for object-component assignment which avoids mentioning the memory array altogether:

$$\frac{Q \to R_E^{/A.f}}{\{Q\}A.f := E\{R\}}$$

Object component substitution $R_E^{/A.f}$ is just like variable substitution except when it is dealing with object component references. Morris's axioms appear to be:

$$\frac{}{(B.g)_E^{/A.f} \triangleq B.g} \ (f \text{ and } g \text{ distinct}) \qquad \frac{}{(B.f)_E^{/A.f} \triangleq \text{if } A = B \text{ then } E \text{ else } B.f \text{ fi}}$$

Formally, this treatment deals only with single occurrences of component names in object component formulae – $p.hd$ and $p.tl$ are dealt with correctly, for example, but

---

[1] I assume, for simplicity, that distinct types of object use distinct component names.

p.hd.tl isn't – so it is valid only with a restricted programming language and a restricted vocabulary of assertion logics. There are similar axioms for assignment to array elements, similarly flawed – $b[i]$ is dealt with, but not $b[b[i]]$.[1]

3.2   Calculating Object-Component Assignment Axioms

It is possible to calculate object-component substitution axioms which work without restriction in Morris's target language. Since objects can't overlap, we can treat the heap as a pointer-indexed collection of objects, each of which is a name-indexed collection of components. An object-component reference $A.f$ in a heap H corresponds to a double indexing, once of the heap and once of the object.

$$\llbracket A.f \rrbracket H \triangleq H\big[\llbracket A \rrbracket H\big][f]$$

Assigning a value to $A.f$ replaces the object $H[A]$ with a new mapping and therefore the heap becomes a new mapping as well:

$$\llbracket F_E^{/A.f} \rrbracket H \triangleq \llbracket F \rrbracket H', \text{ where } H' = \Big(H \oplus \big(\llbracket A \rrbracket H\big) \mapsto \big(H\big[\llbracket A \rrbracket H\big] \oplus f \mapsto \llbracket E \rrbracket H\big)\Big)$$

When f and g are distinct component names:

$$\llbracket (B.g)_E^{/A.f} \rrbracket H = \llbracket B.g \rrbracket H' = H'\big[\llbracket B \rrbracket H'\big][g] = H'\big[\llbracket B_E^{/A.f} \rrbracket H\big][g]$$

$$= \Big(H \oplus \big(\llbracket A \rrbracket H\big) \mapsto \big(H\big[\llbracket A \rrbracket H\big] \oplus f \mapsto \llbracket E \rrbracket H\big)\Big)\big[\llbracket B_E^{/A.f} \rrbracket H\big][g]$$

$$= \Big(\text{if } \llbracket A \rrbracket H = \llbracket B_E^{/A.f} \rrbracket H \text{ then } \big(H\big[\llbracket A \rrbracket H\big] \oplus f \mapsto \llbracket E \rrbracket H\big) \text{ else } H\big[\llbracket B_E^{/A.f} \rrbracket H\big] \text{ fi}\Big)[g]$$

$$= \text{if } \llbracket A \rrbracket H = \llbracket B_E^{/A.f} \rrbracket H \text{ then } \big(H\big[\llbracket A \rrbracket H\big] \oplus f \mapsto \llbracket E \rrbracket H\big)[g] \text{ else } H\big[\llbracket B_E^{/A.f} \rrbracket H\big][g] \text{ fi}$$

$$= \text{if } \llbracket A \rrbracket H = \llbracket B_E^{/A.f} \rrbracket H \text{ then } H\big[\llbracket A \rrbracket H\big][g] \text{ else } H\big[\llbracket B_E^{/A.f} \rrbracket H\big][g] \text{ fi}$$

$$= \text{if } \llbracket A \rrbracket H = \llbracket B_E^{/A.f} \rrbracket H \text{ then } H\big[\llbracket B_E^{/A.f} \rrbracket H\big][g] \text{ else } H\big[\llbracket B_E^{/A.f} \rrbracket H\big][g] \text{ fi}$$

$$= H\big[\llbracket B_E^{/A.f} \rrbracket\big][g] = \llbracket (B_E^{/A.f}).g \rrbracket H$$

With identical component names:

$$\llbracket (B.f)_E^{/A.f} \rrbracket H = \llbracket B.f \rrbracket H' = H'\big[\llbracket B \rrbracket H'\big][f] = H'\big[\llbracket B_E^{/A.f} \rrbracket H\big][f]$$

$$= \Big(H \oplus \big(\llbracket A \rrbracket H\big) \mapsto \big(H\big[\llbracket A \rrbracket H\big] \oplus f \mapsto \llbracket E \rrbracket H\big)\Big)\big[\llbracket B_E^{/A.f} \rrbracket H\big][f]$$

---

[1]   In examples Morris deals with multiple occurrences of component names or array names by sometimes introducing nested substitutions, sometimes introducing constants – replacing $b[b[j]] = j$, for example, by $b[b0] = j \land b[j] = b0$. It may be that his less than formal statement of the mechanism is misleading.

$$= \left(\text{if } [\![A]\!] \, H = [\![B_E^{/A.f}]\!] \, H \text{ then } \left(H \big[[\![A]\!] \, H \big] \oplus f \mapsto [\![E]\!] \, H \right) \text{ else } H \big[[\![B_E^{/A.f}]\!] \, H \big] \text{ fi} \right) [f]$$

$$= \text{if } [\![A]\!] \, H = [\![B_E^{/A.f}]\!] \, H \text{ then } \left(H \big[[\![A]\!] \, H \big] \oplus f \mapsto [\![E]\!] \, H \right) [f] \text{ else } H \big[[\![B_E^{/A.f}]\!] \, H \big] [f] \text{ fi}$$

$$= \text{if } [\![A]\!] \, H = [\![B_E^{/A.f}]\!] \, H \text{ then } [\![E]\!] \, H \text{ else } [\![\left(B_E^{/A.f} \right).f]\!] \, H \text{ fi}$$

$$= [\![\text{ if } A = B_E^{/A.f} \text{ then } E \text{ else } \left(B_E^{/A.f} \right).f \text{ fi}]\!] \, H$$

In each case the calculated equivalence leads to an axiom which is identical to Morris's except that B on the right-hand side of the axiom is replaced by $B_E^{/A.f}$.

3.3   The Component-as-Array Trick

The axioms for object component substitution, following an assignment $A.f := E$, for distinct component names f and g, are

$$\overline{\left(B.g \right)_E^{/A.f}} \triangleq \left(B_E^{/A.f} \right).g \qquad \overline{\left(B.f \right)_E^{/A.f}} \triangleq \text{if } A = B_E^{/A.f} \text{ then } E \text{ else } \left(B_E^{/A.f} \right).f \text{ fi}$$

The standard treatment of an assignment $b[I] := E$ gives us for distinct arrays b and c

$$c[J]_{b \oplus I \mapsto E}^b = c \left[J_{b \oplus I \mapsto E}^b \right] \qquad b[J]_{b \oplus I \mapsto E}^b = \left(b \oplus I \mapsto E \right) \left[J_{b \oplus I \mapsto E}^b \right]$$

$$= \text{if } I = J_{b \oplus I \mapsto E}^b \text{ then } E \text{ else } b \left[J_{b \oplus I \mapsto E}^b \right] \text{ fi}$$

It is clear from the correspondence between these treatments that object-component substitution is formally equivalent to a treatment of object components as pointer-indexed arrays. That is, assignment to component f of an object pointed to by A can be treated as if it were an assignment to the A-indexed component of an array f, and access to the f component of an object pointed to by A as selection of the Ath component of an array f.

This observation is certainly not novel: Burstall gives an equivalent in [6], and it may be that Morris intended this reading in [21]. It is worth stating clearly, however, to clarify what seems otherwise to be imperfectly understood 'folk knowledge'.

The advantages of the component-as-array treatment are considerable. First of all, it is obvious that it enables the calculation of weakest preconditions. Second, it means that we don't need a new structural induction to deal with object component substitution: a considerable advantage when mechanising proof and proof-checking. Finally, and most importantly in the context of this paper, it makes possible a formal treatment of object component substitution into inductively defined formulæ.

I feel it's necessary, despite its advantages, to emphasise that the treatment is doubly a trick. It's a trick built on the array-as-mapping trick of McCarthy and Painter. It's violently at odds with our understanding of how heaps work in practice. It isn't clear how much of it would survive a relaxation of the restrictions we have imposed on our programming language.

$$\frac{Q \to R_E^x}{\{Q\}x:=E\{R\}} \qquad \frac{Q \to R_{f \oplus A \mapsto E}^f}{\{Q\}A.f:=E\{R\}} \qquad \frac{\{Q\}S\{R'\} \quad R' \to R}{\{Q\}S\{R\}}$$

$$\frac{Q \to P \quad \{P \wedge B\}S\{P\} \quad P \wedge \neg B \to R \quad P \wedge B \to t > 0 \quad \{P \wedge B \wedge t = vt\}S\{t < vt\}}{\{Q\} \text{ while } B \text{ do } S \text{ od } \{R\}}$$

$$\frac{\{Q \wedge B\}S_{then}\{R\} \quad \{Q \wedge \neg B\}S_{else}\{R\}}{\{Q\}\text{if } B \text{ then } S_{then} \text{ else } S_{else} \text{ fi}\{R\}} \qquad \frac{\{Q\}S1\{Q'\} \quad \{Q'\}S2\{R\}}{\{Q\}S1;S2\{R\}}$$

Fig. 1. Hoare-triple rules

3.4   Restricted Global Reasoning

If we treat the heap as a global array, and convert all our object component assignments to heap-array element assignments, then we have *global reasoning*, because substitution of a new mapping for the heap array affects every assertion about any part of the heap. By contrast the Floyd-Hoare treatment of variable assignment gives us *local reasoning*: only those assertions which mention the assigned variable are affected by substitution.

Object component substitution and the component-as-array trick each offer a restricted global reasoning. Some locality is achieved effortlessly, when formulæ which only mention component f aren't affected by assignment to component g. But on the other hand the interaction of assignment with inductive definitions, discussed below, needs careful treatment if a global reasoning explosion is to be avoided.

4   Hoare-Triple Rules

I consider a language which has assignment to variables and object components, while-do-od, if-then-else-fi and instruction sequence (fig. 1). The usual caveats apply to the while-do-od rule: vt must be a fresh variable, t must be an integer-valued function of the state. It is useful to include a postcondition-strengthening rule. Component indexing $A.(B \oplus C \mapsto E)$ is equivalent to $($if $A = C$ then E else $A.B$ fi$)$.

I omit from the rules anything which requires definedness of formulæ. Definedness is especially important in pointer-manipulating programs, because nil is such a dangerous value – often in use, of pointer type, and yet not dot-suffixable. Nevertheless, it would add little to the discussion in this paper to deal with definedness, if only because my examples don't attempt to traverse nil pointers.

5   Three Small Examples

Cycles in the heap show pointer aliasing in its rawest form. Three small mechanical proofs, calculated in Jape [5], are shown in full detail except for trivial implications.

```
1:p.b=3→p.b=3                                      {→-I,hyp}
2:p.b=3→p.(a⊕p↦p).b=3                              A.(B⊕A↦E)≜E 1
3:p.b=3→p.(a⊕p↦p).(a⊕p↦p).b=3                      A.(B⊕A↦E)≜E 2
4:p.b=3→p.(a⊕p↦p).(a⊕p↦p).(a⊕p↦p).b=3   A.(B⊕A↦E)≜E 3
5:{p.b=3}(p.a:=p){p.a.a.a.b=3}                     :=4
```

Fig. 2. A single-step cycle

```
1:p.d=3→p.d=3                                            {→-I,hyp}
2:p.d=3→q.b.(c⊕q.b↦p).d=3                               A.(B⊕A↦E)≜E 1
3:p.d=3→p.(a⊕p↦q).b.(c⊕q.b↦p).d=3                       A.(B⊕A↦E)≜E 2
4:p.d=3→q.b.(c⊕q.b↦p).(a⊕p↦q).b.(c⊕q.b↦p).d=3           A.(B⊕A↦E)≜E 3
5:{p.d=3}(q.b.c:=p){q.b.c.(a⊕p↦q).b.c.d=3}              :=4
6:q.b.c.(a⊕p↦q).b.c.d=3→q.b.c.(a⊕p↦q).b.c.d=3           {→-I,hyp}
7:q.b.c.(a⊕p↦q).b.c.d=3→p.(a⊕p↦q).b.c.(a⊕p↦q).b.c.d=3   A.(B⊕A↦E)≜E 6
8:{q.b.c.(a⊕p↦q).b.c.d=3}(p.a:=q){p.a.b.c.a.b.c.d=3}    :=7
9:{p.d=3}(q.b.c:=p;p.a:=q){p.a.b.c.a.b.c.d=3}           sequence 5,8
```

Fig. 3. A multi-step cycle (version 1)

```
1:p.d=3→p.d=3                                            {→-I,hyp}
2:p.d=3→q.b.(c⊕q.b↦p).d=3                               A.(B⊕A↦E)≜E 1
3:p.d=3→p.(a⊕p↦q).b.(c⊕q.b↦p).d=3                       A.(B⊕A↦E)≜E 2
4:p.d=3→q.b.(c⊕q.b↦p).(a⊕p↦q).b.(c⊕q.b↦p).d=3           A.(B⊕A↦E)≜E 3
5:p.d=3→p.(a⊕p↦q).b.(c⊕q.b↦p).(a⊕p↦q).b.(c⊕q.b↦p).d=3   A.(B⊕A↦E)≜E 4
6:{p.d=3}(p.a:=q){p.a.b.(c⊕q.b↦p).a.b.(c⊕q.b↦p).d=3}    :=5
7:p.a.b.(c⊕q.b↦p).a.b.(c⊕q.b↦p).d=3→p.a.b.(c⊕q.b↦p).a.b.(c⊕q.b↦p).d=3   {→-I,hyp}
8:{p.a.b.(c⊕q.b↦p).a.b.(c⊕q.b↦p).d=3}(q.b.c:=p){p.a.b.c.a.b.c.d=3}   :=7
9:{p.d=3}(p.a:=q;q.b.c:=p){p.a.b.c.a.b.c.d=3}           sequence 6,8
```

Fig. 4. A multi-step cycle (version 2)

First a single-step cycle established by a single assignment.

$$\{p.b = 3\}p.a := p\{p.a.a.a.b = 3\}$$

The proof (fig. 2) consists of a use of the assignment rule (line 5) followed by three applications of component-indexing simplification on lines 4, 3 and 2.

Next, a multi-step cycle established by a sequence of two assignments.

$$\{p.d = 3\}q.b.c := p; \; p.a := q\{p.a.b.c.a.b.c.d = 3\}$$

The proof (fig. 3) consists of an application of the sequence rule (line 9), two applications of the assignment rule (lines 8 and 5) and various uses of component-indexing simplification. Note that we can't simplify $q.b.c.(a \oplus p \mapsto q)$ on line 6, but the mapping can be eliminated on line 3, once $q.b.c$ has been simplified to p.

If we make the same cycle with the same instructions, but executed in the reverse order (fig. 4), neither of the mappings generated by the assignment rule on line 8 can be eliminated immediately, but they are dealt with eventually, on lines 4 and 2.

6 Substitution and Auxiliary Definitions

When we make proofs of programs which manipulate heap objects using pointers, our assertions will usually call upon auxiliary definitions of data structures. Auxiliary definitions are useful for all kinds of reasons: they allow us to parameterise important assertions in user-defined predicates, they let us define inductive calculations, they shorten descriptions. But the Floyd/Hoare mechanism, even in the absence of pointer aliasing, has difficulty with assertions which contain arbitrary auxiliary defined formulæ (henceforth *adfs*).

If, for example, we define a predicate

$$F(z) \triangleq (x = z)$$

then $F(y)$ both asserts that y has the same value as x and contains an implicit occurrence of x. Substitution deals only with explicit occurrences, so the variable assignment rule would seem to allow us to conclude mistakenly

$$\{F(y)\}x := x + 1\{F(y)\}$$

The difficulty would disappear if we were to insist that adfs are expanded from their definitions before we use substitution. That would not merely be inconvenient but impossible in general, because inductive definitions can expand indefinitely. If we insist, however, that definitions are program-variable closed – that is, that they have no free occurrences of variable names which can be the target of substitution – then we can deal with them in unexpanded form.

For example, we might define

$$F(u, v) \triangleq u = v$$

and the assignment rule would correctly calculate

$$\{F(x+1, y)\}x := x + 1\{F(x, y)\}$$

The problem of auxiliary definitions of heap data structures is not quite so easy to solve. Reynolds [23] deals with *assertion procedures*, but his intentions and his approach are quite distinct from that developed below.

6.1 Inductive Auxiliary Definitions of Data Structures

Pointer-linked data-structure definitions are usually inductively defined. Indeed it is difficult to see how we could do without induction when specifying programs which manipulate data structures via pointers. Making them program-variable closed doesn't deal with object component assignment, but the component-as-array trick allows us to make them component-array closed as well.

Following Burstall, Morris and Reynolds, an example data structure which uses a component array parameter is the sequence of objects[1] $A \Rightarrow_f B$ generated by starting

---

[1] It's helpful to think of this formula as generating a sequence of objects, but of course it actually generates a sequence of pointer values.

$$A \Rightarrow_f B \stackrel{\wedge}{=} \text{if } A = B \text{ then } \langle \, \rangle \text{ else } \langle A \rangle \, @ \big(A.f \Rightarrow_f B \big) \text{ fi}$$

Fig. 5. An inductive definition of f-linked sequences in the heap

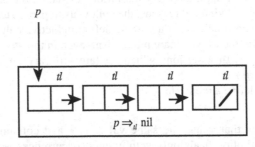

Fig. 6. The sequence $p \Rightarrow_{tl} \text{nil}$

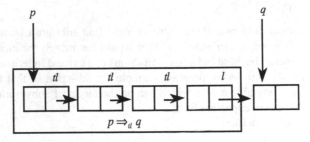

Fig. 7. The sequence $p \Rightarrow_{tl} q$

at the object pointed to by A and following links in f components until a pointer equal to B is encountered.

For various reasons (not least the fact that nil doesn't point to an object), B isn't included in the sequence. The definition is both program-variable and component-array closed: it mentions nothing but constants and its parameters A, B and f. The sequence it generates isn't necessarily a list – that is, a finite sequence with no repetitions – because cycles in the heap may mean that we never reach B. It will not be defined if we attempt to traverse a nil pointer before reaching B.

If we consider objects with hd and tl components, as in the list reversal and list merge examples below, then $p \Rightarrow_{tl} \text{nil}$ can represent what we normally think of as 'the list p' (fig. 6). If p and q point to distinct objects, then $p \Rightarrow_{tl} q$ describes a list fragment, the sequence of objects linked by tl components starting with the one pointed to by p up to but not including the one pointed to by q (fig. 7). In each of these examples I have assumed that the data structure is acyclic.

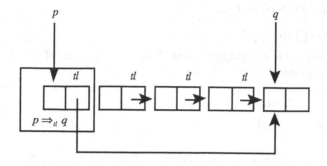

Fig. 8. Effect of the assignment $p.tl := q$ on the sequence $p \Rightarrow_{tl} q$

7 Spatial Separation, Global Reasoning and Inductive Definitions

What imperative graph, tree and list algorithms all seem to do is to work with disjoint bits of data structures, nibbling away at the edges, moving a node from here to there, swinging pointers, altering values in exposed components. The locality of assignment means that changes made in one area of the heap don't affect objects elsewhere. But because pointer aliasing is always a possibility, our reasoning must continually take into account the possibility that the location we are altering is referred to under another name. In practice we take that possibility into account most often in order to dismiss it. Our logic must make this easy to do, and we must choose our assertions to exploit this capability.

Substitution into $x \Rightarrow_f y$, as a result of the assignment $A.f := E$, generates $x \Rightarrow_{f \oplus A \mapsto E} y$. That expands to give a formula which contains indefinitely many occurrences of the mapping $f \oplus A \mapsto E$, in $x.(f \oplus A \mapsto E)$, $x.(f \oplus A \mapsto E).(f \oplus A \mapsto E)$, and so on. This explosion of effects, produced by an assignment which affects only a single location, must either be avoided or effectively dealt with. It arises with any inductive auxiliary definition which has a component-array parameter.

By contrast, assignment is operationally local. Consider, for example the $p \Rightarrow_{tl} q$ data structure of fig. 7. Executing $p.tl := q$ will swing the pointer in the first box to point at the last, changing the data structure to that in fig. 8.

Only one component of the heap changes because of the assignment. The challenge is to imitate this simplicity in our reasoning, to avoid an explosion of mappings and combat what Hoare and Jifeng [12] call 'the complexity of pointer-swing'.

In this particular case the result of substitution is easy to unravel:

$$\left(p \Rightarrow_{tl} q\right)^{tl}_{tl \oplus p \mapsto q} = p \Rightarrow_{tl \oplus p \mapsto q} q$$

$$= \text{if } p = q \text{ then } \langle\,\rangle \text{ else } \langle p \rangle \,@\, p.(tl \oplus p \mapsto q) \Rightarrow_{tl \oplus p \mapsto q} q \text{ fi}$$

$$= \text{if } p = q \text{ then } \langle\,\rangle \text{ else } \langle p \rangle \,@\, q \Rightarrow_{tl \oplus p \mapsto q} q \text{ fi}$$

$$= \text{if } p = q \text{ then } \langle \, \rangle \text{ else } \langle p \rangle \, @\langle \, \rangle \text{ fi}$$

$$= \text{if } p = q \text{ then } \langle \, \rangle \text{ else } \langle p \rangle \text{ fi}$$

Not every example is so straightforward. Consider the effect of the assignment $x.tl := y$ on the postcondition $x \neq \text{nil} \wedge \text{list}(x \Rightarrow_{tl} \text{nil})$, where the list predicate[1] asserts that a sequence is finite and non-repetitive. We may proceed with substitution, expansion and simplification as before:

$$\left(x \neq \text{nil} \wedge \text{list}(x \Rightarrow_{tl} \text{nil}) \right)^{tl}_{tl \oplus x \mapsto y} = x \neq \text{nil} \wedge \text{list}\left(x \Rightarrow_{tl \oplus x \mapsto y} \text{nil} \right)$$

$$= x \neq \text{nil} \wedge \text{list}\left(\text{if } x = \text{nil then } \langle \, \rangle \text{ else } \langle x \rangle \, @ \, x.(tl \oplus x \mapsto y) \Rightarrow_{tl \oplus x \mapsto y} \text{nil fi} \right)$$

$$= x \neq \text{nil} \wedge \text{list}\left(\text{if } x = \text{nil then } \langle \, \rangle \text{ else } \langle x \rangle \, @ \, y \Rightarrow_{tl \oplus x \mapsto y} \text{nil fi} \right)$$

$$= x \neq \text{nil} \wedge \text{list}\left(\langle x \rangle \, @ \, y \Rightarrow_{tl \oplus x \mapsto y} \text{nil} \right)$$

Without further information we can go no further, but we can be sure that this is the weakest precondition, because all we've done is to use component-as-array substitution, expand a definition and evaluate a conditional.

We've by no means achieved local reasoning yet, because there is a mapping $tl \oplus x \mapsto y$ in the argument to an inductively defined auxiliary formula. Observe, however, that when x doesn't point to any of the components of $y \Rightarrow_{tl} \text{nil}$, assignment to $x.tl$ can't affect the meaning of that formula. In those circumstances, therefore, $y \Rightarrow_{tl} \text{nil} = y \Rightarrow_{tl \oplus x \mapsto E} \text{nil}$ for any formula E. (This is easily shown formally by induction on the length of finite sequences.) We might, that is, be content to assume separation of objects in the heap, and to prove the simpler precondition

$$x \neq \text{nil} \wedge x \notin y \Rightarrow_{tl} \text{nil} \wedge \text{list}(\langle x \rangle \, @ \, y \Rightarrow_{tl} \text{nil})$$

Note that the assumption ought to hold, because if x does point into $y \Rightarrow_{tl} \text{nil}$ – that is, if $y \Rightarrow_{tl} \text{nil} \quad y \Rightarrow_{tl} x \Rightarrow_{tl} \text{nil}$ – then we don't have a non-repeating sequence and the precondition is false:

$$x \neq \text{nil} \wedge \text{list}(\langle x \rangle \, @ \, y \Rightarrow_{tl \oplus x \mapsto y} \text{nil})$$

$$= x \neq \text{nil} \wedge \text{list}(\langle x \rangle \, @ \, y \Rightarrow_{tl \oplus x \mapsto y} x \, @ \, x \Rightarrow_{tl \oplus x \mapsto y} \text{nil})$$

$$= x \neq \text{nil} \wedge \text{list}(\langle x \rangle \, @ \, y \Rightarrow_{tl} x \, @\langle x \rangle \, @ \, y \Rightarrow_{tl \oplus x \mapsto y} \text{nil})$$

What's being appealed to by adding $x \notin y \Rightarrow_{tl} \text{nil}$ to the precondition, thereby eliminating a mapping, is the *principle of spatial separation*. There is a set of objects whose components help define the meaning of $y \Rightarrow_{tl} \text{nil}$, and if the object x points to isn't one of that set, then the assignment $x.tl := E$ can't have any effect on $y \Rightarrow_{tl} \text{nil}$.

In practice spatial-separation assertions like $x \notin y \Rightarrow_{tl} \text{nil}$ aren't plucked out of the air – they are found in invariants, as shown in the list reversal, list merge and graph marking examples below.

---

[1] Defined by heap-independent axioms: see section 9.1.

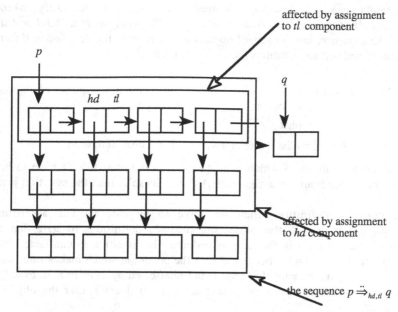

Fig. 9. Offset sequence with different support sets for different components

What's surprising is that lists and sequences aren't a special case. Spatial separation is exactly what we need to deal in general with inductively defined heap data structures. Any data structure in a finite heap depends on the component values of a finite set of objects. If we assign to a component of an object outside that set, the data structure can't be affected. Faced with an adf whose arguments include a mapping $B \oplus A \mapsto E$, therefore, we can either expand it until all the affected objects are exposed – as, for example, we expanded $x \Rightarrow_{tl \oplus x \mapsto y}$ nil above – or we can show that because of spatial separation the mapping is never used, no matter how far we expand the formula – as in the case of $y \Rightarrow_{tl \oplus x \mapsto y}$ nil above – or we can do both steps, one after the other – or we are stuck for the moment, and we have to leave the mapping alone.

7.1   Spatial Separation Examples

Spatial separation of a data structure and an object A can always be expressed as $A \notin S$, where S is a set of objects whose component values define the data structure. In straightforward cases, like the $\Rightarrow_f$ definition of fig. 5, the set of objects is just the data structure itself.

Offset Sequences. Consider the definition

$$A \stackrel{..}{\Rightarrow}_{f,g} B \,\hat{=}\, \text{if } A = B \text{ then } \langle\,\rangle \text{ else } \langle A.f.f \rangle @ A.g \stackrel{..}{\Rightarrow}_{f,g} B \text{ fi}$$

The formula $p \overset{\rightrightarrows}{\Rightarrow}_{hd,tl} q$ describes a sequence of objects not necessarily linked together, and offset by two steps from $p \Rightarrow_{tl} q$ (fig. 9). Assignment to $A.hd$ or $A.tl$ may alter the sequence, but the sets of objects which support the description differ between cases, and neither of them is the sequence itself.

Ordered Sequences. The predicate olist_f asserts that a particular sequence of objects is ordered by $(\leq)$ in its f component:

$$\text{olist}_f\langle\,\rangle \qquad\qquad \text{olist}_f\langle A\rangle$$
$$\text{olist}_f\big(R\,@\langle A,B\rangle\,@\,S\big) \mathrel{\hat{=}} \text{olist}_f\big(R\,@\langle A\rangle\big) \wedge A.f \leq B.f \wedge \text{olist}_f\big(\langle B\rangle\,@\,S\big)$$

The sequence of objects S which $\text{olist}_f(S)$ asserts is ordered don't have to be linked together in the heap. An assignment $A.f := E$ doesn't affect the assertion just when $A \notin S$.

If we combine definitions then we have to be careful. The assertion $\text{olist}_{hd}(x \Rightarrow_{tl} \text{nil})$ uses both the olist_f and the $\Rightarrow_f$ definitions to state that a particular linked sequence in the heap is ordered: the assertion is unaffected by $A.tl := E$ when $A \notin x \Rightarrow_{tl} \text{nil}$ – because that is the condition which makes sure that the sequence $x \Rightarrow_{tl} \text{nil}$ remains the same – and unaffected by $A.hd := E$ in exactly the same circumstances, even though that assignment doesn't alter the object-sequence itself.

Cyclic Graphs. The set of nodes in a directed binary graph reachable through a pointer A is

$$A*_{l,r} \mathrel{\hat{=}} \text{if } A = \text{nil then } \{\,\} \text{ else } \{A\} \cup A.l*_{l,r} \cup A.r*_{l,r} \text{ fi}$$

The assignment $p.l := q$, given the postcondition $p \neq \text{nil} \wedge G\big(p*_{l,r}\big)$, where G is some predicate, will generate the precondition

$$p \neq \text{nil} \wedge G\big(\{p\} \cup q*_{l\oplus p\mapsto q,r} \cup p.r*_{l\oplus p\mapsto q,r}\big)$$

We can expect our graphs to be cyclic, so the occurrences of the mapping $l \oplus p \mapsto q$ in this formula will give us problems.

In this case it is helpful to rewrite the definition to make spatial separation easier to establish. It's simple to calculate reachable nodes using a directed acyclic graph (DAG), breaking cycles by including an exclusion set S in the definition:

$$A*_{l,r,S} = \text{if } A = \text{nil} \vee A \in S \text{ then } \{\,\} \text{ else } \{A\} \cup A.l*_{l,r,S\cup\{A\}} \cup A.r*_{l,r,S\cup\{A\}} \text{ fi}$$

This automatically gives spatial separation between the root node A and the subgraphs generated from the child nodes $A.l$ and $A.r$. Now the assignment $p.l := q$. given the postcondition $p \neq \text{nil} \wedge p \notin S \wedge G\big(p*_{l,r,S}\big)$, will generate

$$p \neq \text{nil} \wedge p \notin S \wedge G\big(\{p\} \cup q*_{l\oplus p\mapsto q,r,S\cup\{p\}} \cup p.r*_{l\oplus p\mapsto q,r,S\cup\{p\}}\big)$$

When $A \in S$ the graph $B*_{l,r,S}$ won't include A – that is, we have spatial separation. Formally we have the equivalence (provable by induction on the height of finite DAGs)

$$A \in S \to \left(B^*_{l \oplus A \mapsto E, r, S} = B^*_{l, r, S}\right)$$

Since p belongs to $S \cup \{p\}$, the precondition can be simplified to

$$p \neq \mathrm{nil} \wedge p \notin S \wedge G\left(\{p\} \cup q^*_{l, r, S \cup \{p\}} \cup p.r^*_{l, r, S \cup \{p\}}\right).$$

8   Heap Reasoning and Structural Reasoning

We can make assertions about a value represented by a heap data structure which are about the value itself and which don't involve knowledge of the heap. If it's a sequence we may remark about its length, its non-cyclic nature, the non-occurrence of 0 elements in its *hd* components, and so on. If it's a tree we may want to talk about its height, the balance between its subtrees, the ordering of its tips, and so on. If it's a graph we may remark about its spanning tree, its connectedness, its colouring, and so on. If we are careful, 'pure' structural reasoning can carry much of the weight of a specification and proof. On the other hand, spatial separation concerns require our heap data structure definitions to be written to expose information about the objects that support particular data structures.

It seems, therefore, that specifications ought to be written at three separate levels:

1. Remarks about the contents of particular variables and objects.
2. Inductive definitions of data structures, including rules which interpret non-hiding assertions.
3. The specification of the problem, in terms of (1) and (2).

We have to make our definitions carefully, both to fit our problem and to permit the easiest and most local forms of reasoning. The $\Rightarrow_f$ definition of fig. 5 is good for acyclic sequences, and makes it easy to reason about assignments near the head of a sequence. It's less good (see the list merge example below) when we assign to the tail of a sequence. It's not very good at all if the sequence can be cyclic, and in that case it seems reasonable to devise a special adf which deals easily with cycles.

It is interesting that remarks about individual heap cells – 'pictures of memory' – seem relatively unimportant in this treatment, in contrast to Reynolds [24]. On the other hand, spatial separation of data structures, a clear echo of Burstall's DNRLS [6] and Reynolds' spatial conjunction, is an essential part of every proof.

9   A Worked Example: In-Place List-Reversal

The in-place list-reversal algorithm (fig. 10) is the lowest hurdle that a pointer-aliasing formalism ought to be able to jump. Burstall deals with it in [6] with essentially the same specification as that below.

$$\{Q\}\ r:=p;\ p:=\text{nil};$$
$$\{P\}\ \text{while}\ r \neq \text{nil do}\ q:=r;\ r:=r.tl;\ q.tl:=p;\ p:=q\ \text{od}\ \{R\}$$

Fig. 10. The in-place list-reversal algorithm

9.1   Definitions

I have not written inductive definitions of functions for the most part. Instead I give useful facts as axioms.

In the invariant I need append ($@$) and rev, and I need to be able to say that a particular cell-sequence S is a list: that is, it is finite length and has no repetitions. I can only reverse finite sequences. I need disjointness ($\pitchfork$) of sequences.

$$\langle\,\rangle @ S \;\hat{=}\; S \qquad S @ \langle\,\rangle \;\hat{=}\; S \qquad\qquad \text{rev}\,\langle\,\rangle \;\hat{=}\; \langle\,\rangle \qquad \text{rev}\,\langle A\rangle \;\hat{=}\; \langle A\rangle$$
$$S @ (T @ U) \;\hat{=}\; (S @ T) @ U \qquad\qquad \text{list}\,A \wedge \text{list}\,B \rightarrow \text{rev}(A @ B) = \text{rev}\,B @ \text{rev}\,A$$

$$\langle\,\rangle \pitchfork S \qquad \langle A\rangle \pitchfork \langle B\rangle \;\hat{=}\; A \neq B \qquad\qquad \text{list}\,\langle\,\rangle \qquad \text{list}\,\langle A\rangle$$
$$S \pitchfork T \;\hat{=}\; T \pitchfork S \qquad\qquad\qquad\qquad\qquad \text{list}(S @ T) \;\hat{=}\; \text{list}\,S \wedge \text{list}\,T \wedge S \pitchfork T$$
$$(S @ T) \pitchfork U \;\hat{=}\; (S \pitchfork U) \wedge (T \pitchfork U)$$

For proof of termination of any list algorithm, it's necessary to do arithmetic on lengths of lists. I haven't attempted a mechanical treatment: instead I've appealed to some obvious facts.

$$\text{list}\,S \rightarrow \text{length}\,\big(\langle A\rangle @ S\big) > \text{length}\,S \qquad \text{length}\,\big(\langle A\rangle @ S\big) > 0$$
$$\text{list}\,S \rightarrow \exists n:(n \geq 0 \wedge \text{length}\,S = n)$$

I use the $\Rightarrow_f$ definition (fig. 5) to describe sequences in the heap. It's possible to prove by induction on the length of finite sequences that

$$\big(\text{list}(B \Rightarrow_{tl} C) \wedge \langle A\rangle \pitchfork B \Rightarrow_{tl} C\big) \rightarrow \big(B \Rightarrow_{tl \oplus A \mapsto E} C = B \Rightarrow_{tl} C\big)$$

– a fact that is appealed to several times in the proof.

9.2   Specification

The algorithm is given in variable p a pointer to a tl–linked list S.

$$Q \;\hat{=}\; \text{list}\big(p \Rightarrow_{tl} \text{nil}\big) \wedge p \Rightarrow_{tl} \text{nil} = S$$

The invariant of the loop is that there is a tl-linked list from p to nil, a similar but distinct list from r to nil, and the reverse of the r list, followed by the p list, is the reverse of the original input.

$$P \;\hat{=}\; \begin{pmatrix} \text{list}\big(p \Rightarrow_{tl} \text{nil}\big) \wedge \text{list}\big(r \Rightarrow_{tl} \text{nil}\big) \wedge p \Rightarrow_{tl} \text{nil} \pitchfork r \Rightarrow_{tl} \text{nil} \wedge \\ \text{rev}\big(r \Rightarrow_{tl} \text{nil}\big) @ p \Rightarrow_{tl} \text{nil} = \text{rev}\,S \end{pmatrix}$$

The loop measure is the length of the r list.

$$t \;\hat{=}\; \text{length}\big(r \Rightarrow_{tl} \text{nil}\big)$$

On termination the p list is the reverse of the original input.

$$R \mathrel{\hat{=}} p \Rightarrow_{tl} \text{nil} = \text{rev } S$$

This specification doesn't say that on termination the hd components of S are what they originally were, though it is obvious from the program that this is so. It would be easy to change the specification to make this point by adding $hd = HD$ to precondition, invariant and postcondition, but it would be just a drop in the ocean of the frame problem.

9.3   Semi-Formal Proofs

These proofs are written backwards: postcondition first, working towards precondition and several substitution steps are compressed into one. The machine-checked proofs available from the web site [4], calculated with the aid of Jape [5], are less compressed.

Initialisation.
$\{P\}$
$r := p;\ p := \text{nil}$

   [substitution]

$$\left\{ \begin{aligned} &\text{list}\big(p \Rightarrow_{tl} \text{nil}\big) \wedge \text{list}\big(\text{nil} \Rightarrow_{tl} \text{nil}\big) \wedge p \Rightarrow_{tl} \text{nil} \curlywedge \text{nil} \Rightarrow_{tl} \text{nil} \wedge \\ &\text{rev}\big(p \Rightarrow_{tl} \text{nil}\big) @ \text{nil} \Rightarrow_{tl} \text{nil} = \text{rev } S \end{aligned} \right\}$$

   [replace $\text{nil} \Rightarrow_{tl} \text{nil}$ by $\langle\,\rangle$; then straightforward sequence calculation]

$$\left\{ \text{list}\big(p \Rightarrow_{tl} \text{nil}\big) \wedge p \Rightarrow_{tl} \text{nil} = S \right\}$$

Loop Body Preserves Invariant
$\{P\}$
$q := r;\ r := r.tl;\ q.tl := p;\ p := q$

   [substitution]

$$\left\{ \begin{aligned} &\text{list}\big(r.tl \Rightarrow_{tl \oplus r \mapsto p} \text{nil}\big) \wedge \text{list}\big(r \Rightarrow_{tl \oplus r \mapsto p} \text{nil}\big) \wedge r.tl \Rightarrow_{tl \oplus r \mapsto p} \text{nil} \curlywedge r \Rightarrow_{tl \oplus r \mapsto p} \text{nil} \wedge \\ &\text{rev}\big(r.tl \Rightarrow_{tl \oplus r \mapsto p} \text{nil}\big) @ r \Rightarrow_{tl \oplus r \mapsto p} \text{nil} = \text{rev } SS \end{aligned} \right\}$$

   [Use $r \neq \text{nil}$ and $\text{list}\big(r \Rightarrow_{tl} \text{nil}\big)$ from invariant to obtain $\text{list}(\langle r \rangle @ r.tl \Rightarrow_{tl} \text{nil})$; thence $\text{list}(r.tl \Rightarrow_{tl} \text{nil})$ and $\langle r \rangle \curlywedge r.tl \Rightarrow_{tl} \text{nil}$, and therefore $r.tl \Rightarrow_{tl \oplus r \mapsto p} \text{nil} = r.tl \Rightarrow_{tl} \text{nil}$.   Use $r \neq \text{nil}$ and $p \Rightarrow_{tl} \text{nil} \curlywedge r \Rightarrow_{tl} \text{nil}$ to   obtain $p \Rightarrow_{tl} \text{nil} \curlywedge (\langle r \rangle @ r.tl \Rightarrow_{tl} \text{nil})$; thence $\langle r \rangle \curlywedge p \Rightarrow_{tl} \text{nil}$ and since $\text{list}(p \Rightarrow_{tl} \text{nil})$, $r \Rightarrow_{tl \oplus r \mapsto p} \text{nil} = \langle r \rangle @ p \Rightarrow_{tl} \text{nil}$. Once all the assignment-induced mappings are eliminated, it's a straightforward sequence calculation.]

$$\left\{ \begin{aligned} &\text{list}\big(p \Rightarrow_{tl} \text{nil}\big) \wedge \text{list}\big(r \Rightarrow_{tl} \text{nil}\big) \wedge p \Rightarrow_{tl} \text{nil} \curlywedge r \Rightarrow_{tl} \text{nil} \wedge \\ &\text{rev}\big(r \Rightarrow_{tl} \text{nil}\big) @ p \Rightarrow_{tl} \text{nil} = \text{rev } S \wedge r \neq \text{nil} \end{aligned} \right\}$$

$\{Q\}$
if $q = \text{nil} \vee\!\!\!\!\vee (p \neq \text{nil} \wedge\!\!\!\wedge p.hd \leq q.hd)$ then $r := p$; $p := p.tl$ else $r := q$; $q := q.tl$ fi; $s := r$
$\{P\}$
while $p \neq \text{nil} \vee q \neq \text{nil}$ do
   if $q = \text{nil} \vee\!\!\!\!\vee (p \neq \text{nil} \wedge\!\!\!\wedge p.hd \leq q.hd)$ then $s.tl := p$; $p := p.tl$ else $s.tl := q$; $q := q.tl$ fi;
   $s := s.tl$
od
$\{R\}$

Fig. 11. The in-place list merge algorithm

Loop Body Reduces Measure

$\{\text{length}(r \Rightarrow_{tl} \text{nil}) < vt\}$
$q := r$; $r := r.tl$; $q.tl := p$; $p := q$

   [substitution]

$\{\text{length}(r.tl \Rightarrow_{tl \oplus r \mapsto p} \text{nil}) < vt\}$

   [use $r \neq \text{nil}$ and $\text{list}(r \Rightarrow_{tl} \text{nil})$ from precondition to obtain $r \pitchfork r.tl \Rightarrow_{tl} \text{nil}$;
   thence $r.tl \Rightarrow_{tl \oplus r \mapsto p} \text{nil} = r.tl \Rightarrow_{tl} \text{nil}$; then straightforward sequence calculation]

$\begin{bmatrix} \text{list}(p \Rightarrow_{tl} \text{nil}) \wedge \text{list}(r \Rightarrow_{tl} \text{nil}) \wedge p \Rightarrow_{tl} \text{nil} \pitchfork r \Rightarrow_{tl} \text{nil} \wedge \\ \text{rev}(r \Rightarrow_{tl} \text{nil}) \,@\, p \Rightarrow_{tl} \text{nil} = \text{rev } S \wedge r \neq \text{nil} \wedge \text{length}(r \Rightarrow_{tl} \text{nil}) = vt \end{bmatrix}$

The While Loop

$\{P\}$ while $r \neq \text{nil}$ do $q := r$; $r := r.tl$; $q.tl := p$; $p := q$ od $\{R\}$

Not shown: it appeals to the invariant and measure proofs above, and is otherwise straightforward sequence calculation.

The Whole Algorithm

$\{Q\}$ $r := p$; $p := \text{nil}$; while $r \neq \text{nil}$ do $q := r$; $r := r.tl$; $q.tl := p$; $p := q$ od $\{R\}$

Trivial, given the previous proofs.

10   An Illustration: In-Place List Merge

The proof of in-place list reversal above is no advance on Burstall's version [6]. In-place list merge (fig. 11) is a more challenging problem, because it works at the tail end of a list. The tests in the program are designed to avoid traversal of nil pointers: $A \vee\!\!\!\!\vee B$ is equivalent to (if A then true else B fi); $A \wedge\!\!\!\wedge B$ is equivalent to (if A then B else false fi).

The program is given two disjoint ordered tl-linked nil-terminated lists via pointers p and q, at least one of which is not empty.

$$Q \triangleq \left(\begin{array}{l} p \Rightarrow_{tl} \text{nil} = SP \wedge q \Rightarrow_{tl} \text{nil} = SQ \wedge \text{olist}_{hd}\left(p \Rightarrow_{tl} \text{nil}\right) \wedge \text{olist}_{hd}\left(q \Rightarrow_{tl} \text{nil}\right) \wedge \\ p \Rightarrow_{tl} \text{nil} \pitchfork q \Rightarrow_{tl} \text{nil} \wedge (p \neq \text{nil} \vee q \neq \text{nil}) \end{array} \right)$$

Writing $A \Rightarrow_f^+ B$ for $A \Rightarrow_f B @ \langle B \rangle$, the invariant states that we can put the list fragment $r \Rightarrow_{tl}^+ s$ before either the p list or the q list to produce an ordered result; that fragment joined with the two lists is a permutation of the original input; and the p and q lists remain disjoint. In order to prove that the result on termination is what we wish, it also has to assert the non-occurrence of nil in the fragment $r \Rightarrow_{tl}^+ s$ and a linkage between the s object and the one or other of the lists.

$$P \triangleq \left(\begin{array}{l} \text{olist}_{hd}\left(r \Rightarrow_{tl}^+ s @ p \Rightarrow \text{nil}\right) \wedge \text{olist}_{hd}\left(r \Rightarrow_{tl}^+ s @ q \Rightarrow \text{nil}\right) \wedge \\ \text{perm}\left(r \Rightarrow_{tl}^+ s @ p \Rightarrow \text{nil} @ q \Rightarrow \text{nil}, SP @ SQ\right) \wedge \\ p \Rightarrow \text{nil} \pitchfork q \Rightarrow \text{nil} \wedge \text{nil} \notin r \Rightarrow_{tl}^+ s \wedge (s.tl = p \vee s.tl = q) \end{array} \right)$$

The measure is the sum of the lengths of the p and q lists.

$t \triangleq \text{length}(p \Rightarrow_{tl} \text{nil} @ q \Rightarrow_{tl} \text{nil})$

On termination r points to an ordered tl-linked nil-terminated list which is a permutation of the original input.

$R \triangleq \text{olist}_{hd}\left(r \Rightarrow_{tl} \text{nil}\right) \wedge \text{perm}\left(r \Rightarrow_{tl} \text{nil}, SP @ SQ\right)$

Problems arise during the proof in showing and exploiting spatial separation between the input lists $p \Rightarrow_{tl} \text{nil}$ and $q \Rightarrow_{tl} \text{nil}$ on the one hand, and the list fragment $r \Rightarrow_{tl}^+ s$ on the other. For example, moving the invariant backward through the sequence $s.tl := p; \ p := p.tl; \ s := s.tl$ – the course of the loop, given that the guard in the if-then-else-fi is true – produces several instances of the fearsome formula $r \Rightarrow_{tl \oplus s \mapsto p}^+ p$. Given

$\text{list}\left(r \Rightarrow_{tl}^+ s\right), \ p \neq \text{nil}, \ p \notin r \Rightarrow_{tl}^+ s$

– each of which is implied by the invariant plus the if guard – then a bit of finite expansion, plus the fact that

$A \Rightarrow_{f \oplus B \mapsto E}^+ B = A \Rightarrow_f^+ B$

makes it possible to show that

$r \Rightarrow_{tl \oplus s \mapsto p}^+ p = r \Rightarrow_{tl}^+ s @ \langle p \rangle$

The rest of the proof is straightforward manipulation.

11   An Illustration: Graph Marking

The Schorr-Waite algorithm is the first mountain that any formalism for pointer aliasing should climb. It's dealt with semi-formally by Morris [21] and mechanically by Suzuki [27]; Kowaltowski [17] gives a wonderful informal proof in pictures of a

$\{Q\}$

$t := root; \ p := \text{nil}$

$\{P\}$

while $p \neq \text{nil} \vee (t \neq \text{nil} \wedge \neg t.m)$ do

   if $t = \text{nil} \vee t.m$ then

     if $p.c$ then

       $q := t; \ t := p; \ p := p.r; \ t.r := q$ /* POP */

     else

       $q := t; \ t := p.r; \ p.r := p.l; \ p.l := q; \ p.c := \text{true}$ /* SWING */

     fi

   else

     $q := p; \ p := t; \ t := t.l; \ p.l := q; \ p.m := \text{true}; \ p.c := \text{false}$ /* PUSH */

   fi

od

$\{R\}$

Fig. 12. The Schorr-Waite graph-marking algorithm

tree-marking variant. Morris's version of the algorithm, modified to permit nil pointers, is shown in fig. 12.

Definitions. The stack starting at A:

$$A\!\uparrow_{l,r,c} \ \hat{=} \ \text{if } A = \text{nil then } \langle\,\rangle \text{ else } \langle A \rangle \ @ \left(\text{if } A.c \text{ then } A.r \text{ else } A.l \text{ fi}\!\uparrow_{l,r,c} \right) \text{ fi}$$

The binary DAG reachable from A but containing none of the objects in set S:

$$A*_{l,r,S} = \text{if } A = \text{nil} \vee A \in S \text{ then } (\,) \text{ else } \left(A, A.l*_{l,r,S\cup\{A\}}, A.r*_{l,r,S\cup\{A\}} \right) \text{ fi}$$

The binary DAG reachable from A which contains only unmarked nodes and none of the objects in set S:

$$A**_{l,r,m,S} \ \hat{=} \ \begin{pmatrix} \text{if } A = \text{nil} \vee A \in S \vee A.m \text{ then } (\,) \\ \text{else } \left(A, A.l**_{l,r,m,S\cup\{A\}}, A.r**_{l,r,m,S\cup\{A\}} \right) \text{ fi} \end{pmatrix}$$

Two sequences zipped together:

$$\langle\,\rangle \, ||| \, S \ \hat{=} \ \langle\,\rangle \qquad\qquad R \, ||| \, \langle\,\rangle \ \hat{=} \ \langle\,\rangle$$

$$(\langle A \rangle \ @ \ R) \, ||| \, (\langle B \rangle \ @ \ S) \ \hat{=} \ \langle (A, B) \rangle \ @ \left(R \, ||| \, S \right)$$

Converting sequences and DAGs to sets:

$$\text{set}\langle\,\rangle \ \hat{=} \ \{\,\} \qquad\qquad\qquad \text{set}(\,) \ \hat{=} \ \{\,\}$$

$$\text{set}\langle A \rangle \ \hat{=} \ \{A\} \qquad\qquad\quad \text{set}(A, T1, T2) \ \hat{=} \ \{A\} \cup \text{set } T1 \cup \text{set } T2$$

$$\text{set}(R \ @ \ S) \ \hat{=} \ \text{set } R \cup \text{set } S$$

Specification. The graph reachable from the root is iG. The whole of the heap is unmarked. Initial values of the control-bit mapping, the left and right subnode mappings, are iC, iL and iR.

$$Q \mathrel{\hat{=}} root^{*}_{l,r,\{\}} = iG \wedge \forall x: \neg x.m \wedge c = iC \wedge l = iL \wedge r = iR$$

Throughout the marking process the stack p is a list, and every node on the stack is marked. Every node in the original graph is reachable from the tip t and/or the stack. Unmarked nodes in the graph are reachable from the tip and/or the right sub-nodes of elements of the stack. If a node is marked then it's in the graph; if it's not marked then its control bit is unchanged; if it's not on the stack then its left and right components are as they were originally. If a node is on the stack then we can reconstruct its left and right components by considering its predecessor node and its control bit.

$$P \mathrel{\hat{=}} \forall x: \begin{pmatrix} list\!\left(p\!\uparrow_{l,r,c}\right) \wedge \forall x:\!\left(x \in set\!\left(p\!\uparrow_{l,r,c}\right) \to x.m\right) \wedge \\[4pt] set\!\left(t^{*}_{l,r,\{\}}\right) \cup set\!\left(p^{*}_{l,r,\{\}}\right) = set\,iG \wedge \forall x:\!\left(x.m \to x \in set\,iG\right) \wedge \\[4pt] \forall x:\!\begin{pmatrix} x \in set\,iG \wedge \neg x.m \to \\ x \in \left(set\!\left(t^{**}_{l,r,m,\{\}}\right) \cup \bigcup\!\left\{ set\!\left(y.r^{**}_{l,r,m,\{\}}\right) \,\middle|\, x \in set\!\left(p\!\uparrow_{l,r,c}\right)\right\}\right) \end{pmatrix} \wedge \\[4pt] \forall x:\!\left(\left(\neg x.m \to x.c = x.iC\right) \wedge \left(x \notin p\!\uparrow_{l,r,c} \to x.l = x.iL \wedge x.r = x.iR\right)\right) \wedge \\[4pt] \forall x,y:\!\begin{pmatrix} (x,y) \in \left(p\!\uparrow_{l,r,c} \,\middle|\!\middle|\!\middle|\, \left(\langle t\rangle @\, p\!\uparrow_{l,r,c}\right)\right) \to \\ \text{if } x.c \text{ then } x.l = x.iL \wedge y = x.iR \text{ else } y = x.iL \wedge x.r = x.iR \text{ fi} \end{pmatrix} \end{pmatrix}$$

The measure of the loop is a triple of the number of unmarked nodes in the graph, the number of nodes on the stack with control bit set to true, and the length of the stack.

On termination all and only the original graph is marked. Unmarked nodes have an unchanged control bit, and the left and right components are as they were on input.

$$R \mathrel{\hat{=}} \forall x:\!\left(\left(x.m \leftrightarrow x \in set\,iG\right) \wedge \left(\neg x.m \to x.c = x.iC\right) \wedge x.l = x.iL \wedge x.r = x.iR\right)$$

Proof. DAGs based on the definitions above are finite height, given a finite heap (provable by induction on the difference between the restriction set S and the heap). That permits inductive proof of all kinds of interesting equivalences, including, for example

$$B \in S \to \left(A^{**}_{l \oplus B \mapsto E, r, m, S} = A^{**}_{l, r, m, S}\right)$$

$$T \subseteq S \to \left(A^{*}_{l,r,m,S} \cup B^{*}_{l,r,m,T} = A^{*}_{l,r,m,S \cup \{B\}} \cup B^{*}_{l,r,m,T}\right)$$

$$E \to \left(A^{**}_{l,r,m \oplus B \mapsto E, S} = A^{**}_{l,r,m,S \cup \{B\}}\right)$$

The marvellous character of the algorithm is not that it reaches every node – a simple recursion would do that – but that it does so without using a stack, modifying nodes it has passed through and – most marvellously of all – restoring them afterwards. Corresponding parts of the proof are large. We have to prove in the SWING arm, for example, that

$$p \neq nil, \quad \neg p.c, \quad \forall x:\left(x \in set\left(p\uparrow_{l,r,c}\right) \to x.m\right), \quad list\left(p.l\uparrow_{l,r,c}\right), \quad \langle p \rangle \pitchfork p.l\uparrow_{l,r,c},$$

$$\forall x:\left(\begin{array}{l} \left(\neg x.m \to x.c = x.iC\right) \wedge \left(x \notin set\left(p\uparrow_{l,r,c}\right) \to \left(x.l = x.iL \wedge x.r = x.iR\right)\right) \wedge \\ \forall y:\left(\begin{array}{l} (x,y) \in set\left(p\uparrow_{l,r,c} ||| \left(\langle t \rangle @ p\uparrow_{l,r,c}\right)\right) \to \\ \text{if } x.c \text{ then } x.l = x.iL \wedge y = x.iR \text{ else } y = x.iL \wedge x.r = x.iR \text{ fi} \end{array}\right) \end{array}\right)$$

$$\vdash \forall x:\left(\begin{array}{l} \left(\neg x.m \to x.(c \oplus p \mapsto \text{true}) = x.iC\right) \wedge \\ \left(\begin{array}{l} x \notin set\left(p\uparrow_{l,r,c}\right) \to \\ \left(x.(l \oplus p \mapsto t) = x.iL \wedge x.(r \oplus p \mapsto p.l) = x.iR\right) \end{array}\right) \wedge \\ \forall y:\left(\begin{array}{l} (x,y) \in set\left(p\uparrow_{l,r,c} ||| \left(\langle p.r \rangle @ p\uparrow_{l,r,c}\right)\right) \to \\ \left(\begin{array}{l} \text{if } x.(c \oplus p \mapsto \text{true}) \text{ then } x.(l \oplus p \mapsto t) = x.iL \wedge y = x.iR \\ \text{else } y = x.iL \wedge x.(r \oplus p \mapsto p.l) = x.iR \text{ fi} \end{array}\right) \end{array}\right) \end{array}\right)$$

It's for the most part straightforward, but it's tedious manipulation. In Burstall's phrase, a great deal of work for such a simple matter.

From the DAG definition it's possible to prove that

$$t*_{l,r,S \cup \{p\}} \cup p*_{l,r,S} = t*_{l,r,S} \cup p*_{l,r,S} = t*_{l,r,S} \cup p*_{l,r,S \cup \{t\}}$$

That gives enough spatial separation to make it easy to prove that the nodes of the original graph are always reachable. It's a little harder to show that the unmarked nodes are always directly reachable: we have to show when dealing with the PUSH arm, for example, that

$$t \neq nil, \neg t.m, list\left(p\uparrow_{l,r,c}\right),$$

$$\forall x:\left(\begin{array}{l} x \in set\, iG \wedge \neg x.m \to \\ x \in \left(set\left(t**_{l,r,m,\{\}}\right) \cup \bigcup\left\{ set\left(y.r**_{l,r,m,\{\}}\right) \mid x \in p\uparrow_{l,r,c} \right\}\right) \end{array}\right)$$

$$\vdash \forall x:\left(\begin{array}{l} x \in set\, iG \wedge \neg x.(m \oplus t \mapsto \text{true}) \to \\ x \in \left(\begin{array}{l} set\left(t.l**_{l \oplus t \mapsto p,r,m \oplus t \mapsto true,\{\}}\right) \cup \\ \bigcup\left\{ set\left(y.r**_{l \oplus t \mapsto p,r,m \oplus t \mapsto true,\{\}}\right) \mid x \in p\uparrow_{l \oplus t \mapsto p,r,c} \right\} \end{array}\right) \end{array}\right)$$

The proof that the stack is invariantly a list sometimes has to deal with some superficially frightening formulæ. The SWING arm, for example, generates

$$p\uparrow_{l \oplus p \mapsto t, r \oplus p \mapsto p.l, c \oplus p \mapsto true}$$

but, with a single step of expansion, plus $p.c$ from the guard and $p \neq nil$ and $list\left(p\uparrow_{l,r,c}\right)$ from the invariant, this simplifies to $p\uparrow_{l,r,c}$.

12 Conclusion

Burstall showed a way towards practical proofs of pointer programs which relatively few have followed. This paper shows that it is possible to reason in Hoare logic about small but moderately complicated pointer programs, using the principle of spatial separation and whatever data structure and other auxiliary definitions suit the problem.

Burstall's DNLRS mechanism achieved local reasoning by restricting itself to particular data structures and particular problems. The treatment of general data structures in this paper doesn't yet approach the elegance of his solution: it substitutes first, tidies up second, and remains rather low-level. To make it more elegant and more practically useful, it will be necessary to make the substitution mechanism mimic the locality of assignment, dealing only with genuine potential aliases and ignoring those which can be dealt with by spatial separation assumptions. If we can do this for a wide range of problems, building on a relatively small collection of data structure inductions, this goal may perhaps be reached.

Acknowledgements. This work springs from discussions with (in temporal order) Keith Clarke, Peter O'Hearn, Dave Streader, Stefano Guerrini, Samin Ishtiaq, Hayo Thielecke, Edmund Robinson and Cristiano Calgagno[1] at QMW, fuelled by the QMW Verified Bytecode project [EPSRC GR/L54578]. Tony Hoare first pointed me to Morris's work, and John Reynolds emphasised the importance of Burstall's. Uday Reddy and Richard Bird impressed upon me the usefulness of the component-as-array trick. Jape is a joint effort with Bernard Sufrin, and the developments which support the Jape-rendered proofs in this document arose out of discussions between us.

References

[1] Appel A.W., Felty A.P.: A Semantic Model of Types and Machine Instructions for Proof-Carrying Code 27th ACM SIGPLAN-SIGACT Symposium on Principles of Programming Languages (POPL '00), pp. 243-253, January 2000.

[2] Arnold K., Gosling, J.: The Java programming language. Addison-Wesley, 1997.

[3] Bijlsma A.: Calculating with Pointers. Science of Computer Programming **12** (1989) 191-205

[4] Bornat R., Machine-checked proofs of list reversal, list merge, Schorr-Waite. Available from http://www.dcs.qmw.ac.uk/~richard/pointers

[5] Bornat R., Sufrin B.A.: Animating formal proof at the surface: the Jape proof calculator. The Computer Journal, 43, 3, 1999, 177-192.

[6] Burstall R.M.: Some techniques for proving correctness of programs which alter data structures. Machine Intelligence 7, D. Michie (ed), American Elsevier, 1972, 23-50.

[7] Cousot P.: Methods and Logics for Proving Programs. In Formal Models and Semantics, J. van Leeuwen (ed.); Volume B of Handbook of Theoretical Computer Science. Elsevier (1990) 843--993

---

[1] Calcagno was on loan from Genova.

[8]   Floyd R.W.: Assigning meaning to programs. Proc. Symp. in App. Math., American Mathematical Society, Vol.19, 1967, 19-32.

[9]   Gries D.: The Schorr-Waite graph marking algorithm. Acta Informatica Vol 11, 1979, 223-232.

[10] Gries D., Levin G.M.: Assignment and procedure call proof rules. ACM Transactions on Programming Languages and Systems 2 (1980) 564-579

[11] Hoare C.A.R.: An axiomatic basis for computer programming, Comm. ACM Vol 12, no 10, 1969, 576-580 and 583.

[12] Hoare C.A.R., Jifeng H.: A Trace Model for Pointers and Objects. Object-Oriented Programming 13th European Conference (ECOOP '99), Lecture Notes in Computer Science, Vol. 1628. Springer Verlag (1999) 1-17

[13] Hoare C.A.R., Wirth N.: An Axiomatic Definition of the Programming Language Pascal. Acta Informatica 2 (1973) 335-355

[14] Jensen K., Wirth N.: Pascal user manual and report. Springer-Verlag (1975)

[15] Kernighan B.W., Ritchie D.M.: The C programming language. Prentice-Hall (1978)

[16] Kowaltowski T.: Data Structures and Correctness of Programs. Journal of the ACM 2, (1979) 283-301

[17] Kowaltowski T.: Examples of Informal but Rigorous Correctness Proofs for Tree Traversing Algorithms. Technical report TR-DCC-92-10, University of Campinas, Brazil.

[18] Leino R.: Toward Reliable Modular Programs. PhD Thesis, California Institute of Technology (1995)

[19] Luckham D.C., Suzuki N.: Verification of Array, Record, and Pointer Operations in Pascal. ACM Transactions on Programming Languages and Systems, Examples of Informal but Rigorous Correctness Proofs for Tree Traversing Algorithms 1 (1979),226-244

[20] McCarthy J., Painter J.A.: Correctness of a Compiler for Arithmetic Expressions. Proceedings Symposium in Applied Mathematics, Mathematical Aspects of Computer Science 19 (1967) 33-41

[21] Morris J.M. A general axiom of assignment. Assignment and linked data structure. A proof of the Schorr-Waite algorithm. In: Theoretical Foundations of Programming Methodology (Proceedings of the 1981 Marktoberdorf Summer School), M Broy and G. Schmidt (eds.) , Reidel (1982) 25-51

[22] Necula G. and Lee P.: Safe, Untrusted Agents using Proof-Carrying Code. Mobile Agents and Security, Lecture Notes in Computer Science, Vol. 1419. Springer-Verlag (1998) 61-91

[23] Reynolds J.C.: The Craft of Programming. Prentice-Hall International (1981)

[24] Reynolds J.C.: Reasoning about Shared Mutable Data Structure, given at the symposium in celebration of the work of C.A.R. Hoare, Oxford, September 1999.

[25] Schorr H., Waite W.M.: An efficient machine-independent procedure for garbage collection in various list structures. Comm. ACM 10 (1967) 501-506

[26] Strachey C.: Towards a Formal Semantics. In: Formal Language Description Languages for Computer Programming, T.B. Steel Jr (ed). North-Holland (1964).

[27] Suzuki N.: Automatic verification of programs with complex data structure. PhD Thesis, Stanford U (1976)

[28] Topor R.W.: The correctness of the Schorr-Waite list marking algorithm. Acta Informatica 11 (1979) 211-221

On Guarded Commands with Fair Choice

Emil Sekerinski

McMaster University
Hamilton, Ontario L8S 4L7, Canada,
emil@mcmaster.ca

Abstract. For the purpose of program development, fairness is typically formalized by verification rules or, alternatively, through refinement rules. In this paper we give an account of (weak) fairness in an algebraic style, extending recently proposed algebraic accounts of iterations and loops using the predicate transformer model of statements.

1 Introduction

The nondeterministic choice known from Dijkstra's guarded commands allows an arbitrary selection to be made each time it is encountered, giving implementations maximal freedom. Alternatively, we can assume that a certain degree of fairness is exercised for repeated choices, a useful assumption for modeling concurrent systems. For the purpose of program development, fairness has been formalized by verification rules, for example in [9,8]. More recently, fairness has been formally treated through refinement rules [5,14].

The goal of this paper is to give an account of fairness in an algebraic style. Doing so, we follow and extend the algebraic accounts of various forms of iterations and of loops in particular [4], which has been used to derive transformation rules for program development techniques like data refinement, atomicity refinement, reordering, and others. Our contribution is to define (weak) fairness algebraically and to derive elementary refinement and verification rules, using predicate transformers as the model of statements.

The next section introduces the basic statements in the predicate transformer model and extends the discussion to various forms of iteration statements defined by fixed points. Section 3 introduced fair choice and gives basic theorems supporting the definition. Section 4 gives the fundamental loop theorem for loops with a fair choice. We conclude with some remarks in Section 5.

2 Statements

We assume the reader is familiar with the principles of weakest precondition semantics and program refinement [2,10,11]. Here we briefly review the fundamentals of statements defined by predicate transformers, following the treatment of [3], using typed, higher-order logic. The iteration statements are based on [1,7] and in particular on [4].

R. Backhouse and J. N. Oliveira (Eds.): MPC 2000, LNCS 1837, pp. 127–139, 2000.
© Springer-Verlag Berlin Heidelberg 2000

State Predicates. State predicates of type $\mathcal{P}\Sigma$ are functions from elements of type Σ to *Bool*, i.e. $\mathcal{P}\Sigma = \Sigma \rightarrow Bool$. On state predicates, conjunction $\wedge$, disjunction $\vee$, implication $\Rightarrow$, and negation $\neg$ are defined by the pointwise extension of the corresponding operations on *Bool*. Likewise, universal and existential quantification of $p_i : \mathcal{P}\Sigma$ are defined by:

$$(\forall i \in I \bullet p_i)\,\sigma \quad \widehat{=} \quad (\forall i \in I \bullet p_i\,\sigma)$$
$$(\exists i \in I \bullet p_i)\,\sigma \quad \widehat{=} \quad (\exists i \in I \bullet p_i\,\sigma)$$

The entailment ordering $\leq$ is defined by universal implication. The state predicates *true* and *false* represent the universally true and false predicates, respectively.

Predicate Transformers. Following Dijkstra, statements are defined by predicate transformers. As only their input-output behavior is of our interest, we identify a statement with its predicate transformer, i.e. we write $S\,p$ rather than $wp(S, p)$. Formally, predicate transformers of type $\Delta \mapsto \Omega$ are functions from predicates over Ω (the postconditions) to predicates over Δ (the preconditions), $\Delta \mapsto \Omega = \mathcal{P}\Omega \rightarrow \mathcal{P}\Delta$. A predicate transformers S is called monotonic if it satisfies $p \leq q \Rightarrow S\,p \leq S\,q$ for any (state) predicates p and q. We use monotonic predicate transformers to model statements.

The sequential composition of predicate transformers S and T is defined by their functional composition:

$$(S; T)\,q \quad \widehat{=} \quad S\,(T\,q)$$

The guard $[p]$ skips if p holds and establishes "miraculously" any postcondition if p does not hold (by blocking execution). The assertion $\{p\}$ skips if p holds and establishes no postcondition if p does not hold (the system crashes):

$$[p]\,q \quad \widehat{=} \quad p \Rightarrow q$$
$$\{p\}\,q \quad \widehat{=} \quad p \wedge q$$

We define *skip* $= [true] = \{true\}$ as the identity predicate transformer, *magic* $= [false]$ as the predicate transformer which always establishes any postcondition, and *abort* $= \{false\}$ as the predicate transformer which always aborts.

The demonic (nondeterministic) choice $\sqcap$ establishes a postcondition only if both alternatives do. The angelic choice $\sqcup$ establishes a certain postcondition if at least one alternative does.

$$(S \sqcap T)\,q \quad \widehat{=} \quad S\,q \wedge T\,q$$
$$(S \sqcup T)\,q \quad \widehat{=} \quad S\,q \vee T\,q$$

Relations of type $\Delta \leftrightarrow \Omega$ are functions from Δ to predicates over Ω. The relational updates $[R]$ and $\{R\}$ both update the state according to relation R. If several final states are possible, then $[R]$ chooses one demonically and $\{R\}$ chooses one angelically. If R is of type $\Delta \leftrightarrow \Omega$, then $[R]$ and $\{R\}$ are of type $\Delta \mapsto \Omega$:

$$[R]\,q\,\delta \quad \widehat{=} \quad (\forall \omega \bullet R\,\delta\,\omega \Rightarrow q\,\omega)$$
$$\{R\}\,q\,\delta \quad \widehat{=} \quad (\exists \omega \bullet R\,\delta\,\omega \wedge q\,\omega)$$

The predicate transformers $[p]$, $\{p\}$, $[R]$, $\{R\}$ are all monotonic and the operators $;$, $\sqcap$, $\sqcup$ preserve monotonicity.

Other statements can be defined in terms of the above ones. For example the guarded statement $p \rightarrow S$ is defined by $[p]; S$ and the conditional by:

$$\text{if } p \text{ then } S \text{ else } T \quad \hat{=} \quad (p \rightarrow S) \sqcap (\neg p \rightarrow T)$$

The enabledness domain (guard) of a statement S is denoted by $grd\, S = \neg S\, false$ and its termination domain by $trm\, S = S\, true$. We have that:

$$grd\, (S \sqcap T) \quad = \quad grd\, S \vee grd\, T \tag{1}$$

$$grd\, T = true \quad \Rightarrow \quad grd\, (S;\, T) = grd\, S \tag{2}$$

Program Variables. Typically the state space is made up of a number of program variables. Thus the state space is of the form $\Gamma_1 \times \ldots \times \Gamma_n$. States are tuples $(x_1, \ldots, x_n)$. The variable names serve for selecting components of the state. For example, if $x : \Gamma$ and $y : \Delta$ are the only program variables, then the assignment $x := e$ updates x and leaves y unchanged:

$$x := e \quad \hat{=} \quad [R] \quad \text{where} \quad R\, (x, y)\, (x', y') = (x' = e) \wedge (y' = y)$$

Refinement Ordering. The refinement ordering $\sqsubseteq$ is defined by universal entailment:

$$S \sqsubseteq T \quad \hat{=} \quad (\forall q \bullet S\, q \leq T\, q)$$

With this ordering, the monotonic predicate transformers form a complete boolean lattice, with top *magic*, bottom *abort*, meet $\sqcap$, and join $\sqcup$. Hence any monotonic function f from predicate transformers to predicate transformers has a unique least fixed point $\mu\, f$ and a unique greatest fixed point $\nu\, f$, also written as $\mu\, x \bullet f\, x$ and $\nu\, s \bullet f\, s$, respectively.

Iterations. Iteration of a statement S is described through solutions of the equation $X = S; X \sqcap skip$. More precisely, we define two fundamental iteration constructs, the strong iteration S^ω and the weak iteration S^*. We use the convention that $;$ binds tighter than $\sqcap$:

$$S^\omega \quad \hat{=} \quad (\mu\, X \bullet S; X \sqcap skip) \tag{3}$$

$$S^* \quad \hat{=} \quad (\nu\, X \bullet S; X \sqcap skip) \tag{4}$$

Both define a demonically chosen number of repetitions of S. However, with S^* the number of repetitions is always finite whereas with S^ω it can be infinite, which is equivalent to abortion. For example, if S is $a := a+1$, then the equation $X = a := a+1; X \sqcap skip$ has two solutions, *abort* and $skip \sqcap a := a+1 \sqcap a := a+2 \sqcap \ldots$. The least solution is given by their demonic choice. As *abort* $\sqcap\, Q = abort$ for any Q, we have that $(a := a + 1)^\omega = abort$. The greatest solution is given by their angelic choice. As *abort* $\sqcup\, Q = Q$ for any Q, we have that $(a := a + 1)^* = skip \sqcap a := a+1 \sqcap a := a+2 \sqcap \ldots$.

From the fixed point definitions we get the following laws for unfolding iterations:

$$S^\omega \quad = \quad S; S^\omega \sqcap skip \qquad (5)$$
$$S^* \quad = \quad S; S^* \sqcap skip \qquad (6)$$

Both weak and strong iteration are monotonic in the sense that $S \sqsubseteq T$ implies $S^\omega \sqsubseteq T^\omega$ and $S^* \sqsubseteq T^*$. Both S^ω and S^* are refined by S itself:

$$S^\omega \quad \sqsubseteq \quad S \qquad (7)$$
$$S^* \quad \sqsubseteq \quad S \qquad (8)$$

Furthermore, from the two unfolding laws we get immediately (as $S = T \sqcap U$ implies $S \sqsubseteq T$ for any S, T) that both are refined by $skip$:

$$S^\omega \quad \sqsubseteq \quad skip \qquad (9)$$
$$S^* \quad \sqsubseteq \quad skip \qquad (10)$$

For the nested application of weak and strong iteration we have:

$$(S^\omega)^* \quad \sqsubseteq \quad S^\omega \qquad (11)$$
$$(S^*)^* \quad \sqsubseteq \quad S^* \qquad (12)$$

However, we note that $(S^\omega)^\omega = abort$ and $(S^*)^\omega = abort$. Intuitively, the inner iteration is refined by $skip$, which then makes $skip^\omega = abort$.

We introduce a derived iteration construct, the positive weak iteration S^+:

$$S^+ \quad = \quad S; S^*$$

Positive weak iteration is also monotonic in the sense that $S \sqsubseteq T$ implies $S^+ \sqsubseteq T^+$, which follows from the monotonicity of weak iteration and sequential composition (in both arguments). Furthermore, S^+ is refined by S itself:

$$S^+ \quad \sqsubseteq \quad S \qquad (13)$$

This follows from the definition of S^+ and (10). Weak iteration can also be defined in terms of positive weak iteration:

$$S^* \quad = \quad S^+ \sqcap skip \qquad (14)$$

This follows immediately from the unfolding law (6) and the definition of S^+. A consequence of this is that S^* is refined by S^+:

$$S^* \quad \sqsubseteq \quad S^+ \qquad (15)$$

For the nested applications of positive weak iterations with weak iteration and strong iteration we get:

$$(S^+)^* \quad = \quad S^* \qquad (16)$$
$$(S^+)^\omega \quad = \quad S^\omega \qquad (17)$$

We show the first one by mutual refinement: $(S^+)^* \sqsubseteq S^*$ holds by (13) and monotonicity of weak iteration. For the refinement $S^* \sqsubseteq (S^+)^*$ we note that the left side is equal to $(S^*)^*$ by (12), hence this is implied by (15).

For the guards of the iteration constructs we get:

$$grd\ S^\omega \quad = \quad true \tag{18}$$
$$grd\ S^* \quad = \quad true \tag{19}$$
$$grd\ S^+ \quad = \quad grd\ S \tag{20}$$

The first two follow immediately from the unfolding laws (5) and 6) as $grd\ skip = true$. The last one follows easily from the definition of S^+, (19) and (2).

The loop **do** S **od** executes its body as long as it is enabled, possibly not terminating (i.e. aborting). This is formally expressed as a strong iteration, followed by a guard statement which ensures that the guard of the body will not hold at exit:

$$\textbf{do}\ S\ \textbf{od} \quad \hat{=} \quad S^\omega; [\neg\ grd\ S]$$

The while loop **while** b **do** S can then be defined as **do** $b \to S$ **od**, provided S is always enabled.

3   Fair Choice

Fairness is associated with the process of repeated selection between alternatives; we restrict our attention to two alternative statements, say S and T, in loops of the form **do** $S \diamond T$ **od**: if S or T is continuously enabled, respectively, it will be eventually taken, a criterion known as *weak fairness* (e.g. [9]). By contrast, in the loop **do** $S \sqcap T$ **od** on each iteration an arbitrary choice between S and T is made.

Following the spirit of the approach, we define the fair choice $S \diamond T$ in isolation, such that the meaning of **do** $S \diamond T$ **od** is defined in a compositional manner. First we introduce an operator $\bar{S}$, read "try S", for a predicate transformer S. If S is enabled, $\bar{S}$ behaves as S, otherwise as *skip*:

$$\bar{S} \quad \hat{=} \quad S \sqcap [\neg\ grd\ S]$$

In the fair choice between S and T we may take S or T arbitrary but finitely often, such that we can give T and S a chance, respectively. We express this in terms of positive weak iterations:

$$S \diamond T \quad \hat{=} \quad S^+; \bar{T} \sqcap T^+; \bar{S}$$

We now consider the construct $S \lhd T$ which guarantees fairness only for S, and dually the construct $S \rhd T$ which guarantees fairness only for T:

$$S \lhd T \quad \hat{=} \quad S^+ \sqcap (T^+; \bar{S})$$
$$S \rhd T \quad \hat{=} \quad (S^+; \bar{T}) \sqcap T^+$$

For reasons of symmetry, we continue only with $S \lhd T$. We state some facts about these operators for supporting our confidence. To this end, we introduce one further operator, $S \Box T$, for the repeated execution of either S or T:

$$S \Box T \quad \hat{=} \quad S^+ \sqcap T^+$$

We notice that $S \Diamond T$, $S \lhd T$, and $S \Box T$ are enabled if either T is enabled or S is enabled:

$$grd\ (S \Diamond T) \quad = \quad grd\ S \vee grd\ T \tag{21}$$
$$grd\ (S \lhd T) \quad = \quad grd\ S \vee grd\ T \tag{22}$$
$$grd\ (S \Box T) \quad = \quad grd\ S \vee grd\ T \tag{23}$$

We prove only the first of these claims as the proofs of the others are similar:

$$grd\ (S \Diamond T)$$
$$= \quad \langle \text{Definition of } \Diamond \rangle$$
$$grd\ (S^+; \bar{T} \sqcap T^+; \bar{S})$$
$$= \quad \langle (1), \text{definition of } S^+ \rangle$$
$$grd\ (S; S^*; \bar{T}) \vee grd\ (T; T^*; \bar{S})$$
$$= \quad \langle grd\ \bar{S} = true \text{ for any } S, (2), (19) \rangle$$
$$grd\ S \vee grd\ T$$

In a loop containing the alternatives S and T, there is no difference whether they are executed exactly once at each iteration, or several times:

Theorem 1. *Let S and T be monotonic predicate transformers. Then:*

$$\textbf{do } S \sqcap T \textbf{ od} \quad = \quad \textbf{do } S \Box T \textbf{ od}$$

Proof. According to the definition of **do S od** we have to show:

$$(S \sqcap T)^\omega; [\neg\ grd\ (S \sqcap T)] \quad = \quad (S \Box T)^\omega; [\neg\ grd\ (S \Box T)]$$

By (1) and (23) we have that $grd\ (S \sqcap T) = grd\ S \vee grd\ T = grd\ (S \Box T)$. Hence it is sufficient to show that $(S \sqcap T)^\omega = (S \Box T)^\omega$ which, by the definition of $\Box$, is equivalent to $(S \sqcap T)^\omega = (S^+ \sqcap T^+)^\omega$. We show this by mutual refinement:

$$(S \sqcap T)^\omega \sqsubseteq (S^+ \sqcap T^+)^\omega$$
$$= \quad \langle (17) \rangle$$
$$((S \sqcap T)^+)^\omega \sqsubseteq (S^+ \sqcap T^+)^\omega$$
$$\Leftarrow \quad \langle \text{monotonicity of } S^\omega \rangle$$
$$(S \sqcap T)^+ \sqsubseteq S^+ \sqcap T^+$$
$$= \quad \langle \text{lattice property} \rangle$$
$$((S \sqcap T)^+ \sqsubseteq S^+) \wedge ((S \sqcap T)^+ \sqsubseteq T^+)$$
$$\Leftarrow \quad \langle \text{monotonicity of } S^+ \rangle$$
$$(S \sqcap T \sqsubseteq S) \wedge (S \sqcap T \sqsubseteq T)$$

The last line follows from the lattice structure. The reverse refinement $(S^+ \sqcap T^+)^\omega \sqsubseteq (S \sqcap T)^\omega$ follows immediately from (13) and the monotonicity of strong iteration.

A loop with a demonic choice between two alternatives is refined by the same loop with a choice which is fair to one of the alternatives:

Theorem 2. *Let S and T be monotonic predicate transformers. Then:*

$$\textbf{do } S \sqcap T \textbf{ od} \quad \sqsubseteq \quad \textbf{do } S \lhd T \textbf{ od}$$

Proof. Applying Theorem 1 we calculate:

$$
\begin{array}{ll}
& \textbf{do } S \;\square\; T \textbf{ od} \sqsubseteq \textbf{do } S \lhd T \textbf{ od} \\[4pt]
= & \langle \text{definition of } \textbf{do } S \textbf{ od} \rangle \\
& (S \;\square\; T)^{\omega}; [\neg\, grd\,(S \;\square\; T)] \sqsubseteq (S \lhd T)^{\omega}; [\neg\, grd\,(S \lhd T)] \\[4pt]
\Leftarrow & \langle \text{as } grd\,(S \;\square\; T) = grd\,(S \lhd T) \text{ by (23) and (22), monotonicity} \rangle \\
& (S \;\square\; T)^{\omega} \sqsubseteq (S \lhd T)^{\omega} \\[4pt]
= & \langle (17) \rangle \\
& ((S \;\square\; T)^{+})^{\omega} \sqsubseteq (S \lhd T)^{\omega} \\[4pt]
\Leftarrow & \langle \text{monotonicity of } S^{\omega} \rangle \\
& (S \;\square\; T)^{+} \sqsubseteq S \lhd T \\[4pt]
\Leftarrow & \langle \text{definition of } \square, \lhd \rangle \\
& (S^{+} \sqcap T^{+})^{+} \sqsubseteq S^{+} \sqcap T^{+}; \bar{S} \\[4pt]
= & \langle \text{lattice property} \rangle \\
& ((S^{+} \sqcap T^{+})^{+} \sqsubseteq S^{+}) \wedge ((S^{+} \sqcap T^{+})^{+} \sqsubseteq T^{+}; \bar{S}) \\[4pt]
\Leftarrow & \langle (13), \text{ monotonicity of } S^{+}, \text{ definition of } \bar{S} \rangle \\
& (S^{+} \sqcap T^{+} \sqsubseteq S^{+}) \wedge ((S^{+} \sqcap T^{+})^{+} \sqsubseteq T^{+}; (S \sqcap [\neg\, grd\, S])) \\[4pt]
\Leftarrow & \langle \text{lattice property, ; distributes over } \sqcap \rangle \\
& (S^{+} \sqcap T^{+})^{+} \sqsubseteq T^{+}; S \sqcap T^{+}; [\neg\, grd\, S] \\[4pt]
\Leftarrow & \langle \text{lattice property, } skip \sqsubseteq [p] \text{ for any } p, S; skip = S \text{ for any } S \rangle \\
& ((S^{+} \sqcap T^{+})^{+} \sqsubseteq T^{+}; S) \wedge ((S^{+} \sqcap T^{+})^{+} \sqsubseteq T^{+}) \\[4pt]
\Leftarrow & \langle \text{definition of } S^{+}, (13), \text{ lattice property} \rangle \\
& (S^{+} \sqcap T^{+}); (S^{+} \sqcap T^{+})^{*} \sqsubseteq T^{+}; S \\[4pt]
\Leftarrow & \langle \text{monotonicity of ;} \rangle \\
& (S^{+} \sqcap T^{+} \sqsubseteq T^{+}) \wedge ((S^{+} \sqcap T^{+})^{*} \sqsubseteq S) \\[4pt]
\Leftarrow & \langle \text{lattice property, (8)} \rangle \\
& S^{+} \sqcap T^{+} \sqsubseteq S
\end{array}
$$

The last line follows from (13) and the lattice structure.

A loop with a demonic choice between two alternatives is also refined by the same loop with a fair choice between the two alternatives. The proof is similar to the previous one:

Theorem 3. *Let S and T be monotonic predicate transformers. Then:*

$$\textbf{do } S \sqcap T \textbf{ od} \quad \sqsubseteq \quad \textbf{do } S \diamond T \textbf{ od}$$

Let us now consider how to implement the loop **do** $S \lhd T$ **od**. One way is to use a round robin scheduler: first we test S; if it is enabled, we execute it and continue with T, otherwise we continue immediately with T. If T is enabled, we execute it. Otherwise, if T is not enabled but S was enabled we start over again. If S was also not enabled, the loop terminates. This is expressed by the loop **do** $S :: T$ **od**, where $S :: T$ is read "S then T":

$$S :: T \quad \hat{=} \quad S; \bar{T} \sqcap [\neg \, grd \, S]; T$$

For example, a loop with a choice which is fair to one alternative can be implemented by a round robin scheduler:

Theorem 4. *Let S and T be monotonic predicate transformers. Then:*

$$\textbf{do } S \vartriangleleft T \textbf{ od} \quad \sqsubseteq \quad \textbf{do } S :: T \textbf{ od}$$

Proof. We note that from the definitions we get $grd \, (S :: T) = grd \, S \vee grd \, T$. We calculate:

$$
\begin{aligned}
& \textbf{do } S \vartriangleleft T \textbf{ od} \sqsubseteq \textbf{do } S :: T \textbf{ od} \\
=\quad & \langle \text{definition of } \textbf{do } S \textbf{ od} \rangle \\
& (S \vartriangleleft T)^{\omega}; [\neg \, grd \, (S \vartriangleleft T)] \sqsubseteq (S :: T)^{\omega}; [\neg \, grd \, (S :: T)] \\
\Leftarrow\quad & \langle \text{as } grd \, (S :: T) = grd \, S \vee grd \, T, \text{ monotonicity of } ; \rangle \\
& (S \vartriangleleft T)^{\omega} \sqsubseteq (S :: T)^{\omega} \\
\Leftarrow\quad & \langle \text{monotonicity of } S^{\omega} \rangle \\
& S \vartriangleleft T \sqsubseteq S :: T \\
\Leftarrow\quad & \langle \text{definition of } \vartriangleleft, :: \rangle \\
& S^{+}; \bar{T} \sqcap T^{+} \sqsubseteq S; \bar{T} \sqcap [\neg \, grd \, S]; T \\
\Leftarrow\quad & \langle (13), \text{ monotonicity of } ; \text{ and } \sqcap \rangle \\
& T^{+} \sqsubseteq [\neg \, grd \, S]; T
\end{aligned}
$$

The last line follows from (13) and $skip \sqsubseteq [p]$ for any p.

Alternatively, we can implement the loop **do** $S \vartriangleleft T$ **od** by a prioritizing scheduler: whenever S is enabled, that is executed. Only if S is not enabled, T is tested and executed if enabled. Otherwise, if neither S nor T are enabled, the loop terminates. This is expressed by the loop **do** $S \mathbin{/\!/} T$ **od**, where $S \mathbin{/\!/} T$, read "S else T", is the prioritized composition as studied in [13]:

$$S \mathbin{/\!/} T \quad \hat{=} \quad S \sqcap [\neg \, grd \, S]; T$$

Using prioritized composition, we can alternatively define $S :: T$ by $S; \bar{T} \mathbin{/\!/} T$.

Theorem 5. *Let S and T be monotonic predicate transformers. Then:*

$$\textbf{do } S \vartriangleleft T \textbf{ od} \quad \sqsubseteq \quad \textbf{do } S \mathbin{/\!/} T \textbf{ od}$$

The proof is similar to the previous one.

4 Verification of Loops with Fair Choice

For the purpose of verifying properties of loops we make use of ranked predicates. Let W be a well-founded set and let $P = \{p_w \mid w \in W\}$ be an indexed collection of predicates, called ranked predicates. Typically, a ranked predicate p_w is the conjunction of an invariant I and a variant t, i.e. $p_w = I \wedge (t = w)$.

For a given set P as above we define $p = (\exists\, w \in W \bullet p_w)$ to be true if some ranked predicate is true and with $W_{<w} = \{v \in W \mid v < w\}$ we define $p_{<w} = (\exists\, v \in W_{<w} \bullet p_v)$ to be true if a predicate with lower rank than p_w is true. The following properties are taken from [3]. Let S be a monotonic predicate transformer and $\{r_w \mid w \in W\}$ a collection of ranked predicates:

$$(\forall\, w \in W \bullet r_w \leq S\ r_{<w}) \quad \Rightarrow \quad r \leq S^\omega\ r \tag{24}$$

By contrast, for the verification of weak iteration we do not have to incorporate a termination argument:

$$p \leq S\ p \quad \Rightarrow \quad p \leq S^* p \tag{25}$$

We first state the basic loop verification theorem, from which we then derive a verification theorem for loops with a demonic choice and finally for loops with a fair choice.

Theorem 6. *Let S be a monotonic predicate transformer and $\{r_w \mid w \in W\}$ a collection of ranked predicates. Then:*

$$(\forall\, w \in W \bullet r_w \leq S\ r_{<w}) \quad \Rightarrow \quad r \leq \mathbf{do}\ S\ \mathbf{od}\ (r \wedge \neg\ grd\ S)$$

Proof. Assuming $(\forall\, w \in W \bullet r_w \leq S\ r_{<w})$ we calculate:

$$
\begin{aligned}
& \mathbf{do}\ S\ \mathbf{od}\ (r \wedge \neg\ grd\ S) \\
=\ & \langle \text{definition of } \mathbf{do}\ S\ \mathbf{od} \rangle \\
& (S^\omega; [\neg\ grd\ S])\ (r \wedge \neg\ grd\ S) \\
=\ & \langle \text{definitions of guard and ;} \rangle \\
& S^\omega(\neg\ grd\ S \Rightarrow r \wedge \neg\ grd\ S) \\
=\ & \langle \text{logic} \rangle \\
& S^\omega\ (grd\ S \vee r) \\
\geq\ & \langle \text{monotonicity of } S \rangle \\
& S^\omega\ r \\
\geq\ & \langle \text{assumption, (24)} \rangle \\
& r
\end{aligned}
$$

The assumption $(\forall\, w \in W \bullet r_w \leq S\ r_{<w})$ expresses that statement S preserves the invariant part of r_w while making progress towards termination by establishing a postcondition of lower rank. If the loop contains a demonic choice between two alternatives, then each of the alternatives has to preserve the invariant and make progress towards termination:

Theorem 7. *Let S be a monotonic predicate transformer and $\{r_w \mid w \in W\}$ a collection of ranked predicates. Let $g = \text{grd } S \vee \text{grd } T$. Then:*

$$(r_w \leq S \ r_{<w}) \ \wedge \ (r_w \leq T \ r_{<w}) \ \Rightarrow \ r \leq \textbf{do } S \sqcap T \textbf{ od } (r \wedge \neg g)$$

Proof. According to (1) and Theorem 6 it is sufficient to show $(\forall w \in W \bullet r_w \leq (S \sqcap T) \ r_{<w})$. For this, we calculate for any $w \in W$:

$$
\begin{aligned}
& r_w \leq (S \sqcap T) \ r_{<w} \\
= \quad & \langle \text{definition of } \sqcap \rangle \\
& r_w \leq S \ r_{<w} \wedge T \ r_{<w} \\
= \quad & \langle \text{logic} \rangle \\
& (r_w \leq S \ r_{<w}) \wedge (r_w \leq T \ r_{<w})
\end{aligned}
$$

The last line is exactly the assumption of the theorem.

Now we consider the loop **do** $S \lhd T$ **od**. In order to ensure termination of this loop, it is sufficient that S makes progress towards termination by establishing a postcondition with lower rank than the precondition, and that T either keeps the rank of the postcondition the same as the precondition but enables S (or keeps S enabled if it was) or otherwise also decreases the rank. In the first case the fairness of S ensures that it will be eventually taken, thus making progress towards termination.

Theorem 8. *Let S be a monotonic predicate transformer and $\{r_w \mid w \in W\}$ a collection of ranked predicates. Let $g = \text{grd } S \vee \text{grd } T$. Then:*

$$
\begin{aligned}
(r_w \leq S \ r_{<w}) \ \wedge \ (r_w \leq T((r_w \wedge \text{grd } S) \vee r_{<w})) \ \Rightarrow \\
r \leq \textbf{do } S \lhd T \textbf{ od } (r \wedge \neg g)
\end{aligned}
$$

We note that $r_{<w} \leq (r_w \wedge \text{grd } S) \vee r_{<w}$. Hence this assumption is indeed weaker than that of Theorem 7.

Proof. First we observe that from $r_w \leq S \ r_{<w}$ we get $r_{<w} \leq S \ r_{<w}$ as $r_{<w} \leq r_w$. By (25) this implies $r_{<w} \leq S^* \ r_{<w}$. As $(r_w \wedge \text{grd } S) \vee r_{<w} \leq r_w$ we get similarly $(r_w \wedge \text{grd } S) \vee r_{<w} \leq T^* ((r_w \wedge \text{grd } S) \vee r_{<w})$. Next we note that according to (22) and Theorem 6 it is sufficient to show $(\forall w \in W \bullet r_w \leq (S \lhd T) \ r_{<w})$. For

this, we calculate for any $w \in W$:

$$r_w \leq (S \lhd T)\ r_{<w}$$
$=$ ⟨definition of $\lhd$ and $\sqcap$⟩
$$r_w \leq S^+\ r_{<w} \wedge (T^+; \bar{S})\ r_{<w}$$
$=$ ⟨definition of S^+ and $;$⟩
$$r_w \leq S(S^*\ r_{<w}) \wedge T^+(\bar{S}\ r_{<w})$$
$=$ ⟨logic⟩
$$(r_w \leq S(S^*\ r_{<w})) \wedge (r_w \leq T^+(\bar{S}\ r_{<w}))$$
$\Leftarrow$ ⟨as $r_{<w} \leq S^*\ r_{<w}$, monotonicity of S⟩
$$(r_w \leq S\ r_{<w}) \wedge (r_w \leq T^+(\bar{S}\ r_{<w}))$$
$\Leftarrow$ ⟨assumption $r_w \leq S\ r_{<w}$, definition of $\bar{S}$⟩
$$r_w \leq T^+((S \sqcap [\neg\ grd\ S])\ r_{<w})$$
$=$ ⟨definition of $\sqcap$ and $[p]$⟩
$$r_w \leq T^+(S\ r_{<w} \wedge (\neg\ grd\ S \Rightarrow r_{<w}))$$
$\Leftarrow$ ⟨assumption $r_w \leq S\ r_{<w}$, monotonicity of T^+, logic⟩

$$r_w \leq T^+(r_w \wedge (grd\ S \vee r_{<w}))$$
$=$ ⟨logic, $r_{<w} \leq r_w$⟩
$$r_w \leq T^+((r_w \wedge grd\ S) \vee r_{<w})$$
$=$ ⟨definition of T^+, $;$⟩
$$r_w \leq T(T^*((r_w \wedge grd\ S) \vee r_{<w}))$$
$=$ ⟨as $(r_w \wedge grd\ S) \vee r_{<w} \leq T^*\ ((r_w \wedge grd\ S) \vee r_{<w})$, (25)⟩
$$r_w \leq T((r_w \wedge grd\ S) \vee r_{<w})$$

The last line is just the second part of the assumption of the theorem.

For reasons of symmetry, we get an analogous theorem for $\mathbf{do}\ S \rhd T\ \mathbf{od}$. Furthermore, with a similar proof, we get following theorem:

Theorem 9. *Let S be a monotonic predicate transformer and $\{r_w \mid w \in W\}$ a collection of ranked predicates. Let $g = grd\ S \vee grd\ T$. Then:*

$$r_w \leq S\ r_{<w} \ \wedge\ r_w \leq T((r_w \wedge grd\ S) \vee r_{<w}) \ \Rightarrow$$
$$r \leq \mathbf{do}\ S \diamond T\ \mathbf{od}\ (r \wedge \neg g)$$

The assumption here is the same as that of Theorem 8. It cannot be weakened to allow S, analogously to T, either to make progress towards termination or to enable T. For example, if both S and T disabled themselves but enable each other, S and T would be selected alternatively and no progress towards termination would be enforced.

5   Discussion

In [12] Dijkstra's calculus is extended by a fair choice operator. The approach relies on temporal predicate transformers like "always" and "eventually" and on syntactic substitutions of fair choice by angelic choice, neither of which is needed here. Interestingly, the resulting notion of (weak) fairness is stronger than ours: For a loop to terminate it is already sufficient if any one alternative makes progress towards termination, whereas we require that one alternative must always make progress. On the other hand, a round robin scheduler is a sound implementation technique here, but not in [12].

In [6] Dijkstra's calculus is also extended by a fair choice operator. Although the definition of **do** $S \diamond T$ **od** looks textually similar, the differences are subtle but substantial: the iteration S^+ is not defined by the greatest fixed point, but in terms of the dovetail operator $\triangledown$ that models fair parallel execution. The definition of dovetail requires the distinction between possible and definite nontermination, which is done by additionally considering weakest liberal preconditions. The expressiveness of the dovetail operator leads to problems with non-monotonicity and to the need for two ordering relations, both of which is avoided here.

In [15] fairness in action systems, a generalization of loops allowing possibly infinite computations, with predicate transformer semantics is considered. The approach there is that unfair non-terminating sequences are explicitly specified, rather than fairness expressed by a fair choice as elsewhere. This allows a wider range of fairness constraints to be expressed compared to the (weak) fairness considered here, though in a different style.

A number of issues found elsewhere have not been treated here. First, Theorem 8 can be weakened by allowing the fair statement S to be "helpful" by decreasing the rank of the precondition only in some states. Such a theorem then makes use of additional invariants characterizing the helpful states [5]. Secondly, we have not considered fairness with more than two statements. Finally, we have not considered other forms of fairness like strong fairness and unconditional fairness [9]. It would be particularly interesting to see whether other forms of fairness can be treated similarly in an algebraic style.

It is worth pointing out that all of our results have been derived without the common assumption of conjunctivity. A predicate transformer S and is called (positively) conjunctive it is satisfies for any set of predicates q_i, $(\forall i \in I \bullet q_i) = (\forall i \in I \bullet S\ q_i)$ where I is a nonempty set. Conjunctivity rules out angelic nondeterminism: the predicate transformers $[p]$, $\{p\}$, $[R]$ are all conjunctive (but not $\{R\}$) and the operators ;, $\sqcap$ preserve conjunctivity (but not $\sqcup$). The combination of demonic and angelic nondeterminism has recently led to a game-theoretic view of predicate transformers [3], with applications to the modeling of interactive systems. Thus our results about fairness carry over to this general setting.

Acknowledgment

We are grateful to the reviewers for their careful reading and their suggestions. We are in particular grateful to Burkhard von Karger for pointing out two errors in the definitions.

References

1. C. Aarts, R. Backhouse, E. Boiten, H. Doorndijk, N. van Gasteren, R. van Geldrop, P. Hoogendijk, T. Voermans, and J. van der Woude. Fixed-point calculus. *Information Processing Letters*, 53(3):131–136, 1995. 127

2. R. J. R. Back. *On the Correctness of Refinement Steps in Program Development*. Ph. D. Thesis, Department of Computer Science, University of Helsinki, 1978. 127

3. R. J. R. Back and J. von Wright. *Refinement Calculus - A Systematic Introduction*. Springer-Verlag, 1998. 127, 135, 138

4. R. J. R. Back and J. von Wright. Reasoning algebraically about loops. *Acta Informatica*, 36(4):295–334, 1999. 127

5. R. J. R. Back and Q. Xu. Refinement of fair action systems. *Acta Informatica*, 35(2):131–165, 1998. 127, 138

6. M. Broy and G. Nelson. Adding fair choice to Dijkstra's calculus. *ACM Transactions on Programming Languages and Systems*, 16(3):924–938, 1994. 138

7. M. J. Butler and C. C. Morgan. Action systems, unbounded nondeterminism and infinite traces. *Formal Aspects of Computing*, 7(1):37–53, 1995. 127

8. K. Mani Chandy and Jayadev Misra. *Parallel Program Design: A Foundation*. Addison-Wesley, 1988. 127

9. N. Francez. *Fairness*. Texts and Monographs in Computer Science. Springer-Verlag, 1986. 127, 131, 138

10. C. C. Morgan. The specification statement. *ACM Transactions on Programming Languages and Systems*, 10(3):403–419, 1988. 127

11. J. M. Morris. A theoretical basis for stepwise refinement and the programming calculus. *Science of Computer Programming*, 9(3), 1987. 127

12. J. M. Morris. Temporal predicate transformers and fair termination. *Acta Informatica*, 27(4):287–313, 1990. 137, 138

13. E. Sekerinski and K. Sere. A theory of prioritising composition. *The Computer Journal*, 39(8):701–712, 1996. 134

14. A. K. Singh. Program refinement in fair transition systems. *Acta Informatica*, 30:503–535, 1993. 127

15. A. Wabenhorst. Developing fairness in terminating and reactive programs. Technical Report PRG-TR-1-96, Oxford University Computing Laboratory, January 1996. 138

Formal Methods and Dependability

Cliff B. Jones

Department of Computing Science,
University of Newcastle, NE1 7RU, UK
cliff.jones@ncl.ac.uk

Abstract. This paper sets out a programme of work in the area of dependability. The research is to be pursued under the aegis of a six-year
Inter-Disciplinary Research Collaboration funded by the UK Engineering and Physical Sciences Research Council. The aim is to to consider
computer-based systems which comprise humans as well as hardware and
software. The aim here is to indicate how formal methods ideas, coupled
with structuring proposals, can help address a problem which clearly also
requires social science input.

Extended Abstract

1 Reasoning about Interference

This section summarises earlier work on formal development methods for concurrent systems.

The essence of concurrency is interference: shared-variable programs must
be designed so as to tolerate state changes; communication-based concurrency
shifts the interference to that from messages. One possible way of specifying
interference is to use rely/guarantee-conditions (see [7,16,17,19,2,4]).

Programming language designers have proposed a series of increasingly sophisticated constructs to control interference; the case for using object-oriented
constructs is set out in [8].

2 Faults as Interference

The essence of this section is to argue that faults can be viewed as interference in
the same way that concurrent processes bring about changes beyond the control
of the process whose specification and design are being considered. Without yet
proposing notation for each case, a range of motivating examples are considered.

The first example is one that re-awakened this author's interest in considering
faults as interference. Faced with the task of specifying a traffic light system,
many computer scientists would confine themselves to the control system and
specify the signals which must be emitted. Michael Jackson (see [6]) considers the
wider issues of the correct wiring of the control system to the physical lights and
the initial state of these lights units. One could widen the specification to address

R. Backhouse and J. N. Oliveira (Eds.): MPC 2000, LNCS 1837, pp. 140–143, 2000.

the overall light system (at one level the requirement is that at least one light must always be red) and record assumptions (as rely-conditions) which state that emitting a signal implies that the light unit changes state. Recording such a rely-condition does not itself result in a dependable system but it ensures that the assumptions are recorded and use of proof rules for development of concurrency should ensure that there are no further hidden assumptions. In fact, one could take this example further by specifying that the real requirement is to reduce the probability of a crash to a certain level and then record probabilities that drivers behave in certain ways when faced with red lights (see, for example, [10] for ways of reasoning about probabilities in design).

A second –trivial– example should again illustrate the shift of view in documenting assumptions. Rather than specifying a control system in terms of the readings delivered by measuring devices, it might be preferable to specify the overall system in terms of the actual temperature etc. and provide a rely-condition which records the acceptable tolerance on the measuring device. Here again, the message is to expose the assumptions.

A more realistic example can be given in the same domain: it would be common for such sensors to be deployed using "triple modular redundancy". The viewpoint of recording the assumptions would suggest that a rely-condition should state that two roughly equal measurements are far less likely to be in error than one which is wildly different (or is perhaps some distinguished error value).

As well as the primary message that exposing assumptions will force their consideration, there is the clear advantage that checking that such rely-conditions are adequate to prove that a system will meet its overall specification will check for any missed assumptions.

3   Fault Containment and Recovery

Significant work has been done on designing architectures for fault-containment and recovery – see for example [11,18].

4   Human Errors and Their Containment

The work in the *Dependability Interdisciplinary Research Collaboration* on which we are embarking will address not just dependable computer systems but will also consider wider systems where the role of the humans involved is seen as critical to overall system dependability. The need for this is emphasized by [9] which reports a large number of computer related accidents which resulted in death and notes that in the majority of cases the key problem related more to the interaction between people and computers than a specific hardware or software malfunction.

There are of course many examples of where a program tries to guard against inadvertent errors of its users: the check in many operating systems asking a user to confirm the request to delete files or the need to retype a new password (being invisible there is no other check) are trivial instances. More interesting is the architecture of the overall system known as Pen& Pad [5] in which software is programmed to warn against possible misprescription of drugs by doctors: no attempt was made to automate prescription but the system would check against dangerous cocktails or specific drugs which might not be tolerable to some other condition that is indicated on the patient's record.

The logical extension of the work outlined in the two preceding sections on purely computer systems is to aim for a more systematic treatment of human errors. Fortunately the work of psychiatrists like Reason (see [12]) in categorising human errors offers the hope of describing and reasoning about the sort of human errors against which a system is designed to guard. The objective would be to minimise the risk of the errors of the computer system and (groups of) humans "lining up" in the way indicated in [13].

5   Further Research

There are many further areas of research related to the themes above. For example:

- Both pre and rely-conditions can record assumptions but if they become complex they might be a warning that an interface has become too messy (cf. [1]) – ways of evaluating interfaces and architectures are needed (see [15]).
- The idea of using rely-conditions to record failure assumptions occurred to the author in a connection with a control system some years ago. One reason for not describing the idea more publicly was that there often appears to be a mismatch of abstraction levels between the specification and the error inducing level. There needs to be more research on whether this can be avoided.
- The role of malicious attacks is being considered in the IST-funded MAFTIA project.
- A key area of system "misuse" is where the user has an incorrect model of what is going on inside the combined control/controlled system – minimizing this risk must be an objective.
- Progress in modelling the human mind (e.g. [3]) should be tracked.

Acknowledgements

There is of course related research and the work of Michael Harrison and his colleagues (who are within the IRC) and John Rushby (see [14]) has influenced the thinking so far. One particular stimulus for this paper was the talk that Michael Jackson gave at the Munich meeting of IFIP's WG2.3 last year – more generally discussions at this working group on Programming Methodology have acted as a sounding board and encouragement to the author.

References

1. Pierre Collette and Cliff B. Jones. Enhancing the tractability of rely/guarantee specifications in the development of interfering operations. In G. D. Plotkin, editor, *Proof, Language and Interaction*, chapter 10, pages 275–305. MIT Press, 2000. 142

2. Pierre Collette. *Design of Compositional Proof Systems Based on Assumption-Commitment Specifications – Application to UNITY*. PhD thesis, Louvain-la-Neuve, June 1994. 140

3. Patricia S. Churchland and Terrance J. Sejnowski. *The Computational Brain*. MIT Press, 1994. 142

4. Jürgen Dingel. *Systematic Parallel Programming*. PhD thesis, Carnegie Mellon University, 1999. 140

5. T. J. Howkins, A. L. Rector, C. A. Horan, A. Nowlan, and A. Wilson. An overview of PEN& PAD. *Lecture Notes in Medical Informatics*, 40:73–78, 1990. 142

6. Michael Jackson. *Problem Frames: Structring and Analysing Software Development Problems*. Addison-Wesley, 2000. 140

7. C. B. Jones. Specification and design of (parallel) programs. In *Proceedings of IFIP'83*, pages 321–332. North-Holland, 1983. 140

8. C. B. Jones. Constraining interference in an object-based design method. In M-C. Gaudel and J-P. Jouannaud, editors, *TAPSOFT'93*, volume 668 of *Lecture Notes in Computer Science*, pages 136–150. Springer-Verlag, 1993. 140

9. Donald MacKenzie. Computer-related accidental death: an empirical exploration. *Science and Public Policy*, 21:233–248, 1994. 141

10. Carroll Morgan, Annabelle McIver, and J. W. Sanders. Refinement-oriented probability for CSP. *Formal Aspects of Computing*, 8(6):617–647, 1996. 141

11. B. Randell. System structure for fault tolerance. *IEEE Transactionns on Software Engineering*, SE-1:220–232, 1975. 141

12. James Reason. *Human Error*. Cambridge University Press, 1990. 142

13. James Reason. *Managing the Risks of Organisational Accidents*. Ashgate Publishing Limited, 1997. 142

14. John Rushby. Using model checking to help discover mode confusions and other automation surprises. In *Proceedings of 3rd Workshop on Human Error*, pages 1–18. HESSD'99, 1999. 142

15. Mary Shaw and David Garlan. *Software Architecture: Perspectives on an Emerging Discipline*. Prentice Hall, 1996. 142

16. C. Stirling. A generalisation of Owicki-Gries's Hoare logic for a concurrent while language. *TCS*, 58:347–359, 1988. 140

17. K. Stølen. *Development of Parallel Programs on Shared Data-Structures*. PhD thesis, Manchester University, 1990. available as UMCS-91-1-1. 140

18. J. Xu, B. Randell, A. Romanovsky, R. J. Stroud, A. F. Zorzo, E. Canver, and F. von Henke. Rigorous development os a safety-critical system based on coordinated atomic actions. In *Proc. of 29th Int. Symp. Fault-Tollerant Computing*. IEEE Computer Society Press, 1999. 141

19. Qiwen Xu. *A Theory of State-based Parallel Programming*. PhD thesis, Oxford University, 1992. 140

Liberating Data Refinement

Eerke Boiten and John Derrick

Computing Laboratory, University of Kent
Canterbury, CT2 7NF, UK.
E.A.Boiten@ukc.ac.uk

Abstract. Traditional rules for refinement of abstract data types suggest a software development process in which much of the detail has to be present already in the initial specification. In particular, the set of available operations and their interfaces need to be fixed. In contrast, many formal and informal software development methods rely on changes of granularity and require introduction of detail in a gradual way during the development process.

This paper discusses several generalisations and extensions of the traditional refinement rules, which are compatible with each other and, more importantly, with the semantic grounding of data refinement. Together they should provide a semantic justification for a larger spectrum of development steps.

The discussion takes place in the context of the formal specification language Z and its relational underpinnings.

Keywords: Refinement, formal methods, Z.

1 Introduction

The theory of data refinement as described in essence by He, Hoare and Sanders [17] (summarised in Section 2) provides a useful model of program development in terms of abstract data types for which the set of operations is known already. In the working out of this theory, the abstract data types (ADTs) were assumed to have identical sets of operations, i.e. they were conformal. The representations of this theory in languages like Z [24] have until recently further restricted this context. The emphasis in the early work on refinement in Z was on the incomplete downward simulation rule, forbidding postponement of non-determinism; and it was implied that input and output were immutable (i.e. in a refinement step, inputs and outputs could not change). Recent work [27,25,5] has relaxed these unnecessary restrictions by more fully exploiting the theory of [17]. In this paper we discuss how these and some other generalisations of data refinement relate to each other and how they can be interpreted in terms of the relational model. In particular it is shown how they represent a number of liberalisations of the notion of conformity of data types, and how these liberalisations are compatible with each other. The comparison between ADTs and process algebra proves to be a recurrent theme which is both inspirational and sometimes confusing.

R. Backhouse and J. N. Oliveira (Eds.): MPC 2000, LNCS 1837, pp. 144–166, 2000.

Our motivation for this work is twofold. The primary motivation stems from using a language like Z for "partial specification", as proposed in e.g. [2,28,6]. In a partial specification approach, a system is not described by a single specification, but by a collection of interlocking ones, possibly written in different languages, each describing a different aspect. (Note that this situation also arises when one uses a notation like UML.) Combination of partial specifications is by construction of a common refinement, whose existence witnesses to the consistency of the partial specifications. From a methodological point of view, it is essential that partial specifications may mention only aspects of the system of relevance to their particular viewpoint. For example, only part of the external interface for an operation may appear in a given viewpoint, and we require that the common refinement can add to, or alter, this interface (i.e. the IO of an operation). This requires a more liberal notion of refinement.

Alternatively, one could view this work as an attempt to provide a semantic justification to a larger number of rigorous, intuitively "correct", steps in program development. Such steps include modifications of inputs and outputs, and changes of granularity of operations.

This paper is organised as follows. Section 2 summarises the data refinement theory as presented in [17], and the traditional [24] representation of data refinement in Z. Readers who are familiar with the area might prefer to skip Section 2 on a first reading, and look at the motivating example in Section 3 first. Section 3 presents a sample ADT in Z, and considers a number of desirable refinements. Subsequent sections present generalised refinement rules and sketches how they are derived from the theory or generalisations of it. The final section contains some conclusions.

2   Data Refinement: The Relational View

In this section, we first summarise the definitions of simulation and refinement as presented for *total* relations by He, Hoare and Sanders [17]. Then we discuss how these definitions can be modified to *partial* relations. Finally we give the traditional presentations of these rules in Z, indicating how input and output can be represented.

2.1   Data Refinement Refined

A seminal paper in the area of data refinement is the paper by He, Hoare and Sanders in ESOP'86 [17], following on from Hoare's earlier paper [18]. It presents conditions for data refinement using upward and downward simulations, removing some of the conditions imposed on such simulations in the VDM literature [19]. We paraphrase their main results below.

We assume the existence of some global data space G.

Definition 1 (Data type). A *data type* is a quadruple $(S, Init, \{Op_i\}_{i \in I}, Fin)$. The operations $\{Op_i\}$, indexed by $i \in I$, are *total* relations on the set S; $Init$ is a relation from G to S; Fin is a relation from S to G.   □

(We omit the extra requirement on so-called conditions here; these are less central once we move to partial relations.)

Data types can be compared if they are conformal:

Definition 2 (Conformal). Two data types are *conformal* if their global data space and the indexing sets of their operations coincide.   □

For the rest of this section, assume that all data types considered are conformal, using some fixed index set I.

The comparison between data types is in terms of programs using them – i.e., these are black box data types.

Definition 3 (Complete program). A *complete program* over a data type $(S, Init, \{Op_i\}_{i \in I}, Fin)$ is an expression of the form $Init \,_9^8\, P \,_9^8\, Fin$, where P, a relation over S, is a *program* over $\{Op_i\}_{i \in I}$.   □

The notion of a program may vary, but should allow at least all operations and be closed under sequential composition. In [17] Dijkstra's guarded command language is used as a programming language; in this paper we will concentrate on a minimal language where every program consists of a *finite sequence* of operations. (This is not a fundamental restriction as any control flow including loops can be represented this way by making the program counter a state variable.) Using the now traditional notation, for a sequence p over I, and data type X, p_X denotes the complete program over X characterised by p. (E.g. if $X = (S, Init, \{Op_1, Op_2, Op_3\}, Fin)$ then $[1, 3, 1]_X$ denotes $Init \,_9^8\, Op_1 \,_9^8\, Op_3 \,_9^8\, Op_1 \,_9^8\, Fin$.) Refinement between data types is then defined by quantification over all programs using them:

Definition 4 (Data refinement). For data types A and C, C *refines* A iff for each finite sequence p over I, $p_C \subseteq p_A$.   □

This is not an easy property to verify as it quantifies over all finite programs.

2.2   Upward and Downward Simulations

Simulations provide a method of checking data refinement in a stepwise fashion, i.e. by comparing concrete and abstract data types per operation (and initialisation and finalisation).

Definition 5 (Simulations). Assume data types $A = (AS, AI, \{AOp_i\}_{i \in I}, AF)$ and $C = (CS, CI, \{COp_i\}_{i \in I}, CF)$.

A *downward* simulation is a relation R from AS to CS satisfying

$$CI \subseteq AI \,_9^8\, R$$
$$R \,_9^8\, CF \subseteq AF$$
$$\forall i : I \bullet R \,_9^8\, COp_i \subseteq AOp_i \,_9^8\, R$$

This is also called a *forward* simulation, or L-simulation [9].

An *upward* simulation is a finitary relation T from CS to AS such that

$$CI \,_9^\circ\, T \subseteq AI$$
$$CF \subseteq T \,_9^\circ\, AF$$
$$\forall i : I \bullet COp_i \,_9^\circ\, T \subseteq T \,_9^\circ\, AOp_i$$

This is also called a *backward* simulation, or L^{-1}-simulation. Simulations are sometimes called *retrieve relations*. □

By structural induction on the programs it can be proved that the existence of either of these simulations is sufficient for data refinement. Moreover:

Theorem 1. *For finitary datatypes, upward and downward simulation are jointly complete, i.e. any data refinement can be proved by a combination of simulations.*

This is proved by first constructing a deterministic equivalent of the "abstract" type, using a powerset construction (this is an upward simulation). A downward simulation can then be found to the "concrete" type.

For canonical data types, i.e. those where all operations are functions, upward and downward simulation coincide. Their difference (and incompleteness) is usually exemplified by data types where the composition of two operations (which are constrained to always occur in sequence) contains non-determinism. In that case, downward simulation allows the non-determinism to be moved only to the first of the two operations and upward simulation allows for the non-determinism to be postponed to the second, but not vice versa.

A single complete rule can be given in the context of predicate transformers [16]. The Z version of this, using powersimulations, is given in [10].

2.3 Dealing with Partial Relations

The rules given above provide a data refinement relation for ADTs whose operations are *total* relations. However, in languages like Z, operations are often specified by partial relations.

There are two fundamentally different approaches to partial operations in the world of state based systems. They are:

- the "contract" approach to ADTs: the domain (precondition) of an operation describes the area within which the operation should be guaranteed to deliver a well-defined result, as specified by the relation. Outside that domain, the operation *may* be applied, but may return any value, even an undefined one (modelling e.g. non-termination). This represents a situation in which the customer employs a black box data type, to be used in their system in situations only when the precondition holds.
- the "behavioural" approach to ADTs: operations may not be applied outside their precondition; doing so anyway leads to an undefined result. This represents the situation where the customer employs an independently operating machine, the operations of the ADT corresponding to possible interactions between the system and its environment.

The first approach is the more common one in Z. The second approach is used in the object-oriented variant Object-Z [22], and in some distributed systems oriented applications in Z ("firing conditions" [26]). Clearly this approach takes its inspiration from process algebra, however it is unclear to which extent this analogy is complete. Process algebra tends to deal with potentially infinite traces, whereas the derivation of data refinement takes only finite programs into account. Attempts to integrate Z with CSP have obviously also used the firing condition interpretation of preconditions [23,15,7].

In either approach, data refinement rules for partial operations are derived from the rules above by modelling partial operations by total operations in a domain enriched with a $\bot$ value. Details of these derivations can be found in [27] for the "contract" approach to ADTs, both upward and downward simulations; and in [7] for downward simulations in the behavioural approach. We summarise these results here.

Let $X_\bot = X \cup \{\bot\}$ for any X and distinguished element $\bot \notin X$.

Definition 6 (Totalisation). For a partial relation Op on $State$, its total-isation is a total relation $\widehat{Op}$ on $State_\bot$, defined by $\widehat{Op} = Op \cup \{(x, y) \in State_\bot \times State_\bot \mid x \notin \operatorname{dom} Op\}$ in the "contract" approach to ADTs, or by $\widehat{Op} = Op \cup \{(x, \bot) \in State_\bot \times State_\bot \mid x \notin \operatorname{dom} Op\}$ in the behavioural approach to ADTs. $\qquad\square$

To preserve undefinedness, simulation relations of particular forms only are considered, viz. those which relate $\bot$ to every other value, or $\bot$ to $\bot$, depending on the ADT interpretation ("lifting" in [27]).

The resulting refinement rules for totalised relations can then be simplified to remove any reference to $\bot$. Here, we give only the refinement rules as they are derived for downward simulation. For the upward simulation rules, see [27,9].

Definition 7 (Downward simulation for partial relations). Assume data types $A = (AS, AI, \{AOp_i\}_{i \in I}, AF)$ and $C = (CS, CI, \{COp_i\}_{i \in I}, CF)$ where the operations may be partial. Assume the "contract" interpretation of ADTs.

A *downward* simulation is a relation R from AS to CS satisfying

$$CI \subseteq AI \,\fatsemi\, R$$
$$R \,\fatsemi\, CF \subseteq AF$$
$$\forall i : I \bullet (\operatorname{dom} AOp_i \lhd R) \,\fatsemi\, COp_i \subseteq AOp_i \,\fatsemi\, R$$
$$\forall i : I \bullet \quad \operatorname{ran}(\operatorname{dom} AOp_i \lhd R) \subseteq \operatorname{dom} COp_i$$

where $A \lhd R = \{(x, y) \in R \mid x \in A\}$. The latter two conditions are commonly referred to as "correctness" and "applicability". The inequalities in these conditions allow strengthening of the postcondition (reduction of non-determinism) and weakening of the precondition (increasing termination), respectively. In the "behavioural" interpretation of ADTs, the latter is not possible, i.e. applicability is strengthened to:

$$\operatorname{ran}(\operatorname{dom} AOp_i \lhd R) = \operatorname{dom} COp_i \qquad\qquad\square$$

2.4   Traditional Z Refinement

Before we can give the Z presentations of these rules, we need to introduce
schemas and in particular the schema "calculus", essentially a predicate calculus
over labelled tuples.

A schema in Z has the following shape:

```
 ┌─ ASchema ──────────────────────────────────────────
 │  Declarations
 │ ──────────────
 │  predicate
 └──────────────────────────────────────────────────────
```

The *Declarations* consist of a list of items of the form *name* : *Set*, and possibly
names of other schemas, possibly with decorations (cf. below). The *predicate* is
a predicate on the names introduced in the declarations (which can be omitted
if it is true). Inclusion of another schema means inclusion of all its names (type
clashes for any of these names should be avoided) in the declarations, and conjunction of its predicate to the including schema's predicate. The conjunction
of two schemas is an anonymous schema that includes both sets of declarations
and has the conjunction of the predicates; the disjunction of two schemas has
the declarations of both, and the disjunction of their predicates. Quantifications
over schemas have the obvious meaning: if *ASchema* is as defined above,

$$\forall ASchema \bullet P \equiv \forall Declarations \bullet predicate \Rightarrow P$$
$$\exists ASchema \bullet P \equiv \exists Declarations \bullet predicate \land P$$

Given a schema *ASchema* as above, the schema *ASchema'* denotes the schema
where all its names have been decorated with a '. A primed schema like that
conventionally denotes the after state of an operation. The schema $\Delta ASchema$
denotes *ASchema* $\land$ *ASchema'*; the schema $\Xi ASchema$ denotes $\Delta ASchema$ extended with a predicate asserting that *name* = *name'* for all names in *ASchema*.
Inputs to operations have names ending in ?, outputs have names ending in !;
?*Op* and !*Op* denote schemas containing only the inputs and outputs of *Op*, respectively. Schemas can be used as predicates in contexts where all their names
have compatible declarations, in which case they denote their predicate plus all
restrictions that follow from their declarations.

The common "states and operations" style of specification used in most text-
books on Z represents an ADT that is not the 4-tuple datatype of Definition 1:
it has no finalisation, no reference to global state, and operations are not defined
on the state only, but also on inputs and outputs. Let us call this the "Standard
Z ADT". For simplicity, let us assume all operations have the same type of input
and the same type of output. (This could be ensured by using sum types, where
the summands are singleton types for absent input or output.)

Definition 8 (Standard Z ADT).   A *standard Z ADT* is a triple
(*State*, *Init*, {*Op_i*}$_{i \in I}$) such that $\emptyset \subset Init \subseteq State$, and *Op_i* are relations between
State × *Input* and *State* × *Output* for particular types *Input* and *Output*. Each
of these components is represented by a schema.

Such a standard Z ADT represents the data type (in the sense of Definition 1) $(State", Init", \{Op_i"\}_{i \in I}, Fin")$ whose components are defined below. Note that the global state $G = \text{seq } Input \times \text{seq } Output$. Variables in and is denote (sequences of) $Input$, o and os denote (sequences of) $Output$.

$$State" = State \times \text{seq } Input \times \text{seq } Output$$
$$Init" = \{((is, os), (s, is, \langle \rangle)) \mid s \in Init\}$$
$$Op_i" = \{(s, <in> \,^\frown is, os), (s', is, os \,^\frown <o>)) \mid ((s, in), (s', o)) \in Op_i\}$$
$$Fin" = \{((s, is, os), (\langle \rangle, os)) \mid s \in State\}$$

□

In other words, the global state (representing what is observable about the ADT's behaviour) consists only of a sequence of inputs (to be consumed) and a sequence of outputs (to be produced). Initialisation involves initialisation of the state plus copying of the input sequence from the global state; in the finalisation the output sequence is copied back to the global state. Note that these denote "complete" programs, not to be composed with other programs, which justifies initialisation discarding all previous output, and finalisation discarding remaining input. Observe that the input and output sequences are part of the global state, and that thus standard Z ADTs can only be conformal if their operations have identical inputs and outputs.

Woodcock and Davies [27] present a detailed derivation of the upward and downward simulation rules for standard Z ADTs, by "unwinding" the rules from the represented (4-tuple) data type. The simulations used are of a particular shape, viz. only those which leave the input and output sequence (components of both abstract and concrete state) unchanged. In the case of downward simulation, the refinement conditions for finalisation reduce to true; for upward simulation they reduce to totality (on the abstract state) of the simulation. This derivation proves the soundness of the standard Z (downward simulation) refinement rule, as presented in Spivey's standard reference [24] and nearly every other Z textbook. The translation from relations and sets to schemas should be obvious. The precondition of a schema plays the rôle of the relation's domain.

Definition 9 (Precondition). The precondition of a Z operation schema Op on state S is a schema on S and the input of Op obtained by hiding (existentially quantifying) the after state (S') and output of Op.

$$\text{pre } Op = \exists S'; !Op \bullet Op$$

Definition 10 (Standard Z refinement).   The standard Z ADT $(AS, AInit, \{AOp_i\}_{i \in I})$ is data refined by $(CS, CInit, \{COp_i\}_{i \in I})$ if they are conformal, and a relation R on $AS \wedge CS$ exists such that

$$\forall CS \bullet CInit \Rightarrow \exists AS \bullet AInit \wedge R$$

and $\forall i : I$

$$\forall AS; \ CS; \ ?AOp_i; \ !AOp_i; \ CS' \bullet \text{pre } AOp_i \wedge R \wedge COp_i \Rightarrow \exists AS' \bullet AOp_i \wedge R'$$
$$\forall AS; \ CS; \ ?AOp_i \qquad \bullet \qquad \text{pre } AOp_i \wedge R \Rightarrow \text{pre } COp_i \qquad \square$$

For the behavioural interpretation of ADTs, the last condition needs to be strengthened to an equality. Note that necessarily (due to conformity) $?AOp_i = ?COp_i$ and $!AOp_i = !COp_i$.

If we leave the state space unchanged, i.e. R equals the identity relation on AS, the simpler conditions of "operation refinement" result.

Definition 11 (Z operation refinement).   The standard Z ADT $(S, AInit, \{AOp_i\}_{i \in I})$ is operation refined by $(S, CInit, \{COp_i\}_{i \in I})$ if they are conformal, and

$$\forall S \bullet (CInit \Rightarrow AInit)$$

and $\forall i : I$

$$\forall S; \ ?AOp_i; \ !AOp_i; \ S' \bullet \operatorname{pre} AOp_i \wedge COp_i \Rightarrow AOp_i$$
$$\forall S; \ ?AOp_i \qquad\qquad \bullet \qquad\quad \operatorname{pre} AOp_i \Rightarrow \operatorname{pre} COp_i \qquad\qquad \square$$

For the remainder of this paper, we will concentrate on downward simulation, and hence when we refer to refinement we are in fact refering to downward simulation only. Similar results can be derived for upward simulation.

3 Examples

A two-dimensional world, in which some object moves about and its movement and position can be observed, is represented by the standard Z ADT $(2D, Init, \{Move, Where\})$ where

---
_2D_____
| $x, y : \mathbb{Z}$

_Init_____
| $2D$
| ‾‾‾‾‾‾‾‾‾
| $x = y = 0$

_Move_____
| $\Delta 2D$

_Where_____
| $\Xi 2D$
| $x!, y! : \mathbb{Z}$
| ‾‾‾‾‾‾‾‾‾
| $x! = x' \wedge y! = y'$

Because the state components x and y are directly observable through the *Where* operation, any data refinement of this ADT would involve reconstructing x and y in *Where*. Therefore we will mostly concentrate on *operation* refinements of this specification. As *Where* is total and deterministic, it cannot be refined any further. Possible operation refinements for *Move* include the following:

_DontMove_____
| $\Xi 2D$

_Swap_____
| $\Delta 2D$
| ‾‾‾‾‾‾‾‾‾
| $x' = y \wedge y' = x$

_StepLeft_____
| $\Delta 2D$
| ‾‾‾‾‾‾‾‾‾
| $x' = x - 1 \wedge y' = y$

_StepRight_____
| $\Delta 2D$
| ‾‾‾‾‾‾‾‾‾
| $x' = x + 1 \wedge y' = y$

As *Move* is total, all of these are refinements in both interpretations ("contract" and "behavioural").

However, the following systems are not traditionally considered refinements of the above ADT. This is in contrast to the fact that we could consider the above ADT a partial or abstract description of every one of them.

Ex1 A system where *Move* does not simply have a non-deterministic result, but there is external control that we were previously unaware of, i.e. *Move* is replaced by

$$\begin{array}{|l}\hline \textit{Translate} \\\hline \Delta 2D \\ x?, y? : \mathbb{Z} \\\hline x' = x + x? \land y' = y + y? \\\hline \end{array}$$

This is not a valid refinement, because *Translate* has inputs that *Move* did not have – the data type interpretations of these Z ADTs are thus not conformal.

Ex2 A system where the output of *Where* is in polar coordinates – also not allowed because conformity enforces identical output types. (The internal representation of the state *can* be changed to polar coordinates, of course.)

Ex3 A system where various kinds of *Move* are possible that we did not distinguish above, e.g. the abstract *Move* is replaced by a choice of two concrete operations *StepLeft* and *StepRight*. Again, this would not be a valid refinement, as the data types involved are not conformal, having different index sets.

Ex4 A system which introduces an internal clock, which is left unchanged by *Move* and *Where* but incremented by an internal operation *Tick*, e.g.

$$\begin{array}{|l}\hline \textit{Timed2D1} \\\hline x, y, clock : \mathbb{Z} \\\hline \end{array}$$

$$\begin{array}{|l}\hline \textit{TInit1} \\\hline \textit{Timed2D1} \\\hline x = y = clock = 0 \\\hline \end{array}$$

$$\begin{array}{|l}\hline \textit{TMove1} \\\hline \Delta \textit{Timed2D1} \\\hline clock' = clock \\\hline \end{array}$$

$$\begin{array}{|l}\hline \textit{TWhere1} \\\hline \Xi \textit{Timed2D1} \\ x!, y! : \mathbb{Z} \\\hline x! = x' \land y! = y' \\\hline \end{array}$$

$$\begin{array}{|l}\hline \textit{Tick1} \\\hline \Delta \textit{Timed2D1} \\\hline clock' = clock + 1 \\ x' = x \land y' = y \\\hline \end{array}$$

Ex5 A variant[1] of **Ex4** where the clock counts down and is set to some value initially and by every *Move* operation:

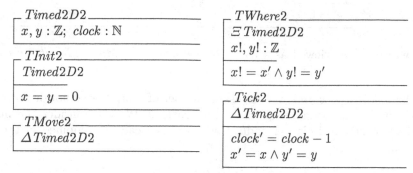

```
┌─ Timed2D2 ──────────────
│ x, y : ℤ;  clock : ℕ
```

```
┌─ TInit2 ────────────────
│ Timed2D2
├─────────────────────────
│ x = y = 0
```

```
┌─ TMove2 ────────────────
│ Δ Timed2D2
```

```
┌─ TWhere2 ───────────────
│ Ξ Timed2D2
│ x!, y! : ℤ
├─────────────────────────
│ x! = x' ∧ y! = y'
```

```
┌─ Tick2 ─────────────────
│ Δ Timed2D2
├─────────────────────────
│ clock' = clock − 1
│ x' = x ∧ y' = y
```

Neither of these is a refinement of $2D$ according to the Spivey rules.

Ex6 Another system where the effect of *Move* is non-deterministic to the observer, but determined elsewhere; *SetNext* must be an "internal" operation:

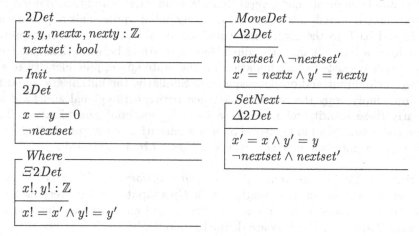

```
┌─ 2Det ──────────────────
│ x, y, nextx, nexty : ℤ
│ nextset : bool
```

```
┌─ Init ──────────────────
│ 2Det
├─────────────────────────
│ x = y = 0
│ ¬nextset
```

```
┌─ Where ─────────────────
│ Ξ2Det
│ x!, y! : ℤ
├─────────────────────────
│ x! = x' ∧ y! = y'
```

```
┌─ MoveDet ───────────────
│ Δ2Det
├─────────────────────────
│ nextset ∧ ¬nextset'
│ x' = nextx ∧ y' = nexty
```

```
┌─ SetNext ───────────────
│ Δ2Det
├─────────────────────────
│ x' = x ∧ y' = y
│ ¬nextset ∧ nextset'
```

Again the internal operation is a "stuttering step" when the obvious simulation is used, but then the precondition of *MoveDet* is stronger than that of *Move* which is not allowed in usual refinement. (The boolean *nextset* is manipulated in such a way that *Move* and *SetNext* can only happen alternately.)

Ex7 A system where an additional (external) operation is available, e.g.

```
┌─ From0 ─────────────────────────────────
│ Ξ2D;
│ d! : ℝ
├─────────────────────────────────────────
│ d! = √(x² + y²)
```

$$d! = \sqrt{x^2 + y^2}$$

or

---

[1] This non-divergent variant was suggested by Stefan Kahrs.

$$\begin{array}{|l}\hline \_\_Reset_____ \\ \quad \Delta 2D \\ \hline \quad x' = y' = 0 \\ \hline \end{array}$$

which is *not* viewed as a concrete occurrence of *Move*. (*Reset* does refine *Move*.) Clearly this would not be allowed for reasons of conformity.

In the following sections, we discuss a number of more liberal notions of refinement, using the examples above as illustrations. We will consider the liberalisations mostly in isolation, indicating how they can be combined in the final section.

4   IO Refinement

It has now been mentioned several times that operations and their more concrete versions are required to have identical inputs and outputs. This requirement can be traced back to the conformity condition on the ADTs when interpreted as 4-tuple data types. It was mentioned that simulations between those interpreted data types consisted of a simulation on the state space, plus identity relations between the input and output sequences. Similarly, the initialisation and finalisation simply copy the relevant sequence between the global and local state. Clearly these identity relations are a focus of potential generalisation. This is explored in full detail in [5], based on a generalisation of the "unwinding" in [27]; the explanation given here is partially suggested by ideas in [25].

Definition 12 (Transformers). An *input transformer IT* for an operation *Op* is a schema whose outputs exactly match *Op*'s inputs, i.e. for every name $x?$ in *Op* there is a name $x!$ in *IT* and vice versa, and all of whose other names are inputs. *Output transformers* are defined analogously.   □

For a formal definition of these notions, and how IO transformers are applied using the schema piping operator $\gg$, cf. [5].

In the relational framework, one should view input transformers as being applied to every input value at initialisation, and output transformers as being applied (inversely) to every output at finalisation. From the refinement requirements on initialisation and finalisation it follows that input transformers must be total on the abstract input: every abstract input must still be allowable. Similarly, output transformers should be injective from abstract output to concrete output: different abstract outputs should be distinguishable by leading to different concrete outputs.

In [5] we present an IO refinement rule which allows IO refinement concurrently with data refinement. However, due to the large number of variables in that rule (all those in the data refinement rule of Definition 10, plus 4 more), we prefer to separate IO refinement steps from other data refinement steps.

Definition 13 (Simple input refinement). A simple input refinement of an ADT $(S, Init, \{Op_i\}_{i \in I})$ is the replacement of an operation Op_i by an operation Op_i", such that for some input transformer IT

$$IT \gg Op_i\text{"} \equiv Op_i$$

In that case, IT needs to be added to the initialisation of the ADT in its interpretation as a 4-tuple data type. $\qquad\qquad\square$

The most obvious instances of simple input refinement are:

– adding an input whose value is not used in the new operation;
– replacing an input by an isomorphic one (total bijective input transformer)

The development in **Ex1** can now be justified in two steps: the first is a simple input refinement step introducing inputs $x?$ and $y?$ which are not used. The corresponding input transformer takes the input of *Move* – there was none, so it is the empty tuple – and relates it to any pair $x?, y? : \mathbb{Z}$. The second step is then an operation refinement, reducing the non-determinism by using $x?$ and $y?$.

Definition 14 (Simple output refinement). A simple output refinement of an ADT $(S, Init, \{Op_i\}_{i \in I})$ is the replacement of an operation Op_i by an operation Op_i", such that for some output transformer OT

$$Op_i\text{"} \gg OT \equiv Op_i$$

In that case, OT needs to be added to the finalisation of the ADT in its interpretation as a 4-tuple data type. $\qquad\qquad\square$

The most obvious instances of simple output refinement are:

– adding an output whose value does not depend on the state;
– replacing an output by an isomorphic one (total bijective output transformer)

Example **Ex2** is of course an instance of a total bijective output transformer.

It is clear that the input and output transformers used in refinement steps (unlike simulation relations which play a similar rôle), need to be preserved in order to recapture the abstract IO. For that reason it might be best to define an alternative kind of ADT which incorporates input and output transformers for every operation.

The central observation made in [5] is that IO refinement rules as presented in this section are (still) a consequence of the data refinement theorems of He, Hoare and Sanders. For that reason, this liberalisation of refinement does not require a generalisation of the notion of refinement as given in Definition 4. Rather, it only requires a generalisation of the embedding of a Z ADT in the 4-tuple data type (Definition 8) which takes into account any input and output transformers used. However, we do not present this generalisation here as it would be dominated by the transformations required to treat all operations as having the same input and output types.

5   Adding Internal Operations

There are two approaches to refining an ADT when we wish to add internal operations: use the existing refinement rules (treating the internal operations separately), or generalise the existing rules.

We can maintain the existing rules by using so called stuttering steps in a verification of a refinement. A stuttering step is an operation which does not change the abstract state, represented in Z by $skip \mathrel{\widehat{=}} [\Xi S]$ if S is the state space. We can then ask that all internal operations in an ADT refine $skip$ when verifying a refinement. Since a stuttering step is total the requirements for refining to a concrete internal operation $CIOp$ are

$R \wedge CIOp \Rightarrow skip$

$R \Rightarrow \mathrm{pre}\, CIOp$

where $skip$ is the stuttering step in the original ADT that is being refined.

For example, example **Ex4** describes a valid refinement if we use stuttering steps. Considering the observable operations we see that $TMove1$ refines $Move$ and $TWhere1$ refines $Where$. In addition, the internal operation $Tick1$ refines $skip \mathrel{\widehat{=}} [\Xi 2D]$ where the retrieve relation is the identity on the common components of the two ADTs (i.e. x and y).

There are a number of problems with this approach though. The more trivial objection is that we have had to break conformity and introduce stuttering steps in the original ADT before we can verify the refinement. This seems rather artificial. More important is the interpretation of internal operations and the potential for divergence through their introduction.

Internal operations are interpreted as being internal because they are not under the control of the environment of the ADT, and in some way they represent operations that the system can invoke whenever their preconditions hold. Because of this we do not want divergence to be introduced by a refinement as a result of their infinitely repeated application. However, refinements of $skip$ have precisely this property. Look at $Tick1$ in **Ex4**. As an internal operation there is nothing to stop it being repeatedly invoked, this causes the system to go into livelock preventing any other operation from occurring.

Related to this issue is a question concerning the meaning of a precondition of an internal operation. For internal operations we need to take a "behavioural" interpretation of their precondition, regardless of the interpretation taken for the observable operations, because we wish them to be applicable only at certain values in the state space. To see this consider an internal protocol timeout being modelled by an internal operation. Clearly we wish the timeout to be invoked only at certain points within the protocol's behaviour. Incorrect refinements would result if we could weaken its precondition and timeout at arbitrary points. Therefore internal operations may not be applied outside their precondition.

In **Ex5** we have attempted to solve the divergence in **Ex4** by only allowing the $Tick$ operation to be invoked a finite number of times. However, this ADT is not a refinement of $2D$ even with stuttering steps. In particular, we fail to have

$R \Rightarrow \mathrm{pre}\, Tick2$

because the precondition of *Tick2* requires that $clock \geq 1$ which we cannot guarantee from R.

A solution to this problem is to draw upon the experience of refining internal operations in process algebras. What we need to do in general is to view refinement in terms of external behaviour, and we can define a set of *weak refinement* rules [13,14] that ensure the observable behaviour of the refined ADT is a valid refinement of the observable behaviour of the original ADT.

We will still assume the sets of observable operations in a refinement are conformal, but we extend the notion of a data type to include a set of internal operations $\{IOp_j\}_{j \in J}$ for some index set J. The definition of conformal is adjusted to require that the indexing sets of *observable* operations coincide. However, we make no requirements on the conformity of the internal operations, and indeed weak refinement will allow the introduction or removal of internal operations during a refinement.

The definition of weak refinement is motivated by the approach taken to internal actions in a process algebra. In particular we move from the application of a single observable operation Op to a situation where a finite number of internal operations are allowed before and after the occurrence of that operation. This corresponds to the change from $P \xrightarrow{a} Q$ to $P \overset{a}{\Longrightarrow} Q$ in a process algebra when internal (i.e. unobservable) actions are taken into account.

Data refinement now requires that for any given program (i.e. choice of observable operations), every complete program over C possibly involving internal operations is contained in some complete program over A (possibly involving internal operations but using the same choice of observable operations). Formally, this leads to the following generalisation of Definition 4.

Definition 15 (Weak data refinement).   Consider data types $A = (AS, AInit, \{AOp_i\}_{i \in I \cup J}, AFin)$ and $C = (CS, CInit, \{COp_i\}_{i \in I \cup K}, CFin)$, where J and K are both disjoint from I; the visible (external) operations in both datatypes are those from I only. (J and K need not be disjoint.) For a program p over I, define its set of programs with internal operations in A as follows (and similarly for C):[2]

$$\hat{p}_A = \{q_A \mid q \in \text{seq}(I \cup J) \wedge q \restriction I = p\}$$

Now C *weakly refines* A iff for each finite sequence p over I,

$$\forall x : \hat{p}_C \bullet \exists y : \hat{p}_A \bullet x \subseteq y \qquad \qquad \square$$

Observe that this is a correct generalisation: when J and K are empty, $\hat{p}_A$ and $\hat{p}_C$ are singleton sets containing only p_A and p_C, respectively.

To verify such weak refinements we adapt the simulation rules given above. To do so we encode the idea of a finite number of internal operations before and after an observable operation in the Z schema calculus. In order to avoid

---

[2] The filtering expression $s \restriction A$ takes from a sequence s only those elements contained in set A.

quantifications over sequences of internal operations in the definition of weak refinement, we encode "all possible finite internal evolution" for a specification as a *single* operation Int (allowing us to write $Int \,\overset{\circ}{,}\, Op \,\overset{\circ}{,}\, Int$). The details of how this is done are in [14]. Internal operations in the concrete and abstract specifications are differentiated by using the subscripts C and A on Int.

The definition of a weak downward simulation then has the same form as the standard Z definition. We typically replace operations Op by $Int \,\overset{\circ}{,}\, Op \,\overset{\circ}{,}\, Int$ to allow for internal evolution before and after. To prevent the introduction of divergence, there are two additional conditions based upon those in [8].

Definition 16 (Weak downward simulation). Given Z data types $A = (AS, AInit, \{AOp_i\}_{i \in I \cup J})$ and $C = (CS, CInit, \{COp_i\}_{i \in I \cup K})$, where J and K (the index sets denoting internal operations) are both disjoint from I. The relation R on $AS \wedge CS$ is a *weak downward simulation* from A to C if

$$\forall CS \bullet (CInit \,\overset{\circ}{,}\, Int_C) \Rightarrow \exists AS \bullet (AInit \,\overset{\circ}{,}\, Int_A) \wedge R$$

and $\forall i : I \cup (J \cap K)$

$$\forall AS;\ CS;\ CS' \bullet \mathrm{pre}(Int_A \,\overset{\circ}{,}\, AOp_i) \wedge R \wedge (Int_C \,\overset{\circ}{,}\, COp_i \,\overset{\circ}{,}\, Int_C)$$
$$\Rightarrow \exists AS' \bullet R' \wedge (Int_A \,\overset{\circ}{,}\, AOp_i \,\overset{\circ}{,}\, Int_A)$$
$$\forall AS;\ CS \bullet \mathrm{pre}(Int_A \,\overset{\circ}{,}\, AOp_i) \wedge R \Rightarrow \mathrm{pre}(Int_C \,\overset{\circ}{,}\, COp_i)$$

where we have elided quantification over inputs and outputs (as in Definition 10) and (for technical reasons) redefine the precondition of an internal operation IOp acting on state S as

$$\mathrm{pre}\,IOp = \mathrm{pre}\,\Xi S = S$$

In addition, we require the existence of a well-founded set WF with partial order $<$, and a variant E which is an expression in the concrete state variables satisfying the following conditions:

D1 $R \vdash E \in WF$
D2 $\forall i : K \bullet R \wedge COp_i \vdash E' < E$ $\square$

Note that although internal operations decrease the variant, there are no constraints on observable operations, which are allowed to increase the variant. This means that an internal operation can be invoked an infinite number of times, but not in an infinite sequence between observable operations.

With these definitions in place we can see that **Ex4** does not describe a weak refinement of $2D$ because the internal operation $Tick1$ can introduce divergence, i.e. it breaks the divergence criteria D1 and D2.

However, **Ex5** does represent a weak refinement of $2D$. To see this note first that there are no internal operations in $2D$, secondly we note that $Tick2$ does not change the effect of any other variable apart from $clock$, and therefore does not alter the effect of the observable operations. This means that the conditions on the observable operations hold. The remaining conditions are to verify the correctness of $Tick2$, but since $R \wedge Tick2 \Rightarrow \Xi 2D$ this follows, and the divergence criteria which in this case is trivial ($\mathbb{N}$ being the set WF).

Weak refinement can also be used to verify **Ex6**. Here $SetNext$ is the internal operation. With a retrieve relation being the identity on x and y, correctness and divergence for $SetNext$ are trivial. However, $MoveDet$ does not refine $Move$ without consideration of the internal $SetNext$. But since applicability in weak refinement just requires that

$$\text{pre } Move \wedge R \Rightarrow \text{pre}(SetNext \, \raisebox{0.2ex}{$\substack{\circ\\\circ}$} \, MoveDet)$$

and similarly for correctness, the conditions for weak refinement are met.

6   Adding Visible Operations

Ideas from process algebra served to motivate a generalisation of Definition 4 that allows internal actions. From the fact that most refinement relations in process algebra do not allow addition of new observable actions ("extension of the alphabet") we might then conclude that refinement of ADTs should not lead to extended sets of visible operations either.

In the behavioural approach this appears to be a defensible position. When our specification is some usual drinks machine using actions *coin*, *coffee*, and *tea*, we would be distinctly unhappy if the implementing machine came with a button that allowed the removal of all the money from the machine. Such an operation, which clearly disrupts the system state, should not be possible. However, adding an operation which displayed the amount of coffee left in the machine (without changing the state) would maybe not be as harmful.

However, in the "contract" interpretation it is less clear that allowing extra operations should be unsound. The canonical view of an ADT in this interpretation is of a software component whose operations are only required to function as specified when their preconditions hold. There being additional operations available in the component besides the ones the customer intends to use does not appear to be a problem. Indeed, it would require some disingenuity to distinguish between an operation that "does not exist" and one whose precondition is universally false. The consequence of identifying those is the obvious one: in the behavioural approach, no extra operations may be added; in the contract approach, they may be added at will.

The corresponding generalisation of Definition 4 is given below. Implicitly it generalises the notion of conformity to the concrete index set *containing* the abstract index set, and as before it quantifies over all *abstract* programs only, not making any restrictions on programs containing indices not in the abstract index set. This is in contrast to weak refinement, where all concrete behaviours are considered.

Definition 17 (Data refinement with alphabet extension).
Consider data types $A = (AS, AInit, \{AOp_i\}_{i \in I}, AFin)$ and
$C = (CS, CInit, \{COp_i\}_{i \in I \cup J}, CFin)$. Now C *refines* A *with alphabet extension*

iff for each finite sequence p over I,

$$p_C \subseteq p_A \qquad \qquad \square$$

Observe that this is a correct generalisation: when J is empty, this reduces to Definition 4. The informal justification of this definition is that it ensures that the concrete system behaves like the abstract one when executing any sequence of instructions that the abstract one allowed.

In this view, it is fine to add operations (like *Reset* and *From0* in **Ex7**) in the contract interpretation. In the behavioural interpretation, neither is allowed, although adding *From0* appears harmless. However, this is not only due to the fact that *From0* leaves the state unchanged, but also to it presenting information that was derivable from the other "observing" operation, i.e. *Where*. (For a more extensive discussion on observing operations and their refinement rules, cf. [4].)

However, this generalisation does not cover the case where in the abstract ADT we have a single operation which has multiple concrete representations. Example **Ex3** suggested that an abstract *Move* could actually be reflected in various sorts of concrete move operations, e.g. *StepLeft* and *StepRight*. In other words, we would like to link *Move* to *StepLeft* ∨ *StepRight*. Allowing this requires a further generalisation of Definition 17 and in particular the notion of conformity: we would give an explicit mapping from the abstract index set to the concrete index set. We shall call this an *alphabet translation*. It would be total (every abstract operation has at least one concrete counterpart) and injective (every concrete operation reflects at most one abstract operation).

Definition 18 (Data refinement with alphabet translation).
Consider data types $A = (AS, AInit, \{AOp_i\}_{i \in I}, AFin)$ and
$C = (CS, CInit, \{COp_i\}_{i \in J}, CFin)$. Let α be a total and injective mapping from I to J. Define the extension $\alpha*$ of α to sequences by

$$(s, t) \in \alpha* \equiv \#s = \#t \wedge \forall i : 1..\#s \bullet (s\,i, t\,i) \in \alpha$$

Then *C refines A with alphabet translation α* iff

$$\forall p : \text{seq}\,I \bullet \exists q : \text{seq}\,J \bullet (p, q) \in \alpha* \wedge q_C \subseteq p_A \qquad \square$$

Observe that this is a correct generalisation of Definition 17: the identity relation on I is a total and injective mapping from I to $I \cup J$, and its extension to sequences is the identity over $\text{seq}\,I$.

7   Splitting Operations

In Section 5 we relaxed the notion of conformity to allow the introduction of internal operations, and then in Section 6 we allowed the abstract operations to be a subset of the concrete ones. In fact we can go even further and relax the requirement of conformity between the sets of observable operations, and the purpose of doing so is to support action (or non-atomic) refinement.

Action refinement is when a single operation in the original ADT is refined by, not one, but a sequence of concrete operations in the refined data type. Such action refinements arise in a number of settings quite naturally (see [1]) and they allow initial specifications to be described independently of the structure of the eventual implementation. The desired final structure can then be introduced by non-atomic refinements which supports a change of operation granularity absent if we require conformity. [11] discusses how action refinement can be supported in Z, and we survey that approach here.

We are now in a situation where data types A and C have different indexing sets (I_A and I_C respectively) for their observable operations, so to discuss refinement we need to be informed of the relationship between them. In general this could be an arbitrary relation, but we consider here a mapping $\rho : I_A \to \text{seq}\, I_C$, so that ρ describes the concrete counterparts for each operation in A. For example, if $\rho(3) = \langle 6, 4\rangle$ then this means that operation AOp_3 is refined by the sequence $COp_6 \,\S\, COp_4$. Our liberalised notion of refinement then becomes

Definition 19 (Action refinement). C action refines A with respect to ρ iff for each finite sequence p over I_A, $(\frown/(\rho \circ p))_C \subseteq p_A$.[3]   □

For example, if AOp_1 is refined by the sequence $COp_1 \,\S\, COp_2$ then action refinement requires that, amongst others, $CI \,\S\, COp_1 \,\S\, COp_2 \,\S\, CF \subseteq AI \,\S\, AOp_1 \,\S\, AF$. This is a sort of liveness condition: to every abstract program there is an equivalent concrete one. However, the liberalisation comes at the expense of safety: there might be concrete programs that have no abstract counterpart. For example, $CI \,\S\, COp_2 \,\S\, CF$ might not correspond to anything at the abstract level. The requirements of safety are discussed in more detail in [11], here we briefly sketch the consequences of Definition 19.

Simulations can be used to make step-by-step comparisons as before. To ease the presentation let us suppose that in the two data types the indexes coincide except that one of the abstract operations AOp is refined by the sequence $COp_1 \,\S\, COp_2$. When we consider the applicability and correctness conditions from Definition 10 in this new setting they become three conditions, namely:

$$(\text{dom}\, AOp \lhd R \,\S\, COp_1 \,\S\, COp_2) \subseteq AOp \,\S\, R$$
$$\text{ran}((\text{dom}\, AOp) \lhd R) \subseteq \text{dom}\, COp_1$$
$$\text{ran}((\text{dom}\, AOp) \lhd R \,\S\, COp_1) \subseteq \text{dom}\, COp_2$$

These have obvious counterparts in Z which we give now (we have elided the quantification over inputs and outputs). This is called action refinement without IO transformations because we have not considered how to deal with input and output as yet.

Definition 20 (Action refinement without IO transformations).
Let R be the retrieve relation between data types $(AS, AI, \{AOp\})$ and

---

[3] This Z expression (ab)uses the representation of sequences by functions in Z. Functional programmers might be happier with $(concat(map\ \rho\ p))_C \subseteq p_A$

$(CS, CI, \{COp_1, COp_2\})$. R is an action downward simulation if the following hold

$$\forall AS;\ CS;\ CS' \bullet \mathrm{pre}\,AOp \wedge (COp_1 \,\mathring{9}\, COp_2) \wedge R \Rightarrow \exists\, Astate' \bullet R' \wedge AOp$$
$$\forall AS;\ CS \bullet \mathrm{pre}\,AOp \wedge R \Rightarrow \mathrm{pre}\,COp_1$$
$$\forall AS;\ CS \bullet \mathrm{pre}\,AOp \wedge R \wedge COp_1 \Rightarrow \mathrm{pre}\,COp_2$$

together with the initialisation condition.   □

As an example, we could consider Example **Ex6** as an action refinement, refining *Move* into two *observable* operations, *SetNext* followed by *MoveDet*. It is easy to check that this is a correct action refinement.

What is the price of liberalisation though? Well, since *SetNext* and *MoveDet* are both observable operations, a valid program might only include one half of the concrete decomposition. The simulation rules provide no regulation to ensure that nothing bad happens. We can however introduce some extra policing to ensure the operations in the concrete decomposition are well behaved.

For example, we know that if COp_2 happens straight after COp_1, then the composition refines AOp. But what happens if we are in a concrete state that was not a result of a COp_1 invocation? We could now require that COp_2 had no effect, i.e. outside the range of COp_1, COp_2 should be *skip*. This can be formalised as[4]

$$R \,\mathring{9}\, (\mathrm{ran}\,COp_1 \lhd COp_2) \subseteq R$$

An alternative policy is that if COp_1 has occurred, then the only operation to have an effect should be COp_2, i.e. other operations cannot interfere with a concrete transaction yet to be completed. This is modelled by saying that COp_1 followed by any other operation (apart from COp_2) is the same as COp_1:

$$COp_1 \,\mathring{9}\, Op \subseteq COp_1 \qquad \text{for all } Op \neq COp_2$$

The opposite way to achieve a safety property on the first part of a decomposition is to require the cancellation of a half completed sequence of concrete operations, that is

$$COp_1 \,\mathring{9}\, Op \subseteq Op \qquad \text{for all } Op \neq COp_2$$

We should note here in passing that these properties, although preserved if we take the weakest refinement, are not preserved by arbitrary refinements.

7.1 Inputs and Outputs

The action refinement of *Move* into *SetNext* followed by *MoveDet* is rather trivial. The real challenge in action refinement is to deal with operations containing input and output, and ask how we can decompose this IO across the sequence

---

[4] $\lhd$ denotes domain anti-restriction, i.e. $S \lhd R = \{(x, y) \in R \mid x \notin S\}$.

of concrete operations. For example, we might wish to refine *Translate* in **Ex1** into two operations each of which translates a single coordinate.

This can be supported if we combine the above action refinement rules with IO refinement discussed in Section 4. We will not go into all the details here, but essentially we use input and output transformers whose structure is identical to that of the mapping $\rho : I_A \to \text{seq } I_C$.

Thus instead of input and output transformers IT and OT which change the input/output of one operation into another, we use mappings r_{in} and r_{out} where

$$r_{in} : Ainput \longrightarrow \text{seq } Cinput$$
$$r_{out} : Aoutput \longrightarrow \text{seq } Coutput$$

This allows input and output to be split across an action refinement (details of the full definition are in [11]). For example, *Translate* can be action refined into *TranslateX* ⨾ *TranslateY* where

$TranslateX$
$\Delta 2D$
$x? : \mathbb{Z}$
$x' = x + x?$
$y' = y$

$TranslateY$
$\Delta 2D$
$y? : \mathbb{Z}$
$x' = x$
$y' = y + y?$

8   Conclusions and Related Work

We have presented an overview of refinement relations that could be used for abstract data types in (a language like) Z, going from the traditional rules to a collection of more liberal rules. All of these have been motivated as consequences or extensions of the data refinement theory set forth by He, Hoare and Sanders.

The generalisations proposed are compatible with each other. First, IO refinement can be combined with the other generalisations, as it (like traditional refinement) derives from Definition 4, which is generalised by the other definitions. Weak refinement and alphabet translation are orthogonal, as in Definition 18 it is possible to generalise by taking the closures of p and q under composition with internal behaviour, with the appropriate extra quantification. The same sort of construction could be applied to Definition 19 to combine action refinement with weak refinement. The combination of alphabet translation and action refinement is obtained by taking the decomposition mapping ρ to be an *arbitrary* total relation between abstract indices and sequences of concrete indices. Injectivity of alphabet translation may need to be weakened or reinterpreted in that situation. The combination of all three generalisations seems feasible theoretically, although mind-boggling in practice. As is already the case with operation refinement and data refinement, it is probably advisable to perform refinement in "one dimension at a time".

Most of the refinement relations considered have been shown to be useful in our work on viewpoint specification in Z [3,6]. We now have a refinement relation which allows the omission of operations, inputs, and outputs from the specification of viewpoints to which they are of no concern. Action refinement will, in addition to that, allow viewpoints at different levels of granularity.

With the exception of the considerations on adding external operations, the refinement rules have been presented in our earlier papers [13,14,5,11], some also in work by Woodcock and others [7,25]. However, the relationship between these rules and (generalisations of) Definition 4 has not previously been made explicit, and we have not previously analysed the compatibility of these rules. Further details are expected to appear in [12].

A comprehensive and detailed overview of the semantic foundations of data refinement with an extensive bibliography can be found in [9].

The issue of providing extra methods in subtypes/subclasses while preserving a semantical ("refinement") interpretation of inheritance has been studied extensively, most notably in [21,20].

Acknowledgements

We would like to thank Ralph Miarka and Chris Taylor. Our weekly discussions with them have been a great help in clarifying many of the thoughts in this paper.

Many thanks go to the MPC referees and in particular Lindsay Groves, who made many useful suggestions for improvements.

References

1. L. Aceto. *Action refinement in process algebras.* CUP, London, 1992. 161 .
2. M. Ainsworth, A. H. Cruickshank, P. J. L. Wallis, and L. J. Groves. Viewpoint specification and Z. *Information and Software Technology*, 36(1):43–51, February 1994. 145
3. E. Boiten, H. Bowman, J. Derrick, and M. Steen. Viewpoint consistency in Z and LOTOS: A case study. In J. Fitzgerald, C.B. Jones, and P. Lucas, editors, *FME'97: Industrial Application and Strengthened Foundations of Formal Methods*, volume 1313 of *Lecture Notes in Computer Science*, pages 644–664. Springer-Verlag, September 1997. 163
4. E. A. Boiten and J. Derrick. Grey box data refinement. In J. Grundy, M. Schwenke, and T. Vickers, editors, *International Refinement Workshop & Formal Methods Pacific '98*, Discrete Mathematics and Theoretical Computer Science, pages 45–59, Canberra, September 1998. Springer-Verlag. 160
5. E. A. Boiten and J. Derrick. IO-refinement in Z. In A. Evans, D. Duke, and T. Clark, editors, *3rd BCS-FACS Northern Formal Methods Workshop*. Springer-Verlag, September 1998. http://www.ewic.org.uk/. 144, 154, 155, 164
6. E. A. Boiten, J. Derrick, H. Bowman, and M. Steen. Constructive consistency checking for partial specification in Z. *Science of Computer Programming*, 35(1):29–75, September 1999. 145, 163
7. C. Bolton, J. Davies, and J. Woodcock. On the refinement and simulation of data types and processes. In K. Araki, A. Galloway, and K. Taguchi, editors, *International conference on Integrated Formal Methods 1999 (IFM'99)*, pages 273–292, York, July 1999. Springer. 148, 164

8. M. Butler. An approach to the design of distributed systems with B AMN. In J. P. Bowen, M. G. Hinchey, and D. Till, editors, *ZUM'97: The Z formal specification notation*, LNCS 1212, pages 223–241, Reading, April 1997. Springer-Verlag. 158

9. W.-P. de Roever and K. Engelhardt. *Data Refinement: Model-Oriented Proof Methods and their Comparison*, volume 47 of *Cambridge Tracts in Theoretical Computer Science*. Cambridge University Press, 1998. 146, 148, 164

10. J. Derrick. A single complete refinement rule for Z. *Logic and Computation*, 2000. To appear. 147

11. J. Derrick and E. A. Boiten. Non-atomic refinement in Z. In J. M. Wing, J. C. P. Woodcock, and J. Davies, editors, *FM'99*, volume 1708 of *Lecture Notes in Computer Science*, pages 1477–1496. Springer, 1999. 161, 163, 164

12. J. Derrick and E. A. Boiten. *Refinement in Z and Object-Z: Foundations and Advanced Applications*. Springer-Verlag, 2001. In preparation. 164

13. J. Derrick, E. A. Boiten, H. Bowman, and M. Steen. Weak refinement in Z. In J. P. Bowen, M. G. Hinchey, and D. Till, editors, *ZUM '97: The Z Formal Specification Notation*, volume 1212 of *Lecture Notes in Computer Science*, pages 369–388. Springer-Verlag, 1997. 157, 164

14. J. Derrick, E. A. Boiten, H. Bowman, and M. Steen. Specifying and refining internal operations in Z. *Formal Aspects of Computing*, 10:125–159, 1998. 157, 158, 164

15. C. Fischer. CSP-OZ - a combination of CSP and Object-Z. In H. Bowman and J. Derrick, editors, *Second IFIP International conference on Formal Methods for Open Object-based Distributed Systems*, pages 423–438. Chapman & Hall, July 1997. 148

16. P. H. B. Gardiner and C. Morgan. A single complete rule for data refinement. *Formal Aspects of Computing*, 5:367–382, 1993. 147

17. He Jifeng, C. A. R. Hoare, and J. W. Sanders. Data refinement refined. In B. Robinet and R. Wilhelm, editors, *Proc. ESOP 86*, volume 213 of *Lecture Notes in Computer Science*, pages 187–196. Springer-Verlag, 1986. 144, 145, 146

18. C. A. R. Hoare. Proof of correctness of data representations. *Acta Informatica*, 1:271–281, 1972. 145

19. C. B. Jones. *Software Development: a Rigorous Approach*. Prentice Hall, 1980. 145

20. K. R. M. Leino. Data groups: Specifying the modification of extended state. In *OOPSLA '98*, pages 144–153, 1998. 164

21. B. H. Liskov and J. M. Wing. A behavioural notion of subtyping. *ACM Transactions on Programming Languages and Systems*, 16(6):1811–1841, 1994. 164

22. G. Smith. *The Object-Z Specification Language*. Kluwer Academic Publishers, 2000. 148

23. G. Smith and J. Derrick. Refinement and verification of concurrent systems specified in Object-Z and CSP. In M. Hinchey and Shaoying Liu, editors, *First IEEE International Conference on Formal Engineering Methods (ICFEM '97)*, pages 293–302, Hiroshima, Japan, November 1997. IEEE Computer Society. 148

24. J. M. Spivey. *The Z Notation: A Reference Manual*. Prentice Hall International Series in Computer Science, 2nd edition, 1992. 144, 145, 150

25. S. Stepney, D. Cooper, and J. Woodcock. More powerful data refinement in Z. In J. P. Bowen, A. Fett, and M. G. Hinchey, editors, *ZUM'98: The Z Formal Specification Notation*, volume 1493 of *Lecture Notes in Computer Science*, pages 284–307. Springer-Verlag, September 1998. 144, 154, 164

26. B. Strulo. How firing conditions help inheritance. In J. P. Bowen and M. G. Hinchey, editors, *Ninth Annual Z User Workshop*, LNCS 967, pages 264–275, Limerick, September 1995. Springer-Verlag. 148

27. J. Woodcock and J. Davies. *Using Z: Specification, Refinement, and Proof.* Prentice Hall, 1996. 144, 148, 150, 154

28. P. Zave and M. Jackson. Where do operations come from? A multiparadigm specification technique. *IEEE Transactions on Software Engineering*, 22(7):508–528, July 1996. 145

Theorems about Composition

Michel Charpentier[1] and K. Mani Chandy[2]

[1] Computer Science Department, University of New Hampshire,
Durham, NH 03824.
charpov@cs.unh.edu
[2] Computer Science Department, California Institute of Technology,
Pasadena, CA 91125.
mani@cs.caltech.edu

Abstract. Compositional designs require component specifications that can be composed: Designers have to be able to deduce system properties from components specifications. On the other hand, components specifications should be abstract enough to allow component reuse and to hide substantial parts of correctness proofs in components verifications. Part of the problem is that too abstract specifications do not contain enough information to be composed. Therefore, the right balance between abstraction and composability must be found. This paper explores the systematic construction of abstract specifications that can be composed through specific forms of composition called *existential* and *universal*.

1 Motivations

1.1 Specifications and Proofs in Compositional Design

This paper explores proofs of correctness of systems constructed by composing components. The promise of component technology is that the same component can be used in many systems, and thus the effort that goes into specifying, proving and implementing components can be exploited many times. Compositional design is productive when the effort required to find and compose components is less than the effort required to design an entire system from scratch. Therefore, greater productivity is achieved by using components that embody substantial effort. Rapidly growing commercial efforts into developing libraries of software components (using, for instance, Java beans, Microsoft DNA or CORBA) are witnesses to the industrial interest in component-based designs.

In this paper, we explore the appropriate level of detail for component specifications. Specifications that are too abstract may be too weak to be useful in composition. Specifications that are too detailed are difficult to reuse and may require systems designers to derive more useful and more abstract specifications from the detailed ones. Component designers should identify those component properties that they expect systems designers to need, and design their components to have these properties. This may require putting a substantial amount of effort into proving that a component has properties that are useful in composition. However, these proofs are achieved at the component level and will be reused each time the component is part of a new system.

R. Backhouse and J. N. Oliveira (Eds.): MPC 2000, LNCS 1837, pp. 167–186, 2000.

Figure 1 depicts specifications and proofs in a compositional design. Proofs labeled with 'T' are those component-correctness proofs that are left unchanged through composition and that can be reused in the design of several systems. Proofs labeled with 'C' are proofs of composition, i.e., proofs of system properties from component properties. The way components are specified, and especially the level of abstraction of their specifications, influences the amount of effort that has to be put in T-proofs and in C-proofs. A good framework for composition should allow us to put most of the effort in T-proofs and keep C-proofs as simple as possible.

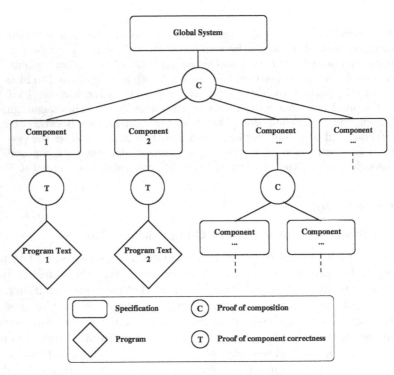

Fig. 1. A compositional design

1.2   Abstract Specifications that Compose

We introduce an informal concept of *compositional properties* to motivate our exploration, and define terms precisely later. Compositional properties are those classes of properties that allow us to deduce system properties from component properties using simple rules. For example, mass is a compositional property because the mass of a system can be deduced in a simple way from the masses of components: the system mass is the sum of component masses. By contrast, heat emitted does not appear to be a compositional property because the heat emitted by a system depends in very complex ways on the shapes, masses, insulation properties and locations of the components. However, engineers have to compute properties of composed systems given properties of components, whether the properties are compositional or not.

In this paper, we restrict ourselves to properties that are predicates on systems. A compositional property is a property whose truth can be established using simple rules from properties of components. The questions that we are exploring are the following:

- What are interesting compositional properties and what are the corresponding proof rules?
- How can we deduce any system property from conjunctions of these compositional properties?

The simplest rules are those that establish that a property X holds for a system given that (i) property X holds for at least one component, or (ii) property X holds for all components. In this paper, we focus our attention on two kinds of compositional properties: *existential properties* and *universal properties*. A property is an existential property exactly when for all systems, a system has the property if there exists a component of the system that has the property. A property is a universal property exactly when for all systems, a system has the property if all components of the system have the property.

Many interesting properties are neither universal nor existential. So, we deduce such system properties in two steps:

- First, we specify components as conjunctions of universal and existential properties so that we can readily derive universal and existential system properties from component properties,
- then we derive the system properties we need from these universal and existential system properties.

1.3   An Illustrative Digression

The next few paragraphs give the reader some intuition of the tradeoff between too much detail and too little detail in component specification by considering the difference between two kinds of properties of reactive systems: invariants and always. This issue has been discussed earlier, for instance in [15,14].

In the context of systems (and components) defined by their infinite computations (reactive systems), a state predicate is an *invariant property* of a program exactly when

- the predicate holds in the initial state of all computations of the program, and
- all atomic transitions from states in which the predicate holds are to states in which the predicate continues to hold.

A state predicate is an *always property* of a program exactly when it holds in all states of all computations of the program.

Invariants tell us about transitions from all states, whether reachable or unreachable. By contrast, always properties tell us about reachable states only.

All invariant properties are always properties. An always property need not be an invariant property because the system may have a transition from an *unreachable state* for which the property holds to a state in which the property does not hold.

An invariant property is universal. If all components of a system enjoy an invariant property then the composed system also enjoys that invariant property. By contrast, an always property is not necessarily universal.

Properties relevant to a system in isolation (i.e., a system that is not composed with other systems) are different from properties relevant to components that we expect to compose with other components. When we study the behavior of a system in isolation, its always properties are relevant, and it is not helpful to know whether an always property is also an invariant property. In this context, always properties offer the appropriate degree of abstraction.

We cannot, however, deduce system properties from always properties of components. The concurrent composition of systems, all of which have the always property that a bank account is nonnegative, may yield a system in which the bank account does indeed become negative. This is because a state that is unreachable when a system executes in isolation may be reachable when that system is composed with other systems.

Thus, always properties are too weak to be helpful in composition even though they have the right degree of abstraction for systems in isolation. However, invariant properties are helpful in composition because they are universal properties. Then, we can weaken invariants to obtain desired always properties.

In our research, we are looking for simple rules that allow us to prove system properties from component properties, for certain restricted kinds of properties. We don't expect to find simple rules for deducing arbitrary kinds of system properties from arbitrary kinds of component properties. The challenge is to find appropriate kinds of compositional properties, and then deduce desired properties by weakening conjunctions of compositional properties.

1.4   Predicate Transformers for Composition

Consider the following problem. A designer of a component F would like to demonstrate that any system that has F as a component enjoys a property X. If property X is an existential property, and if F has property X, then any system that has F as a component will enjoy property X. What if X is not existential?

If we could define a predicate transformer $\mathcal{E}$ where $\mathcal{E}.X$ is existential and at least as strong as X, and if we could demonstrate that component F has property $\mathcal{E}.X$, then any system that includes component F would also have existential property $\mathcal{E}.X$, and therefore would also enjoy the weaker property X. Therefore, component designers can ensure that all systems that contains their components have a property X by proving that their components have a stronger existential property $\mathcal{E}.X$.

What requirements should we place on predicate transformer $\mathcal{E}$ other than that $\mathcal{E}.X$ must be stronger than X? The obvious answer is that $\mathcal{E}.X$ should be as weak as possible. Ideally, it should be the weakest existential property stronger than X, provided that such a property exists.

Now consider the analogous case for universal properties. We would like to prove that a system has a property X if all its components have property X even though X is not a universal property. So, we attempt to introduce a predicate transformer $\mathcal{U}$ with the requirement that $\mathcal{U}.X$ is universal and stronger than X. If we can prove that all components of a system have property $\mathcal{U}.X$ then we can conclude that the system enjoys this property and hence also enjoys the weaker property X.

Can we require that $\mathcal{U}.X$ be the weakest universal property stronger than X? We can show that we cannot do so because there does not exist, in general, a weakest universal property stronger than X. The idea of a predicate transformer $\mathcal{U}$ where $\mathcal{U}.X$ is universal and is stronger than X will indeed help in engineering systems by composing components, but we must define $\mathcal{U}$ in some way other than being the weakest. We do not define a transformer $\mathcal{U}$ in this paper. We only show that $\mathcal{U}.X$ cannot be defined as the weakest universal property stronger than X.

1.5   Overview

Our components are abstract entities. They are not necessarily programs and they may not have "states" or "computations". We consider composition operators that have certain algebraic properties such as associativity and explore theorems that are derived from these properties.

In the next section we introduce components, their properties and the composition law. We also introduce a simple model of components that is used as an example throughout the paper, as well as our notation and vocabulary. Section 3 presents the definition of *existential* and *universal* properties. In this section we introduce a special form of existential properties called *guarantees*. The main results of the paper are presented in section 4 where a property transformer $\mathcal{E}$ for existential composition is defined. Theorems with regard to this property transformer are presented, and the reasons why a property transformer for universal composition is *not* defined in the same way are explored. An example, that uses the simple model previously defined, concludes that section. In section 5, the work is compared with other proposed approaches and some remaining questions are formulated. Finally, conclusions are drawn in section 6.

2   Terminology and Notations

2.1   Predicates, Components and Properties

Function application is denoted with a dot, which has higher precedence than boolean operators and which associates to the left (i.e., $a.b.c = (a.b).c$). The application of function A to parameter x is denoted by $A.x$. Predicates are boolean valued functions. We denote predicates with the capital letters X, Y, Z, ... Components are denoted with the capital letters F, G, H, ... Properties are predicates on components: $X.F$ is the boolean "property X holds in component F".

2.2   Everywhere Operator

Following [11], we use square brackets to denote that a predicate is *"everywhere true"*. For any property X, $[X]$ is the boolean "X holds for all systems".

2.3   Composition

We restrict our attention to a single composition operator $\circ$. We postulate the existence of a binary relation $\sqrt{}$ between components, and we restrict our attention to composition of components that satisfy this relation. We denote by $F\sqrt{}G$ the fact that components F and G can be composed, and then their composition is denoted by $F{\circ}G$.

We assume the existence of a *UNIT* component such that, for any F:

$$UNIT\sqrt{}F \;\land\; F\sqrt{}UNIT \;\land\; (UNIT{\circ}F = F{\circ}UNIT = F) . \tag{1}$$

Furthermore, we assume that $\circ$ is associative and that, for any F, G and H:

$$F\sqrt{}G \;\land\; (F{\circ}G)\sqrt{}H \;\equiv\; G\sqrt{}H \;\land\; F\sqrt{}(G{\circ}H) . \tag{2}$$

The left-hand side and the right-hand side denote (equivalently) that F, G and H can be composed (in that order). We introduce the shortcut $F\sqrt{}G\sqrt{}H$ to represent either side of the equivalence.

Note that we do not assume here any other property of the operator $\circ$, such as symmetry or idempotency.

2.4   Bags of Colored Balls

To illustrate the results presented in this paper, we use a model for components defined as follows:

 − components are bags of colored balls;
 − bags can always be composed ($F\sqrt{}G$ for all F and G) and composition is the union of contents of the component bags in the composed bag;
 − the *UNIT* element is the empty bag. Note that properties of the form *"all balls in the bag are red"* hold in *UNIT*.

Composition here is always defined and is symmetric (Abelian monoid). This needs not be the case for more interesting models. For instance, sequential composition of programs is not symmetric and parallel composition of processes may not always be possible (for example, if a process references a local variable from another process).

3   Existential and Universal Composition

We start our exploration of compositional properties by studying properties that obey certain rules of universal and existential quantification.

3.1   Existential Properties

A property X is existential (denoted by the boolean $exist.X$) exactly when

$$exist.X \; \triangleq \; \langle \forall F, G : F\sqrt{G} : X . F \vee X . G \Rightarrow X . F{\circ}G \rangle \; . \tag{3}$$

A system enjoys an existential property if it has a component that enjoys that property.

3.2   Universal Properties

A property X is universal (denoted by the boolean $univ.X$) exactly when:

$$univ.X \; \triangleq \; \langle \forall F, G : F\sqrt{G} : X . F \wedge X . G \Rightarrow X . F{\circ}G \rangle \; . \tag{4}$$

A system enjoys a universal property if all its components enjoy that property. Note that any existential property is also universal:

$$exist.X \; \Rightarrow \; univ.X \; .$$

3.3   "*guarantees*" Properties

In this section, we show that there is a systematic way to build existential properties from any property. We introduce a function *guarantees*, from pairs of properties to properties:

$$X \; guarantees \; Y . F$$
$$\triangleq \tag{5}$$
$$\langle \forall H, K : H\sqrt{F}\sqrt{K} : X . H{\circ}F{\circ}K \Rightarrow Y . H{\circ}F{\circ}K \rangle \; .$$

Properties of the form X *guarantees* Y are called *guarantees properties*.

An important result about *guarantees* properties is that, for any X and Y, X *guarantees* Y is existential:

Proposition 1 $exist.(X \; guarantees \; Y)$

Proof: See corollary of proposition 12.   □

3.4 Basic Rules

In this section, we give basic rules relating existential properties, universal properties and *guarantees* [4]. Let E and E' be existential properties and U and U' be universal properties. Then, it can easily be proved that:

$$exist \cdot (E \wedge E'), \qquad exist \cdot (E \vee E'),$$
$$univ \cdot (U \wedge U'), \qquad univ \cdot (U \vee E).$$

Note that the disjunction of universal properties is not universal in general, and that strengthening or weakening existential or universal properties does not preserve their existential or universal characteristics.

Furthermore, for any properties X, Y, X', Y' and any existential property E:

$$E \cdot UNIT \equiv [E \equiv true],$$
$$[X \Rightarrow Y] \equiv [X \ guarantees \ Y],$$
$$[(X \ guarantees \ Y) \Rightarrow (X \Rightarrow Y)],$$
$$[(X \ guarantees \ Y) \wedge (Y \ guarantees \ Z) \Rightarrow (X \ guarantees \ Z)],$$
$$[(X \ guarantees \ Y) \wedge (X' \ guarantees \ Y') \Rightarrow (X \wedge X' \ guarantees \ Y \wedge Y')],$$
$$[(X \ guarantees \ Y) \wedge (X' \ guarantees \ Y') \Rightarrow (X \vee X' \ guarantees \ Y \vee Y')].$$

3.5 Example

In the bag of colored balls model:

> $exist$ · (bag contains at least 3 balls),
> $exist$ · (bag contains at least 2 red balls and at least 1 blue ball),
> $exist$ · (bag contains at least 1 red ball) *guarantees* (bag contains
> · at least 2 colors),
> $univ$ · (all balls in bag are black),
> $univ$ · (all balls in bag are red, or bag contains at least 1 blue ball).

The following properties are neither existential nor universal:

(all balls in the bag are red, or all balls in the bag are blue),
(if the bag contains at least 1 red ball, then the bag contains at least 2 colors).

4   The Property Transformer $\mathcal{E}$

4.1 $\mathcal{E}$ and $\mathcal{E}'$

In this section, we show that, for any property X, there exists a weakest existential property stronger than X, denoted by $\mathcal{E}.X$. Note that X holds in any system containing a component for which $\mathcal{E}.X$ holds.

We provide two equivalent formulations for $\mathcal{E}$:

$$\mathcal{E}.X \triangleq \langle \exists Y : [Y \Rightarrow X] \wedge exist.Y : Y \rangle, \tag{6}$$
$$\mathcal{E}'.X.F \triangleq \langle \forall H, K : H \surd F \surd K : X . H \circ F \circ K \rangle . \tag{7}$$

Instead of proving directly that $[\mathcal{E} = \mathcal{E}']$, we prove that $\mathcal{E}.X$ is the weakest existential property stronger than X, and that $\mathcal{E}'.X$ also is the weakest existential property stronger than X. From the uniqueness of such a weakest property, we conclude that $[\mathcal{E} = \mathcal{E}']$.

Note that, by construction, $\mathcal{E}.X$ is weaker than any existential property stronger than X, but we have to prove that $\mathcal{E}.X$ is existential. On the other hand $\mathcal{E}'.X$ is defined to be existential, but we have to prove that it is the weakest existential property stronger than X.

4.2 $\mathcal{E}.X$ is the Weakest Existential Property Stronger than X

We consider the equation (in predicates):

$$Y : [Y \Rightarrow X] \wedge exist.Y \ . \tag{8}$$

It is well known [11] that such an equation has a weakest solution exactly when the disjunction of all solutions is itself a solution, and then this disjunction is the weakest solution.

From definition (6), $\mathcal{E}.X$ is the disjunction of all the solutions of equation (8). Therefore, $\mathcal{E}.X$ is the weakest existential property stronger than X if and only if $\mathcal{E}.X$ is a solution of equation (8). The proof obligation is:

$$[\mathcal{E}.X \Rightarrow X] \wedge exist.(\mathcal{E}.X) \ .$$

Proposition 2 $\qquad\qquad\qquad\qquad [\mathcal{E}.X \Rightarrow X]$

Proof:

$\quad \mathcal{E}.X$
$= \ \{\text{Definition of } \mathcal{E} \ (6)\}$
$\quad \langle \exists Y : [Y \Rightarrow X] \wedge exist.Y : Y \rangle$
$\Rightarrow \ \{[Y \Rightarrow X] \wedge exist.Y \Rightarrow [Y \Rightarrow X], \text{ and } \exists Y \text{ is monotonic}\}$
$\quad \langle \exists Y : [Y \Rightarrow X] : Y \rangle$
$\Rightarrow \ \{[[Y \Rightarrow X] \wedge Y \Rightarrow X], \text{ and } \exists Y \text{ is monotonic}\}$
$\quad \langle \exists Y :: X \rangle$
$= \ \{\text{No free } Y \text{ in } X\}$
$\quad X \qquad\qquad\qquad\qquad\qquad\qquad\qquad\qquad\qquad\qquad\qquad\qquad \square$

Proposition 3 $\qquad\qquad\qquad\qquad exist.(\mathcal{E}.X)$

Proof: We consider two components F and G such that $F\sqrt{}G$ and we prove that $\mathcal{E}.X . F \Rightarrow \mathcal{E}.X . F{\circ}G$. By a similar argument, $\mathcal{E}.X . G \Rightarrow \mathcal{E}.X . F{\circ}G$, and therefore we deduce that $\mathcal{E}.X . F \vee \mathcal{E}.X . G \Rightarrow \mathcal{E}.X . F{\circ}G$, i.e., that $\mathcal{E}.X$ is existential.

$\mathcal{E}.X \, . \, F \wedge F \sqrt{G}$

$= \{$Definition of $\mathcal{E}$ (6)$\}$

$\quad \langle \exists Y : [Y \Rightarrow X] \wedge exist.Y : Y \rangle \, . \, F \wedge F \sqrt{G}$

$= \{$Predicate calculus$\}$

$\quad \langle \exists Y : [Y \Rightarrow X] \wedge exist.Y : Y.F \wedge F \sqrt{G} \rangle$

$= \{$Duplicate and expand $exist.Y$ (3)$\}$

$\quad \langle \exists Y : [Y \Rightarrow X] \wedge exist.Y :$
$\quad\quad \langle \forall F', G' : F' \sqrt{G'} : Y.F' \vee Y.G' \Rightarrow Y.F' \circ G' \rangle \wedge Y.F \wedge F \sqrt{G} \rangle$

$\Rightarrow \{$Choose $F' := F$ and $G' := G\}$

$\quad \langle \exists Y : [Y \Rightarrow X] \wedge exist.Y : (F \sqrt{G} \Rightarrow (Y.F \vee Y.G \Rightarrow Y.F \circ G)) \wedge Y.F \wedge F \sqrt{G} \rangle$

$\Rightarrow \{$Modus ponens$\}$

$\quad \langle \exists Y : [Y \Rightarrow X] \wedge exist.Y : Y.F \circ G \rangle$

$= \{$Predicate calculus$\}$

$\quad \langle \exists Y : [Y \Rightarrow X] \wedge exist.Y : Y \rangle \, . \, F \circ G$

$= \{$Definition of $\mathcal{E}$ (6)$\}$

$\quad \mathcal{E}.X \, . \, F \circ G$ $\qquad\qquad\qquad\qquad\qquad\qquad \square$

Proposition 4 *For any property X, there exists a weakest existential property stronger than X and it is $\mathcal{E}.X$.*

Proof: From propositions 2 and 3 and the characterization of extreme solutions of equations in predicates. $\qquad\qquad \square$

4.3 $\mathcal{E}'.X$ is the Weakest Existential Property Stronger than X

In this section, we prove that $\mathcal{E}'.X$ also is the weakest existential property stronger than X. We prove first that $\mathcal{E}'.X$ is solution of equation (8), and then that any other solution is stronger than $\mathcal{E}'.X$.

Proposition 5 $\qquad\qquad\qquad\qquad\qquad [\mathcal{E}'.X \Rightarrow X]$

Proof:

$\quad \mathcal{E}'.X \, . \, F$

$= \{$Definition of $\mathcal{E}'$ (7)$\}$

$\quad \langle \forall H, K : H \sqrt{F} \sqrt{K} : X \, . \, H \circ F \circ K \rangle$

$\Rightarrow \{$Choose $H := UNIT$ and $K := UNIT\}$

$\quad (UNIT \sqrt{F} \sqrt{UNIT} \Rightarrow X \, . \, UNIT \circ F \circ UNIT)$

$= \{$Axiom about $UNIT$ (1)$\}$

$\quad X \, . \, F$ $\qquad\qquad\qquad\qquad\qquad\qquad\qquad \square$

Proposition 6 $\qquad\qquad\qquad\qquad\qquad exist.(\mathcal{E}'.X)$

Proof:

$exist.(\mathcal{E}'.X)$

$=$ {Definition of existential properties}

$\langle \forall F, G : F\sqrt{G} : \mathcal{E}'.X\,.\,F \vee \mathcal{E}'.X\,.\,G \Rightarrow \mathcal{E}'.X\,.\,F{\circ}G\rangle$

$=$ {Predicate calculus}

$\langle \forall F, G : F\sqrt{G} : \mathcal{E}'.X\,.\,F \Rightarrow \mathcal{E}'.X\,.\,F{\circ}G\rangle$
$\wedge \;\langle \forall F, G : F\sqrt{G} : \mathcal{E}'.X\,.\,G \Rightarrow \mathcal{E}'.X\,.\,F{\circ}G\rangle$

In order to prove these two proof obligations, we choose two components F and G such that $F\sqrt{G}$, and we prove first that

$$\mathcal{E}'.X\,.\,F \Rightarrow \mathcal{E}'.X\,.\,F{\circ}G$$

and then that

$$\mathcal{E}'.X\,.\,G \Rightarrow \mathcal{E}'.X\,.\,F{\circ}G\;.$$

(The two proofs are different, because $\sqrt{}$ and $\circ$ may not be symmetric.)

$\mathcal{E}'.X\,.\,F \;\wedge\; F\sqrt{G}$

$=$ {Definition of $\mathcal{E}'$ (7)}

$\langle \forall H, K : H\sqrt{F}\sqrt{K} : X\,.\,H{\circ}F{\circ}K\rangle \wedge F\sqrt{G}$

$\Rightarrow$ {For K' s.t. $G\sqrt{K'}$, replace K with $G{\circ}K'$}

$\langle \forall H, K' : G\sqrt{K'} \wedge H\sqrt{F}\sqrt{G{\circ}K'} : X\,.\,H{\circ}F{\circ}G{\circ}K'\rangle \wedge F\sqrt{G}$

$=$ {Axiom about $\sqrt{}$ (2), using the shortcut}

$\langle \forall H, K' : F\sqrt{G} \wedge H\sqrt{F{\circ}G}\sqrt{K'} : X\,.\,H{\circ}F{\circ}G{\circ}K'\rangle \wedge F\sqrt{G}$

$\Rightarrow$ {Modus ponens}

$\langle \forall H, K' : H\sqrt{(F{\circ}G)}\sqrt{K'} : X\,.\,H{\circ}(F{\circ}G){\circ}K'\rangle$

$=$ {Definition of $\mathcal{E}'$ (7)}

$\mathcal{E}'.X\,.\,F{\circ}G$

$\mathcal{E}'.X\,.\,G \;\wedge\; F\sqrt{G}$

$=$ {Definition of $\mathcal{E}'$ (7)}

$\langle \forall H, K : H\sqrt{G}\sqrt{K} : X\,.\,H{\circ}G{\circ}K\rangle \wedge F\sqrt{G}$

$\Rightarrow$ {For H' s.t. $H'\sqrt{F}$, replace H with $H'{\circ}F$}

$\langle \forall H', K : H'\sqrt{F} \wedge H'{\circ}F\sqrt{G}\sqrt{K} : X\,.\,H'{\circ}F{\circ}G{\circ}K\rangle \wedge F\sqrt{G}$

$=$ {Axiom about $\sqrt{}$ (2), using the shortcut}

$\langle \forall H', K : F\sqrt{G} \wedge H'\sqrt{F{\circ}G}\sqrt{K} : X\,.\,H'{\circ}F{\circ}G{\circ}K\rangle \wedge F\sqrt{G}$

$\Rightarrow$ {Modus ponens}

$\langle \forall H', K : H'\sqrt{(F{\circ}G)}\sqrt{K} : X\,.\,H'{\circ}(F{\circ}G){\circ}K\rangle$

$=$ {Definition of $\mathcal{E}'$ (7)}

$\mathcal{E}'.X\,.\,F{\circ}G$ $\square$

This completes the proof that $\mathcal{E}'.X$ is solution of equation (8). We now prove that any other solution of (8) is stronger than $\mathcal{E}'.X$.

Proposition 7 $exist.X \;\equiv\; [\mathcal{E}'.X \equiv X]$

Proof:

$\boxed{\Leftarrow}$

$[\mathcal{E}'.X \equiv X]$
$= \quad$ {From proposition 6}
$\quad [\mathcal{E}'.X \equiv X] \wedge exist.(\mathcal{E}'.X)$
$\Rightarrow \quad$ {Leibniz}
$\quad exist.X$

$\boxed{\Rightarrow}$ Assume $exist.X$, prove that $X.F \equiv \mathcal{E}'.X.F$, for any F.

$X.F$
$= \quad$ {Introduce and expand $exist.X$}
$\quad X.F \wedge \langle \forall H, G : H \sqrt{G} : X.H \vee X.G \Rightarrow X.H{\circ}G \rangle$
$\Rightarrow \quad$ {Choose $G := F$}
$\quad X.F \wedge \langle \forall H : H \sqrt{F} : X.H \vee X.F \Rightarrow X.H{\circ}F \rangle$
$\Rightarrow \quad$ {Modus ponens}
$\quad \langle \forall H : H \sqrt{F} : X.H{\circ}F \rangle$
$= \quad$ {Introduce and expand $exist.X$}
$\quad \langle \forall H : H \sqrt{F} : X.H{\circ}F \wedge \langle \forall G, K : G \sqrt{K} : X.G \vee X.K \Rightarrow X.G{\circ}K \rangle \rangle$
$\Rightarrow \quad$ {Choose $G := H{\circ}F$}
$\quad \langle \forall H : H \sqrt{F} : X.H{\circ}F \wedge \langle \forall K : H{\circ}F \sqrt{K} : X.H{\circ}F \vee X.K \Rightarrow X.H{\circ}F{\circ}K \rangle \rangle$
$= \quad$ {Move $\forall K$ outside}
$\quad \langle \forall H, K : H \sqrt{F} : X.H{\circ}F \wedge (H{\circ}F \sqrt{K} \Rightarrow (X.H{\circ}F \vee X.K \Rightarrow X.H{\circ}F{\circ}K)) \rangle$
$\Rightarrow \quad$ {Predicate calculus, $\forall H, K$ is monotonic}
$\quad \langle \forall H, K : H \sqrt{F} \wedge H{\circ}F \sqrt{K} : X.H{\circ}F{\circ}K \rangle$
$= \quad$ {Axiom about $\sqrt{}$ (2), introducing the shortcut}
$\quad \langle \forall H, K : H \sqrt{F} \sqrt{K} : X.H{\circ}F{\circ}K \rangle$
$= \quad$ {Definition of $\mathcal{E}'$ (7)}
$\quad \mathcal{E}'.X.F$

Since $[\mathcal{E}'.X \Rightarrow X]$ (prop. 5), this completes the proof of $X.F \equiv \mathcal{E}'.X.F$. $\square$

Proposition 8 ($\mathcal{E}'$ is universally conjunctive) *For any set S:*

$$[\mathcal{E}'.\langle \forall X : X \in S : X \rangle \;\equiv\; \langle \forall X : X \in S : \mathcal{E}'.X \rangle] \;.$$

Proof:

$$\mathcal{E}'.\langle \forall X : X \in S : X \rangle.F$$
$= \{\text{Definition of } \mathcal{E}' \ (7)\}$
$$\langle \forall H, K : H\sqrt{F}\sqrt{K} : \langle \forall X : X \in S : X \rangle.H \circ F \circ K \rangle$$
$= \{\text{Predicate calculus}\}$
$$\langle \forall H, K : H\sqrt{F}\sqrt{K} : \langle \forall X : X \in S : X.H \circ F \circ K \rangle \rangle$$
$= \{\text{Interchange of universal quantifiers}\}$
$$\langle \forall X : X \in S : \langle \forall H, K : H\sqrt{F}\sqrt{K} : X.H \circ F \circ K \rangle \rangle$$
$= \{\text{Definition of } \mathcal{E}' \ (7)\}$
$$\langle \forall X : X \in S : \mathcal{E}'.X . F \rangle$$
$= \{\text{Predicate calculus}\}$
$$\langle \forall X : X \in S : \mathcal{E}'.X \rangle.F \qquad \qquad \Box$$

Proposition 9 ($\mathcal{E}'$ is monotonic)

$$[X \Rightarrow Y] \Rightarrow [\mathcal{E}'.X \Rightarrow \mathcal{E}'.Y]$$

Proof:

$$[X \Rightarrow Y]$$
$= \{\text{Predicate calculus}\}$
$$[X \equiv X \wedge Y]$$
$\Rightarrow \{\text{Leibniz}\}$
$$[\mathcal{E}'.X \equiv \mathcal{E}'.(X \wedge Y)]$$
$= \{\mathcal{E}' \text{ is conjunctive from prop. 8}\}$
$$[\mathcal{E}'.X \equiv \mathcal{E}'.X \wedge \mathcal{E}'.Y]$$
$= \{\text{Predicate calculus}\}$
$$[\mathcal{E}'.X \Rightarrow \mathcal{E}'.Y] \qquad \qquad \Box$$

Proposition 10 *For any property X, there exists a weakest existential property stronger than X and it is $\mathcal{E}'.X$.*

Proof: From propositions 5 and 6, we know that $\mathcal{E}'.X$ is solution of equation (8). It remains to show that any solution Z of (8) is stronger than $\mathcal{E}'.X$:

$$[Z \Rightarrow X] \wedge exist.Z$$
$= \{[\mathcal{E}'.Z \equiv Z] \text{ from prop. 7}\}$
$$[Z \Rightarrow X] \wedge [\mathcal{E}'.Z \equiv Z]$$
$\Rightarrow \{\mathcal{E}' \text{ is monotonic from prop. 9}\}$
$$[\mathcal{E}'.Z \Rightarrow \mathcal{E}'.X] \wedge [\mathcal{E}'.Z \equiv Z]$$
$\Rightarrow \{\text{Leibniz}\}$
$$[Z \Rightarrow \mathcal{E}'.X] \qquad \qquad \Box$$

Proposition 11 $\qquad\qquad\qquad\qquad [\mathcal{E} = \mathcal{E}']$

Proof: From the uniqueness of a weakest element, when it exists. $\qquad \Box$

4.4   Relationship with "*guarantees*"

Proposition 12 $[X \; guarantees \; Y \; \equiv \; \mathcal{E}'.(X \Rightarrow Y)]$

Proof:

$\quad X \; guarantees \; Y . F$

$= \{\text{Definition of } guarantees \text{ (def. 5)}\}$

$\quad \langle \forall H, K : H\sqrt{F}\sqrt{K} : X . H{\circ}F{\circ}K \Rightarrow Y . H{\circ}F{\circ}K \rangle$

$= \{\text{Predicate calculus}\}$

$\quad \langle \forall H, K : H\sqrt{F}\sqrt{K} : (X \Rightarrow Y) . H{\circ}F{\circ}K \rangle$

$= \{\text{Definition of } \mathcal{E}'\}$

$\quad \mathcal{E}'.(X \Rightarrow Y) . F$ $\square$

Corollary: $exist.(X \; guarantees \; Y)$

4.5   A Property Transformer $\mathcal{U}$?

The reason why, for any property X, there exists a weakest existential property stronger than X, which allowed us to define the property transformer $\mathcal{E}$, is that any disjunction of existential properties in existential. This is not true for universal properties. Indeed, we can demonstrate a property X such that there is no unique weakest universal property stronger than X. This fact prevents us from defining a property transformer $\mathcal{U}$ in the same manner as we defined $\mathcal{E}$.

Proposition 13 (No $\mathcal{U}$ transformer) *There exists nontrivial models in which some properties do not have a unique weakest universal property stronger than them.*

Proof: To prove this claim, we use the model of bags of colored balls and we consider the property P defined by:

$$P_0 \overset{\triangle}{=} (\text{all balls are white}),$$
$$P_1 \overset{\triangle}{=} (\text{all balls are black}),$$
$$P \overset{\triangle}{=} P_0 \vee P_1 \; .$$

Clearly, P_0 and P_1 are universal and, if black and white balls exist at all, P is not. Let W, if it exists, be the weakest universal property stronger than P. Then:

$\quad\quad [P_0 \Rightarrow W]$ because P_0 is universal and stronger than P,
$\quad\quad [P_1 \Rightarrow W]$ because P_1 is universal and stronger than P,
$\quad\quad [P \Rightarrow W]$ from the two above,
$\quad\quad [W \Rightarrow P]$ by definition of W,
$\quad\quad [W \equiv P]$ from the two above.

But W is universal (by definition) and P is not, which leads us to a contradiction. Therefore, no such W exists. $\square$

4.6   Example

Let's consider the following question: In the world of bags of colored balls, what is the property: (at least 1 red ball) *guarantees* (at least 2 colors)? Obviously, the answer is: $\mathcal{E}.((\text{at least 1 red ball}) \Rightarrow (\text{at least 2 colors}))$, but can we find a simpler, equivalent, formulation?

In this part, we prove the following equivalence:

$$[\mathcal{E}.((\text{at least 1 red ball}) \Rightarrow (\text{at least 2 colors})) \equiv (\text{at least 1 non red ball})]^{[1]}. \quad (9)$$

We introduce two specific properties, $UNIT_=$ ("being the unit") and its negation $UNIT_{\neq}$ ("not being the unit"):

$$UNIT_= . F \;\triangleq\; (F = UNIT),$$
$$UNIT_{\neq} . F \;\triangleq\; (F \neq UNIT) .$$

We will prove equivalence (9) by first proving the following proposition:

Proposition 14 $\neg exist. UNIT_{\neq} \vee [X \equiv UNIT_{\neq}] \vee [\mathcal{E}.(UNIT_= \vee X) \equiv \mathcal{E}.X]$

Proof:
Assume $exist. UNIT_{\neq}$ and $\neg[X \equiv UNIT_{\neq}]$, and prove $[\mathcal{E}.(UNIT_= \vee X) \equiv \mathcal{E}.X]$.
First case: $F \neq UNIT$

$\mathcal{E}.(UNIT_= \vee X).F$
$= \{[\mathcal{E} = \mathcal{E}']$ from prop. 11, definition of $\mathcal{E}'$ (7)$\}$
    $\langle \forall H, K : H\sqrt{F}\sqrt{K} : (UNIT_= \vee X).H \circ F \circ K \rangle$
$= \{$From hypotheses $F \neq UNIT$ and $exist. UNIT_{\neq}$, $\neg(UNIT_= . H \circ F \circ K)\}$
    $\langle \forall H, K : H\sqrt{F}\sqrt{K} : X.H \circ F \circ K \rangle$
$= \{$Definition of $\mathcal{E}'$ (7), $[\mathcal{E} = \mathcal{E}']$ from prop. 11$\}$
    $\mathcal{E}.X.F$

Second case: $F = UNIT$

$\mathcal{E}.(UNIT_= \vee X).UNIT$
$= \{exist.(\mathcal{E}.Y)$ from prop. 3, basic rules of existential properties$\}$
    $[\mathcal{E}.(UNIT_= \vee X) \equiv true]$
$= \{[\mathcal{E}.true \equiv true]$ and $[\mathcal{E}.Y \Rightarrow Y]$ from prop. 2$\}$
    $[UNIT_= \vee X \equiv true]$
$= \{$Predicate calculus ($UNIT$ is the only component where X *may* not hold)$\}$
    $[X \equiv true] \vee [X \equiv UNIT_{\neq}]$
$= \{$Hypothesis $\neg[X \equiv UNIT_{\neq}]\}$

---

[1] This example also shows that $\mathcal{E}$ is not disjunctive, i.e., $\mathcal{E}.X \vee \mathcal{E}.Y$ is, in general, strictly stronger that $\mathcal{E}.(X \vee Y)$.

$[X \equiv true]$

$= \{[\mathcal{E}.true \equiv true] \text{ and } [E.Y \Rightarrow Y] \text{ from prop. 2}\}$

$[\mathcal{E}.X \equiv true]$

$= \{exist.(\mathcal{E}.Y) \text{ from prop. 3, basic rules of existential properties}\}$

$\mathcal{E}.X \,.\, UNIT$ $\hfill \square$

We can now apply proposition 14 to prove formula (9):

$\mathcal{E}.((\text{at least 1 red ball}) \Rightarrow (\text{at least 2 colors}))$

$= \{\text{Definition of implication}\}$

$\mathcal{E}.((\text{no red balls}) \vee (\text{at least 2 colors}))$

$= \{\text{Nonempty bags contain balls: } UNIT_= \vee (\text{at least 1 ball}) \equiv true\}$

$\mathcal{E}.(((UNIT_= \vee (\text{at least 1 ball})) \wedge (\text{no red balls})) \vee (\text{at least 2 colors}))$

$= \left\{ \begin{array}{l} \text{Simplify using (at least 1 non red ball)} \equiv \\ ((\text{at least 1 non red ball}) \wedge (\text{no red balls})) \vee (\text{at least 2 colors}) \end{array} \right\}$

$\mathcal{E}.(UNIT_= \vee (\text{at least 1 non red ball}))$

$= \left\{ \begin{array}{l} exist.\,UNIT_{\neq} \text{ in bags model, assume there exist red balls, hence} \\ \neg[(\text{at least 1 non red ball}) \equiv UNIT_{\neq}], \text{ apply prop. 14} \end{array} \right\}$

$\mathcal{E}.(\text{at least 1 non red ball})$

$= \{exist.(\text{at least 1 non red ball})\}$

$(\text{at least 1 non red ball})$

In other words, to ensure that any system that uses a certain component F will have at least two balls of different colors provided that it contains at least one red ball, it is sufficient and necessary that the component F contains at least one non red ball. This is consistent with our intuition.

Note that instead of guessing the desired property of F and then prove that any system composed from F satisfies (at least 1 red ball) $\Rightarrow$ (at least 2 colors), we *calculate* the desired property of F. This provides us with both the property and the proof at the same time, and avoids dealing explicitly with the universal quantification over components.

5   Related Work

5.1   Existential/Universal versus Assumption-Commitment

Traditional *"assumption-commitment"* (or *"rely-guarantee"*) approach to composition of concurrent systems [1,2,13,17,10,8,9,12] relies on an explicit specification of a component's possible environments. It is defined in terms of "open system computations", in which some steps are labeled "environment steps". In some sense, components are "prepared" to be composed, by leaving room for interaction with the outside world. Interaction with the environment is present from the start. If nothing is specified about the environment, few component properties can be proved. Properties like *always* are meaningless in this context.

The approach presented here is the dual of assumption-commitment. In contrast to much of the work in assumption-commitment, we deal with properties of components, not components coupled to specific environments. There are no "environment steps" in our theory. Indeed, we want to deal with systems in which steps and computations may not exist. So, we do not use automata-based models or process models nor do we assume specific forms of computations such as open-system computations.

In our approach, we do not study composition in terms of specific languages or logics such as TLA [1,2], linear temporal logic [13,12], UNITY [17,10,8,9], CSP, or process algebras. Instead, we deal with component properties and composition in the abstract. We postulate simple rules for the composition operator (such as associativity and the existence of a unit element), and then base a theory on these rules.

A potential weakness of our approach is that by exploiting only theorems that we can prove from a limited set of rules we obtain less useful results than by working with a specific programming language and its associated logic (say TLA or UNITY). Despite this weakness, we believe that explorations such as these can help to identify the relationships between central results about compositional design and the postulates about composition and component properties.

5.2 The Benefits of "*guarantees*"

Existential and universal properties, as well as the *guarantees* operator were first introduced in [4] (with slightly different definitions). The *guarantees* operator has several advantages compared to corresponding operators in the assumption-commitment theory.

Firstly, because *guarantees* properties do not reference an environment, but only deal with component and (global) system properties, they avoid a well-known circularity problem [1,3] (due to the fact that components are environments of each other). The price we pay is that we cannot assume a property X of the environment to prove the same property X of the system, and such assumptions have proved to be useful in assumption-commitment specifications. To describe such behavior, we cannot use *guarantees* and instead we rely on universal properties (see, for instance, examples in [6]).

Secondly, because X *guarantees* Y is existential, regardless of the properties X and Y, *guarantees* can be used with *progress* properties in its left-hand side. Indeed, system proofs can be simplified considerably by using *guarantees* properties with progress properties on the left-hand side [7]. For instance, a useful property of a distributed resource manager is: All clients *eventually* return the resources they are given *guarantees* the server *eventually* satisfies all requests from clients. By contrast, much of the literature on assumption-commitment specifications deals only with assumptions that are safety properties [1,2].

An advantage of having progress properties on the left-hand side of *guarantees* is that component designers can prove complex (progress) properties that can be used directly in proving composed systems.

5.3 $\mathcal{E}$ and $\mathcal{E}'$ versus "*guarantees*"

In [4], *guarantees* properties are the basic elements of the theory. In this paper, we rely on $\mathcal{E}$ instead. This use of predicate transformers leads to more concise definitions and simpler proofs.

In particular, a simple but important theorem is that X *guarantees* Y is merely the application of predicate transformer $\mathcal{E}$ to the property $X \Rightarrow Y$. This theorem explains why *guarantees* is easy to reason with (it behaves like implication) and useful in specifying components (it does not strengthen implication too much).

Two equivalent formulations of $\mathcal{E}$ are given in this report. The first is in terms of an extreme solution to an equation in predicates. This form is useful to deduce theorems about existential properties and *guarantees*. The second form uses an explicit quantification over components. This form has been useful in deducing proof rules for *guarantees* properties in the context of concurrent programs, namely UNITY logic. (These rules are not given here.)

5.4 Predicate Transformers and Universal Properties

In section 4.5, we proved that, for some properties, there does not exist a weakest universal strengthening. Consequently, it is impossible to define a predicate transformer $\mathcal{U}$ that would be to universal composition what the transformer $\mathcal{E}$ is to existential composition.

Universal properties are useful where *guarantees* properties cannot be used. However, elementary properties like *always* are not universal. Therefore, we are interested in studying universal properties that are stronger than specific properties such as *always*. *Invariant* is one possible strengthening of *always*, but *invariant* properties turn out to be too strong. Intermediate universal properties, between *invariant* and *always*, can be defined [9,17], but we need to experiment with using these properties on proving systems to determine if they have the appropriate level of abstraction. The existence of a weakest universal property stronger than *always* is still an open question.

6   Conclusions

Component technology allows designers to develop systems by composing subsystems. Compositional design is simpler than designing systems from scratch if designers have access to large libraries of components, provided appropriate components in the library can be discovered easily, and there are simple rules for deducing system properties from component properties. This paper reports on an ongoing exploration of rules for deducing system properties from component properties.

We have explored properties of composition that can be deduced from algebraic properties of the composition operator: associativity and the existence of a unit component. Though the exploration reported in this study is abstract and is independent of specific types of systems, we are particularly concerned with applying the results to parallel and sequential composition of programs. Since Hoare triples and weakest preconditions handle sequential composition very well, the practical results of our explorations are particularly important for concurrent composition. The concurrent composition operator, as defined in UNITY, is symmetric (commutative) and idempotent in addition to being associative. This allows us to prove additional theorems about $\mathcal{E}$ for this special case and, for instance, to deduce proof rules for *guarantees* that are specific to the UNITY model. We have applied these rules and the theorems discussed here to the compositional design of several message-passing programs [7] and shared-memory programs [6].

Requiring components to be specified in terms of conjunctions of existential and universal properties may seem too restrictive. We have found, however, that this requirement is at the appropriate level of specificity for compositional design. Existential properties are a surprisingly rich class of properties, especially since many properties can be expressed as *guarantees* properties.

For example, we specify a first-in first-out single input, single output, message channel by the characteristic that the sequence of messages output "follows" [5,16,7] the sequence of messages input. More precisely, such a specification is a *guarantees* property whose right-hand side is the conjunction of an *always* property (the output sequence is a prefix of the input sequence) and a *progress* property (any prefix of the input sequence is eventually a prefix of the output sequence).

We have shown that there are some properties X for which there does not exist a weakest universal property stronger than X. For some properties of interest in specific domains, however, there may exist weakest universal properties stronger than them. For example, there may exist a weakest universal property stronger than any *always* property. We wish to explore such strengthening properties because properties such as *always* are important for the specification of reactive systems.

References

1. Martín Abadi and Leslie Lamport. Composing specifications. *ACM Transactions on Programming Languages and Systems*, 15(1):73–132, January 1993. 182, 183
2. Martín Abadi and Leslie Lamport. Conjoining specifications. *ACM Transactions on Programming Languages and Systems*, 17(3):507–534, May 1995. 182, 183
3. Martín Abadi and Stephan Merz. An abstract account of composition. In Jivrí Wiedermann and Petr Hajek, editors, *Mathematical Foundations of Computer Science*, volume 969 of *Lecture Notes in Computer Science*, pages 499–508. Springer-Verlag, September 1995. 183
4. K. Mani Chandy and Beverly Sanders. Reasoning about program composition. Submitted for publication.
   http://www.cise.ufl.edu/~sanders/pubs/composition.ps. 174, 183, 184
5. Michel Charpentier. *Assistance à la Répartition de Systèmes Réactifs*. Thèse de doctorat, Institut National Polytechnique de Toulouse, November 1997. 185

6. Michel Charpentier and K. Mani Chandy. Examples of program composition illustrating the use of universal properties. In J. Rolim, editor, *International workshop on Formal Methods for Parallel Programming: Theory and Applications (FMPPTA'99)*, volume 1586 of *Lecture Notes in Computer Science*, pages 1215–1227. Springer-Verlag, April 1999. 183, 185

7. Michel Charpentier and K. Mani Chandy. Towards a compositional approach to the design and verification of distributed systems. In J. Wing, J. Woodcock, and J. Davies, editors, *World Congress on Formal Methods in the Development of Computing Systems (FM'99), (Vol. I)*, volume 1708 of *Lecture Notes in Computer Science*, pages 570–589. Springer-Verlag, September 1999. 183, 185

8. Pierre Collette. Composition of assumption-commitment specifications in a UNITY style. *Science of Computer Programming*, 23:107–125, 1994. 182, 183

9. Pierre Collette. *Design of Compositional Proof Systems Based on Assumption-Commitment Specifications. Application to UNITY*. Doctoral thesis, Faculté des Sciences Appliquées, Université Catholique de Louvain, June 1994. 182, 183, 184

10. Pierre Collette and Edgar Knapp. Logical foundations for compositional verification and development of concurrent programs in UNITY. In *International Conference on Algebraic Methodology and Software Technology*, volume 936 of *Lecture Notes in Computer Science*, pages 353–367. Springer-Verlag, 1995. 182, 183

11. Edsger W. Dijkstra and Carel S. Scholten. *Predicate calculus and program semantics*. Texts and monographs in computer science. Springer-Verlag, 1990. 172, 175

12. J. L. Fiadeiro and T. Maibaum. Verifying for reuse: foundations of object-oriented system verification. In I. Makie C. Hankin and R. Nagarajan, editors, *Theory and Formal Methods*, pages 235–257. World Scientific Publishing Company, 1995. 182, 183

13. Zohar Manna and Amir Pnueli. *The Temporal Logic of Reactive and Concurrent Systems: Specification*. Springer-Verlag, 1992. 182, 183

14. Jayadev Misra. A logic for concurrent programming: Safety. *Journal of Computer and Software Engineering*, 3(2):239–272, 1995. 169

15. Beverly A. Sanders. Eliminating the substitution axiom from UNITY logic. *Formal Aspects of Computing*, 3(2):189–205, April–June 1991. 169

16. Paolo A. G. Sivilotti. *A Method for the Specification, Composition, and Testing of Distributed Object Systems*. PhD thesis, California Institute of Technology, 256-80 Caltech, Pasadena, California 91125, December 1997. 185

17. Rob T. Udink. *Program Refinement in UNITY-like Environments*. PhD thesis, Utrecht University, September 1995. 182, 183, 184

The Universal Resolving Algorithm: Inverse Computation in a Functional Language

Sergei Abramov[1] and Robert Glück[2]*

[1] Program Systems Institute, Russian Academy of Sciences
RU-152140 Pereslavl-Zalessky, Russia
`abram@botik.ru`
[2] Department of Information and Computer Science,
School of Science and Engineering, Waseda University
Shinjuku-ku, Tokyo 169-8555, Japan
`glueck@acm.org`

Abstract. We present an algorithm for inverse computation in a first-order functional language based on the notion of a perfect process tree. The Universal Resolving Algorithm (URA) introduced in this paper is sound and complete, and computes each solution, if it exists, in finite time. The algorithm has been implemented for TSG, a typed dialect of S-Graph, and shows some remarkable results for the inverse computation of functional programs such as pattern matching and the inverse interpretation of While-programs.

1 Introduction

While standard computation is the calculation of the output of a program for a given input ('forward execution'), inverse computation is the calculation of the possible input of a program for a given output ('backward execution'). Inverse computation is an important and useful concept in many different areas. Advances in this direction have been achieved in the area of logic programming, based on solutions emerging from logic and proof theory.

But inversion is not restricted to the context of logic programming. Reversibility is an important concept in any programming language, *e.g.*, if one direction of an algorithm is easier to define than the other, or if both directions are needed (*cf.* encoding and decoding). Interestingly, inversion has spanned relatively little interest in the area of functional programming (exceptions are [5,9,18,20,21,25]), even though it is an essential concept in mathematics.

We distinguish between two approaches for solving inversion problems: an *inverse interpreter* that performs inverse computation and an *inverse compiler* that performs program inversion. Determining for a given program P and output y an input x of P such that $[\![P]\!]x = y$ is inverse computation. A program that produces P^{-1}, is an inverse compiler (also called program inverter). Using P^{-1} will then determine input x of P.

---

* On leave from DIKU, Department of Computer Science, University of Copenhagen.

R. Backhouse and J. N. Oliveira (Eds.): MPC 2000, LNCS 1837, pp. 187–212, 2000.

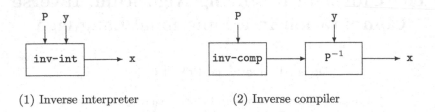

(1) Inverse interpreter   (2) Inverse compiler

As shown in [3,4], inverse computation and program inversion can be related conveniently using the Futamura projections known from partial evaluation: a program inverter is a generating extension of an inverse interpreter. In the remainder of this paper we shall focus on inverse computation.

As example of inverse computation, consider a pattern matcher which takes two strings as input, pat and str, and returns SUCCESS if pat is a substring of str; FAILURE otherwise. For instance, computation with pattern "BC" and string "ABCD" returns SUCCESS, and the same string with pattern "CB" returns FAILURE.

$$\text{match ["BC", "ABCD"]} \stackrel{*}{\Rightarrow} \text{'SUCCESS}$$
$$\text{match ["CB", "ABCD"]} \stackrel{*}{\Rightarrow} \text{'FAILURE}$$

standard computation

Given string str, we may want to ask inverse questions such as: Which patterns are substrings of str, or which patterns are *not* substrings of str? To compute the answer, we can either implement new programs, in general a time consuming and error prone task, or we can use an inverse interpreter ura to extract the answer from the original program. We do so by fixing the output to SUCCESS (or FAILURE) and the string to str, while leaving the pattern unspecified (placeholders X_1, X_2).

$$\text{ura [match, } [X_1, \text{ "ABCD"], 'SUCCESS]} \stackrel{*}{\Rightarrow} ans_1$$
$$\text{ura [match, } [X_2, \text{ "ABCD"], 'FAILURE]} \stackrel{*}{\Rightarrow} ans_2$$

inverse computation

The answer tells us which values the placeholders may take. In general, computability of the answer is not guaranteed, even with sophisticated inversion strategies. Some inversions are too resource consuming, while others are undecidable. When a program is not injective in the missing input, the answer can either be universal (all possible inputs) or existential (one of the possible inputs). We will only consider universal solutions, hence the name for our algorithm.

Most of the earlier work on this topic (*e.g.*, [5,6,7,16,17]) has been program transformation by hand: specify a problem as the inverse of an easy computation, and then derive an efficient algorithm by manual application of transformation rules. By contrast, our approach aims for mechanical inversion. The first observation [4] is that to do this, it suffices, in principle, to stage an inverse interpreter: via the Futamura projections this will give an inverse compiler. This is convenient because inverse computation is simpler than program inversion. The second key idea is to use the notion of a *perfect process tree* [12] to systematically trace the space of possible execution paths by *standard computation*, in order to find the inverse computation.

The *Universal Resolving Algorithm* (URA) introduced in this paper is sound and complete, and computes each solution, if it exists, in finite time. The algorithm has been designed for a first-order functional language with S-expressions as data structures. However, the principles and methods developed here are not limited to this language, but can be extended to other programming languages.

The main contributions in this paper are:

- an approach to inverse computation, its organization and structure,
- a formal specification of a Universal Resolving Algorithm for a first-order functional language based on the notion of a perfect process tree,
- an implementation of the algorithm and experiments with inverse computation of programs such as pattern matchers and interpreters,
- a constructive representation of sets of S-expressions allowing operations such as contractions and perfect splits.

The paper is organized as follows. In Section 2 we formalize a set representation of S-expressions and in Section 3 we define our source language. A program-related extension of the set representation is introduced in Section 4. Sections 5–7 present the three steps to inverse computation. Implementation and experiments are discussed in Section 8 and 9. We conclude with a discussion of related work in Section 10 and future work in Section 11.

2   A Set Representation of S-Expressions

This section introduces the basic notions needed for inverse computation using a source language with S-expressions. In particular, we define a set representation of S-expressions and related operations such as substitution and concretization, contraction and splitting.

A simple and elegant way to represent subsets of a value domain is to use *variables*, *expressions with variables* and *restrictions on variables*. Let us consider an example from mathematics. The definition of a set of 3D-points

$$P = \{ (x, y, x + y) \mid x > 0, y > x \}$$

is expressed by means of (i) variables x and y (typed variables, in fact: it is assumed that x and y range over the set of reals), (ii) expression $(x, y, x + y)$ with variables, and (iii) restrictions $x > 0$ and $y > x$ on variables. We will use the same approach for representing sets of S-expressions and introduce similar notions: c-variables, c-expressions and restrictions.

2.1   S-Expressions

We use S-expressions known from Lisp as value domain for our programs. The syntax of S-expressions is given by the grammar in Fig. 1. Values are build recursively from an infinite set of symbols using **atom** and **cons** as constructors. A value $d \in$ Dval is *ground*. We will use $'z$ as shorthand for (**atom** z).

S-Expressions	C-Expressions
$d \quad ::= \quad (\textbf{cons } d \ d) \mid da$	$\widehat{d} \quad ::= \quad (\textbf{cons } \widehat{d} \ \widehat{d}) \mid Xe \mid \widehat{da}$
$da \quad ::= \quad (\textbf{atom } z)$	$\widehat{da} \quad ::= \quad (\textbf{atom } z) \mid Xa$
	$X \quad ::= \quad Xe \mid Xa$

Value Domains

$$d \quad \in \quad \text{Dval} \qquad \widehat{d} \quad \in \quad \text{Cexp}$$
$$da \quad \in \quad \text{DAval} \qquad \widehat{da} \quad \in \quad \text{CAexp}$$
$$Xe \quad \in \quad \text{CEvar} \qquad X \quad \in \quad \text{Cvar}$$
$$Xa \quad \in \quad \text{CAvar} \qquad z \quad \in \quad \text{Symb}$$

Fig. 1. S-expressions and c-expressions

2.2 Representing Sets of S-Expressions

Expressions with variables, called *c-expressions* (Fig. 1), represent sets of S-expressions by means of two types of variables: *ca-variables* Xa and *ce-variables* Xe, where variables Xa range over DAval, and variables Xe range over Dval. To further refine our set representation we introduce restrictions on variables (Fig. 2). A *restriction* is a set of inequalities defining a set of values a ca-variable Xa must not be equal to. An *inequality* can be expressed between ca-variables and atoms.

Finally, we form pairs of c-expressions and restrictions, short *cr-pairs* (Fig. 2). This will be our main method for representing and manipulating sets of S-expressions in a constructive way. These structures may contain c-variables and for notational convenience we indicate this by notation $\widehat{\cdot}$.

Definition 1 (c-expression). *A* c-expression *is an expression* $\widehat{d} \in$ Cexp *as defined in Fig. 1. By* $\text{var}(\widehat{d})$ *we denote the set of all c-variables occurring in* $\widehat{d}$.

Definition 2 (c-construction). *A* c-expression *is a* c-construction $\widehat{cc} \in$ Ccon. *We define* Ccon = Cexp.[1]

Definition 3 (inequality, restriction). *An* inequality *ineq* $\in$ Ineq *is an unordered pair* $(\widehat{da}_1 \# \widehat{da}_2)$ *with* $\widehat{da}_1, \widehat{da}_2 \in$ CAexp, *or the symbol* **contra**. *A restriction* $\widehat{r} \in$ Restr *is a finite set of inequalities. By* $\text{var}(\widehat{r})$ *we denote the set of all ca-variables occurring in* $\widehat{r}$.

Definition 4 (tautology, contradiction). *A tautology is an inequality of the form* $(\widehat{da}_1 \# \widehat{da}_2) \in$ Ineq *where* $\widehat{da}_1, \widehat{da}_2$ *are ground and* $\widehat{da}_1 \neq \widehat{da}_2$. *A contradiction is either an inequality of the form* $(\widehat{da} \# \widehat{da}) \in$ Ineq *or the symbol* **contra**. *By* Tauto *and* Contra *we denote the set of tautologies and the set of contradictions, respectively.*

---

[1] In Sect. 4 we will extend the definition of domain Ccon with program-related constructions: c-state $\widehat{s}$, c-environment $\widehat{\sigma}$, etc.

CR-Pairs   Restrictions

$\widehat{cr}$ ::= $\langle \widehat{cc}, \widehat{r} \rangle$ $\widehat{r}$ ::= $ineq^*$

$\widehat{cc}$ ::= $\widehat{d}$ (see Fig. 1) $ineq$ ::= $(\widehat{da} \# \widehat{da})$ | contra

Value Domains

$\widehat{cr}$ ∈ CRpair $\widehat{r}$ ∈ Restr
$\widehat{cc}$ ∈ Ccon $ineq$ ∈ Ineq

Fig. 2. CR-pairs and restrictions

Definition 5 (cr-pair). *A cr-pair $\widehat{cr}$ ∈ CRpair is a pair $\langle \widehat{cc}, \widehat{r} \rangle$ where $\widehat{cc}$ ∈ Ccon is a c-construction and $\widehat{r}$ ∈ Restr is a restriction. By var($\widehat{cr}$) we denote the set of c-variables occurring in $\widehat{cr}$: var($\widehat{cr}$) = var($\widehat{cc}$) ∪ var($\widehat{r}$).*

Example 1. The following expressions are cr-pairs:

$$\widehat{cr}_1 = \langle (\textbf{cons } Xa \ (\textbf{cons } Xe \ 'Z)), \emptyset \rangle$$
$$\widehat{cr}_2 = \langle (\textbf{cons } Xa \ (\textbf{cons } Xa \ 'Z)), \emptyset \rangle$$
$$\widehat{cr}_3 = \langle (\textbf{cons } Xa \ (\textbf{cons } Xa \ 'Z)), \{ (Xa \# 'A) \} \rangle$$
$$\widehat{cr}_4 = \langle (\textbf{cons } Xa_1 \ (\textbf{cons } Xa_2 \ 'Z)), \{ (Xa_1 \# Xa_2) \} \rangle .$$

2.3 Substitution and Concretization

We now define substitution and concretization. The semantics of applying a *substitution* θ to a cr-pair $\widehat{cr}$ is defined in Fig. 3. Substitution will be used to define *concretization* $\lceil \widehat{cr} \rceil$, namely the set of S-expressions represented by $\widehat{cr}$.

Definition 6 (substitution). *A substitution $\theta = [X_1 \mapsto \widehat{d}_1, \ldots, X_n \mapsto \widehat{d}_n]$ is a sequence of typed bindings such that c-variables X_i are pairwise distinct, $\widehat{d}_i$ are c-expressions, and X_i ∈ CAvar implies $\widehat{d}_i$ ∈ CAexp, $i = 1 \ldots n$. Substitution θ is ground if all $\widehat{d}_i$ are ground. By dom(θ) we denote the set $\{X_1, \ldots, X_n\}$.*

Definition 7 (substitution on c-construction). *Let $\widehat{cc}$ ∈ Ccon be a c-construction, and let $\theta = [X_1 \mapsto \widehat{d}_1, \ldots, X_n \mapsto \widehat{d}_n]$ ∈ CCsub be a substitution, then the result of applying θ to $\widehat{cc}$, denoted $\widehat{cc}/\theta$, is the c-construction obtained by replacing every occurrence of X_i in $\widehat{cc}$ by $\widehat{d}_i$ for every $X_i \mapsto \widehat{d}_i$ in θ.*

Definition 8 (full substitution). *Let $\widehat{cc}$ be a c-construction (or restriction, or cr-pair), let θ be a substitution. Then θ is a full substitution for $\widehat{cc}$ iff θ is ground and var($\widehat{cc}$) ⊆ dom(θ). By FS($\widehat{cc}$) we denote the set of all full substitutions for $\widehat{cc}$.*

Definition 9 (substitution on restriction). *Let θ ∈ CCsub, let $\widehat{r}$ ∈ Restr, then the result of applying θ to $\widehat{r}$, denoted $\widehat{r}/\theta$, is defined by*

$$\widehat{r}/\theta \overset{\text{def}}{=} \begin{cases} \{\text{contra}\} & \text{if } \widehat{r}' \cap \text{Contra} \neq \emptyset \\ \widehat{r}' \setminus \text{Tauto} & \text{otherwise,} \end{cases}$$
$$\text{where } \widehat{r}' = \{ ineq/\theta \mid ineq \in \widehat{r} \} .$$

$$\begin{aligned}
\textit{CR-Pair:} \qquad \langle \widehat{cc}, \widehat{r} \rangle / \theta &= \langle \widehat{cc}/\theta, \widehat{r}/\theta \rangle \\
\textit{C-Expression:} \\
X/\theta &= \begin{cases} \theta(X) & \text{if } X \in dom(\theta) \\ X & otherwise \end{cases} \\
(\textbf{atom } z)/\theta &= (\textbf{atom } z) \\
(\textbf{cons } \widehat{d_1}\ \widehat{d_2})/\theta &= (\textbf{cons } \widehat{d_1}/\theta\ \widehat{d_2}/\theta) \\
\textit{Inequality:} \\
\textsf{contra}/\theta &= \textsf{contra} \\
(\widehat{da_1} \mathbin{\#} \widehat{da_2})/\theta &= (\widehat{da_1}/\theta \mathbin{\#} \widehat{da_2}/\theta) \\
\textit{Restriction:} \\
\widehat{r}/\theta &= \begin{cases} \{\textsf{contra}\} & \text{if } \widehat{r}' \cap \text{Contra} \neq \emptyset \\ \widehat{r}' \setminus \text{Tauto} & otherwise, \end{cases} \\
& \qquad \text{where } \widehat{r}' = \{\, ineq/\theta \mid ineq \in \widehat{r} \,\}
\end{aligned}$$

Fig. 3. Definition of substitutions $\widehat{cr}/\theta$, $\widehat{d}/\theta$, $ineq/\theta$ and $\widehat{r}/\theta$

The definition says that the result of applying a substitution θ to a restriction $\widehat{r}$ is either a contradiction, which means it is impossible to satisfy the new restriction, or a new set of inequalities from which all tautologies have been removed.[2]

Let $ineq$ be an inequality such that $var(ineq) = \emptyset$. According to Def. 4 we have: $ineq$ is either a tautology or a contradiction. This fact allows us to prove the following proposition.

Proposition 1. *Let $\widehat{r} \in$ Restr be a restriction and let $\theta \in FS(\widehat{r})$ be a full substitution for $\widehat{r}$, then either $\widehat{r}/\theta = \emptyset$ or $\widehat{r}/\theta = \{\,\textsf{contra}\,\}$.*

Definition 10 (substitution on cr-pair). *Let $\widehat{cr} = \langle \widehat{cc}, \widehat{r} \rangle \in$ CRpair be a cr-pair and $\theta \in$ CCsub be a substitution, then the result of applying θ to $\widehat{cr}$, denoted $\widehat{cr}/\theta$, is defined by*

$$\widehat{cr}/\theta \stackrel{\text{def}}{=} \langle \widehat{cc}/\theta, \widehat{r}/\theta \rangle \ .$$

Definition 11 (cr-concretization). *The set of data represented by cr-pair $\langle \widehat{cc}, \widehat{r} \rangle \in$ CRpair, denoted $\lceil \langle \widehat{cc}, \widehat{r} \rangle \rceil$, is defined by*

$$\lceil \langle \widehat{cc}, \widehat{r} \rangle \rceil \stackrel{\text{def}}{=} \{\, \widehat{cc}/\theta \mid \theta \in FS(\langle \widehat{cc}, \widehat{r} \rangle), \widehat{r}/\theta = \emptyset \,\} \ .$$

Example 2. The cr-pairs from Example 1 represent the following sets of values:

$$\begin{aligned}
\lceil \widehat{cr}_1 \rceil &= \{\, (\textbf{cons } da\ (\textbf{cons } d\ 'Z)) \mid da \in \text{DAval}, d \in \text{Dval} \,\} \\
\lceil \widehat{cr}_2 \rceil &= \{\, (\textbf{cons } da\ (\textbf{cons } da\ 'Z)) \mid da \in \text{DAval} \,\} \\
\lceil \widehat{cr}_3 \rceil &= \{\, (\textbf{cons } da\ (\textbf{cons } da\ 'Z)) \mid da \in \text{DAval}, da \neq 'A \,\} \\
\lceil \widehat{cr}_4 \rceil &= \{\, (\textbf{cons } da_1\ (\textbf{cons } da_2\ 'Z)) \mid da_1, da_2 \in \text{DAval}, da_1 \neq da_2 \,\} \ .
\end{aligned}$$

---

[2] Even though from a formal point of view it is not necessary to remove all tautologies, it is convenient to check for empty set after applying a full substitution (*cf.* Prop. 1).

2.4 Contraction and Splitting

To narrow the set of values represented by a cr-pair, we introduce contractions. A *contraction* κ is either a substitution θ or a restriction $\widehat{r}$. A *split* is a pair of contractions (κ_1, κ_2) that partitions a set of values into two disjoint sets. A *perfect split* guarantees that no elements will be lost, and no elements will be added when partitioning a set.

Definition 12 (contraction). *A contraction* $\kappa \in \text{Contr}$ *is either a substitution* $\theta \in \text{CCsub}$ *or a restriction* $\widehat{r} \in \text{Restr}$.

Definition 13 (contracting). *The result of contracting cr-pair* $\langle \widehat{cc}, \widehat{r} \rangle \in \text{CRpair}$ *by contraction* $\kappa \in \text{Contr}$, *denoted* $\langle \widehat{cc}, \widehat{r} \rangle / \kappa$, *is a cr-pair defined by*

$$\langle \widehat{cc}, \widehat{r} \rangle / \kappa \stackrel{\text{def}}{=} \begin{cases} \langle \widehat{cc}, \widehat{r} \rangle / \kappa & \text{if } \kappa \in \text{CCsub} \\ \langle \widehat{cc}, \widehat{r} \cup \kappa \rangle & \text{if } \kappa \in \text{Restr} . \end{cases}$$

For notational convenience we also define

$$\widehat{r} / \kappa \stackrel{\text{def}}{=} \begin{cases} \widehat{r} / \kappa & \text{if } \kappa \in \text{CCsub} \\ \widehat{r} \cup \kappa & \text{if } \kappa \in \text{Restr} . \end{cases}$$

It is easy to show that $\lceil \widehat{cr} / \kappa \rceil \subseteq \lceil \widehat{cr} \rceil$ for all $\widehat{cr} \in \text{CRpair}$ and for all $\kappa \in \text{Contr}$. That is, a contraction κ does never enlarge the set represented by a cr-pair.

Definition 14. *Define two special contractions: identity* $\kappa_{\text{id}} \stackrel{\text{def}}{=} [\,] \in \text{CCsub}$ *and contradiction* $\kappa_{\text{contra}} \stackrel{\text{def}}{=} \{\text{contra}\} \in \text{Restr}$.

It is easy to show that for all $\widehat{cr} \in \text{CRpair}$:

$$\lceil \widehat{cr} / \kappa_{\text{id}} \rceil = \lceil \widehat{cr} \rceil \quad \text{and} \quad \lceil \widehat{cr} / \kappa_{\text{contra}} \rceil = \emptyset .$$

Definition 15 (split). *A split* $sp \in \text{Split}$ *is a pair* (κ_1, κ_2) *where* $\kappa_1, \kappa_2 \in \text{Contr}$.

Definition 16 (perfect splitting). *A split* $(\kappa_1, \kappa_2) \in \text{Split}$ *is perfect for* $\widehat{cr} \in \text{CRpair}$ *if* (κ_1, κ_2) *divides* $\lceil \widehat{cr} \rceil$ *into two disjoint sets* $\lceil \widehat{cr} / \kappa_1 \rceil$ *and* $\lceil \widehat{cr} / \kappa_2 \rceil$ *such that*

$$\lceil \widehat{cr} / \kappa_1 \rceil \cup \lceil \widehat{cr} / \kappa_2 \rceil = \lceil \widehat{cr} \rceil \quad \text{and} \quad \lceil \widehat{cr} / \kappa_1 \rceil \cap \lceil \widehat{cr} / \kappa_2 \rceil = \emptyset .$$

Theorem 1 (perfect splits). *For all cr-pairs* $\langle \widehat{cc}, \widehat{r} \rangle \in \text{CRpair}$ *the following four splits are perfect:*

1. $(\kappa_{\text{id}}, \kappa_{\text{contra}})$
2. $([Xa_1 \mapsto da], \{(Xa_1 \# da)\})$
3. $([Xa_1 \mapsto Xa_2], \{(Xa_1 \# Xa_2)\})$
4. $([Xe_3 \mapsto Xa^\circ], [Xe_3 \mapsto (\textbf{cons } Xe_h^\circ \ Xe_t^\circ)])$

where $Xa_1, Xa_2, Xe_3 \in \text{var}(\widehat{cc})$, $Xa^\circ, Xe_h^\circ, Xe_t^\circ \notin \text{var}(\widehat{cc}) \cup \text{var}(\widehat{r})$, $da \in \text{DAval}$. *Remark: we use notation* $^\circ$ *to denote fresh c-variables for* $\langle \widehat{cc}, \widehat{r} \rangle$.

Proof: Omitted. $\qquad\qquad\qquad\qquad\qquad\qquad\qquad\qquad\qquad\qquad\qquad\qquad$ $\square$

Grammar

p	$::=$	q^+	Program
q	$::=$	$(\textbf{define } f \ x^* \ t)$	Definition
t	$::=$	$(\textbf{call } f \ e^*) \ \mid \ (\textbf{if } k \ t \ t) \ \mid \ e$	Term
k	$::=$	$(\textbf{eqa? } ea \ ea) \ \mid \ (\textbf{cons? } e \ xe \ xe \ xa)$	Condition
e	$::=$	$(\textbf{cons } e \ e) \ \mid \ xe \ \mid \ ea$	Expression
ea	$::=$	$(\textbf{atom } z) \ \mid \ xa$	Atomic Expression
x	$::=$	$xe \ \mid \ xa$	Typed Variable

Syntax Domains

p	$\in$ Program	f	$\in$ Fname	x	$\in$ Pvar
q	$\in$ Definition	z	$\in$ Symb	xe	$\in$ PEvar
t	$\in$ Term	e	$\in$ Pexp	xa	$\in$ PAvar
k	$\in$ Cond	ea	$\in$ PAexp		

Fig. 4. Abstract syntax of typed S-Graph (TSG)

3   Source Language

We consider the following first-order functional language, called TSG, as our source language. The language is a typed dialect of S-Graph [12]. The syntax of TSG is given by the grammar in Fig. 4; the operational semantics is defined in Fig. 5. An example program in concrete syntax is shown in Fig. 13. This family of languages has been used earlier for work on program transformation [2,11,12].

Syntax. A TSG-program is a sequence of function definitions where each definition contains the name, the parameters and the body of the function. The body of a function is a term which is either a function call **call**, a conditional **if**, or an expression e. Values can be constructed by **atom**, **cons**, and tested and/or decomposed by **eqa?**, **cons?**. Variables xa range over atoms, variables xe range over arbitrary values. The language is restricted to tail-recursion.

We assume that every TSG-program p we consider is *well-formed* in the sense that every function name that appears in a call in p is defined in p, that the types of arguments and parameters are compatible, and that every variable x used in the body of a definition q is a parameter of q or defined in an enclosing conditional. The first definition in a program is called *main function*. A program p is represented by a *program map* Γ which maps a function name f to the corresponding definition in p.

Semantics. The evaluation of a term updates a program's *state* (t, σ) which consists of a term t and an environment σ. The meaning of each term is then a *state transformation* computing the effect of the term on the state. We consider the *input* of a program to be the arguments of a call to the program's main

Condition Eqa?

$$\frac{ea_1/\sigma = ea_2/\sigma}{\sigma \vdash_{if} (\textbf{eqa? } ea_1\ ea_2)\ t_1\ t_2 \Rightarrow (t_1,\sigma)} \qquad \frac{ea_1/\sigma \neq ea_2/\sigma}{\sigma \vdash_{if} (\textbf{eqa? } ea_1\ ea_2)\ t_1\ t_2 \Rightarrow (t_2,\sigma)}$$

Condition Cons?

$$\frac{e/\sigma = (\textbf{cons } d_1\ d_2) \qquad \sigma' = \sigma[xe_1 \mapsto d_1, xe_2 \mapsto d_2]}{\sigma \vdash_{if} (\textbf{cons? } e\ xe_1\ xe_2\ xa_3)\ t_1\ t_2 \Rightarrow (t_1,\sigma')}$$

$$\frac{e/\sigma = (\textbf{atom } z) \qquad \sigma' = \sigma[xa_3 \mapsto e/\sigma]}{\sigma \vdash_{if} (\textbf{cons? } e\ xe_1\ xe_2\ xa_3)\ t_1\ t_2 \Rightarrow (t_2,\sigma')}$$

Terms

$$\frac{\sigma \vdash_{if} k\ t_1\ t_2 \Rightarrow (t_i,\sigma') \qquad i \in \{1,2\}}{\vdash_T ((\textbf{if } k\ t_1\ t_2),\sigma) \Rightarrow (t_i,\sigma')}$$

$$\frac{\Gamma(f) = (\textbf{define } f\ x_1 \dots x_n\ t) \qquad \sigma' = [x_1 \mapsto e_1/\sigma, \dots, x_n \mapsto e_n/\sigma]}{\vdash_T ((\textbf{call } f\ e_1 \dots e_n),\sigma) \Rightarrow (t,\sigma')}$$

Transition

$$\frac{\vdash_T s \Rightarrow s'}{\Vdash_T s \to s'}$$

Semantic Values

$$s \in \text{PDstate} = \text{Term} \times \text{PDenv}$$
$$\sigma \in \text{PDenv} = (\text{Pvar} \times \text{Dval})^*$$
$$\Gamma \in \text{ProgMap} = \text{Fname} \rightharpoonup \text{Definition}$$

Fig. 5. Operational semantics of TSG-programs

function, and the *output* of a program (if it exists) to be the value returned by evaluating this call. The semantics of TSG relies on the following definitions.

Values and variables. Values $d \in$ Dval are defined by the grammar in Fig. 1. In addition, we use tuples of values $ds = [d_1, \dots, d_n]$ as input for programs $(0 \leq n)$. The set of all value tuples will be denoted by Dvals. A program contains two types of variables $x \in$ Pvar. Variables $xa \in$ PAvar range over DAval, variables $xe \in$ PEvar range over Dval. Recall that DAval $\subseteq$ Dval.

Environment. An *environment* $\sigma = [x_1 \mapsto d_1, \dots, x_n \mapsto d_n] \in$ PDenv is a sequence of typed bindings such that variables x_i are pairwise distinct, d_i are values, and $x_i \in$ PAvar implies $d_i \in$ DAval $(i = 1 \dots n)$. An environment σ holds the values of the program variables.

We write $\sigma[x \mapsto d]$ to denote the environment that is just like σ except that variable x is bound to value d, and we write $\sigma(x)$ to denote the value of x in σ. Let $e \in$ Pexp and $\sigma \in$ PDenv, then e/σ denotes *the value of e on σ* defined as the result of replacing every variable x occurring in e by value $\sigma(x)$. If a program is well-formed, then σ in the rules of Fig. 5 defines a value for every x in e.

State. A *state* $s = (t, \sigma) \in$ PDstate is a term-environment pair that represents the current state of computation. A state of the form $s = (e, \sigma)$ with $e \in$ Pexp is a *terminal* state; otherwise s is a *non-terminal* state.

Evaluation. Figure 5 defines a transition relation $\rightarrow$ between states. The rules are straightforward. The rule for **call** states that a call to a function f returns a new state (t, σ') that contains the body t of f's definition and a new environment σ' that binds each parameter x_i of f to the value obtained by e_i/σ.

The rule for **if** states that, depending on the evaluation of condition k under environment σ, a new state (t_i, σ') is returned that contains one of the two branches t_1 or t_2, and an updated environment σ'.

The two rules for **eqa?** state that, depending on the equality of values ea_1/σ and ea_2/σ, a new state is formed containing term t_1 or t_2, and unchanged environment σ. The two rules for **cons?** state that, depending on value e/σ, a new state is formed containing term t_1 or t_2, and an updated environment σ'. If value e/σ has outermost constructor **cons**, environment σ is extended with variables xe_1, xe_2 bound to head and tail component of the value, respectively. Otherwise, environment σ is extended with variable xa_3 bound to atom e/σ.

Finally, the Γ-indexed transition relation $\rightarrow_\Gamma \subseteq$ (PDstate $\times$ PDstate) defines a transition from a state s to a state s' in a program represented by program map Γ. Even though the rule's formulation in Fig. 5 is trivial, we keep it for later extension. We write $\rightarrow_\Gamma$ in infix notation and drop the Γ-index when it is clear from the context. For example, we write $s \rightarrow s'$ when $(s, s') \in \rightarrow_\Gamma$.

Definition 17 (program evaluation). *Let p be a well-formed TSG-program with main function $q = (\textbf{define } f \; x_1 \ldots x_n \; t)$, and let $ds = [d_1, \ldots, d_n] \in$ Dvals. We define initial state $s^\circ(p, ds) \overset{\text{def}}{=} (t_0, \sigma_0)$ where $t_0 = (\textbf{call } f \; x_1 \ldots x_n)$ and $\sigma_0 = [x_1 \mapsto d_1, \ldots, x_n \mapsto d_n]$. We define program evaluation $\llbracket \cdot \rrbracket$ as follows:*

$$\llbracket p \rrbracket \, ds \overset{\text{def}}{=} \begin{cases} e/\sigma & \text{if } s^\circ(p, ds) \rightarrow^* (e, \sigma) \\ \text{undefined} & \text{otherwise .} \end{cases}$$

4   Program-Related Extension of the Set Representation

We extend the set representation introduced in Sect. 2 to program-related constructions needed for inverse computation of TSG-programs, such as state, environment, and input. These notions are language dependent and relate to the operational semantics of TSG.

First, we extend the definition of c-construction $\widehat{cc}$ to include *c-state* $\widehat{s}$, *c-binding* $\widehat{b}$, *c-environment* $\widehat{\sigma}$, and *c-input* $\widehat{ds}$ (Fig. 6). That is, domain Ccon (Def. 2) is extended to include all of these sets. Second, we extend the application of substitution to all program-related c-constructions (Fig. 7). Beside these

---

Extended C-Constructions

$$\begin{aligned}
\widehat{cc} &::= \widehat{s} \mid \widehat{b} \mid \widehat{\sigma} \mid \widehat{ds} \mid \widehat{d} & &\text{C-Construction}\\
\widehat{s} &::= (t, \widehat{\sigma}) & &\text{C-State}\\
\widehat{b} &::= xa \mapsto \widehat{da} \mid xe \mapsto \widehat{d} & &\text{C-Binding}\\
\widehat{\sigma} &::= [\widehat{b}^*] & &\text{C-Environment}\\
\widehat{ds} &::= [\widehat{d}^*] & &\text{C-Input}\\
\widehat{d} &::= (\text{defined in Fig. 1}) & &\text{C-Expression}
\end{aligned}$$

Value Domains

$$\begin{aligned}
\widehat{s} &\in \text{PCstate} & \widehat{cc} &\in \text{Ccon}\\
\widehat{b} &\in \text{PCbind} & \widehat{ds} &\in \text{Cexps}\\
\widehat{\sigma} &\in \text{PCenv} & &
\end{aligned}$$

Fig. 6. A program-related extension of c-constructions

C-State:	$(t, \widehat{\sigma})/\theta = (t, \widehat{\sigma}/\theta)$
C-Binding:	$(x \mapsto \widehat{d})/\theta = (x \mapsto \widehat{d}/\theta)$
C-Environment:	$[\widehat{b}_1, \ldots, \widehat{b}_n]/\theta = [\widehat{b}_1/\theta, \ldots, \widehat{b}_n/\theta]$
C-Input:	$[\widehat{d}_1, \ldots, \widehat{d}_n]/\theta = [\widehat{d}_1/\theta, \ldots, \widehat{d}_n/\theta]$

Fig. 7. Substitution on program-related c-constructions

---

extensions, all definitions and results from Sect. 2 remain valid. In particular, Thm. 1 (perfect splits) holds for the extended set of c-constructions.

The extension of domain Ccon leads to new cr-pairs. A cr-pair containing a c-state $\widehat{s}$ is called *configuration*. A cr-pair containing a c-input $\widehat{ds}$ is called *class*. Each of them represents a set of states and a set of value tuples, respectively.

Definition 18 (class, configuration). *A cr-pair* $\langle \widehat{ds}, \widehat{r} \rangle$ *where* $\widehat{ds} \in$ Cexps *is a class. A cr-pair* $\langle \widehat{s}, \widehat{r} \rangle$ *where* $\widehat{s} \in$ PCstate *is a configuration. By* Class *and* Conf *we denote the set of classes and the set of configurations, respectively.*

Definition 19 (well-formed input class, initial configuration). *Let* p *be a well-formed TSG-program with main function* $q = ($**define** $f \, x_1 \ldots x_n \, t)$, *and let* $cls = \langle [\widehat{d}_1, \ldots, \widehat{d}_n], \widehat{r} \rangle \in$ Class. *We say that* cls *is a well-formed input class for* p *if* $\lceil cls \rceil \neq \emptyset$ *and variable* $x_i \in$ PAvar *implies* $\widehat{d}_i \in$ CAexp $(i = 1 \ldots n)$. *We define initial configuration* $c^\circ(p, cls) \stackrel{\text{def}}{=} \langle (t_0, \widehat{\sigma}_0), \widehat{r} \rangle$ *where* cls *is a well-formed input class for* p, $t_0 = ($**call** $f \, x_1 \ldots x_n)$ *and* $\widehat{\sigma}_0 = [x_1 \mapsto \widehat{d}_1, \ldots, x_n \mapsto \widehat{d}_n]$.

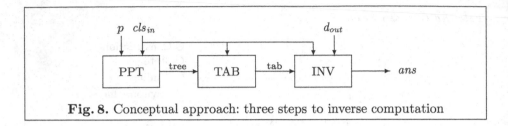

Fig. 8. Conceptual approach: three steps to inverse computation

5   Three Steps to Inverse Computation

Inverse computation can be organized into three steps: walking through a perfect process tree, then tabulating the input-output pairs, and finally extracting the answer to the inversion problem from the input-output pairs.

The key idea used in our approach is based on the notion of a *perfect process tree* which represents the computation of a program with missing input by a tree of all possible computation traces. Each fork in the tree partitions the input class into disjoint classes. Our algorithm then constructs, breadth-first and lazily, a perfect process tree for a given program p and input class cls_{in}. We shall not be concerned with different implementation techniques, but with a rigorous development of the principles and foundations of inverse computation.

In general, inverse computation using *ura* takes the form

$$[\![ura]\!][p, [cls_{in}, d_{out}]] = ans$$

where p is a program, cls_{in} is an input class, and d_{out} the output. We say, tuple $[cls_{in}, d_{out}]$ is a *request* for inverse computation where class cls_{in} specifies the set of admissible input (the search space), and d_{out} is the fixed output. The set *ans* is a *solution* of the given inversion problem. It is a set of substitution-restriction pairs $ans = \{(\theta_1, \widehat{r}_1), \ldots\}$ which represents the largest subset of $\lceil cls_{in} \rceil$ such that $[\![p]\!] ds_{in} = d_{out}$ for all elements $(\theta_i, \widehat{r}_i)$ of the solution and $ds_{in} \in \lceil cls_{in} \rceil$. More formally, a correct solution to an inversion problem is specified by

$$\bigcup_i \lceil cls_{in}/\theta_i/\widehat{r}_i \rceil = \{ ds_{in} \mid ds_{in} \in \lceil cls_{in} \rceil, [\![p]\!] ds_{in} = d_{out} \} .$$

In the following sections we present each of the three steps:

1. **Perfect Process Tree**: tracing program p under standard computation with cls_{in}.
2. **Tabulation**: forming the table of input-output pairs from the perfect process tree and class cls_{in}.
3. **Inversion**: extracting the answer for given output d_{out} from the table of input-output pairs.

The structure of the algorithm is illustrated in Fig. 5. Since our method is sound and complete, and since TSG is a universal programming language, which follows from the fact that the Universal Turing Machine can be defined in it, we can apply inverse computation, in principle, to any computable function. Thus our method of inverse computation has full generality.

The organization of inverse computation given here can be used for virtually any programming language. TSG is only a means to develop and fully formalize an algorithm for inverse computation. In fact, the set representation introduced in Sect. 2 can be used for any programming language with S-expressions, for example, for a subset of Lisp, or a simple flowchart language with S-expressions. Only the notions of state and configuration may change depending on the language. Changing the source language affects the construction of the perfect process tree, while the tabulation and inversion steps are not affected.

6   Walking the Perfect Process Tree

The transition relation in Fig. 9 defines walks through a *perfect process tree* [12]. Starting from a partially specified input, the goal is to follow all possible walks a standard evaluation may take under this generalized input. This will be the basis for inverse computation where the input of a program is only partially specified.

Process tree. A computation process is a potentially infinite sequence of states and transitions. Each state and transition in a deterministic computation is fully defined. The set of computation processes captures the semantics of a program as a whole. A *process tree* is used to examine the set of computation processes when the computation is not deterministic (because the input is only partly specified). Each node in a process tree contains a set of states represented by a *configuration*. A configuration which branches to two or more configurations in a process tree corresponds to a conditional transition from one set of program states to two or more sets of program states.

As defined in [12], a walk w in a process tree g is *feasible* if at least one initial state exists which selects w. A node n in a process tree g is feasible if it belongs at least to one feasible walk w in g. A process tree g is *perfect* if all walks in g are feasible.

Role of perfectness. The two most important operations when developing a process tree are:

1. applying perfect splits at branching configurations,
2. cutting infeasible branches in the tree.

Cutting infeasible branches is important because an infeasible branch is either non-terminating, or terminating in an unreachable node. The risk of entering non-terminating branches makes inverse computation less terminating (but completeness of the solution can be preserved). A terminating branch leads to a terminal state that can only be associated with an empty set of input in the solution (but soundness of the solution is preserved). Short, the correctness of the solution can be guaranteed, but an algorithm for inverse computation becomes less terminating and less efficient. The correctness of the solution cannot

Condition Eqt?

$$\frac{ea_1/\widehat{\sigma} = ea_2/\widehat{\sigma}}{\widehat{\sigma} \vdash_{if} (\textbf{eqa?}\ ea_1\ ea_2)\ t_1\ t_2 \Rightarrow \langle (t_1,\widehat{\sigma}), \kappa_{id} \rangle}$$

$$\frac{ea_1/\widehat{\sigma} \neq ea_2/\widehat{\sigma} \quad (ea_1/\widehat{\sigma}\ \#\ ea_2/\widehat{\sigma}) \notin \text{Tauto} \quad \kappa = [\,mkBind(ea_1/\widehat{\sigma}, ea_2/\widehat{\sigma})\,]}{\widehat{\sigma} \vdash_{if} (\textbf{eqa?}\ ea_1\ ea_2)\ t_1\ t_2 \Rightarrow \langle (t_1,\widehat{\sigma}), \kappa \rangle}$$

$$\frac{ea_1/\widehat{\sigma} \neq ea_2/\widehat{\sigma} \quad \kappa = \{(ea_1/\widehat{\sigma}\ \#\ ea_2/\widehat{\sigma})\}}{\widehat{\sigma} \vdash_{if} (\textbf{eqa?}\ ea_1\ ea_2)\ t_1\ t_2 \Rightarrow \langle (t_2,\widehat{\sigma}), \kappa \rangle}$$

Condition Cons?

$$\frac{e/\widehat{\sigma} = (\textbf{cons}\ \widehat{d_1}\ \widehat{d_2}) \quad \widehat{\sigma}' = \widehat{\sigma}[x_1 \mapsto \widehat{d_1}, x_2 \mapsto \widehat{d_2}]}{\widehat{\sigma} \vdash_{if} (\textbf{cons?}\ e\ x_1\ x_2\ x_3)\ t_1\ t_2 \Rightarrow \langle (t_1,\widehat{\sigma}'), \kappa_{id} \rangle}$$

$$\frac{e/\widehat{\sigma} = \widehat{da} \quad \widehat{\sigma}' = \widehat{\sigma}[x_3 \mapsto \widehat{da}]}{\widehat{\sigma} \vdash_{if} (\textbf{cons?}\ e\ x_1\ x_2\ x_3)\ t_1\ t_2 \Rightarrow \langle (t_2,\widehat{\sigma}'), \kappa_{id} \rangle}$$

$$\frac{e/\widehat{\sigma} = Xe \quad \widehat{\sigma}' = \widehat{\sigma}[x_1 \mapsto Xe_1^\circ, x_2 \mapsto Xe_2^\circ] \quad \kappa = [Xe \mapsto (\textbf{cons}\ Xe_1^\circ\ Xe_2^\circ)]}{\widehat{\sigma} \vdash_{if} (\textbf{cons?}\ e\ x_1\ x_2\ x_3)\ t_1\ t_2 \Rightarrow \langle (t_1,\widehat{\sigma}'), \kappa \rangle}$$

$$\frac{e/\widehat{\sigma} = Xe \quad \widehat{\sigma}' = \widehat{\sigma}[x_3 \mapsto Xa^\circ] \quad \kappa = [Xe \mapsto Xa^\circ]}{\widehat{\sigma} \vdash_{if} (\textbf{cons?}\ e\ x_1\ x_2\ x_3)\ t_1\ t_2 \Rightarrow \langle (t_2,\widehat{\sigma}'), \kappa \rangle}$$

Terms

$$\frac{\widehat{\sigma} \vdash_{if} k\ t_1\ t_2 \Rightarrow \langle (t_i,\widehat{\sigma}'), \kappa \rangle \quad i \in \{1,2\}}{\vdash_T ((\textbf{if}\ k\ t_1\ t_2), \widehat{\sigma}) \Rightarrow \langle (t_i,\widehat{\sigma}'), \kappa \rangle}$$

$$\frac{\Gamma(f) = (\textbf{define}\ f\ x_1 \ldots x_n\ t) \quad \widehat{\sigma}' = [x_1 \mapsto e_1/\widehat{\sigma}, \ldots, x_n \mapsto e_n/\widehat{\sigma}]}{\vdash_T ((\textbf{call}\ f\ e_1 \ldots e_n), \widehat{\sigma}) \Rightarrow \langle (t,\widehat{\sigma}'), \kappa_{id} \rangle}$$

Transition

$$\frac{\vdash_T \widehat{s} \Rightarrow \langle \widehat{s}', \kappa \rangle \quad \widehat{r}/\kappa \neq \{\text{contra}\}}{\Vdash_T \langle \widehat{s}, \widehat{r} \rangle \mapsto \langle \widehat{s}', \widehat{r} \rangle / \kappa}$$

Semantic Values

$$\widehat{s} \in \text{PCstate} = \text{Term} \times \text{PCenv}$$
$$\widehat{\sigma} \in \text{PCenv} = (\text{Pvar} \times \text{Cexp})^*$$
$$\Gamma \in \text{ProgMap} = \text{Fname} \rightharpoonup \text{Definition}$$

Fig. 9. Trace semantics for perfect process trees of TSG-programs

be guaranteed without *applying perfect splits* because in this case empty sets of input cannot be detected neither during the development of the tree nor in the solution. Our formulation of the transition relation includes both operations.

Walking a process tree. Fig. 9 defines a transition relation $\mapsto$ between configurations. The transition relation does not actually construct a tree, but allows to perform all walks in a perfect process tree. The transition relation is nondeterministic when a condition (**eqa?**, **cons?**) cannot be decided. In this case the rules permit us to follow any of the two possible branches.

The transition rule states that a configuration $\langle \hat{s}, \hat{r} \rangle$ is transformed into a new configuration which is obtained by evaluating c-state $\hat{s}$ to a new c-state $\hat{s}'$, and applying contraction κ of the associated perfect split to configuration $\langle \hat{s}', \hat{r} \rangle$ if this does not lead to a contradiction (which would mean the transition is not feasible). The rule ensures perfect splitting and cutting of infeasible branches.

The rules for **if** and **call** are similar to the rules for the operational semantics in Fig. 5 except that they take a c-state to a new c-state and an associated contraction κ. In case of a call, identity contraction κ_{id} is returned (no split), in case of a conditional, contraction κ produced by evaluating condition k is returned.

We now describe the rules for conditions in more detail. The three rules for **eqa?** state that, depending on the equality of ca-expressions $ea_1/\hat{\sigma}$ and $ea_2/\hat{\sigma}$, a new c-state is formed which is associated with a contraction κ. The first equality rule applies if ca-expressions $ea_1/\hat{\sigma}$ and $ea_2/\hat{\sigma}$ are equal, which means they represent the same set of values. The second and third rule may apply at the same time. This is the case when $ea_1/\hat{\sigma}$ and $ea_2/\hat{\sigma}$ are not equal and at least one of the two ca-expressions is a c-variable (*i.e.*, inequality $(ea_1/\hat{\sigma} \# ea_2/\hat{\sigma})$ is not a tautology). Then c-states $(t_1, \hat{\sigma})$ and $(t_2, \hat{\sigma})$ are associated with the corresponding contraction of the *perfect split* (Thm. 1, split 2, 3): $(t_1, \hat{\sigma})$ is equipped with a substitution binding the ca-variable to the other ca-expression, and $(t_2, \hat{\sigma})$ is equipped with an inequality between $ea_1/\hat{\sigma}$ and $ea_2/\hat{\sigma}$. Auxiliary function *mkBind* makes a binding of its arguments ensuring that a ca-variable appears on the left hand side of that binding.

The four rules for **cons?** associate a new c-state with a contraction κ. The first two rule correspond to the two cons rules in Fig. 5 except that $e/\hat{\sigma}$ is a c-expression. If $e/\hat{\sigma}$ has outermost constructor **cons** then the true-branch is entered, otherwise, the false-branch is entered. In case $e/\hat{\sigma}$ is a ce-variable Xe, the third and fourth rule apply and c-states $(t_1, \hat{\sigma}_1)$ and $(t_2, \hat{\sigma}_2)$ are equipped with the corresponding contraction of the perfect split (Thm. 1, split 4): $(t_1, \hat{\sigma}_1)$ is equipped with a substitution instantiating Xe to a new cons-expression (where $Xe_1^\diamond$ and $Xe_2^\diamond$ are fresh ce-variables), and $(t_2, \hat{\sigma}_2)$ is equipped with a substitution binding ce-variable Xe to a fresh ca-variable $Xa^\diamond$.

Correctness. Proving the trace semantics for perfect process trees (Fig. 9) correct *wrt* the operational semantics of TSG must consist of a soundness and completeness argument. First, we state the correctness of an initial configuration and a transition step, and then state the main correctness result. We shall not be concerned with the technical details of the proofs in this paper, only with the fact [2] that the trace semantics is correct *wrt* the operational semantics.

Theorem 2 (correctness of initial configuration). *Let p be a well-formed* TSG-*program, let cls be well-formed input class for p, then* *Completeness and Soundness:* $\lceil c^\circ(p, cls) \rceil = \{ s^\circ(p, ds) \mid ds \in \lceil cls \rceil \}$.

Transition

$$\frac{\vdash_\Gamma \hat{s} \Rightarrow \langle \hat{s}', \kappa \rangle \quad \hat{r}/\kappa \neq \{\text{contra}\}}{\Vdash_\Gamma (cls, \langle \hat{s}, \hat{r} \rangle) \rightarrow_{tab} (cls/\kappa, \langle \hat{s}', \hat{r} \rangle/\kappa)}$$

Semantic Values

$$tab \in \text{Tab} = \text{Class} \times \text{Cexp}$$

Fig. 10. Tabulation of TSG-programs

Theorem 3 (correctness of ppt-transition). *Let p be a well-formed TSG-program, and let c be a well-formed configuration for p, then*
Completeness: $\forall s \in \lceil c \rceil \,.\, \forall s' \,.\, (\Vdash_\Gamma s \rightarrow s') \Rightarrow (\exists c' \,.\, (\Vdash_\Gamma c \mapsto c' \wedge s' \in \lceil c' \rceil))$
Soundness: $\quad \forall c' \,.\, (\Vdash_\Gamma c \mapsto c') \Rightarrow (\forall s' \in \lceil c' \rceil \,.\, \exists s \in \lceil c \rceil \,.\, \Vdash_\Gamma s \rightarrow s') \,.$

Theorem 4 (correctness of ppt). *Let p be a well-formed TSG-program, let cls be well-formed input class for p, then*
Completeness:
$$\forall ds \in \lceil cls \rceil \,.\, \forall s_0 \ldots s_n \,.\, s_0 = s^\circ(p, ds) \wedge (\wedge_{i=0}^{n-1} \Vdash_\Gamma s_i \rightarrow s_{i+1}) \Rightarrow$$
$$\exists c_0 \ldots c_n \,.\, c_0 = c^\circ(p, cls) \wedge (\wedge_{i=0}^{n-1} \Vdash_\Gamma c_i \mapsto c_{i+1}) \wedge (\wedge_{i=0}^{n} s_i \in \lceil c_i \rceil)$$

Soundness:
$$\forall c_0 \ldots c_n \,.\, c_0 = c^\circ(p, cls) \wedge (\wedge_{i=0}^{n-1} \Vdash_\Gamma c_i \mapsto c_{i+1}) \Rightarrow$$
$$\exists ds \in \lceil cls \rceil \,.\, \exists s_0 \ldots s_n \,.\, s_0 = s^\circ(p, ds) \wedge (\wedge_{i=0}^{n-1} \Vdash_\Gamma s_i \rightarrow s_{i+1}) \wedge (\wedge_{i=0}^{n} s_i \in \lceil c_i \rceil) \,.$$

Proof: Omitted (base case Thm. 2, induction step Thm. 3). $\qquad\square$

7 Tabulation and Inversion

Before defining the solution of inverse computation, we define the tabulation of a program p for a given input class cls_{in}. Tabulation divides input class cls_{in} into disjoint input classes each of which is associated with a leave (output) in the process tree. All input-output pairs are collected in a set $TAB(p, cls_{in})$. For this we define a transition relation $\rightarrow_{tab}$ (Fig. 10) that carries an input class and applies to it every contraction κ encountered while following a path in the process tree. Finally, we define the solution of inverse computation as the set $ANS(p, cls_{in}, d_{out})$.

Definition 20 (tabulation). *Let p be a well-formed TSG-program, let cls_{in} be a well-formed input class for p. Define tabulation of p on cls_{in} as follows:*

$$TAB(p, cls_{in}) \stackrel{\text{def}}{=} \{ (cls, e/\hat{\sigma}) \mid (cls_{in}, c^\circ(p, cls_{in})) \rightarrow^*_{tab} (cls, \langle (e, \hat{\sigma}), \hat{r} \rangle) \} \,.$$

Definition 21 (inverse computation). *Let p be a well-formed TSG-program, let cls_{in} be a well-formed input class for p, and let $d_{out} \in \text{Dval}$. Define inverse computation of p on cls_{in} and d_{out} as follows:*

$$ANS(p, cls_{in}, d_{out}) \stackrel{\text{def}}{=} \{ (\theta, \hat{r}) \mid (cls, \hat{d}) \in TAB(p, cls_{in}), \; \theta, \theta' \in \text{CCsub},$$
$$\hat{r} \in \text{Restr}, \; \hat{d}/\theta' = d_{out}, \; cls_{in}/\theta/\hat{r} = cls/\theta' \} \,.$$

Correctness. Proving the correctness of tabulation $TAB(p, cls_{in})$ must consist of a soundness and completeness argument. For completeness we must prove that for each evaluation $[\![p]\!][d_1, \ldots, d_n] = d$, there is a input-output pair $(cls, \widehat{d}) \in TAB(p, cls_{in})$ such that $[d_1, \ldots, d_n] \in \lceil cls \rceil$ and $d \in \lceil \widehat{d} \rceil$. For soundness we must prove that each $(cls, \widehat{d}) \in TAB(p, cls_{in})$ and each $[d_1, \ldots, d_n] \in \lceil cls \rceil$ implies $[\![p]\!][d_1, \ldots, d_n] = d$ and $d \in \lceil \widehat{d} \rceil$. The corresponding argument for set $ANS(p, cls_{in}, d_{out})$ is based on the correctness of the tabulation. We shall not be concerned with the technical details of the proofs, only with the fact [2] that tabulation and inversion are correct *wrt* the operational semantics.

Theorem 5 (correctness of TAB). *Let p be a well-formed TSG-program, let cls_{in} be a well-formed input class for p, and let $T = TAB(p, cls_{in})$, then completeness and soundness:*

$$\{ (ds_{in}, d) \mid ds_{in} \in \lceil cls_{in} \rceil, [\![p]\!] ds_{in} = d \} =$$
$$\{ (\widehat{ds}/\theta, \widehat{d}/\theta) \mid (\langle \widehat{ds}, \widehat{r} \rangle, \widehat{d}) \in T, \theta \in FS(\langle \widehat{ds}, \widehat{r} \rangle), \widehat{r}/\theta = \emptyset \} .$$

Theorem 6 (correctness of ANS). *Let p be a well-formed TSG-program, let cls_{in} be a well-formed input class for p, let $d_{out} \in$ Dval and $A = ANS(p, cls_{in}, d_{out})$, then completeness and soundness:*

$$\{ ds_{in} \mid ds_{in} \in \lceil cls_{in} \rceil, [\![p]\!] ds_{in} = d_{out} \} = \bigcup_{(\theta, \widehat{r}) \in A} \lceil cls_{in}/\theta/\widehat{r} \rceil .$$

The most important property of set $TAB(p, cls_{in})$ is *the perfectness property*—this allows us to inverse all input-output pairs independently and in any order.

Theorem 7 (perfectness of TAB). *Let p be a well-formed TSG-program, let cls_{in} be a well-formed input class for p, and let $(cls_1, \widehat{d}_1)$ and $(cls_2, \widehat{d}_2)$ be two different input-output pairs from $TAB(p, cls_{in})$, then $\lceil cls_1 \rceil \cap \lceil cls_2 \rceil = \emptyset$.*

8   Algorithmic Aspects

In this section we discuss algorithmic aspects related to the Universal Resolving Algorithm and presents our Haskell implementation. While Def. 21 specifies the solution obtained from the tabulation of the perfect process tree, an algorithm for inverse computation must actually traverse the process tree according to some algorithmic strategy and extract the solution from the leaves.

The algorithm is fully implemented in Hugs, a dialect of Haskell, a lazy functional language (321 lines of pretty-printed source text).[3] The algorithm is structured into three separate functions: (1) function `ppt` that builds a potentially infinite process tree, (2) function `tab` that consumes the tree to perform the tabulation, and (3) function `inv` that enumerates set $ANS(p, cls_{in}, d_{out})$.

The main function `ura` which performs inverse computation is defined by

---

[3] Hugs-script available by `http://www.botik.ru/AbrGlu/URA/MPC2000`

```
ppt :: ProgTSG -> Class -> Tree
ppt   p cls@(ces, r) = evalT c p i
           where (DEFINE f xs _): _ = p
                 env = mkEnv xs ces
                 c   = ((CALL f xs, env), r)
                 i   = freeind 0 cls

evalT :: Conf -> ProgTSG -> FreeInd -> Tree
evalT c@(( CALL f es , env), r) p i = NODE c [ (kId, evalT c' p i) ]
           where DEFINE _ xs t = getDef f p
                 env' = mkEnv xs (es/.env)
                 c'   = ((t,env'),r)

evalT c@(( IF cond t1 t2 , env), r) p i = NODE c (brT++brF)
           where ((kT,kF),bindsT,bindsF,i') = ccond cond env i
                 brT = mkBr t1 kT bindsT
                 brF = mkBr t2 kF bindsF
                 mkBr t k binds = case r' of
                                     [CONTRA] -> []
                                     _        -> [(k, evalT c' p i')]
                                  where ((_,env'), r') = c/.k
                                        c' = ((t, env'+.binds), r')

evalT c@((e,env),r) p i = LEAF c

ccond :: Cond -> PCenv -> FreeInd -> (Split,PCenv,PCenv,FreeInd)
ccond (EQA? ea1 ea2) env i =
         let cea1 = ea1/.env; cea2 = ea2/.env in case (cea1, cea2) of
           (a,     b   )|a==b -> ( (kId,kContra), [],[],i)
           (ATOM _,ATOM _)    -> ( (kContra,kId), [],[],i)
           (XA _,  cea )      -> (splitA cea1 cea,[],[],i)
           (cea,   XA _ )      -> (splitA cea2 cea,[],[],i)

ccond (CONS? e xh xt xa) env i =
         let ce = e/.env in case ce of
           CONS ceh cet -> ((kId,kContra),[xh:=ceh,xt:=cet],[],i )
           ATOM a       -> ((kContra,kId),[],            [xa:=ce],i )
           XA _         -> ((kContra,kId),[],            [xa:=ce],i )
           XE _         -> (split, [xh:=cxh,xt:=cxt],[xa:=cxa],i')
                           where
                           (split,i') = splitE ce i
                           (S[_:->(CONS cxh cxt)],S[_:->cxa])=split
```

Fig. 11. Function ppt for constructing perfect process trees (written in Haskell)

```
ura :: ProgTSG -> Class -> Dval -> [(CCsub,Restr)]
ura p cls out = inv (tab (ppt p cls) cls) cls out
```

Given source program p, class cls and output out, function ura returns a list of substitution-restriction pairs (CCsub,Restr). Due to the lazy evaluation strategy of Haskell, the process tree and the tabulation are only developed on demand by

```
type Tab = [(Class, Cexp)]
tab  :: Tree -> Class -> Tab
tab  tree cls = tab' [(cls, tree)]
     where tab' [] = []
           tab' ((cls,LEAF ((e,env),_)):cts) = (cls,e/.env):(tab' cts)
           tab' ((cls,NODE _ brs)    :cts) =
                    tab' (cts++(map (\(k,tree) -> (cls/.k,tree)) brs))
inv  :: Tab -> Class -> Dval -> [(CCsub,Restr)]
inv  tab cls out = concat (map ans tab)
     where ans (cls_i, ce_i) =
             case (clash [ce_i] [out]) of
             (False, _) -> []
             (True,sub') -> case cls_i' of
                            (_, [CONTRA]) -> []
                            _             -> [(sub, r)]
                          where cls_i' = cls_i/.sub'
                                (sub, r) = subClassCntr cls cls_i'
```

Fig. 12. Functions `tab` and `inv` for tabulation and inversion (written in Haskell)

function `ura`. The type definitions `Class`, `Dval`, `CCsub` and `Restr` correspond to the domains Class, Dval, CCsub, and Restr; the source program is typed `ProgTSG`. The implementation of the functions `ppt`, `tab`, `inv` is shown in Figs. 11 and 12.

Function `ppt` in Fig. 11 implements the trace semantics from Fig. 9 such that all applicable rules are fired at the same time. The function makes use of a tree structure to record all walks:

```
data Tree = LEAF Conf              type Branch = (Contr, Tree)
          | NODE Conf [Branch]
```

For each rule that applies a branch is added (one branch if the transition is deterministic, two branches if the transition is non-deterministic). Each node is labeled with the current configuration c, and each branch with the contraction κ used to split c (the contraction κ is needed for tabulation). Function `ppt` is the initial function, function `evalT` constructs the tree, and function `ccond` evaluates a condition. The reader may notice the format returned by function `ccond`: a tuple that contains the split to be performed on the current configuration, possibly updated bindings for the true- and false-branch, and a free index i (used for generating fresh variables). Infix operator `/.` implements substitution $/$, and infix operator `+.` implements update $\hat{\sigma}[x_1 \mapsto \hat{d}_1, \ldots, x_n \mapsto \hat{d}_n]$.

Auxiliary functions `splitA` and `splitE` return the perfect splits for ca- and ce-variables, respectively (as defined in Thm. 1, perfect splits):

```
splitA :: CAvar -> CAexp -> Split            -- Thm.1: split 2,3
splitA cxa cea = (S[cxa:->cea], R[cxa:#:cea])
```

```
splitE :: CAvar -> FreeInd -> (Split,FreeInd)     -- Thm.1: split 4
splitE cxe i = ((S[cxe:->(CONS cxe'h cxe't)], S[cxe:->cxa]), i')
              where cxe'h = newCEvar(i);     cxa = newCAvar(i+2)
                    cxe't = newCEvar(i+1);   i' = i+3
```

Function `tab` in Fig. 12 consumes the process tree produced by `ppt` using a *breadth-first strategy*[4] in order to ensure that all leaves on finite branches will eventually be visited. This is important because a depth-first strategy may 'fall' into an infinite branch, never visiting other branches.

Function `inv` in Fig. 12 enumerates the set $ANS(p, cls_{in}, d_{out})$ according to Def. 21. Two auxiliary functions `clash` and `subClassCntr` are used. Given $\widehat{ds_1}, \widehat{ds_2} \in$ Cexps, the auxiliary function `clash` returns $(\texttt{True}, \theta)$ if a substitution $\theta \in$ CCsub exists such that $\widehat{ds_1}/\theta = \widehat{ds_2}$ and $dom(\theta) = var(\widehat{ds_1})$; otherwise $(\texttt{False}, [])$. The requirement for the domain of θ ensures that no redundant bindings are added and that, if a solution exists, we produce a unique θ.

Given $cls, cls' \in$ Class where cls' can be obtained from cls by several contractions, the auxiliary function `subClassCntr` returns $(\theta, \widehat{r})$ where $\theta \in$ CCsub, $\widehat{r} \in$ Restr such that $cls' = (cls/\theta)/\widehat{r}$ and $dom(\theta) = var(cls)$.

Termination. Of course, inverse computation is undecidable, so an algorithm cannot be sound, complete, and terminating. Our algorithm is sound and complete, but not always terminating. Each solution, if it exists, is computed in finite time due to the breadth-first strategy. The algorithm does not always terminate because the search for solutions in a process tree may continue infinitely (even though all elements of the solution were found). The algorithm terminates if all branches in a process tree are finite.

9   Experiments and Results

This section illustrates the Universal Resolving Algorithm by means of examples. The first example illustrates inverse computation of a pattern matcher, the second example demonstrates the inverse interpretation of While-programs.[5]

Pattern matching. We performed the two inversion tasks from Sect. 1 using a naive pattern matcher written in TSG (Fig. 13).

- **Task 1**: Find the set of strings `pattern` which *are* substrings of `"ABC"`. To perform this task we leave input `pattern` unknown (Xe_1), set input `string = "ABC"` and the desired output to `'SUCCESS`.
- **Task 2**: Find the set of strings `pattern` which *are not* substrings of `"AAA"`. To perform this task we use a setting similar to Task 1 (`pattern = Xe_1`, `string = "AAA"`), but the desired output is set to `'FAILURE`.

---

[4] The breadth-first strategy is implemented in the last line of function `tab` by appending the list of next-level-nodes produced by `map` to the end of list `cts`.

[5] Run times given for Hugs 98, PC/Intel Pentium MMX-233MHz, MS Windows 95.

```
match =
  [(DEFINE "Match"[p,s]                    (DEFINE "NextPos" [p,s]
     (CALL"CheckPos"[p,s,p,s]) ),             (IF (CONS? s sh st a)
   (DEFINE "CheckPos" [p,s,pp,ss]             (CALL "Match" [p,st])
     (IF (CONS? p ph pt a)                    'FAILURE ) ) ]
       (IF (CONS? ph _ _ a'ph)
       'ERROR:Atom_expected
       (IF (CONS? s sh st a)
         (IF (CONS? sh _ _ a'sh)
         'ERROR:Atom_expected
         (IF (EQA? a'ph a'sh)
           (CALL "CheckPos"[pt,st,pp,ss])
           (CALL "NextPos" [pp,ss]) ) )
       'FAILURE ) )
     'SUCCESS ) ),
```

Fig. 13. Naive pattern matcher written in concrete TSG syntax

Figure 14 shows the results of applying URA to the matcher. The answer for Task1 is a finite representation of all possible substrings of string "ABC", Fig. 14(i). The answer for Task 2 is a finite representation of all strings which are not substrings of "AAA", Fig. 14(ii). URA terminates after 0.5 seconds (Task 1, Task 2).

Interpreter inversion. As proven in [3,4], inverse computation can be performed in a programming language N given a standard interpreter $intN$ for N written in L, and an inverse interpreter for L. The result obtained by inverse computation of N's interpreter is a solution for inverse computation in N. The theorem guarantees that the solution is *correct* for all N-program regardless of $intN$'s operational properties. Since TSG is a universal programming language we can, in principle, perform inverse computation in any programming language.

According to this result, we should now be able to apply our algorithm to programs written in languages other than TSG. To put this theorem to a practical trial, we implemented an interpreter for an imperative language, called MP, in TSG. MP [27] is a small *imperative language* with assignments (<==), conditionals (oIF) and loops (oWHILE). An MP-program operates over a store consisting of parameters and local variables. The semantics is conventional Pascal-style semantics. The MP-interpreter has 309 lines of pretty-printed source text, 30 functions in TSG, and is the largest TSG-program we implemented.

To compare the results with inverse computation in TSG, we rewrote the naive pattern matcher in MP. Figure 14 shows the results for the inversion of the MP-matcher. The answer for Task 1 is a finite representation of all possible substrings of string "ABC", Fig. 14(iii). The answer for Task 2 is a finite representation of all strings which are not substrings of "AAA", Fig. 14(iv). URA terminates after 36 sec (Task 1) and after 34 sec (Task 2).

(i)   ura [match, [([Xe_1, str"ABC"],[]), 'SUCCESS]] $\overset{*}{\Rightarrow}$

   [(([$Xe_1 \mapsto Xa_4$], []),   --str""
    ([$Xe_1 \mapsto$ (CONS 'A Xa_{10})], []),   --str"A"
    ([$Xe_1 \mapsto$ (CONS 'A (CONS 'B Xa_{16}))], []),   --str"AB"
    ([$Xe_1 \mapsto$ (CONS 'B Xa_{10})], []),   --str "B"
    ([$Xe_1 \mapsto$ (CONS 'A (CONS 'B (CONS 'C Xa_{22})))], []), --str"ABC"
    ([$Xe_1 \mapsto$ (CONS 'B (CONS 'C Xa_{16}))], []),   --str "BC"
    ([$Xe_1 \mapsto$ (CONS 'C Xa_{10})], [])]   --str "C"

(ii) ura [match, [([Xe_1, str"AAA"],[]), 'FAILURE]] $\overset{*}{\Rightarrow}$

   [([$Xe_1 \mapsto$ (CONS 'A (CONS 'A (CONS 'A (CONS Xa_{25} Xe_{21}))))],[]),
    ([$Xe_1 \mapsto$ (CONS Xa_7 Xe_3)],[Xa_7:#:'A]),
    ([$Xe_1 \mapsto$ (CONS 'A (CONS 'A (CONS Xa_{19} Xe_{15})))],[Xa_{19}:#:'A]),
    ([$Xe_1 \mapsto$ (CONS 'A (CONS Xa_{13} Xe_9))],[Xa_{13}:#:'A])]

(iii) ura [intMP, [[matchMP, ([Xe_1, str"ABC"],[])], 'SUCCESS]] $\overset{*}{\Rightarrow}$

   [([$Xe_1 \mapsto Xa_4$], []),   --str""
    ([$Xe_1 \mapsto$ (CONS 'A Xa_{10})], []),   --str"A"
    ([$Xe_1 \mapsto$ (CONS 'A (CONS 'B Xa_{16}))], []),   --str"AB"
    ([$Xe_1 \mapsto$ (CONS 'B Xa_{10})], []),   --str "B"
    ([$Xe_1 \mapsto$ (CONS 'A (CONS 'B (CONS 'C Xa_{22})))], []), --str"ABC"
    ([$Xe_1 \mapsto$ (CONS 'B (CONS 'C Xa_{16}))], []),   --str "BC"
    ([$Xe_1 \mapsto$ (CONS 'C Xa_{10})], [])]   --str "C"

(iv) ura [intMP, [[matchMP, ([Xe_1, str"AAA"],[])], 'FAILURE]] $\overset{*}{\Rightarrow}$

   [([$Xe_1 \mapsto$ (CONS 'A (CONS 'A (CONS 'A (CONS Xe_{20} Xe_{21}))))],[]),
    ([$Xe_1 \mapsto$ (CONS Xa_7 Xe_3)],[Xa_7:#:'A]),
    ([$Xe_1 \mapsto$ (CONS 'A (CONS 'A (CONS Xa_{19} Xe_{15})))],[Xa_{19}:#:'A]),
    ([$Xe_1 \mapsto$ (CONS 'A (CONS Xa_{13} Xe_9))],[Xa_{13}:#:'A])]

Fig. 14. Inverse computation of pattern matcher (i, ii) and interpreter (iii, iv)

Inverse computation in MP (implemented by ura and intMP) produces results very similar[6] to inverse computation in TSG (implemented directly by ura). This is noteworthy because inverse computation in MP is done through a *standard interpreter* for MP (and not by an inverse interpreter for MP). It demonstrates that inverse computation can be ported successfully, here, from a functional language to an imperative language. Inverse computation in MP takes longer than in TSG due to the additional interpretive overhead (about 70 times).

In earlier work [4], inverse computation was ported from TSG to a small assembler-like programming language (called Norma). The only other experimental work we are aware of that ported inverse computation, inverses imperative programs by treating their relational semantics as logic program [26]. Our

---

[6] The results differ slightly (Fig. 14: compare (ii) line 2 and (iv) line 2) due to small differences in the implementation of the source programs.

experiment gives further practical evidence for the idea of porting inverse computation from one language to another.

10   Related Work

The first work on program inversion appears to be [22], suggesting a *generate and test approach* for Turing machines; this will correctly find an inverse when it exists, but is computationally infeasible. Several efforts have gone into *imperative programs* [16,7,17,6] but use non-automatic (sometimes heuristic) methods for deriving the inverse program. For example, the technique suggested in [7] provides for inverting programs symbolically, but requires that the programmer provide inductive assertions on conditionals and loop statements.

Few papers have been devoted to inversion of *functional programs* [5,9,18,20] [21,25] in a similar manner, sometimes automatically. The work in functional languages is usually on program inversion. An automatic system for synthesizing recursive programs from first-order functional programs is InvX [20]. The inverse of functions has been paid attention to, at least conceptually, in program analysis and program verification (*e.g.*, [8,24]).

An early result [28] for inverse computation in a functional language was obtained in 1972 by a unification-based transformation technique called *driving* [29] which was used to perform subtraction by inverse computation of binary addition. Later, universal resolving algorithms were implemented using methods from supercompilation [29] for first-order functional programs by combining them with a mechanical extraction of answers (*cf.* [1,25]).

We know of two techniques for inverse computation in functional languages: the universal resolving algorithm (see [1,4]) and walk grammars for inverse interpretation [30,23]. The universal resolving algorithm in this paper uses methods from supercompilation [29], in particular driving, and is based on perfect process trees [12]. Connections between inverse computation and logic programming are discussed in [1,4]; partial deduction and driving were formally related in [14]. An abstract framework for describing partial evaluation and supercompilation is [19]. A comprehensive bibliography on supercompilation can be found in [15].

To conclude, there exists only a small number of papers addressing inverse computation in the context of functional languages. With the exception of [26,4], we know of no paper addressing inverse computation in imperative languages.

11   Conclusion and Future Work

We presented an algorithm for inverse computation in a first-order functional language based on the notion of a perfect process tree, discussed the general organization and structure of inverse computation, stated the main correctness results, and illustrated our Haskell implementation with several examples.

Among others, a motivation for our work was the thesis [13] that program inversion is one of the three fundamental operations on programs (beside program specialization and program composition). We believe that to achieve full generality of program manipulation, ultimately all three operations have to be mastered. So far, progress has been achieved mostly on program specialization.

For future work it is desirable, though not difficult, to extend our algorithm to user-defined constructor domains. This requires an extension of the set representation in Sect. 2 and an extension of the source language (*e.g.*, case-expressions). In this paper we focused on a rigorous development of the principles and foundations of inverse computation and used S-expressions familiar from Lisp.

In general, cutting all infeasible branches from a process tree cannot be guaranteed, in particular, when the underlying logic of the set representation is undecidable for certain logic formulas (or too time consuming to prove). For example, this is the case when using a tree developer based on generalized partial computation [10]. In this case, the solution of inverse computation may contain elements which represent empty sets of input (the correctness of the solution can be preserved). The set representation we used expresses structural properties of values that can always be resolved. Perfect splits are essential to guarantee the correctness of the solution, cutting infeasible branches improves termination and efficiency of the algorithm.

The question of a more efficient implementation is also left for future work. Our algorithm is fully implemented in Haskell and serves our experimental purposes quite well. In particular, Haskell's lazy evaluation strategy allowed us to use a modular approach very close to the theoretical definition of the algorithm (where the development of perfect process trees and the inversion of the tabulation are conveniently separated). The design of a more efficient algorithm would require to merge these steps. Compilation techniques and strategies developed for logic programming may be beneficial for a more practical implementation.

Finally, the relation to narrowing used in logic-functional programming and term rewriting should be studied more formally (reference [14] relates driving and partial deduction).

Acknowledgments

The authors would like to thank their colleagues from the Refal group for various discussions related to this work. Special thanks are due to Jeremy Gibbons for suggesting to submit this material to MPC, to the five anonymous referees for valuable comments, and to Kazuhiko Kakehi for careful proofreading. The second author would like to thank Michael Leuschel for joint work leading to some of the material in Section 10. Special thanks are due to Yoshihiko Futamura for generous support of this research. The authors were also supported by the Japan Society for the Promotion of Science and the Danish Natural Sciences Research Council.

References

1. S. M. Abramov. Metavychislenija i logicheskoe programmirovanie (Metacomputation and logic programming). *Programmirovanie*, 3:31–44, 1991. (In Russian). 209

2. S. M. Abramov. *Metavychislenija i ikh prilozhenija (Metacomputation and its applications).* Nauka-Fizmatlit, Moscow 1995. (In Russian). 194, 201, 203
3. S. M. Abramov, R. Glück. From standard to non-standard semantics by semantics modifiers. *International Journal of Foundations of Computer Science,* to appear. 188, 207
4. S. M. Abramov, R. Glück. Semantics modifiers: an approach to non-standard semantics of programming languages. In M. Sato, Y. Toyama (eds.), *Third Intern. Symposium on Functional and Logic Programming,* 247–270. World Scientific, 1998. 188, 207, 208, 209
5. R. Bird, O. de Moor. *Algebra of Programming.* International Series in Computer Science. Prentice Hall, 1997. 187, 188, 209
6. W. Chen, J. T. Udding. Program inversion: More than fun! *Science of Computer Programming,* 15:1–13, 1990. 188, 209
7. E. W. Dijkstra. EWD671: Program inversion. In *Selected Writings on Computing: A Personal Perspective,* 351–354. Springer-Verlag, 1982. 188, 209
8. P. Dybjer. Inverse image analysis generalises strictness analysis. *Information and Computation,* 90(2):194–216, 1991. 209
9. D. Eppstein. A heuristic approach to program inversion. In *Intern. Joint Conf. on Artificial Intelligence (IJCAI-85),* 219–221. William Kaufmann Inc., 1985. 187, 209
10. Y. Futamura, K. Nogi, A. Takano. Essence of generalized partial computation. *Theoretical Computer Science,* 90(1):61–79, 1991. 210
11. R. Glück, J. Hatcliff, J. Jørgensen. Generalization in hierarchies of online program specialization systems. In P. Flener (ed.), *Logic-Based Program Synthesis and Transformation. Proceedings,* LNCS 1559, 179–198. Springer-Verlag, 1999. 194
12. R. Glück, A. V. Klimov. Occam's razor in metacomputation: the notion of a perfect process tree. In P. Cousot et al. (eds.), *Static Analysis. Proceedings,* LNCS 724, 112–123. Springer-Verlag, 1993. 188, 194, 199, 209
13. R. Glück, A. V. Klimov. Metacomputation as a tool for formal linguistic modeling. In R. Trappl (ed.), *Cybernetics and Systems'94,* 1563–1570. World Scientific, 1994. 209
14. R. Glück, M. H. Sørensen. Partial deduction and driving are equivalent. In M. Hermenegildo, J. Penjam (eds.), *Programming Language Implementation and Logic Programming. Proceedings,* LNCS 844, 165–181. Springer-Verlag, 1994. 209, 210
15. R. Glück, M. H. Sørensen. A roadmap to metacomputation by supercompilation. In O. Danvy et al. (eds.), *Partial Evaluation. Proceedings,* LNCS 1110, 137–160. Springer-Verlag, 1996. 209
16. D. Gries. Inverting programs (chapter 21). In *The Science of Programming,* 265–274. Springer-Verlag, 1981. 188, 209
17. D. Gries, J. L. A. van de Snepscheut. Inorder traversal of a binary tree and its inversion. In E. W. Dijkstra (ed.), *Formal Development of Programs and Proofs,* 37–42. Addison Wesley, 1990. 188, 209
18. P. G. Harrison, H. Khoshnevisan. On the synthesis of function inverses. *Acta Informatica,* 29:211–239, 1992. 187, 209
19. N. D. Jones. The essence of program transformation by partial evaluation and driving. In N. D. Jones et al. (eds.), *Logic, Language and Computation.* LNCS 792, 206–224. Springer-Verlag, 1994. 209
20. H. Khoshnevisan, K. M. Sephton. InvX: An automatic function inverter. In N. Dershowitz (ed.), *Rewriting Techniques and Applications (RTA'89),* LNCS 355, 564–568. Springer-Verlag, 1989. 187, 209

21. R. E. Korf. Inversion of applicative programs. In *Proceedings of the Seventh Intern. Joint Conference on Artificial Intelligence (IJCAI-81)*, 1007–1009. William Kaufmann, Inc., 1981. 187, 209

22. J. McCarthy. The inversion of functions defined by Turing machines. In C. E. Shannon, J. McCarthy (eds.), *Automata Studies*, 177–181. Princeton University Press, 1956. 209

23. A. P. Nemytykh, V. A. Pinchuk. Program transformation with metasystem transitions: experiments with a supercompiler. In D. Bjørner et al. (eds.), *Perspectives of System Informatics*, LNCS 1181, 249–260. Springer-Verlag, 1996. 209

24. M. Ogawa. Automatic verification based on abstract interpretation. In A. Middeldorp, T. Sato (eds.), *Functional and Logic Programming. Proceedings*, LNCS 1722, 131–146. Springer-Verlag, 1999. 209

25. A. Y. Romanenko. The generation of inverse functions in Refal. In D. Bjørner et al. (eds.), *Partial Evaluation and Mixed Computation*, 427–444. North-Holland, 1988. 187, 209

26. B. J. Ross. Running programs backwards: the logical inversion of imperative computation. *Formal Aspects of Computing*, 9:331–348, 1997. 208, 209

27. P. Sestoft. The structure of a self-applicable partial evaluator. Technical Report 85/11, DIKU, University of Copenhagen, Denmark, 1985. 207

28. V. F. Turchin. Ehkvivalentnye preobrazovanija rekursivnykh funkcij na Refale (Equivalent transformations of recursive functions defined in Refal). In *Teorija Jazykov i Metody Programmirovanija (Proceedings of the Symp. on the Theory of Languages and Programming Methods)*, 31–42, 1972. (In Russian). 209

29. V. F. Turchin. The concept of a supercompiler. *ACM Transactions on Programming Languages and Systems*, 8(3):292–325, 1986. 209

30. V. F. Turchin. Program transformation with metasystem transitions. *Journal of Functional Programming*, 3(3):283–313, 1993. 209

Metacomputation-Based Compiler Architecture

William L. Harrison[1] and Samuel N. Kamin[2]

[1] Department of Computer Science, Indiana University
Bloomington, IN 47401
wlh@cs.indiana.edu
[2] Department of Computer Science, University of Illinois
Urbana, Illinois 61801
kamin@cs.uiuc.edu

Abstract. This paper presents a modular and extensible style of language specification based on metacomputations. This style uses two monads to factor the static and dynamic parts of the specification, thereby staging the specification and achieving strong binding-time separation. Because metacomputations are defined in terms of monads, they can be constructed modularly and extensibly using monad transformers. A number of language constructs are specified: expressions, control-flow, imperative features, and block structure. Metacomputation-style specification lends itself to semantics-directed compilation, which we demonstrate by creating a modular compiler for a block-structured, imperative while language.

Keywords: Compilers, Partial Evaluation, Semantics-Based Compilation, Programming Language Semantics, Monads, Monad Transformers, Pass Separation.

1 Introduction

Metacomputations—computations that produce computations—arise naturally in the compilation of programs. Figure 1 illustrates this idea. The source language program s is taken as input by the compiler, which produces a target language program t. So, compiling s produces another computation—namely, the computation of t. Observe that there are two entirely distinct notions of computation here: the compilation of s and the execution of t. The reader will recognize this distinction as the classic separation of static from dynamic. Thus, *staging* is an instance of metacomputation.

The main contributions of this paper are: (1) *Compiler architecture based on metacomputations:* Metacomputation-based compiler architecture yields substantially simpler language definitions than in [8], while still retaining its modular "mix and match" approach to compiler construction. Combining the metacomputation-based "reusable compiler building blocks" is also much simpler than combining those in [8] (as is proving their correctness). (2) *A modular and extensible method of staging denotational specifications based on metacomputations:* A style of language specification based on metacomputation is proposed

R. Backhouse and J. N. Oliveira (Eds.): MPC 2000, LNCS 1837, pp. 213–229, 2000.

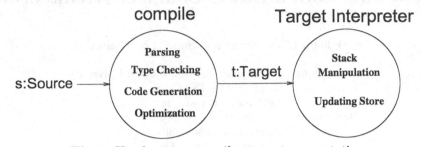

Fig. 1. Handwritten compiler as metacomputation

in which the static and dynamic parts of a language specification are factored into distinct monads[7,13,16,24]. (3) *Direct-style specifications:* instead of writing all specifications in continuation-passing style, here we write in direct style, invoking the CPS monad transformer only when needed. This naturally simplifies many of the equations, and although less essential than (1) and (2), it also helps to make the approach more practical.

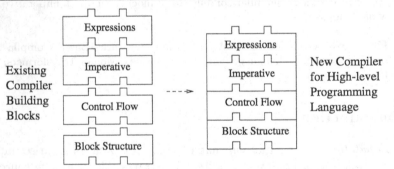

Fig. 2. Modular Compilers: Existing compiler building blocks combine to make new compiler

We believe this style of language specification may have many uses, but in this paper we concentrate on one: modular compilation. *Modular compilers* are compilers built from building blocks that represent *language features* rather than *compilation phases*, as illustrated in Figure 2. Espinosa [7] and Liang, Hudak, & Jones [13] showed how to construct modular *interpreters* using the notion of *monads* [7,13,16,24] — or, more precisely, monad *transformers*.

The current authors built on those ideas to produce modular *compilers* in [8]. However, there the notion of *staging*, though conceptually at the heart of the approach, was not *explicit* in the compiler building blocks we constructed. As in traditional monadic semantics, the monadic structure was useful in creating the domains, but those domains, once constructed, were "monolithic;" that is, they gave no indication of which parts were for dynamic aspects of the computation and which for static aspects. The result was awkwardness in communicating between these aspects of the domain, which meant that "gluing together" compiler blocks was sometimes delicate. However, metacomputation-based compiler architecture *completely* alleviates this awkwardness, so that combining compiler blocks is simply a matter of applying the appropriate monad transformers.

Indeed, metacomputation is *purposely* avoided in [7,13,8]. A key aspect of that work is that monad transformers are used to create the single monad used to interpret or compile the language. The problem that inspired it was that monads don't compose nicely. Given monads M and M', the composed monad $M \circ M'$ — corresponding to an M-computation that produces an M' computation — usually does not produce the "right" monolithic domain. However, there may exist monad transformers T_M and $T_{M'}$ such that T_M Id $= M$ and $T_{M'}$ Id $= M'$, where $(T_M \circ T_{M'})$Id does give the "right" domain. The difference between composing monads and composing monad transformers is what makes these approaches work — monad transformers are a way to *avoid* metacomputation.

In this paper, we show that, for some purposes, metacomputation may be exactly what one wants: *Defining a compiler block via the metacomputation of two monads gives an effective representation of staging.* We are not advocating abandoning monad transformers: the two monads can be constructed using them, with the attendant advantages of that approach. We are simply saying that having two monads — what might be called the *static* and *dynamic* monads — and composing them seems to give the "right" domain for modular compilation.

The next section explains the advantages for modular compilation of metacomputation-based language specification over the monolithic style. Section 3 reviews the most relevant related work. In Section 4, we review the theory of monads and monad transformers and their use in language specification. Section 5 presents a case study in metacomputation-style language specification; its subsections present metacomputation-style specifications for expressions, control flow, block structure, and imperative features, respectively. Section 6 shows how to combine these compiler building blocks into a compiler for the combined language, and presents a compiler and an example compilation. Section 7 discusses the impact of metacomputation-based specification on compiler correctness. Finally, Section 8 summarizes this work and outlines future research.

2   Why Metacomputations?

In this section, we will describe at a high level why two monads are better than one for modular compilation. Using metacomputations instead of a single monolithic monad simplifies the use of the "code store" (defined below) in the specification of reusable compiler building blocks.

In [8], we borrowed a technique from denotational semantics[23] for modeling jumps, namely storing command continuations in a "code store" and denoting "jump L" as "execute the continuation at label L in the code store." Viewing command continuations as machine code is a common technique in semantics-directed compilation[25,22]. Because our language specifications were in monadic style, it was a simple matter to add label generator and code store states to the underlying monad. Indeed, the primary use for monads in functional programming seems to be that of adding state-like features to purely functional languages and programs[24,20], and the fact that we structured our monads in [8] with monad transformers made adding the new states simple.

The use of a code store is integral to the modular compilation technique described in [8]. We use it to compile control-flow and procedures, and the presence of the code store in our language specifications allowed us to make substantial improvements over Reynolds[22] (e.g., avoiding infinite programs through jumps and labels). Yet the mixing of static with dynamic data into one "monolithic" monad causes a number of problems with using the code store. Consider the program "if b then (if b' then c)". Compiling the outer "if" with initial continuation **halt** and label 0 will result in the continuation "[if b' then c]; **halt**" being stored at label 0 and the label counter being incremented. The problem here is that trying to compile this continuation via partial evaluation will fail. Why? Because having been *stored* rather than *executed*, it will not have access to the next label 1. Instead, the partial evaluator will try to increment a (dynamic) variable rather than an actual (static) integer, and this will cause an error (e.g., a partial evaluator can evaluate "1+1" but not "x+1"). In [8], the monolithic style specifications forced all static data to be explicitly passed to stored command continuations, although this was at the expense of modularity. In fact to compile **if-then-else**, the snapback operator had to be used. These complications also make reasoning about compilers constructed in [8] difficult. We shall demonstrate in Section 5 that using metacomputations results in vastly simpler compiler specifications than in [8] and that this naturally makes them easier to reason about.

3   Related Work

Espinosa [7] and Hudak, Liang, and Jones [13] use monad transformers to create modular, extensible interpreters. Liang [12,14] addresses the question of whether compilers can be developed similarly, but since he does not compile to machine language, many of the issues we confront—especially staging—do not arise.

A syntactic form of metacomputation can be found in the two-level λ-calculus of Nielson[19]. Two-level λ-calculus contains two distinct λ-calculi—representing the static and dynamic *levels*. Expressions of mixed level, then, have strongly separated binding times by definition. Nielson[18] applies two-level λ-calculus to code generation for a typed λ-calculus, and Nielson[19] presents an algorithm for static analysis of a typed λ-calculus which converts one-level specifications into two-level specifications. Mogensen[15] generalizes this algorithm to handle variables of mixed binding times. The present work offers a semantic alternative to the two-level λ-calculus. We formalize distinct levels (in the sense of Nielson[19]) as distinct monads, and the resulting specifications have all of the traditional advantages of monadic specifications (reusability, extensibility, and modularity). While our binding time analysis is not automatic as in [19,15], we consider a far wider range of programming language features than they do.

Danvy and Vestergaard [5] show how to produce code that "looks like" machine language, by expressing the source language semantics in terms of machine language-like combinators (e.g., "popblock", "push"). When the interpreter is closed over these combinators, partial evaluation of this closed term with respect to a program produces a completely *dynamic* term, composed of a sequence of combinators, looking very much like machine language. This approach is key to making the monadic structure useful for compilation.

Reynolds' [22] demonstration of how to produce efficient code in a compiler derived from the functor category semantics of an Algol-like language was an original inspiration for this study. Our approach to compilation improves on Reynolds's in two ways: it is monad-structured—that is, built from interchangeable parts—and it includes jumps and labels where Reynolds simply allowed code duplication and infinite programs.

4   Monads and Monad Transformers

In this section, we review the theory of monads [16,24] and monad transformers [7,13]. Readers familiar with these topics may skip the section.

A *monad* is a type constructor M together with a pair of functions (obeying certain algebraic laws that we omit here):

$$\star_M : M\tau \to (\tau \to M\tau') \to M\tau'$$
$$\mathbf{unit}_M : \tau \to M\tau$$

A value of type $M\tau$ is called a τ-*computation*, the idea being that it yields a value of type τ while also performing some other computation. The $\star_M$ operation generalizes function application in that it determines how the computations associated with monadic values are combined. $\mathbf{unit}_M$ defines how a τ value can be regarded as a τ-computation; it is usually a trivial computation.

To see how monads are used, suppose we wish to define a language of integer expressions containing constants and addition. The standard definition might be:

$$[\![e_1 + e_2]\!] = [\![e_1]\!] + [\![e_2]\!]$$

where $[\![-]\!] : Expression \to int$. However, this definition is inflexible; if expressions needed to look at a store, or could generate errors, or had some other feature not planned on, the equation would need to be changed.

Monads can provide this needed flexibility. To start, we rephrase the definition of $[\![-]\!]$ in monadic form (using infix bind $\star$, as is traditional) so that $[\![-]\!]$ has type $Expression \to M\,int$:

$$[\![e_1 + e_2]\!] = [\![e_1]\!] \star (\lambda x.[\![e_2]\!] \star (\lambda y.\mathbf{add}(x, y)))$$

We must define an operation $\mathbf{add}$ of type $int \times int \to M\,int$.

Identity Monad Id:

$$\text{Id}\,\tau = \tau$$
$$\text{unit}_{\text{Id}}\,x = x$$
$$x \star_{\text{Id}} f = f\,x$$

Environment Monad Transformer $\mathcal{T}_{\text{Env}}$:

$$\text{M}'\tau = \mathcal{T}_{\text{Env}}\,Env\,\text{M}\,\tau = Env \to \text{M}\tau$$
$$\text{unit}_{\text{M}'}\,x = \lambda\rho : Env.\,\text{unit}_{\text{M}}\,x$$
$$x \star_{\text{M}'} f = \lambda\rho : Env.\,(x\,\rho) \star_{\text{M}} (\lambda a.f\,a\,\rho)$$
$$lift_{\text{M}\tau \to \text{M}'\tau}\,x = \lambda\rho : Env.\,x$$
$$\textbf{rdEnv} : \text{M}'Env = \lambda\rho : Env.\,\text{unit}_{\text{M}}\rho$$
$$\textbf{inEnv}(\rho : Env, x : \text{M}'\tau) = \lambda\_.\,(x\,\rho) : \text{M}'\tau$$

CPS Monad Transformer $\mathcal{T}_{\text{CPS}}$:

$$\text{M}'\tau = \mathcal{T}_{\text{CPS}}\,ans\,\text{M}\,\tau =$$
$$(\tau \to \text{M}\,ans) \to \text{M}\,ans$$
$$\text{unit}_{\text{M}'}\,x = \lambda\kappa.\,\kappa\,x$$
$$x \star_{\text{M}'} f = \lambda\kappa.\,x(\lambda a.f\,a\,\kappa)$$
$$lift_{\text{M}\tau \to \text{M}'\tau}\,x = \star_{\text{M}}$$
$$\textbf{callcc} : ((a \to \text{M}b) \to \text{M}a) \to \text{M}a$$
$$\textbf{callcc}\,f = \lambda\kappa.f(\lambda a.\lambda\_.\kappa\,a)\,\kappa$$

State Monad Transformer $\mathcal{T}_{\text{St}}$:

$$\text{M}'\tau = \mathcal{T}_{\text{St}}\,store\,\text{M}\,\tau = store \to \text{M}(\tau \times store)$$
$$\text{unit}_{\text{M}'}\,x = \lambda\sigma : store.\,\text{unit}_{\text{M}}(x,\sigma)$$
$$x \star_{\text{M}'} f = \lambda\sigma_0 : store.(x\sigma_0) \star_{\text{M}} (\lambda(a,\sigma_1).fa\sigma_1)$$
$$lift_{\text{M}\tau \to \text{M}'\tau}\,x = \lambda\sigma.x \star_{\text{M}} \lambda y.\,\text{unit}_{\text{M}}(y,\sigma)$$
$$\textbf{update}(\Delta : store \to store) = \lambda\sigma.\text{unit}_{\text{M}}(\bullet, \Delta\sigma)$$
$$\textbf{getStore} = \lambda\sigma.\,\text{unit}_{\text{M}}(\sigma,\sigma)$$

Fig. 3. The Identity Monad, and Environment, CPS, and State Monad Transformers

---

The beauty of the monadic form is that the meaning of $[\![-]\!]$ can be reinterpreted in a variety of monads. Monadic semantics separate the *description* of a language from its *denotation*. In this sense, it is similar to *action semantics*[17] and *high-level semantics*[11].

The simplest monad is the identity monad, shown in Figure 3. Given the identity monad, we can define **add** as ordinary addition. $[\![-]\!]$ would have type $Expression \to int$.

Perhaps the best known monad is the state monad, which represents the notion of a computation as something that modifies a store:

$$\text{M}_{St}\tau = Sto \to \tau \times Sto$$
$$x \star f = \lambda\sigma.\,\textbf{let}\,(x',\sigma') = x\sigma\,\textbf{in}\,fx'\sigma'$$
$$\textbf{unit}\,v = \lambda\sigma.(v,\sigma)$$
$$\textbf{add}\,(x,y) = \lambda\sigma.(x+y,\sigma)$$

The $\star$ operation handles the bookkeeping of "threading" the store through the computation. Now, $[\![-]\!]$ has type $Expression \to Sto \to int \times Sto$. This might be an appropriate meaning for addition in an imperative language. To define operations that actually have side effects, we can define a function:

$$\textbf{updateSto} : (Sto \to Sto) \to \text{M}_{St}\textbf{void}$$
$$: f \mapsto \lambda\sigma.(\bullet, f\sigma)$$
$$\textbf{getSto} \quad : \text{M}_{St}Sto$$
$$: \lambda\sigma.(\sigma,\sigma)$$

updateSto applies a function to the store and returns a useless value (we assume a degenerate type void having a single element, which we denote •). getSto returns the store.

Now, suppose a computation can cause side effects on two separate stores. One could define a new "double-state" monad M_{2St}:

$$M_{2St}\tau = Sto \times Sto \to \tau \times Sto \times Sto$$

that would thread the two states through the computation, with separate updateSto and getSto operations for each copy of Sto. One might expect to get $M_{2St}\tau$ by applying the ordinary state monad twice. Unfortunately, $M_{St}(M_{St}\tau)$ and $M_{2St}\tau$ are very different types. This points to a difficulty with monads: they do not compose in this simple manner.

The key contribution of the work [7,13] on *monad transformers* is to solve this composition problem. When applied to a monad M, a monad transformer $\mathcal{T}$ creates a new monad M'. For example, the state monad transformer, $\mathcal{T}_{St}$ *store*, is shown in Figure 3. (Here, the *store* is a type argument, which can be replaced by any value which is to be "threaded" through the computation.) Note that $\mathcal{T}_{St}$ *Sto* Id is identical to the state monad, but here we get a useful notion of composition: $\mathcal{T}_{St}$ *Sto* $(\mathcal{T}_{St}$ *Sto* Id$)$ is equivalent to the two-state monad $M_{2St}\tau$. The state monad transformer also provides updateSto and getSto operations appropriate to the newly-created monad. When composing $\mathcal{T}_{St}$ *Sto* with itself, as above, the operations on the "inner" state need to be *lifted* through the outer state monad; this is the main technical issue in [7,13].

In our work in [8], we found it convenient to factor the state monad into two parts: the state proper and the address allocator. This was really a "staging transformation," with the state monad representing dynamic computation and the address allocator static computation, but, as mentioned earlier, it led to significant complications. In the current paper, we are separating these parts more completely, by viewing compilation as metacomputation.

4.1   A Semantics for Metacomputation

We can formalize this notion of metacomputation using monads[7,13,16,24] and use the resulting framework as a basis for staging computations. Given a monad M, the *computations* of type a is the type M a. So given two monads M and N, the *metacomputations* of type a is the type M(N a), because the M-computation produces as a value a N-computation. This definition is not superfluous; as we have noted, M $\circ$ N is not generally a monad, so metacomputations are generally a different notion altogether from computations.

5   A Case Study in Metacomputation-Based Compiler Architecture: Modular Compilation for the While Language

In this section, we present several compiler building blocks. In section 6, they will be combined to create a compiler. For the first two of these blocks, we also give monolithic versions, drawn from [8], to illustrate why metacomputation is helpful. Of particular importance to the present work, Section 5.2 presents the reusable compiler building block for control flow, which demonstrates how metacomputation-based compiler architecture solves the difficulties with the monolithic approach we outlined in Section 2.

5.1   Integer Expressions Compiler Building Block

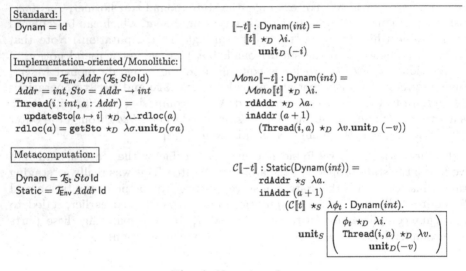

Fig. 4. Negation, 3 ways

Consider the standard monadic-style specification of negation[7,13,24] displayed in Figure 4. To use this as a compiler specification for negation, we need to make a more implementation-oriented version, which might be defined informally as:

$$[\![-t]\!] = [\![t]\!] \star_D \lambda i. \text{ ``Store } i \text{ at } a \text{ and return contents of } a\text{''} \star_D \lambda v.\text{unit}_D (-v)$$

Let us assume that this is written in terms of a monad Dynam with bind and unit operations $\star_D$ and unit_D. Observe that this implementation-oriented definition calculates the same value as the standard definition, but it stores the intermediate value i as well. But where do addresses and storage come from? In [8], we added them to the Dynam monad using monad transformers[7,13] as in the "Implementation-oriented" specification in Figure 4. In that definition, rdAddr reads the current top of stack address a, inAddr increments the top of stack, and Thread stores i at a. The monad (Dynam) is used to construct the domain containing both static and dynamic data.

$$
\begin{aligned}
&\mathcal{C}[\![e_1 + e_2]\!] : \mathsf{Static}(\mathsf{Dynam}\ int) = \\
&\quad \texttt{rdAddr} \star_S \lambda a. \\
&\quad \mathcal{C}[\![e_1]\!] \star_S \lambda\phi_{e_1}. \\
&\quad \texttt{inAddr}\ (a+2) \\
&\quad \mathcal{C}[\![e_2]\!] \star_S \lambda\phi_{e_2}. \\
&\quad\quad\ \texttt{unit}_S \left(
\begin{array}{l}
\phi_{e_1} \star_D \lambda i : int. \\
\phi_{e_2} \star_D \lambda j : int. \\
\texttt{Thread}(i, a) \star_D \lambda v_1. \\
\texttt{Thread}(j, (a+1)) \star_D \lambda v_2. \\
\quad \texttt{unit}_D(v_1 + v_2)
\end{array}
\right)
\end{aligned}
$$

Fig. 5. Specification for Addition

In the "metacomputation"-style specification, we use two monads, Static, to encapsulate the static data, and Dynam to encapsulate the dynamic data. The meaning of the phrase is a metacomputation—the Static monad produces a computation of the Dynam monad. Clear separation of binding times is thus achieved. (In our examples, we have set the dynamic parts of the computation in a box for emphasis.)

Figure 5 displays the specification for addition, which is similar to negation. Multiplication and subtraction are defined analogously.

5.2   Control-Flow Compiler Building Block

We now present an example where separating binding times in specifications with metacomputations has a very significant advantage over the monolithic approach. Consider the three definitions of the conditional **if-then** statement in Figure 6. The first is a dual continuation "control-flow" semantics, found commonly in compilers[2]. If B is true, then the first continuation, $[\![c]\!] \star_D \kappa$, is executed, otherwise c is skipped and just κ is executed. A more implementation-oriented (informal) specification might be:

$[\![\textbf{if } b \textbf{ then } c]\!] =$
   $[\![b]\!] \star_D \lambda B.$
   "get two new labels L_c, L_κ" $\star_D \lambda\langle L_c, L_\kappa\rangle.$
   $\texttt{callcc } (\lambda\kappa.$
       "store κ at L_κ, then $([\![c]\!] \star_D$ ("jump to L_κ")) at L_c" $\star_D \lambda\_.$
       $B\langle$"jump to L_c", "jump to L_κ"$\rangle)$

To formalize this specification, we use a technique from denotational semantics for modeling jumps. We introduce a continuation store, $Code$, and a label state $Label$. A jump to label L simply invokes the continuation stored at L. The second definition in Figure 6 presents an implementation-oriented specification of **if-then** in monolithic style (that is, where $Code$ and $Label$ are both added to Dynam). Again, this represents our approach in [8].

Control-Flow:

$\text{Dynam} = \mathcal{T}_{\text{CPS}} \text{ void } \text{Id}$
$\text{Bool} = \forall \alpha.\alpha \times \alpha \to \alpha$

$[\![\textbf{if } b \textbf{ then } c]\!] : \text{Dynam(void)} =$
   $[\![b]\!] \star_D \lambda B : Bool.$
   $\texttt{callcc } (\lambda\kappa.$
       $B\langle[\![c]\!] \star_D \kappa, \kappa\rangle)$

Implementation-oriented/Monolithic:

$\text{Dynam} = \mathcal{T}_{\text{CPS}} \text{ void } (\mathcal{T}_{\text{St}} \text{ } Label \text{ } (\mathcal{T}_{\text{St}} \text{ } Code \text{ Id}))$
$Label = int, Code = \text{void} \to \text{Dynam void}$
$\text{jump } L = \text{getCode} \star_D (\lambda\Pi : Code.\Pi L)$
$\text{newlabel} : \text{Dynam}(Label) =$
   $\text{getLabel} \star_D \lambda l : Label.$
   $\text{updateLabel}[L \mapsto L+1] \star_D \lambda\_.$
   $\textbf{unit}_D(l)$

$\mathcal{M}ono[\![\textbf{if } b \textbf{ then } c]\!] : \text{Dynam(void)} =$
   $\mathcal{M}ono[\![b]\!] \star_D \lambda B : Bool.$
   $\text{newlabel} \star_D \lambda L_\kappa.$
   $\text{newlabel} \star_D \lambda L_c.$
   $\texttt{callcc } (\lambda\kappa.$
       $\text{newSegment}(L_\kappa, \kappa) \star_D \lambda\_.$
       $\text{newSegment}(L_c, \mathcal{M}ono[\![c]\!] \star_D (\text{jump } L_\kappa)) \star_D$
       $B\langle\text{jump } L_c, \text{jump } L_\kappa\rangle)$

Metacomputation:

$\text{Dynam} = \mathcal{T}_{\text{CPS}} \text{ void } (\mathcal{T}_{\text{St}} \text{ } Code \text{ Id}), \text{Static} = \mathcal{T}_{\text{St}} \text{ } Label \text{ Id}$
$\text{IfThen} : \text{Dynam}(Bool) \times \text{Dynam(void)} \times Label \times Label \to \text{Dynam(void)}$
$\text{IfThen}(\phi_B, \phi_c, L_c, L_\kappa) =$
   $\phi_B \star_D \lambda B : Bool.$
   $\texttt{callcc } (\lambda\kappa.$
       $\text{updateCode}[L_\kappa \mapsto \kappa] \star_D \lambda\_.$
       $\text{updateCode}[L_c \mapsto \phi_c \star_D (\text{jump } L_\kappa)] \star_D \lambda\_.$
       $B\langle\text{jump } L_c, \text{jump } L_\kappa\rangle)$

$\mathcal{C}[\![\textbf{if } b \textbf{ then } c]\!] : \text{Static(Dynam void)} =$
   $\mathcal{C}[\![b]\!] \star_S \lambda\phi_B.$
   $\mathcal{C}[\![c]\!] \star_S \lambda\phi_c.$
   $\text{newlabel} \star_S \lambda L_c.$
   $\text{newlabel} \star_S \lambda L_\kappa.$
   $\textbf{unit}_S (\text{IfThen}(\phi_B, \phi_c, L_c, L_\kappa))$

Fig. 6. if-then: 3 ways

One very subtle problem remains: what is "$\texttt{newSegment}$"? One's first impulse is to define it as a simple update to the $Code$ store (i.e., $\text{updateCode}[L_\kappa \mapsto \kappa]$), but here is where the monolithic approach greatly complicates matters. Because the monolithic specification mixes static and dynamic computation, the continuation κ may contain both kinds of computation. But because it is *stored* and not *executed*, κ will not have access to the current label count and any other static data necessary for proper staging. Therefore, newSegment must explicitly pass the current label count and any other static intermediate data structure to the continuation it stores[1].

$\mathcal{C}[\![e_1 \leq e_2]\!]$: Static(Dynam *Bool*) =
  rdAddr $\star_S$ λa.
  $\mathcal{C}[\![e_1]\!]$ $\star_S$ $\lambda\phi_{e_1}$.
  inAddr $(a + 2)$
    $\mathcal{C}[\![e_2]\!]$ $\star_S$ $\lambda\phi_{e_2}$.

$$\mathbf{unit}_S \left(\begin{array}{l} \phi_{e_1} \star_D \lambda i : int. \\ \phi_{e_2} \star_D \lambda j : int. \\ \mathbf{Thread}(i, a) \star_D \lambda v_1. \\ \mathbf{Thread}(j, (a+1)) \star_D \lambda v_2. \\ \quad \mathbf{unit}_D \left(\begin{array}{l} \lambda\langle\kappa_T, \kappa_F\rangle. \\ ((v_1 \leq v_2) \rightarrow \kappa_T, \kappa_F) \end{array} \right) \end{array} \right)$$

$\mathcal{C}[\![\textbf{while } b \textbf{ do } c]\!]$: Static(Dynam **void**) =
  $\mathcal{C}[\![b]\!]$ $\star_S$ $\lambda\phi_B$.
  $\mathcal{C}[\![c]\!]$ $\star_S$ $\lambda\phi_c$.
  newlabel $\star_S$ λL_{test}.
  newlabel $\star_S$ λL_c.
  newlabel $\star_S$ λL_κ.

$$\mathbf{unit}_S \left(\begin{array}{l} \texttt{callcc } \lambda\kappa. \\ \quad \phi_B \star_D \lambda B : Bool. \\ \quad \texttt{updateCode}[L_\kappa \mapsto \kappa] \star_D \lambda_-. \\ \quad \texttt{updateCode}[L_c \mapsto \phi_c \star_D (\texttt{jump } L_{test})] \star_D \\ \quad \texttt{updateCode}[L_{test} \mapsto \phi_B \star_D \lambda B.((B\langle\texttt{jump } L_c, \texttt{jump } L_\kappa\rangle\bullet)] \star_D \\ \quad \texttt{jump } L_{test} \end{array} \right)$$

Fig. 7. Specification for $\leq$ and **while**

The last specification in Figure 6 defines **if-then** as a metacomputation and is much simpler than the monolithic-style specification. Observe that Dynam does not include the *Label* store, and so the continuation κ now includes only dynamic computations. Therefore, there is no need to pass in the label count to κ, and so, κ may simply be stored in *Code*. **This is a central advantage of the metacomputation-based specification:** because of the separation of static and dynamic data into two monads, the complications outlined in Section 2

---

[1] A full description of newSegment is found in [8].

associated with storing command continuations in [8] (e.g., explicitly passing static data and use of a *snapback* operator) are *completely* unnecessary.

Figure 7 contains the specifications for $\leq$ and **while**, which are very similar to the specifications of addition and **if-then**, respectively, that we have seen already.

5.3   Block Structure Compiler Building Block

Dynam = Id

Static = $\mathcal{T}_{Env}$ *Env* ($\mathcal{T}_{Env}$ *Addr* Id)

set $a = \lambda v.$updateSto$(a \mapsto v)$

get $a = $ getSto $\star_D$ $\lambda\sigma.$unit$_D(\sigma\, a)$

$\mathcal{C}[\![\textbf{new } x \textbf{ in } c]\!] : \text{Static}(\text{Dynam void}) =$
  rdAddr $\star_S$ $\lambda a.$
  inAddr $(a + 1)$
  rdEnv $\star_S$ $\lambda\rho.$
  inEnv $(\rho[x \mapsto \textbf{unit}_S \langle \textbf{set } a, \textbf{get } a\rangle]) \, \mathcal{C}[\![c]\!]$

Fig. 8. Compiler Building Block for Block Structure

The block structure language includes **new** x **in** c, which declares a new program variable x in c. The compiler building block for this language appears in Figure 9. The static part of this specification allocates a free stack location a, and the program variable x is bound to an accepter-expresser pair[21] in the current environment ρ. In an *accepter-expresser* pair $\langle acc, exp\rangle$, acc accepts an integer value and sets the value of its variable to the value, and the expresser exp simply returns the current value of the variable. **set** and **get** set and return the contents of location a, respectively. c is then compiled in the updated environment and larger stack $(a + 1)$.

5.4   Imperative Features Compiler Building Block

Dynam = $\mathcal{T}_{St}$ *Sto* Id, Static = $\mathcal{T}_{Env}$ *Env* Id

$\mathcal{C}[\![c_1;c_2]\!] : \text{Static}(\text{Dynam void}) =$
  $\mathcal{C}[\![c_1]\!] \star_S \lambda\phi_{c_1}.$
  $\mathcal{C}[\![c_2]\!] \star_S \lambda\phi_{c_2}.$
    unit$_S$ $\boxed{(\phi_{c_1} \star_D \lambda\_.\phi_{c_2})}$

$\mathcal{C}[\![x := t]\!] : \text{Static}(\text{Dynam void}) =$
  rdEnv $\star_S$ $\lambda\rho.$
  $(\rho\, x) \star_S \lambda\langle acc, \_\rangle.$
  $\mathcal{C}[\![t]\!] \star_S \lambda\phi_t.$
    unit$_S$ $\boxed{(\phi_t \star_D \lambda i : int.(acc\; i))}$

Fig. 9. Compiler Building Block for Imperative Features

The simple imperative language includes assignment (:=) and sequencing (;). The compiler building block for this language appears in Figure 9. For sequencing, the static part of the specification compiles c_1 and c_2 in succession, while the dynamic (boxed) part runs them in succession. For assignment, the static part of the specification retrieves the accepter[21] *acc* for program variable x from the current environment ρ and compiles t, while the dynamic part calculates the value of t and passes it to *acc*.

6   Combining Compiler Building Blocks

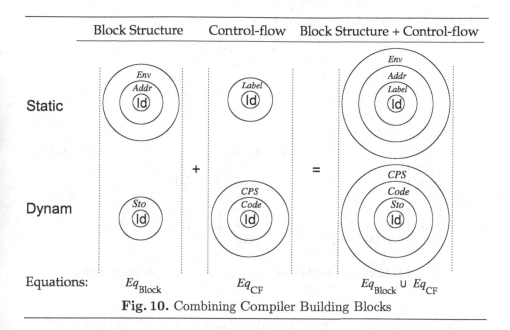

	Block Structure	Control-flow	Block Structure + Control-flow

Static

Dynam

Equations: Eq_{Block} Eq_{CF} $Eq_{\text{Block}} \cup Eq_{\text{CF}}$

Fig. 10. Combining Compiler Building Blocks

Figure 10 illustrates the process of combining the compiler building blocks for the block structure and control-flow languages. It is important to emphasize that this is much simpler than in [8], in that there is no explicit passing of static data needed. The process is nothing more than applying the appropriate monad transformers to create the Static and Dynam monads for the combined language. Recall that for the block structure language:

$$\text{Static} = \mathcal{T}_{\text{Env}} \, Env \, (\mathcal{T}_{\text{Env}} \, Addr \, \text{Id}), \text{ and } \text{Dynam} = \text{Id}$$

For the control flow language:

$$\text{Static} = \mathcal{T}_{\text{St}} \, Label \, \text{Id}, \text{ and } \text{Dynam} = \mathcal{T}_{\text{CPS}} \, \text{void} \, (\mathcal{T}_{\text{St}} \, Code \, (\mathcal{T}_{\text{St}} \, Sto \, \text{Id}))$$

To combine the compiler building blocks for these languages, one simply combines the respective monad transformers:

$$\text{Static} = \mathcal{T}_{\text{Env}} \, Env \, (\mathcal{T}_{\text{Env}} \, Addr \, (\mathcal{T}_{\text{St}} \, Label \, \text{Id})), \text{ and}$$
$$\text{Dynam} = \mathcal{T}_{\text{CPS}} \, \text{void} \, (\mathcal{T}_{\text{St}} \, Code \, (\mathcal{T}_{\text{St}} \, Sto \, \text{Id}))$$

Now, the specifications for both of the smaller languages, Eq_{Block} and Eq_{CF}, apply for the "larger" Static and Dynam monads, and so we have the compiler for the combined language is specified by $Eq_{Block} \cup Eq_{CF}$.

Compiler:

Dynam $= \mathcal{T}_{CPS}$ void $(\mathcal{T}_{St}$ Code $(\mathcal{T}_{St}$ Sto Id$))$, Static $= \mathcal{T}_{Env}$ Env $(\mathcal{T}_{Env}$ Addr $(\mathcal{T}_{St}$ Label Id$))$

Language $=$ Expressions $\cup$ Imperative $\cup$ Control-flow $\cup$ Block structure $\cup$ Booleans

Equations $= Eq_{Expressions} \cup Eq_{Imperative} \cup$
$\qquad Eq_{Control\text{-}flow} \cup Eq_{Block\ structure} \cup Eq_{Booleans}$

Source Code:

$$\textbf{new } x \textbf{ in new } y \textbf{ in}$$
$$x := 5;\ y := 1;$$
$$\textbf{while } (1 \le x)\ \textbf{do}$$
$$y := y^*x;\ x := x\text{-}1;$$

Target Code:

```
         0 := 5;          2:  2 := [1];          3:  halt;
         1 := 1;              3 := [0];
         jump 1;              1 := [2] * [3];
                              2 := [0];
     1:  2 := 1;              3 := 1;
         3 := [0];            0 := [2] - [3];
         BRLEQ [2] [3] 2 3;   jump 1;
```

Fig. 11. Compiler for While language and example compilation

Code is generated via type-directed partial evaluation[4] using the method of Danvy and Vestergaard[5]. Figure 11 contains the compiler for the while language, and an example program and its pretty-printed compiled version. All that was necessary was to combine the compiler building blocks developed in this section combined as discussed in Section 6.

7   Correctness

In this section, we outline an example correctness specification for a reusable compiler building block written in metacomputation style. In particular, we illustrate the advantages w.r.t. compiler correctness of metacomputation-based compiler specifications over the monolithic style specifications of [8] and also of the general usefulness of monads and monad transformers w.r.t. compiler correctness. Although lack of space makes a full exposition of metacomputation-based compiler correctness impossible here, we hope to convey the basic issues[2].

---

[2] The interested reader may consult the first author's forthcoming doctoral dissertation.

The correctness of a reusable compiler building block for a source language feature is specified by comparing the *compilation semantics* $\mathcal{C}[\![-]\!]$ with the *standard semantics* $[\![-]\!]$ for that feature. Let us take as an example the conditional **if-then**. Its standard and compilation semantics are presented in Figure 6. A (slightly informal) specification of **if-then** is: If $L_c \neq L_\kappa$ and L_c, L_κ are unbound in the code store, then

$$\mathsf{IfThen}([\![b]\!], [\![c]\!], L_c, L_\kappa) \star_D \lambda\_.\mathtt{initCode} = [\![\textbf{if } b \textbf{ then } c]\!] \star_D \lambda\_.\mathtt{initCode}$$

where $\mathtt{initCode} = \mathtt{updateCode}(\lambda\_.\Pi)$ for arbitrary constant $\Pi : Code$. Because $\mathsf{IfThen}([\![b]\!],[\![c]\!],L_c,L_\kappa)$ will affect the code store and $[\![\textbf{if } b \textbf{ then } c]\!]$ will not, $\mathsf{IfThen}([\![b]\!], [\![c]\!], L_c, L_\kappa) \neq [\![\textbf{if } b \textbf{ then } c]\!]$. But by "masking out" the code store state on both sides with $\mathtt{initCode}$—which sets the code store to constant Π—we require that both sides of the above equation have the same action on the value store Sto.

The above specification is easier to prove than the analogous one in monolithic style because the metacomputation-based definition in Figure 6 just stores the continuation κ while the monolithic-style definition manipulates κ as was outlined in Sections 2 and 5.2. Furthermore, here is an example of how monad transformers help with compiler correctness proofs. Although the above equation holds in $\mathsf{Dynam} = \mathcal{T}_{\mathsf{CPS}} \, Void \, (\mathcal{T}_{\mathsf{St}} \, Label \, (\mathcal{T}_{\mathsf{St}} \, Sto \, \mathsf{Id}))$, other monad transformers could be applied to Dynam for the purposes of adding new source language features and the specification would still hold[3]. So, the use of monad transformers in this work yields a kind of proof reuse for metacomputation-based compiler correctness[14].

8   Conclusions and Future Work

Metacomputations are a simple and elegant structure for representing staged computation within the semantics of a programming language. This paper presents a modular and extensible style of language specification based on metacomputation. This style uses two monads to factor the static and dynamic parts of the specification, thereby staging the specification and achieving strong binding-time separation. Because metacomputations are defined in terms of monads, they can be constructed modularly and extensibly using monad transformers. We exploit this fact to create modular *compilers*.

Future work focuses on two areas: specifying other language constructs like objects, classes, and exceptions; and exploring the use of metacomputations in the semantics of two-level languages.

---

[3] Given certain fairly weak conditions on the order of monad transformer application. See [12,13,14] for details.

Acknowledgements

The authors would like to thank Uday Reddy and the rest of the functional programming research group at UIUC for offering many helpful suggestions that led to significant improvements in the presentation.

References

1. A. V. Aho, R. Sethi, and J. D. Ullman *Compilers: Principles, Techniques, and Tools,* Addison-Wesley, 1986.
2. A. Appel, *Modern Compiler Implementation in ML,* Cambridge University Press, New York, 1998. 221
3. A. Appel, *Compiling with Continuations,* Cambridge University Press, New York, 1992.
4. O. Danvy, "Type-Directed Partial Evaluation," *Proceedings of the ACM Conference on the Principles of Programming Languages,* 1996. 226
5. O. Danvy and R. Vestergaard, "Semantics-Based Compiling: A Case Study in Type-Directed Partial Evaluation," *Eighth International Symposium on Programming Language Implementation and Logic Programming,* 1996, pages 182-197. 217, 226
6. R. Davies and F. Pfenning, "A Modal Analysis of Staged Computation," *Proceedings of the ACM Conference on the Principles of Programming Languages,* 1996.
7. D. Espinosa, "Semantic Lego," Doctoral Dissertation, Columbia University, 1995. 214, 215, 216, 217, 219, 220, 221
8. W. Harrison and S. Kamin, "Modular Compilers Based on Monad Transformers," *Proceedings of the IEEE International Conference on Programming Languages,* 1998, pages 122-131. 213, 214, 215, 216, 219, 220, 221, 222, 223, 224, 225, 226
9. N. D. Jones, C. K. Gomard, and P. Sestoft, *Partial Evaluation and Automatic Program Generation,* Prentice-Hall 1993.
10. U. Jorring and W. Scherlis, "Compilers and Staging Transformations," *Proceedings of the ACM Conference on the Principles of Programming Languages,* 1986.
11. P. Lee, *Realistic Compiler Generation,* MIT Press, 1989. 218
12. S. Liang, "A Modular Semantics for Compiler Generation," *Yale University Department of Computer Science Technical Report TR-1067,* February 1995. 216, 227
13. S. Liang, P. Hudak, and M. Jones, Monad Transformers and Modular Interpreters. *Proceedings of the ACM Conference on the Principles of Programming Languages,* 1995. 214, 215, 216, 217, 219, 220, 221, 227
14. S. Liang, "Modular Monadic Semantics and Compilation," Doctoral Thesis, Yale University, 1997. 216, 227
15. T. Mogensen. "Separating Binding Times in Language Specifications," *Proceedings of the ACM Conference on Functional Programming and Computer Architecture,* pp 12-25, 1989. 216, 217
16. E. Moggi, "Notions of Computation and Monads," *Information and Computation 93(1),* pp. 55-92, 1991. 214, 217, 219
17. P. Mosses, *Action Semantics,* Cambridge University Press, 1992. 218
18. H. Nielson and F. Nielson, "Code Generation from two-level denotational meta-languages," in *Programs as Data Objects,* Lecture Notes in Computer Science **217** (Springer, Berlin, 1986). 216

19. H. Nielson and F. Nielson, "Automatic Binding Time Analysis for a Typed λ-calculus," *Science of Computer Programming* 10, 2 (April 1988), pp 139-176. 216, 217

20. S. L. Peyton-Jones and Philip Wadler. "Imperative Functional Programming," *Twentieth ACM Symposium on Principles of Programming Languages*, 1993. 216

21. J. Reynolds. "The Essence of Algol," *Algorithmic Languages, Proceedings of the International Symposium on Algorithmic Languages*, pp. 345-372, 1981. 224, 225

22. J. Reynolds, "Using Functor Categories to Generate Intermediate Code," *Proceedings of the ACM Conference on the Principles of Programming Languages*, pages 25–36, 1995. 216, 217

23. J. E. Stoy, *Denotational Semantics: the Scott-Strachey Approach to Programming Language Theory*, MIT Press, 1977. 215

24. P. Wadler, "The essence of functional programming," *Proceedings of the ACM Conference on the Principles of Programming Languages*, pages 1–14, 1992. 214, 216, 217, 219, 220

25. M. Wand, "Deriving Target Code as a Representation of Continuation Semantics," *ACM Transactions on Programming Languages and Systems*, Vol. 4, No. 3, pp. 496-517, 1982. 216

A Metalanguage for Programming with Bound Names Modulo Renaming

Andrew M. Pitts[1] and Murdoch J. Gabbay[2]

[1] Cambridge University Computer Laboratory
Cambridge CB2 3QG, UK
Andrew.Pitts@cl.cam.ac.uk
[2] Department of Pure Mathematics and Mathematical Statistics,
Cambridge University, Cambridge CB2 1SB, UK
M.J.Gabbay@dpmms.cam.ac.uk

Abstract. This paper describes work in progress on the design of an ML-style metalanguage FreshML for programming with recursively defined functions on user-defined, concrete data types whose constructors may involve variable binding. Up to operational equivalence, values of such FreshML data types can faithfully encode terms modulo α-conversion for a wide range of object languages in a straightforward fashion. The design of FreshML is 'semantically driven', in that it arises from the model of variable binding in set theory with atoms given by the authors in [7]. The language has a type constructor for abstractions over names (= atoms) and facilities for declaring locally fresh names. Moreover, recursive definitions can use a form of pattern-matching on bound names in abstractions. The crucial point is that the FreshML type system ensures that these features can only be used in well-typed programs in ways that are insensitive to renaming of bound names.

1 Introduction

This paper concerns the design of functional programming languages for *metaprogramming*, by which we mean the activity of creating software systems—interpreters, compilers, proof checkers, proof assistants, and so on—that manipulate syntactical structures. An important part of such activity is the design of data structures to represent the terms of formal languages. The nature of such an *object language* will of course depend upon the particular application. It might be a language for programming, or one for reasoning, for example. But one thing is certain: in all but the most trivial cases, the object language will involve variable binding, with associated notions of free and bound variables, renaming of bound variables, substitution of terms for free variables, and so on. It is this aspect of representing object languages in metaprogramming languages upon which we focus here.

Modern functional programming languages permit user-defined data types, with pattern matching in definitions of functions on these data types.[1] For object

---

[1] As far as we know, this feature was introduced into functional programming by Rod Burstall: see [2,1].

R. Backhouse and J. N. Oliveira (Eds.): MPC 2000, LNCS 1837, pp. 230–255, 2000.
© Springer-Verlag Berlin Heidelberg 2000

languages without variable binding, this reduces the work involved in designing representations to a mere act of declaration: a specification of the abstract syntax of the object language gives rise more or less directly to the declaration of some algebraic data types (mutually recursive ones in general). Consider the familiar example of the language of terms of the untyped lambda calculus

$$t ::= x \mid t\,t \mid \lambda x.t \tag{1}$$

and a corresponding ML data type

```
datatype ltree = Vr of string                    (2)
               | Ap of ltree * ltree
               | Lm of string * ltree
```

where x ranges over some fixed countably infinite set of variable symbols which we have chosen to represent by values of the ML type `string` of character strings. This gives a one-one representation of the abstract syntax trees of all (open or closed) untyped lambda terms as closed ML values of type `ltree`. However, the ML declaration takes no account of the fact that the term former $\lambda x.(-)$ involves variable binding. Thus, if one wishes to identify terms of the object language up to renaming of bound variables (as one often does), such representations are too concrete. It is entirely up to programmers to ensure that their term manipulating programs respect the renaming discipline—an obligation which becomes irksome and error prone for complex object languages, or large programs.

A common way round this problem is to introduce a new version of the object language that eliminates variable binding constructs through the use of de Bruijn indices [4]. For example, 'nameless' lambda terms are given by

$$t' ::= n \mid t'\,t' \mid \lambda\,t' \tag{3}$$

and a corresponding ML data type by

```
datatype ltree' = Vr' of nat                     (4)
                | Ap' of ltree' * ltree'
                | Lm' of ltree'
```

where the indices n are natural numbers, represented by the values of a suitable ML data type `nat`. Closed ML values of type `ltree'` correspond to nameless terms t', which in turn correspond to α-equivalence classes of ordinary lambda terms t (open or closed). Hence functions manipulating lambda terms modulo α-conversion can be defined, and their properties proved, using structural recursion and induction for the algebraic data type `ltree'`. This approach has been adopted for a number of large systems written in ML involving syntax manipulation (such as HOL [8] and Isabelle [14], for example). However, it does have some drawbacks. Firstly, nameless terms are hard for humans to understand and they need translation and display functions relating them to the usual syntax with named bound variables. Secondly, some definitions (such as substitution and weakening the context of free variables) are non-intuitive and error-prone when cast in terms of de Bruijn indices. Lastly, and most importantly, the ML language does not have any built-in support that might alleviate these problems: one usually starts with a specification of an object language in terms of context free grammars and some indication of the binding constructs and has to craft its 'name free' representation by hand. Perhaps more can be done automatically? In this paper we describe an ML-like language with features that address these difficulties and provide improved automatic support for metaprogramming with variable binding constructs. The key innovation is to deduce at compile-time not only traditional type information, but also information about the 'freshness' of object-level variables. This information is used to guarantee that at run-time the observable behaviour of well-typed meta-level expressions is insensitive to renaming bound object-level variables. Thus, users are notified at compile-time if their syntax-manipulating code descends below the level of abstraction which identifies α-equivalent object-level expressions.

Our language design is guided by the mathematical model of binding operations introduced in [7] using a Fraenkel-Mostowski permutation model of sets with atoms. A key feature of this model is that it provides a syntax-independent notion of a name (i.e. an atom) being *fresh* for a given object. For this reason the resulting programming language is called FreshML. Figure 1 gives some sample FreshML declarations which continue the running example of the untyped lambda calculus.[2] They will be used in the rest of this paper to illustrate the features of the new language. We attempt to explain FreshML without assuming knowledge of the mathematics underlying our model of binding; for the interested reader, the intended model of FreshML is sketched in an Appendix to this paper. Sections 2–5 describe the novel features of FreshML compared with ML, namely *atoms*, *freshness*, *atom abstraction/concretion* and pattern matching with *abstraction patterns*. Sections 6–8 discuss the interaction of these features with standard ones for equality, recursive functions and types not involving atoms. It should be stressed that the design of FreshML is still evolving: section 9 discusses some of the possibilities and reviews related work.

Note (Meta-level versus object-level binding). The metalanguage FreshML provides a novel treatment of binding operations in object languages. However, in describing FreshML syntax we treat its various binding constructs in a conventional way—by first giving their abstract syntax and then defining what the free, bound and binding identifiers are in such expressions. This in turn gives rise to a conventional definition of the capture-avoiding substitution $[exp/\text{x}]exp'$ of a FreshML expression exp for all free occurrences of an identifier x in an expression exp'. We write $\text{fv}(exp)$ for the finite set of free identifiers in exp.

---

[2] It will be seen from these declarations that the syntax of function declarations (and case expressions) in FreshML is more like that of CAML [3] than that of Standard ML [12].

```
(* Lambda terms, modulo alpha conversion. *)
datatype lam = Var of atm
             | App of lam * lam
             | Lam of [atm]lam;

(* Encoding of a couple of familiar combinators. *)
val I = new a in Lam a.(Var a) end;
val K = new a in new b in Lam a.(Lam b.(Var a)) end end;

(* A function sub:lam * [atm]lam -> lam
   implementing capture avoiding substitution. *)
fun sub =
 { (t, a.(Var b)) where b=a => t
 | (t, a.(Var b)) where b#a => Var b
 | (t, a.(App(u,v))) => App(sub(t, a.u), sub(t, a.v))
 | (t, a.(Lam b.u)) => Lam b.(sub(t, a.u)) };

(* A function cbv: lam -> lam
   implementing call-by-value evaluation. *)
fun cbv =
 { App(t,u) => case (cbv t) of {Lam e => cbv(sub(cbv u, e))}
 | v => v };

(* A function rem: [atm](atm list) -> (atm list)
   taking a list of atoms with one atom abstracted and removing it. *)
fun rem =
 { a.nil => nil
 | a.(x::xs) where x=a => rem a.xs
 | a.(x::xs) where x#a => x::(rem a.xs) };

(* A function fv: lam -> (atm list)
   which lists the free variables of a lambda term,
   possibly with repeats. *)
fun fv =
 { Var a => a::nil
 | App(t,u) => append(fv t)(fv u)
 | Lam a.t => rem a.(fv t) };

(* Unlike the previous function, the following function, which tries
   to list the bound variables of a lambda term, does not type check
   ---good! *)
fun bv =
 { Var a => nil
 | App(t,u) => append(bv t)(bv u)
 | Lam a.t => a::(bv t) };
```

Fig. 1. Sample FreshML declarations

2   Freshness

Variables of object languages are represented in FreshML by value identifiers of a special built-in type atm of *atoms*.[3] Operationally speaking, atm behaves somewhat like the ML type unit ref, but the way in which dynamically created values of type atm (which are drawn from a fixed, countably infinite set $A = \{a, a', \ldots\}$ of *semantic atoms*) can be used is tightly constrained by the FreshML type system, as described below. Just as addresses of references do not occur explicitly in ML programs, semantic atoms do not occur explicitly in the syntax of FreshML. Rather, they can be referred to via a local declaration of the form

$$\text{new a in } exp \text{ end} \tag{5}$$

where a is an identifier implicitly of type atm. This is a binding operation: free occurrences of a in the expression *exp* are bound in new a in *exp* end. Its behaviour is analogous to the Standard ML declaration

$$\text{let val a = ref () in } exp \text{ end} \tag{6}$$

in that the expression in (5) is evaluated by associating a with the first semantic atom unused by the current value environment and then evaluating *exp* in that augmented value environment. (We formulate this more precisely at the end of this section.) As in ML, evaluation in FreshML is done after type checking, and it is there that an important difference between the expressions in (5) and (6) shows up. Compared with ML's type-checking of the expression in (6), the FreshML type system imposes a restriction on the expression in (5) which always seems to be present in uses of 'fresh names' in informal syntax-manipulating algorithms, namely that

> *expressions in the scope of a fresh name a only use it in ways that are insensitive to renaming.*

For example, although let val a = ref () in a end has type unit ref in ML, the expression new a in a end is not typeable in FreshML—the meaning of a is clearly sensitive to renaming a. On the other hand, in the next section we introduce atom-abstraction expressions such as a.a, whose meaning (either operationally or denotationally) is insensitive to renaming a even though they contain free occurrences of a, giving rise to well typed expressions such as new a in a.a end. (Some other examples of well typed new-expressions are given in Fig. 1.)

Type System. To achieve the restrictions mentioned above, the FreshML type system deduces for an expression *exp* judgments not only about its type, $\Gamma \vdash exp : ty$, but also about which atoms a are *fresh* with respect to it,

$$\Gamma \vdash exp \# a. \tag{7}$$

---

[3] In the current experimental version of FreshML, there is only one such type. Future versions will allow the programmer to declare as many distinct copies of this type as needed, for example, for the distinct sorts of names there are in a particular object language.

Here a is some value identifier assigned type atm by the typing context Γ. Fresh-ML typing contexts may contain both typing assumptions about value identifiers, $x : ty$, and freshness assumptions about them, x # a (if Γ contains such an assumption it must also contain a : atm and $x : ty$ for some type ty). The intended meaning of statements such as 'x # a' is that, in the given value environment, the denotation of x (an element of an *FM-set*) does not contain the semantic atom associated to a in its *support*—the mathematical notions of 'FM-set' and 'support' are explained in the Appendix (see Definitions A.1 and A.2). Here we just give rules for inductively generating typing and freshness judgements that are sound for this notion. In fact it is convenient to give an expression's typing and freshness properties simultaneously, using assertions of the form $exp : ty \# \{a_1, \ldots, a_n\}$ standing for the conjunction

$$exp : ty \ \& \ exp \# a_1 \ \& \ \cdots \ \& \ exp \# a_n .$$

Thus the FreshML type system can be specified using judgments of the form

$$\Gamma \vdash exp : ty \# \overline{a} \tag{8}$$

where

$$\Gamma = (x_1 : ty_1 \# \overline{a}_1), \ldots, (x_n : ty_n \# \overline{a}_n) \tag{9}$$

and

- $x_1, \ldots, x_n$ are distinct value identifiers which include all the free identifiers of the FreshML expression exp;
- $ty_1, \ldots, ty_n$ and ty are FreshML types[4];
- $\overline{a}_1, \ldots, \overline{a}_n$ and $\overline{a}$ are finite sets of value identifiers with the property that each $a \in \overline{a}_1 \cup \ldots \cup \overline{a}_n \cup \overline{a}$ is assigned type atm by the typing context, i.e. is equal to one of the x_i with $ty_i = $ atm.

We write $\Gamma \vdash exp : ty$ as an abbreviation for $\Gamma \vdash exp : ty \# \emptyset$. When discussing just the freshness properties of an expression, we write $\Gamma \vdash exp \# a$ to mean that $\Gamma \vdash exp : ty \# \{a\}$ holds for some type ty.

The rule for generating type and freshness information for new-expressions is (11) in Fig. 2. The notation a : atm $\otimes \Gamma$ used there indicates the context obtained from Γ by adding the assumptions a : atm and x # a for each value identifier x declared in Γ (where we assume a does not occur in Γ). For example, if $\Gamma = (x : $ atm$), (y : ty \# \{x\})$, then

$$a : atm \otimes \Gamma = (a : atm), (x : atm \# \{a\}), (y : ty \# \{a, x\}) .$$

The side condition a $\notin$ dom$(\Gamma) \cup \overline{a}$ in rule (11) is comparable to ones for more familiar binding constructs, such as function abstraction; given Γ and $\overline{a}$, within the α-equivalence class of the expression new a in exp end we have room to choose the bound identifier a so that the side condition is satisfied.

---

[4] In the current experimental version of FreshML, we just consider monomorphic types built up from basic ones like atm and string using products, functions, recursively defined data type constructions and the atom-abstraction type constructor described in the next section. Introducing type schemes and ML-style polymorphism seems unproblematic in principle, but remains a topic for future work.

$$\frac{(\mathbf{x}: ty \mathbin{\#} \overline{\mathbf{a}}') \in \varGamma \quad \overline{\mathbf{a}} \subseteq \overline{\mathbf{a}}'}{\varGamma \vdash \mathbf{x}: ty \mathbin{\#} \overline{\mathbf{a}}} \tag{10}$$

$$\frac{\mathbf{a}: \mathbf{atm} \otimes \varGamma \vdash exp: ty \mathbin{\#} (\{\mathbf{a}\} \cup \overline{\mathbf{a}}) \quad \mathbf{a} \notin \mathrm{dom}(\varGamma) \cup \overline{\mathbf{a}}}{\varGamma \vdash (\mathbf{new\ a\ in}\ exp\ \mathbf{end}): ty \mathbin{\#} \overline{\mathbf{a}}} \tag{11}$$

$$\frac{\varGamma \vdash exp: ty \mathbin{\#} (\overline{\mathbf{a}} \smallsetminus \{\mathbf{a}\}) \quad \varGamma(\mathbf{a}) = \mathbf{atm}}{\varGamma \vdash \mathbf{a}.\,exp: [\mathbf{atm}]\,ty \mathbin{\#} \overline{\mathbf{a}}} \tag{12}$$

$$\frac{\varGamma \vdash exp: [\mathbf{atm}]\,ty \mathbin{\#} (\{\mathbf{a}\} \cup \overline{\mathbf{a}}) \quad \varGamma \vdash \mathbf{a}: \mathbf{atm} \mathbin{\#} \overline{\mathbf{a}}}{\varGamma \vdash exp\ \mathbb{Q}\ \mathbf{a}: ty \mathbin{\#} \overline{\mathbf{a}}} \tag{13}$$

$$\frac{\varGamma \vdash exp: [\mathbf{atm}]\,ty \mathbin{\#} \overline{\mathbf{a}} \quad \mathbf{a}, \mathbf{x} \notin \mathrm{dom}(\varGamma) \cup \overline{\mathbf{a}}'}{(\mathbf{a}: \mathbf{atm} \otimes \varGamma), (\mathbf{x}: ty \mathbin{\#} \overline{\mathbf{a}}) \vdash exp': ty' \mathbin{\#} (\{\mathbf{a}\} \cup \overline{\mathbf{a}}')}{\varGamma \vdash \mathbf{case}\ exp\ \mathbf{of}\ \{\mathbf{a}.\mathbf{x} \Rightarrow exp'\}: ty' \mathbin{\#} \overline{\mathbf{a}}'} \tag{14}$$

$$\frac{\varGamma(\mathbf{a}) = \varGamma(\mathbf{b}) = \mathbf{atm} \quad \varGamma \vdash exp: ty \mathbin{\#} \overline{\mathbf{a}} \quad \varGamma[\mathbf{a} \mathbin{\#} \mathbf{b}] \vdash exp': ty \mathbin{\#} \overline{\mathbf{a}}}{\varGamma \vdash \mathbf{ifeq}(\mathbf{a},\mathbf{b})\ \mathbf{then}\ exp\ \mathbf{else}\ exp': ty \mathbin{\#} \overline{\mathbf{a}}} \tag{15}$$

$$\frac{\varGamma(\mathbf{a}) = \mathbf{atm}\ \text{ for all } \mathbf{a} \in \overline{\mathbf{a}}}{\varGamma \vdash (): \mathbf{unit} \mathbin{\#} \overline{\mathbf{a}}} \tag{16}$$

$$\frac{\varGamma \vdash exp_1: ty_1 \mathbin{\#} \overline{\mathbf{a}} \quad \varGamma \vdash exp_2: ty_2 \mathbin{\#} \overline{\mathbf{a}}}{\varGamma \vdash (exp_1, exp_2): ty_1 * ty_2 \mathbin{\#} \overline{\mathbf{a}}} \tag{17}$$

$$\frac{\varGamma \vdash exp: ty_1 * ty_2 \mathbin{\#} \overline{\mathbf{a}} \quad \mathbf{x}, \mathbf{y} \notin \mathrm{dom}(\varGamma)}{\varGamma, (\mathbf{x}: ty_1 \mathbin{\#} \overline{\mathbf{a}}), (\mathbf{y}: ty_2 \mathbin{\#} \overline{\mathbf{a}}) \vdash exp': ty' \mathbin{\#} \overline{\mathbf{a}}'}{\varGamma \vdash \mathbf{case}\ exp\ \mathbf{of}\ \{(\mathbf{x},\mathbf{y}) \Rightarrow exp'\}: ty' \mathbin{\#} \overline{\mathbf{a}}'} \tag{18}$$

$$\frac{\varGamma \vdash exp: ty \mathbin{\#} \overline{\mathbf{a}} \quad \varGamma, (\mathbf{x}: ty \mathbin{\#} \overline{\mathbf{a}}) \vdash exp': ty' \mathbin{\#} \overline{\mathbf{a}}' \quad \mathbf{x} \notin \mathrm{dom}(\varGamma)}{\varGamma \vdash \mathbf{let\ val}\ \mathbf{x} = exp\ \mathbf{in}\ exp'\mathbf{end}: ty' \mathbin{\#} \overline{\mathbf{a}}'} \tag{19}$$

$$\frac{\varGamma, (\mathbf{f}: ty \mathbin{\text{->}} ty'), (\mathbf{x}: ty) \vdash exp: ty' \quad \mathbf{f}, \mathbf{x} \notin \mathrm{dom}(\varGamma)}{\varGamma(\mathbf{a}) = \mathbf{atm},\ \text{for all } \mathbf{a} \in \overline{\mathbf{a}} \quad \varGamma \vdash \mathbf{x}_i: ty_i \mathbin{\#} \overline{\mathbf{a}},\ \text{for all } \mathbf{x}_i \in \mathrm{fv}(exp) \smallsetminus \{\mathbf{f}, \mathbf{x}\}}{\varGamma \vdash \mathbf{fun}\ \mathbf{f} = \{\mathbf{x} \Rightarrow exp\}: (ty \mathbin{\text{->}} ty') \mathbin{\#} \overline{\mathbf{a}}} \tag{20}$$

$$\frac{\varGamma \vdash exp_1: (ty \mathbin{\text{->}} ty') \mathbin{\#} \overline{\mathbf{a}} \quad \varGamma \vdash exp_2: ty \mathbin{\#} \overline{\mathbf{a}}}{\varGamma \vdash exp_1\ exp_2: ty' \mathbin{\#} \overline{\mathbf{a}}} \tag{21}$$

$$\frac{ty\ \text{pure} \quad \varGamma \vdash exp: ty \quad \varGamma(\mathbf{a}) = \mathbf{atm},\ \text{for all } \mathbf{a} \in \overline{\mathbf{a}}}{\varGamma \vdash exp: ty \mathbin{\#} \overline{\mathbf{a}}} \tag{22}$$

Fig. 2. Excerpt from the type system of FreshML

To understand rule (11) better, consider the special case when Γ and $\bar{a}$ are empty. This tells us that a closed expression of the form **new a in** *exp* **end** has type *ty* if not only a : atm $\vdash$ *exp* : *ty*, but also a : atm $\vdash$ *exp* # a. This second property guarantees that although *exp* may involve the atom a, its meaning is unchanged if we rename a—and hence it is meaningful to 'anonymise' a in *exp* by forming the expression **new a in** *exp* **end**.

But how do we generate the freshness assertions needed in the hypothesis of rule (11) in the first place? One rather trivial source arises from the fact that if a is fresh for all the free identifiers in an expression *exp*, then it is fresh for *exp* itself (this is a derivable property of the FreshML type system); so in particular a is always fresh for closed expressions. However, it can indeed be the case that $\Gamma \vdash exp$ # a holds with a occurring freely in *exp*. Section 3 introduces the principal source of such non-trivial instances of freshness.

Operational Semantics. At the beginning of this section we said that the operational behaviour of the FreshML expression **new a in** *exp* **end** is like that of the ML expression **let val a = ref()** in *exp* **end**. In order to be more precise, we need to describe the operational semantics of FreshML. The current experimental version of FreshML is a pure functional programming language, in the sense that the only effects of expression evaluation are either to produce a value or to not terminate. We describe evaluation of expressions *exp* using a judgement of the form

$$E \vdash exp \Rightarrow v$$

where E is a *value environment* (whose domain contains the free value identifiers of *exp*) and v is a *semantic value*. These are mutually recursively defined as follows: E is a finite mapping from value identifiers to semantic values; and, for the fragment of FreshML typed in Fig. 2, we can take v to be given by the grammar

$$v ::= a \mid abs(a, v) \mid unit \mid pr(v, v) \mid fun(\mathbf{x}, \mathbf{x}, exp, E)$$

where a ranges over semantic atoms, $\mathbf{x}$ over value identifiers, and *exp* over expressions. The rule for evaluating **new**-expressions is (24) in Fig. 3. The notation $fa(E)$ used in that rule stands for the finite set of 'synthetically' free semantic atoms of a value environment E; this is defined by

$$fa(E) \;=\; \bigcup_{\mathbf{x} \in \mathrm{dom}(E)} fa(E(\mathbf{x}))$$

where $fa(a) = \{a\}$, $fa(abs(a, v)) = fa(v) \smallsetminus \{a\}$, $fa(pr(v_1, v_2)) = fa(v_1) \cup fa(v_2)$, $fa(unit) = \emptyset$ and $fa(fun(\mathbf{f}, \mathbf{x}, exp, E)) = \bigcup_{\mathbf{y} \in \mathrm{fv}(exp) \smallsetminus \{\mathbf{f}, \mathbf{x}\}} fa(E(\mathbf{y}))$.

It should be emphasised that the rules in Fig. 3 are only applied to well-typed expressions. Evaluation preserves typing and freshness information in the following sense.

Theorem 2.1 (Soundness of the type system with respect to evaluation). *If* $\Gamma \vdash exp : ty$ # $\bar{a}$, $E \vdash exp \Rightarrow v$ *and* $E : \Gamma$, *then* $v : ty$ *and* $fa(v) \cap \{ E(a) \mid a \in \bar{a} \} = \emptyset$. *(The definitions of '$E : \Gamma$' and '$v : ty$' for the fragment of FreshML typed in Fig. 2 are given in Fig. 4)*

$$\frac{E(\mathbf{x}) = v}{E \vdash \mathbf{x} \Rightarrow v} \tag{23}$$

$$\frac{E[\mathbf{a} \mapsto a] \vdash exp \Rightarrow v \quad a \notin fa(E)}{E \vdash \mathbf{new\ a\ in}\ exp\ \mathbf{end} \Rightarrow v} \tag{24}$$

$$\frac{E \vdash exp \Rightarrow v \quad E(\mathbf{a}) = a}{E \vdash \mathbf{a}.\, exp \Rightarrow abs(a, v)} \tag{25}$$

$$\frac{E \vdash exp \Rightarrow abs(a', v') \quad E(\mathbf{a}) = a \quad v = (a'\ a) \cdot v'}{E \vdash exp\ \mathbf{@\ a} \Rightarrow v} \tag{26}$$

$$\frac{E \vdash exp \Rightarrow abs(a, v) \qquad a' \notin fa(E) \cup fa(abs(a, v))}{v'' = (a'\ a) \cdot v \qquad E[\mathbf{a} \mapsto a', \mathbf{x} \mapsto v''] \vdash exp' \Rightarrow v'}{E \vdash \mathbf{case}\ exp\ \mathbf{of}\ \{\mathbf{a}.\mathbf{x} \Rightarrow exp'\} \Rightarrow v'} \tag{27}$$

$$\frac{E(\mathbf{a}) = E(\mathbf{b}) \quad E \vdash exp \Rightarrow v}{E \vdash \mathbf{ifeq(a,b)\ then}\ exp\ \mathbf{else}\ exp' \Rightarrow v} \tag{28}$$

$$\frac{E(\mathbf{a}) \neq E(\mathbf{b}) \quad E \vdash exp' \Rightarrow v'}{E \vdash \mathbf{ifeq(a,b)\ then}\ exp\ \mathbf{else}\ exp' \Rightarrow v'} \tag{29}$$

$$E \vdash () \Rightarrow unit \tag{30}$$

$$\frac{E \vdash exp_1 \Rightarrow v_1 \quad E \vdash exp_2 \Rightarrow v_2}{E \vdash (exp_1, exp_2) \Rightarrow pr(v_1, v_2)} \tag{31}$$

$$\frac{E \vdash exp \Rightarrow pr(v_1, v_2) \quad E[\mathbf{x} \mapsto v_1, \mathbf{y} \mapsto v_2] \vdash exp' \Rightarrow v'}{E \vdash \mathbf{case}\ exp\ \mathbf{of}\ \{(\mathbf{x}, \mathbf{y}) \Rightarrow exp'\} \Rightarrow v'} \tag{32}$$

$$\frac{E \vdash exp \Rightarrow v \quad E[\mathbf{x} \mapsto v] \vdash exp' \Rightarrow v'}{E \vdash \mathbf{let\ x} = exp\ \mathbf{in}\ exp'\ \mathbf{end} \Rightarrow v'} \tag{33}$$

$$E \vdash \mathbf{fun\ f} = \{\mathbf{x} \Rightarrow exp\} \Rightarrow fun(\mathbf{f}, \mathbf{x}, exp, E) \tag{34}$$

$$\frac{E \vdash exp_1 \Rightarrow v_1 \qquad E \vdash exp_2 \Rightarrow v_2}{v_1 = fun(\mathbf{f}, \mathbf{x}, exp, E_1) \qquad E_1[\mathbf{f} \mapsto v_1, \mathbf{x} \mapsto v_2] \vdash exp \Rightarrow v}{E \vdash exp_1\ exp_2 \Rightarrow v} \tag{35}$$

Fig. 3. Excerpt from the operational semantics of FreshML

$$\frac{a \in A}{a : \mathtt{atm}} \qquad \frac{a \in A \quad v : ty}{abs(a,v) : [\mathtt{atm}]\,ty} \qquad unit : \mathtt{unit} \qquad \frac{v_1 : ty_1 \quad v_2 : ty_2}{pr(v_1, v_2) : ty_1 * ty_2}$$

$$\frac{\Gamma, (\mathtt{f} : ty \mathrel{-\!\!>} ty'), (\mathtt{x} : ty) \vdash exp : ty \mathrel{-\!\!>} ty' \quad \mathtt{f}, \mathtt{x} \notin \mathrm{dom}(\Gamma) \quad E : \Gamma}{fun(\mathtt{f}, \mathtt{x}, exp, E) : ty \mathrel{-\!\!>} ty'}$$

$$\frac{\mathrm{dom}(E) = \mathrm{dom}(\Gamma)}{E(\mathtt{x}_i) : ty_i \text{ and } fa(E(\mathtt{x}_i)) \cap \{\, E(\mathtt{a}) \mid \mathtt{a} \in \overline{\mathtt{a}}_i \,\} = \emptyset, \text{ for all } (\mathtt{x}_i : ty_i \,\#\, \overline{\mathtt{a}}_i) \in \Gamma}{E : \Gamma}$$

Fig. 4. Typing semantics values and value environments

3   Atom Abstraction

FreshML user-declared data types can have value constructors involving binding, via a type constructor $[\mathtt{atm}](-)$ for *atom abstractions*. The data type $\mathtt{lam}$ declared in Fig. 1 provides an example of this, with its constructor $\mathtt{Lam}$: $[\mathtt{atm}]\mathtt{lam} \mathrel{-\!\!>} \mathtt{lam}$. Expressions of an atom abstraction type $[\mathtt{atm}]\,ty$ are introduced with a syntactic form which is written $\mathtt{a}.\,exp$, where $\mathtt{a}$ is a value identifier of type $\mathtt{atm}$ and exp an expression of type ty. Such *atom abstraction expressions* behave like pairs in which the first component is hidden, in a way comparable to hiding in abstract data types [13]. The operations for accessing the second component are discussed in Sects 4 and 5. We claim that two such expressions, $\mathtt{a}.\,exp$ and $\mathtt{a}'.\,exp'$, are contextually equivalent (i.e. are interchangeable in any complete FreshML program without affecting the observable results of evaluating it) if and only if

> *for some (any) fresh $\mathtt{a}''$, $(\mathtt{a}''\,\mathtt{a}) \cdot exp$ and $(\mathtt{a}''\,\mathtt{a}') \cdot exp'$ are contextually equivalent expressions of type ty*

where $(\mathtt{a}''\,\mathtt{a}) \cdot exp$ indicates the expression obtained by interchanging all occurrences of $\mathtt{a}''$ and $\mathtt{a}$ in exp. It is for this reason that values of type $\mathtt{lam}$ correspond to α-equivalence classes of lambda terms: see [7, Theorem 2.1].

Atom abstraction expressions $\mathtt{a}.\,exp$ are evaluated using rule (25) in Fig. 3; and their typing and freshness properties are given by rule (12) in Fig. 2. In that rule, the notation $\overline{\mathtt{a}} \smallsetminus \{\mathtt{a}\}$ means the finite set $\{\, \mathtt{a}' \in \overline{\mathtt{a}} \mid \mathtt{a}' \neq \mathtt{a} \,\}$; and the side-condition $\Gamma(\mathtt{a}) = \mathtt{atm}$ means that, with Γ as in equation (9), $\mathtt{a} = \mathtt{x}_i$ for some i with $ty_i = \mathtt{atm}$. To understand rule (12) better, consider the special case when $\overline{\mathtt{a}} = \{\mathtt{a}\}$: then the rule tells us that provided $\Gamma(\mathtt{a}) = \mathtt{atm}$ and exp is typeable in context Γ, then $\mathtt{a}$ *is always fresh for* $\mathtt{a}.\,exp$, i.e. $\Gamma \vdash (\mathtt{a}.\,exp) \,\#\, \mathtt{a}$. This is the principal source of freshness assertions in FreshML. For example:

Example 3.1. Given the declarations in Fig. 1 and some straightforward rules for typing data type constructors (which we omit, but which are analogous to the rules (16) and (17) for unit and pairs in Fig. 2), from rule (12) we have

$$\mathtt{a} : \mathtt{atm} \vdash (\mathtt{a}.(\mathtt{Var}\ \mathtt{a})) : [\mathtt{atm}]\mathtt{lam} \,\#\, \{\mathtt{a}\}$$

and then

$$a : \mathtt{atm} \vdash (\mathtt{Lam}\, a.(\mathtt{Var}\ a)) : \mathtt{lam}\ \#\ \{a\}.$$

Applying rule (11) to this yields

$$\vdash (\mathtt{new}\ a\ \mathtt{in}\ \mathtt{Lam}\, a.(\mathtt{Var}\ a)\ \mathtt{end}) : \mathtt{lam}.$$

This closed expression of type `lam` is a FreshML representation of the lambda term $\lambda a.a$.

Note that *atom abstraction is not a binder* in FreshML: the free identifiers of `a.`*exp* are `a` and all those of *exp*. The syntactic restriction that the expression to the left of the 'abstraction dot' be an identifier is needed because we only consider freshness assertions '*exp* $\#$ `a`' with `a` an identifier rather than a compound expression (in order to keep the type system as simple as possible). This does not really restrict the expressiveness of FreshML, since a more general form of atom abstraction '*atexp*.*exp*' (with *atexp* of type `atm`) can be simulated with the `let`-expression `let val a = `*atexp*` in a.`*exp*` end`. (The typing rule for `let`-expressions is (19) in Fig. 2.)

Remark 3.2 (binding = renameability + name hiding). Example 3.1 illustrates the fact that, unlike metalanguages that represent object-level binding via lambda abstraction, FreshML separates the renaming and the hiding aspects of variable binding. On the one hand `a` is still a free identifier in `a.`*exp*, but on the other hand the fact that `new a in − end` is a statically scoped binder can be used to hide the name of an atom (subject to the freshness conditions discussed in Sect. 2). We illustrate why this separation of the renaming and the hiding aspects of variable binding can be convenient in Example 4.1 below. To give the example we first have to discuss mechanisms for computing with expressions of atom abstraction type `[atm]` *ty*. FreshML offers two related alternatives: *concretion* expressions, *exp* `@ a`, and `case`-expressions using *abstraction patterns*, such as `case `*exp*` of {a.x => `*exp′*`}`. We discuss each in turn.

4   Concretion

Values of atom abstraction type have a double nature. So far we have seen their pair-like aspect; but as noted in [7, Lemma 4.1], they also have a function-like aspect: we can choose the name `a` of the first component in an atom abstraction *exp* : `[atm]` *ty* as we like, subject to a certain freshness restriction, and then the second component turns out to be a function of that choice, which we write as `a` $\mapsto$ *exp* `@ a`. We call *exp* `@ a` the *concretion*[5] of the atom abstraction *exp* at the atom `a`. The typing and freshness properties of concretions are given by rule (13) in Fig. 2. Note in particular (taking $\overline{a} = \emptyset$ in the rule) that given $\Gamma \vdash exp : [\mathtt{atm}]\, ty$, in order to deduce $\Gamma \vdash exp\,@\,a : ty$ we need to know not only that $\Gamma(a) = \mathtt{atm}$, but also that $\Gamma \vdash exp\ \#\ a$. The denotational justification for

---

[5] The terminology is adopted from [11, Sect. 12.1].

this is given by Proposition A.2 of the Appendix. Operationally, the behaviour of concretion is given by rule (26) in Fig. 3. Thus evaluation of exp @ a proceeds by first evaluating exp; if a semantic value of the form $abs(a', v')$ is returned and the semantic atom associated with a in the current value environment is a, then the result of evaluating exp @ a is the semantic value $(a'\,a) \cdot v'$ obtained from v' by interchanging all occurrences of a' and a in v'. By analogy with β-conversion for λ-abstraction and application, it is tempting to replace the use of transposition $(a'\,a)\cdot(-)$ by substitution $[a/a'](-)$, but this would not be correct. The reason for this has to do with the fact that while a.$(-)$ is used to represent binding in object languages, it is not itself a binding operation in FreshML; so the substitution $[a/a'](-)$ can give rise to capture at the object-level in a way which $(a'\,a) \cdot (-)$ cannot. Here is an example to illustrate this: the result of evaluating

$$(a'.(a.(Var\ a'))) @ a$$

in the value environment $E = \{a \mapsto a, a' \mapsto a'\}$ is $abs(a', Var\ a)$. Using $[a/a'](-)$ instead of $(a'\,a) \cdot (-)$ one would obtain the wrong value, namely $abs(a, Var\ a)$, which is semantically distinct from $abs(a', Var\ a)$ (in as much as the two semantic values have different denotations in the FM-sets model—see Sect. A.4).

Here is an example combining atom abstraction, concretion and local freshness expressions (together with standard **case**-expressions and function declaration).

Example 4.1. One of the semantic properties of the atom abstraction set-former in the model in [7] (and the related models in [5]) which distinguish it from function abstraction is that it commutes with disjoint unions up to natural bijection. We can easily code this bijection in FreshML as follows.

```
(* A type constructor for disjoint unions. *)
datatype ('a,'b)sum = Inl of 'a | Inr of 'b;
(* A bijection i:[atm](('a,'b)sum) -> ([atm]'a,[atm]'b)sum. *)
fun i = { e => new a in
                case e@a of
                  { Inl x => Inl(a.x)
                  | Inr y => Inr(a.y) }
              end }
```

This illustrates the use of the fact mentioned in Remark 3.2 that name abstraction and name hiding are separated in FreshML: note that in the definition of i, the locally fresh atom a is not used in an abstraction immediately, but rather at two places nested within its scope (a.x and a.y).

The bijection in this example can be coded even more perspicuously using pattern matching:

```
fun i' = { a.(Inl x) => Inl(a.x)
         | a.(Inr y) => Inr(a.y) }
```

Expressions like 'a.(Inl x)' are *abstraction patterns*. The fact that there is a useful matching mechanism for them is one of the major innovations of FreshML and we discuss it next.

5   Matching with Atom Abstraction Patterns

It is not possible to split semantic values of type $[\mathtt{atm}]\,ty$ into (atom,value)-pairs uniquely, because given $abs(a,v)$ then for any $a' \notin fa(v)$, $abs(a,v)$ has the same denotation as $abs(a',(a'\,a)\cdot v)$. However, if we only use the second component $(a'\,a)\cdot v$ in a way that is insensitive to which particular fresh a' is chosen, we get a well-defined means of specifying a function on atom abstractions via matching against an *abstraction pattern*. The simplest example of such a pattern takes the form $\mathtt{a.x}$, where $\mathtt{a}$ and $\mathtt{x}$ are distinct identifiers. Rule (14) in Fig. 2 gives the typing and freshness properties and rule (27) in Fig. 3 the evaluation properties for a $\mathtt{case}$-expression with a single match using such a pattern. (In the expression $\mathtt{case}\ exp\ \mathtt{of}\ \{\mathtt{a.x} => exp'\}$, the distinct identifiers $\mathtt{a}$ and $\mathtt{x}$ are binders with exp' as their scope.)

Figure 1 gives some examples of declarations involving more complicated, nested abstraction patterns. We omit the formal definition of matching against such patterns, but the general idea is that atom identifiers to the left of an 'abstraction dot' in a pattern represent semantic atoms that are fresh in the appropriate sense; and by checking freshness assertions, the type system ensures that the expression to the right of '=>' in a match uses such identifiers in a way that is insensitive to renaming. For example, this implicit freshness in matching is what ensures that $\mathtt{sub}$ in Fig. 1 implements *capture-avoiding* substitution—in the last match clause, $\mathtt{b}$ is automatically fresh for $\mathtt{t}$ and so it makes sense to apply the substitution function $\mathtt{sub(t,\ a.\,-)}$ under $\mathtt{Lam\ b.-}$. Another example is the declaration $\mathtt{bv}$ in Fig. 1, which does not type check because in the last match clause $\mathtt{a}$ is not fresh for $\mathtt{a::(bv\ t)}$.

In the current experimental version of FreshML, all uses of abstraction patterns are eliminated by macro-expanding them using concretion and local freshness. For example, as rules (14) and (27) may suggest, $\mathtt{case}\ exp\ \mathtt{of}\ \{\mathtt{a.x} => exp'\}$ can be regarded as an abbreviation for

$$\mathtt{new}\ a'\ \mathtt{in\ case}\ exp\ @\ a'\ \mathtt{of}\ \{\mathtt{x} => [a'/\mathtt{a}]exp'\}\ \mathtt{end}$$

(where $a' \notin fv(exp)$). However, to accommodate the more general notions of abstraction mentioned at the end of Sect. 9, we expect that matching with abstraction patterns will have to be a language primitive.

Remark 5.1 (Comparison with Standard ML). According to its Definition [12], in Standard ML during type checking a pattern *pat* elaborates in the presence of a typing context Γ to a piece of typing context Γ' (giving the types of the identifiers in the pattern) and a type ty (the overall type of the pattern); then a match *pat* => *exp'* elaborates in the context Γ to a function type $ty \rightarrow ty'$ if *exp'* has type ty' in the augmented context $\Gamma \oplus \Gamma'$. Pattern elaboration is a little more complicated in FreshML. For abstraction patterns generate not only a piece of typing context Γ', but also two kinds of freshness assumptions: ones that modify Γ (cf. the use of $\mathtt{a} : \mathtt{atm} \otimes \Gamma$ in rule (14)); and ones that impose freshness restrictions on *exp'* in a match *pat* => *exp'* (cf. the use of $exp' : ty'\ \#\ (\{\mathtt{a}\} \cup \bar{\mathtt{a}}')$ in rule (14)).

Example 5.2. In Example 4.1 we gave an example where the use of abstraction patterns allows a simplification compared with code written just using the combination of **new**-expressions and concretion. Sometimes the reverse is the case. For example, in informal practice when specifying a function of finitely many abstractions, it is convenient to use the *same* name for the abstracted variable (and there is no loss of generality in doing this, up to α-conversion). This is not possible using FreshML patterns because, as in ML, we insist that they be *linear*: an identifier must occur at most once in a pattern. However, it is possible through explicit use of a locally fresh atom. Here is a specific example.

In the FM-sets model (see the Appendix), the atom abstraction set-former commutes with cartesian products up to natural bijection. We can code this bijection in FreshML using pattern-matching as follows.

```
(* A bijection ([atm]'a)*([atm]'b) -> [atm]('a * 'b)  *)
fun p1 = { (a.x, b.y) => b.((a.x)@b, y) }
```

Better would be

```
fun p2 = { (e, b.y) => b.(e@b, y) }
```

but an arguably clearer declaration (certainly a more symmetric one) uses local freshness explicitly:

```
fun p3 = { (e, f) => new a in a.(e@a, f@a) end }
```

Simplest of all would be the declaration

```
fun p4 = { (a.x, a.y) => a.(x, y) }
```

but this is not legal, because (a.x, a.y) is not a linear pattern. As we discuss in the next section, atm is an equality type; so matching patterns with repeated occurrences of identifiers of that type is meaningful (although patterns like (a.x, a.y) involve a further complication, in that the repeated identifier is in a 'negative position', i.e. to the left of the 'abstraction dot'). We have insisted on linear patterns in the current version of FreshML in order not to further complicate a notion of matching which, as we have seen, is already more complicated than in ML.

6   Atom Equality

Algorithms for manipulating syntax frequently make use of the decidability of equality of names (of object level variables, for example). Accordingly, the type atm of atoms in FreshML admits equality. In particular if *atexp* and *atexp'* are two expressions of type atm, then eq(*atexp*, *atexp'*) is a boolean expression which evaluates to *true* if *atexp* and *atexp'* evaluate to the same semantic atom and evaluates to *false* if they evaluate to different ones. What more need one say? In fact, when it comes to type checking there is more to say. To see why, consider the following declaration of a function taking a list of atoms with one atom abstracted and removing it.

```
fun rem2 = { e => new a in
                 case e@a of
                     { nil => nil
                     | b::bs => ifeq(b,a) then (rem2 a.bs)
                                else b::(rem2 a.bs) }
             end }
```

This makes use of a form of conditional

$$\texttt{ifeq(a,b) then } exp \texttt{ else } exp'$$

which branches on the equality of a and b—see rules (28) and (29) in Fig. 3. For the above declaration of rem2 to type-check as a function [atm](atm list) -> (atm list), one has to apply rule (11) to the subphrase new a in ...end. Amongst other things, this requires one to prove

$$\texttt{(ifeq(b,a) then (rem2 a.bs) else b::(rem2 a.bs))} \mathbin{\#} \texttt{a}$$

in a typing context whose only freshness assumptions are rem2 # a and e # a. For this to be possible we have to give a typing rule for ifeq(a,b) then − else − which, while checking the second branch of the conditional, adds the semantically correct information a # b to the typing context. Such a typing rule is (15) in Fig. 2. (This uses the notation $\Gamma[\texttt{a} \mathbin{\#} \texttt{b}]$ to indicate the typing context obtained from Γ by adding the assumption a # b; we omit the straightforward formal definition of this for the typing contexts defined as in equation (9).) Although we take account of the fact that a and b denote distinct atoms when checking the second branch of the conditional, we have not found a need in practice to take account of the fact that they denote the same atom when checking the first branch (by strengthening the second hypothesis of this rule to $[\texttt{a/b}](\Gamma \vdash exp : ty \mathbin{\#} \bar{\texttt{a}})$, for example.)

To get information about atom equality to where it is needed for type checking, FreshML also permits the use of *guarded patterns*

$$pat \texttt{ where a = b} \quad \text{and} \quad pat \texttt{ where a } \mathbin{\#} \texttt{ b}$$

where a and b are value identifiers of type atm. Such guards are inter-definable with the ifeq(− , −) then − else − construct, but often more convenient. Figure 1 gives several examples of their use. We omit the precise definition of matching such guarded patterns. Note also that the atom equality test expression eq(*atexp*, *atexp'*) can be regarded as a macro for

```
let val a = atexp in
    let val b = atexp' in
        ifeq(a,b) then true else false
    end
end .
```

7   Functions

Recall from Sect. 2 that the intended meaning of freshness assertions in Fresh-ML has to do with the notion of the 'support' of an element of an FM-set (see Definition A.1 in the Appendix). The nature of this notion is such that in any reasonable (recursively presented) type system for FreshML, the provable freshness assertions will always be a proper subset of those which are satisfied by the FM-sets model. This is because of the logical complexity of the statement

'the semantic atom associated with the identifier a is not in the support
of the denotation of the function expression fn{x => exp}'

which involves extensional equality of mathematical functions. So if 'provable freshness' only gives an approximation to 'not in the support of', we should expect that not every denotationally sensible expression will receive a type. (Of course, such a situation is not uncommon for static analyses of properties of functional languages.)

What approximation of the support of a function should be used to infer sound freshness information for function expressions in FreshML? We certainly want type-checking to be decidable. In the current experimental version of Fresh-ML, we take a simple approach (which does ensure decidability) making use of the following general property of freshness

*if a is fresh for all the free identifiers in an expression exp, then it is
fresh for exp itself*

which is certainly sound for the denotational semantics in **FM-Set**. Applying this in the case when exp is a recursive function expression

$$\text{fun } f = \{x => exp\} \tag{36}$$

we arrive the typing rule (20) given in Fig. 2. As usual, free occurrences of f and x in exp become bound in the expression (36). We can regard non-recursive function expressions fn{x => exp} as the special case of expression (36) in which f $\notin$ fv(exp).

Example 7.1. Consider the following FreshML declaration of a function fv2 for computing the list (possibly with repetitions) of free variables of a lambda term encoded as a value of the data type lam in Fig. 1.

```
fun fv2 =
 { Var a => a::nil
 | App(t,u) => append(fv2 t)(fv2 u)
 | Lam a.t => remove a (fv2 t) }
```

This uses auxiliary functions append for joining two lists, and remove : atm ->
(atm list) -> (atm list) for removing an atom from a list of atoms (using the
fact that atm is an equality type), whose standard definitions we omit.

One might hope that `fv2` is assigned type `lam->(atm list)`, but the current FreshML type system rejects it as untypeable. The problem is the last match clause, `Lam a.t => remove a (fv2 t)`. As explained in Sect. 5, for this to type check we have to prove

$$(a : \mathtt{atm}), (\mathtt{fv2} : (\mathtt{lam} \mathbin{\texttt{->}} (\mathtt{atm\ list})) \mathbin{\#} \{a\}), (e : [\mathtt{atm}]\mathtt{lam} \mathbin{\#} \{a\})$$
$$\vdash \mathtt{remove}\, a\, (\mathtt{fv2}(e@a)) : \mathtt{atm\ list} \mathbin{\#} \{a\} \qquad (37)$$

This is denotationally correct, because the denotation of `remove` maps a semantic atom a and a list of semantic atoms as to the list $as \smallsetminus \{a\}$; and the support of the latter consists of all the semantic atoms in the list as that are not equal to a. However, the typing rules in Fig. 2 are not sufficiently strong to deduce (37).

It seems that this problem, and others like it, can be solved by using a richer notion of type in which expressions like '$ty \mathbin{\#} \bar{a}$' become first-class types which can be mixed with the other type constructors (in particular, with function types). We have made some initial investigations into the properties of such richer type systems (and associated notions of subtyping induced by making $ty \mathbin{\#} \bar{a}$ a subtype of ty), but much remains to be done. However, for this particular example there is a simple work-around which involves making better use of atom-abstractions and the basic fact (12) about their support. Thus the declaration of `fv` in Fig. 1 makes use of the auxiliary function `rem : [atm](atm list) -> (atm list)` for which

$$(a : \mathtt{atm}), (\mathtt{fv} : (\mathtt{lam} \mathbin{\texttt{->}} (\mathtt{atm\ list})) \mathbin{\#} \{a\}), (e : [\mathtt{atm}]\mathtt{lam} \mathbin{\#} \{a\})$$
$$\vdash (\mathtt{rem}\, a.(\mathtt{fv}(e@a))) : \mathtt{atm\ list} \mathbin{\#} \{a\}$$

can be deduced using (12). It follows that `fv` does yield a function of type `lam -> (atm list)` (and its denotation is indeed the function returning the list of free variables of a lambda term).

Remark 7.2. Note that freshness is not a 'logical relation': just because a function maps all arguments not having a given atom in their support to results not having that atom in their support, it does not follow that the atom is fresh for the function itself. Thus the following rule is unsound.

$$\frac{\Gamma, (\mathtt{f} : (ty \mathbin{\texttt{->}} ty') \mathbin{\#} \bar{a}), (\mathtt{x} : ty \mathbin{\#} \bar{a}) \vdash exp : ty' \mathbin{\#} \bar{a} \qquad \mathtt{f}, \mathtt{x} \notin \mathrm{dom}(\Gamma)}{\Gamma \vdash \mathtt{fun\ f} = \{\mathtt{x} \mathbin{\texttt{=>}} exp\} : (ty \mathbin{\texttt{->}} ty') \mathbin{\#} \bar{a}} \text{ (wrong!)}$$

To see this, consider the following example. From rule (12) we have

$$a : \mathtt{atm}, x : \mathtt{atm} \mathbin{\#} \{a\} \vdash a.x : [\mathtt{atm}]\mathtt{atm} \mathbin{\#} \{a\}$$

and so using the above rule (wrong!) we would be able to deduce

$$a : \mathtt{atm} \vdash \mathtt{fn}\{x \mathbin{\texttt{=>}} a.x\} : (\mathtt{atm} \mathbin{\texttt{->}} [\mathtt{atm}]\mathtt{atm}) \mathbin{\#} \{a\}.$$

This is denotationally incorrect, because the denotation of `fn{x => a.x}` does contain the denotation of `a` in its support. Correspondingly, the operational behaviour of this function expression depends on which semantic atom is associated with a: if we replace a by a′ in fn{x => a.x}, then under the assumption a # a′ we get a contextually inequivalent function expression, fn{x => a′.x}. For applying these function expressions to the same argument a yields contextually inequivalent results (in the first case an expression equivalent to a.a and in the second case one equivalent to a′.a).

8   Purity

Consider the following declaration of a function count for computing the number of lambda abstractions in a lambda term encoded as a value of the data type lam in Fig. 1.

```
fun count =
  { Var a => 0
  | App(t,u) => (count t)+(count u)
  | Lam a.t => (count a)+1 }
```

For this to type check as a function lam -> int, the last match clause requires

$$(a : \text{atm}), (\text{count} : (\text{lam} \to \text{int}) \mathbin{\#} \{a\}), (t : \text{lam})$$
$$\vdash ((\text{count } t)+1) : \text{int} \mathbin{\#} \{a\}$$

to be proved. The interpretation of this judgement holds in the FM-sets model because the denotation of int is a 'pure' FM-set, i.e. one whose elements all have empty support. Accordingly, we add rule (22) in Fig. 2 to the FreshML type system; using it, we do indeed get that count has type lam -> int. The condition '*ty* pure' in the hypothesis of this rule is defined by induction on the structure of the type *ty* and amounts to saying that *ty* does not involve atm or ->[6] in its construction.

The current experimental version of FreshML is a pure functional programming language, in the sense that the only effects of expression evaluation are either to produce a value or to not terminate. This has an influence on the soundness of rule (22). For example, if we add to the language an exception mechanism in which exception packets contain values involving atoms, then it may no longer be the case that an integer expression *exp* : int satisfies *exp* # a for *any* atom a. To restore the soundness of rule (22) in the presence of such computational effects with non-trivial support, one might consider imposing a 'value restriction', by insisting that the rule only applies to expressions *exp* that are non-expansive in the sense of [12, Sect. 4.7]. However, note that the rule (19) for let-expressions rather undoes such a value-restriction. For using rule (19), the freshness properties of *exp* which we could have deduced from the unrestricted rule (22) can be deduced for the semantically equivalent expression let val x = *exp* in x end from the value-restricted version. This highlights

---

[6]   For Theorem 2.1 to hold, in rule (22) we need that *ty* pure implies *fa*(*v*) = ∅ for any semantic value *v* of type *ty*; excluding the use of function types (as well as atm) in pure types is a simple way of ensuring this.

the fact that the soundness of rule (19), and also rules (14) and (18) in Fig. 2, depends upon the evaluation of *exp* not producing an effect with non-empty support. Should one try to restrict these rules as well? Probably it is better to curtail the computational effects. For example, although it is certainly desirable to add an exception-handling mechanism to the current version of the language, it may be sufficient to have one which only raises packets containing values with empty support (character strings, integers, etc). Investigation of this is a matter for future work—which brings us to our final section.

9   Related and Future Work

Related work

The model presented in [7] was one of three works on the metamathematics of syntax with binders using categories of (pre)sheaves which appeared simultaneously in 1999—the other two being [5] and [9]. The starting point for these works is a discovery, made independently by several of the authors, which can be stated roughly as follows.

> *The quotient by α-equivalence of an inductively defined set of abstract syntax trees (for some signature involving binders) can be given an initial algebra semantics provided one works with initial algebras of functors not on sets, but on categories of 'variable' sets, i.e. certain categories of sheaves or presheaves.*

There is a strong connection between initial algebras for functors and recursive data types, so this observation should have some consequences for programming language design, and more specifically, for new forms of user declared data type. That is what we have investigated here. For us, the notion of (finite) *support*, which is a key feature of the model in [7], was crucial—giving rise as it does to FreshML's idiom of computing with freshness. While the presheaf models considered in [5] have weaker notions of support (or 'stage') than does the FM-sets model, it seems that they too can model languages with notions of abstraction similar to the one in FreshML (Plotkin, private communication).

Miller [10] proposed tackling the problems motivating the work in this paper by incorporating the techniques of *higher order abstract syntax*, HOAS [16], into an ML-like programming language, ML_λ, with intentional function types $ty \Rightarrow ty'$. Compared with HOAS, the approach in [7] and [5] is less ambitious in what it seeks to lift to the metalevel: like HOAS we promote object-level renaming to the metalevel, but unlike HOAS we leave object-level substitution to be defined case-by-case using structural recursion. The advantage is that FreshML data types using [atm] *ty* retain the pleasant recursion/induction properties of classical first order algebraic data types: see Sect. 5 of [7]. It is also the case that names of bound variables are inaccessible to the ML_λ programmer, whereas they are accessible to a FreshML programmer in a controlled way.

Formal properties of FreshML

In this paper we have mostly concentrated on explaining the ideas behind our approach and giving examples, rather than on presenting the formal properties of the language. Such properties include:

1. Decidability of type/freshness inference.
2. Correspondence results connecting the operational and denotational semantics.
3. The correctness of the encoding of the set of terms over a 'binding signature' [5, Sect. 2], modulo renaming of bound variables, as a suitable FreshML data type. For example, values of type lam in Fig. 1 modulo contextual equivalence (or equality of denotations) correspond to α-equivalence classes of untyped lambda terms, with free identifiers of type atm corresponding to free variables.
4. Transfer of principles of structural induction for inductively defined FM-sets involving atom abstraction (cf. [7, Sect. 5]) to induction principles for FreshML data types. More generally, the 'И-quantifier' introduced in [7] should feature in an LCF-style program logic for FreshML.

Some of the details will appear in the second author's forthcoming PhD thesis [6]. At this stage, just as important as proving such properties is accumulating experience with programming in FreshML, to see if the idiom it provides for metaprogramming with bound names modulo renaming is a useful one.

Future work

To improve the usefulness of FreshML for programming with bound names, it is already clear that we must investigate richer syntactic forms of abstraction. At the moment we permit abstraction over a single type of atoms. We already noted in Sect. 2 that it would be a good idea to allow the declaration of distinct sorts of atoms (for example, to more easily encode distinct sorts of names in an object language). Indeed, it might be a good idea to allow atom polymorphism via Haskell-style type classes [15], with a type class for 'types of atoms'. But even with a single sort of atoms, there is good reason to consider notions of abstraction in which the data to the left of the 'abstraction dot' is structurally more complicated than just single atoms. For example, some object languages use operators that bind varying numbers of variables rather than having a fixed 'arity' (for example, the free identifiers in an ML match m, however many there may be, become bound in the function expression fn $\{m\}$). To encode such operators we can make use of the following FreshML data type construction

```
datatype 'a abs = Val of 'a | Abs of [atm]('a abs)
```

whose values Abs a1.(Abs a2. $\cdots$ Val val) are some finite number of atom-abstractions of a value val of type 'a. When specifying a function on 'a abs by structural recursion, one has to recurse on the list of binders in such a value, whereas in practice one usually wants to recurse directly on the structure of the inner most value *val*. Therefore it would be useful to have 'atom-list abstraction types' [atm list] *ty* (denotationally isomorphic to *ty* abs) and abstraction expressions of the form *as . exp*, where *as* is a value of type atm list and *exp* is an expression of type *ty*. But if one abstracts over atom-lists, why not over other concrete types built up from atoms? Indeed, in addition to such concrete types, it appears to be useful to abstract with respect to certain abstract types, such as finite sets of atoms, or finite mappings defined on atoms. So it may be appropriate to consider a general form of abstraction type, [*ty*] *ty'*, for arbitrary types *ty* and *ty'*. To do so would require some changes to the nature of the freshness judgement (7), whose details have yet to be worked out. In fact, the FM-sets model contains a set-former for such a general notion of abstraction, so there is a firm semantic base from which to explore this extension of FreshML. Emphasising this firm semantic base is a good note on which to finish. Having reached this far, we hope the reader agrees that FreshML has some novel and potentially useful features for metaprogramming modulo renaming of bound variables. But whatever the particularities of FreshML, we believe the real source of this potential is the FM-sets model, which appears to provide a simple, elegant and useful mathematical foundation for computing and reasoning about name binding modulo renaming. It is certainly the case that without it, we would not have reached the language design described in this paper. (So please read the Appendix!)

A   Appendix: FM-Sets

Naïvely speaking, ML types and expressions denote sets and functions. By contrast, FreshML types and expressions are intended to denote *FM-sets* and *equivariant functions*. This appendix gives a brief review these notions; more details can be found in [7]. Of course, the presence of recursive features and computational effects in ML means that a denotational semantics for it really involves much more complicated mathematical structures than mere sets. Similarly, to account for the recursive features of the present version of FreshML, we should really give it a denotational semantics using domains and continuous functions in the category of FM-sets. For simplicity's sake we suppress these domain-theoretic details here.

Notation. Let $\mathbb{A} = \{a, a', \ldots\}$ be a fixed countably infinite set, whose elements we call *semantic atoms*. Let $S_\mathbb{A}$ denote the group of all permutations of $\mathbb{A}$. Thus the elements π of $S_\mathbb{A}$ are bijections from $\mathbb{A}$ to itself. The group multiplication takes two such bijections π and π' and composes them—we write the composition of π followed by π' as $\pi'\pi$. The group identity is the identity function on $\mathbb{A}$, denoted by $id_\mathbb{A}$.

Recall that an *action* of the group $S_\mathbb{A}$ on a set X is a function $(-) \cdot_X (-)$ mapping pairs $(\pi, x) \in S_\mathbb{A} \times X$ to elements $\pi \cdot_X x \in X$ and satisfying

$$\pi' \cdot_X (\pi \cdot_X x) = (\pi'\pi) \cdot_X x \quad \text{and} \quad id_\mathbb{A} \cdot_X x = x$$

for all $\pi, \pi' \in S_\mathbb{A}$ and $x \in X$. For example, if Λ is the set of syntax trees of lambda terms with variable symbols from $\mathbb{A}$

$$\Lambda = \{t ::= a \mid t\,t \mid \lambda a.t \; (a \in \mathbb{A})\} \tag{38}$$

then there is a natural action of $S_\mathbb{A}$ on Λ: for each $\pi \in S_\mathbb{A}$ and $t \in \Lambda$, $\pi \cdot_\Lambda t$ is the tree which results from permuting all the atoms occurring in t according to π.

In general, an action of $S_\mathbb{A}$ on a set X gives us an abstract way of regarding the elements x of X as somehow 'involving atoms from $\mathbb{A}$ in their construction', in as much as the action tells us how permuting atoms changes x—which turns out to be all we need for an abstract theory of renaming and binding. An important part of this theory is the notion of *finite support*. This generalises the property of an abstract syntax tree that it only involves finitely many atoms in its construction to the abstract level of an element of any set equipped with an $S_\mathbb{A}$-action.

Definition A.1 (Finite support). Given a set X equipped with an action of $S_\mathbb{A}$, a set of semantic atoms $\omega \subseteq \mathbb{A}$ is said to *support* an element $x \in X$ if all permutations $\pi \in S_\mathbb{A}$ which fix every element of ω also fix x:

$$(\forall a \in \omega . \pi(a) = a) \Rightarrow \pi \cdot_X x = x \; . \tag{39}$$

We say that x is *finitely supported* if there is some finite subset $\omega \subseteq \mathbb{A}$ supporting it. It is not too hard to show that if x is finitely supported, then there is a smallest finite subset of $\mathbb{A}$ supporting it: we call this the *support* of x, and denote it by $supp_X(x)$.

Definition A.2 (The category FM-Set). An *FM-set* is a set X equipped with an action of the permutation group $S_\mathbb{A}$ in which every element $x \in X$ is finitely supported. These are the objects of a category, **FM-Set**, whose morphisms $f : X \longrightarrow Y$ are *equivariant functions*, i.e. functions from X to Y satisfying

$$f(\pi \cdot_X x) = \pi \cdot_Y f(x)$$

for all $\pi \in S_\mathbb{A}$ and $x \in X$.

Example A.3. The set Λ of untyped lambda terms, defined as in (38) and with the $S_\mathbb{A}$-action mentioned there, is an FM-set. The support of $t \in \Lambda$ is just the finite set of *all* variable symbols occurring in the tree t (whether free, bound, or binding). Note that if two lambda terms are α-equivalent, $t =_\alpha t'$, then for any permutation π one also has $\pi \cdot_\Lambda t =_\alpha \pi \cdot_\Lambda t'$. It follows that $(-) \cdot_\Lambda (-)$ induces an action on the quotient set $\Lambda/=_\alpha$. It is not hard to see that this is also an FM-set, with the support of an α-equivalence class of lambda terms being the finite set of *free* variable symbols in any representative of the class (it does not matter which). This turns out to be the denotation of the data type `lam` declared in Fig. 1 (using [7, Theorem 5.1]).

It should be emphasised that the above definitions are not novel, although the use to which we put them is. They are part of the rich mathematical theory of continuous actions of topological groups. $S_\mathbb{A}$ has a natural topology as a subspace of the countably infinite product of the discrete space $\mathbb{A}$, which makes it a topological group. Given an action of $S_\mathbb{A}$ on a set X, all the elements of X have finite support if and only if the action is a continuous function $S_\mathbb{A} \times X \longrightarrow X$ when X is given the discrete topology. Thus **FM-Set** is an example of a category of 'continuous G-sets' and as such, much is known about its properties: see [7, Sect. 6] for references. Here we just recall its cartesian closed structure.

A.1   Products in FM-Set

These are given by taking the cartesian product of underlying sets

$$X \times Y = \{ (x, y) \mid x \in X \text{ and } y \in Y \}.$$

The permutation action is given componentwise by that of X and Y:

$$\pi \cdot_{X \times Y} (x, y) \triangleq (\pi \cdot_X x, \pi \cdot_Y y) \qquad (\pi \in S_\mathbb{A}).$$

Each pair $(x, y) \in X \times Y$ does indeed have finite support, namely $supp_X(x) \cup supp_Y(y)$.

A.2   Exponentials in FM-Set

Given any function (not necessarily an equivariant one) $f : X \longrightarrow Y$ between FM-sets X and Y, we can make permutations of $\mathbb{A}$ act on f by defining

$$\pi \cdot_{X \to Y} f \triangleq \lambda x \in X. (\pi \cdot_Y f(\pi^{-1} \cdot_X x)) . \qquad (40)$$

By applying the property (39) with $\cdot_{X \to Y}$ in place of $\cdot_X$, it makes sense to ask whether f has finite support. The subset of all functions from X to Y which do have finite support in this sense, together with the action $\cdot_{X \to Y}$ given by (40), forms an FM-set which is the exponential $X \to Y$ in **FM-Set**. Note that (40) implies that for all $\pi \in S_\mathbb{A}$, $f \in (X \to Y)$ and $x \in X$

$$\pi \cdot_Y f(x) = (\pi \cdot_{X \to Y} f)(\pi \cdot_X x)$$

and hence evaluation $(f, x) \mapsto f(x)$ determines an equivariant function $ev : (X \to Y) \times X \longrightarrow Y$. Given any $f : Z \times X \longrightarrow Y$ in **FM-Set**, its exponential transpose $cur(f) : Z \longrightarrow (X \to Y)$ is given by the usual 'curried' version of f, for the following reason: given any $z \in Z$, if $\pi \in S_\mathbb{A}$ fixes each semantic atom in $supp_Z(z)$, then it is not hard to see from definition (40) and the equivariance of f that π fixes the function $\lambda x \in X. f(z, x)$ as well; so this function has finite support and hence is in $X \to Y$. So defining $cur(f)(z)$ to be $\lambda x \in X. f(z, x)$, we get a function $cur(f) : Z \longrightarrow (X \to Y)$; it is equivariant because f is and clearly has the property required for it to be the exponential transpose of f.

In the rest of this appendix we indicate the structures in the category **FM-Set** used to model the key novelties of FreshML: locally fresh atoms, atom abstraction and concretion of atom abstractions.

A.3   Locally Fresh Atoms

The set $\mathbb{A}$ of atoms becomes an object of **FM-Set** once we endow it with the action:

$$\pi \cdot_{\mathbb{A}} a \triangleq \pi(a) \quad (\pi \in S_{\mathbb{A}}, a \in \mathbb{A}).$$

(The support of $a \in \mathbb{A}$ is just $\{a\}$.) This FM-set is the denotation of the type atm of atoms in FreshML.

The meaning of **new a in** exp **end** in **FM-Set** is given by the following proposition (whose straightforward proof we omit). It makes use of the following construction in the category **FM-Set**: given an FM-set G, define

$$\mathbb{A} \otimes G \triangleq \{ (a, g) \in \mathbb{A} \times G \mid a \notin supp_G(g) \} \ .$$

This becomes an FM-set if we define a permutation action by

$$\pi \cdot_{\mathbb{A} \otimes G} (a, g) \triangleq (\pi(a), \pi \cdot_G g) \ .$$

Proposition A.1. *Given a morphism* $e : \mathbb{A} \otimes G \longrightarrow T$ *in* **FM-Set** *satisfying*

$$a \notin supp_T(e(a, g)) \quad \text{for all } (a, g) \in \mathbb{A} \otimes G \tag{41}$$

then there is a unique morphism $new(e) : G \longrightarrow T$ *such that*

$$new(e)(g) = e(a, g) \quad \text{for all } g \in G \text{ and } a \notin supp_G(g) \tag{42}$$

is satisfied.   □

If a typing context Γ has denotation G and if $\mathsf{a} \notin dom(\Gamma)$, then the denotation of the typing context $(\mathsf{a} : \mathsf{atm}) \otimes \Gamma$ used in rule (11) of Fig. 2 is the FM-set $\mathbb{A} \otimes G$. Suppose the denotation of $(\mathsf{a} : \mathsf{atm}) \otimes \Gamma \vdash exp : ty$ is the equivariant function $e : \mathbb{A} \otimes G \longrightarrow T$. We can use Proposition A.1 to give a denotation to $\Gamma \vdash (\mathbf{new\ a\ in}\ exp\ \mathbf{end}) : ty$ as $new(e) : G \longrightarrow T$, using the fact that the freshness part of the hypothesis of (11) means that e satisfies condition (41). The soundness of rule (11) follows from the defining property (42) of $new(e)$.

A.4   Abstraction and Concretion

If the denotation of the FreshML type ty is the FM-set T, the denotation of the atom abstraction type [atm] ty is the FM-set $[\mathbb{A}]T$ introduced in Sect. 4 of [7]. Its underlying set is the quotient of the cartesian product $\mathbb{A} \times T$ by the equivalence relation $\sim_{\mathbb{A}}$ defined as follows: $(a, t) \sim_{\mathbb{A}} (a', t')$ holds if and only if

$$(a''\ a) \cdot_T t = (a''\ a') \cdot_T t'$$

holds for some (or equivalently, any) a'' not in the support of $a, a', t,$ or t' (where $(a''\ a) \in S_{\mathbb{A}}$ denotes the permutation interchanging a'' and a). We write $a.t$ for the $\sim_\mathbb{A}$-equivalence class determined by (a,t).[7] The action of a permutation $\pi \in S_\mathbb{A}$ on elements of $[\mathbb{A}]T$ is given by:

$$\pi \cdot_{[\mathbb{A}]T} (a.t) \triangleq (\pi(a)).(\pi \cdot_T t) \ .$$

This does indeed determine a well-defined FM-set, with the support of $a.t$ being the finite set $supp_T(t) \smallsetminus \{a\}$.

If a is associated with the semantic atom $a \in \mathbb{A}$ (in some given value environment) and the denotation of $exp : ty$ is $t \in T$, then the denotation of the atom abstraction expression $a. exp$ is $a.t \in [\mathbb{A}]T$.

On the other hand, the meaning of concretion expressions (Sect. 4) uses the following property of FM-sets.

Proposition A.2. *Given an FM-set T, for each atom-abstraction $e \in [\mathbb{A}]T$ and semantic atom $a \in \mathbb{A}$, if $a \notin supp_{[\mathbb{A}]T}(e)$ then there is a unique element $e@a$ of T such that $e = a.(e@a)$.*

When $e = a'.t$ then $a \notin supp_{[\mathbb{A}]T}(e)$ if and only if $a = a'$ or $a \notin supp_T(t)$; and in this case $(a',t) \sim_\mathbb{A} (a,(a\,a') \cdot_T t)$. So when $a = a'$ or $a \notin supp_T(t)$, it follows from the uniqueness part of the defining property of $e@a$ that

$$(a'.t)@a = (a\,a') \cdot_T t \tag{43}$$

holds. □

The partial function $e, a \mapsto e@a$ is used to give the denotational semantics of concretion expressions, $exp@a$. The soundness of rule (13) follows from the easily verified fact that $supp_T(e@a) \subseteq supp_{[\mathbb{A}]T}(e) \cup \{a\}$.

Acknowledgements

The authors thank members of the Cambridge University *Logic and Semantics* group, Mark Shinwell (who is carrying out an implementation of FreshML), Simon Peyton Jones and the anonymous referees for constructive comments on the work presented here. This research was partially supported by the ESPRIT Working Group Nr 26142 on Applied Semantics (APPSEM).

References

1. R. Burstall, D. MacQueen, and D. Sannella. HOPE: An experimental applicative language. In *Proc. LISP Conference, Stanford CA, 1980*, pages 136–143. Stanford University, 1980. 230
2. R. M. Burstall. Design considerations for a functional programming language. In *Proc. of the Infotech State of the Art Conference, Copenhagen, 1977*. 230
3. G. Cousineau and M. Mauny. *The Functional Approach to Programming*. Cambridge University Press, 1998. 232

---

[7] The notation $[a]t$ was used for this in [7].

4. N. G. de Bruijn. Lambda calculus notation with nameless dummies, a tool for automatic formula manipulation, with application to the Church-Rosser theorem. *Indag. Math.*, 34:381–392, 1972. 231

5. M. P. Fiore, G. D. Plotkin, and D. Turi. Abstract syntax and variable binding. In *14th Annual Symposium on Logic in Computer Science*, pages 193–202. IEEE Computer Society Press, Washington, 1999. 241, 248, 249

6. M. J. Gabbay. *A Theory of Inductive Definitions with α-Conversion: Semantics, Implementation, and Meta-Language*. PhD thesis, Cambridge University, in preparation. 249

7. M. J. Gabbay and A. M. Pitts. A new approach to abstract syntax involving binders. In *14th Annual Symposium on Logic in Computer Science*, pages 214–224. IEEE Computer Society Press, Washington, 1999. 230, 232, 239, 240, 241, 248, 249, 250, 251, 252, 253, 254

8. M. J. C. Gordon and T. F. Melham. *Introduction to HOL*. Cambridge University Press, 1993. 231

9. M. Hofmann. Semantical analysis of higher-order abstract syntax. In *14th Annual Symposium on Logic in Computer Science*, pages 204–213. IEEE Computer Society Press, Washington, 1999. 248

10. D. Miller. An extension to ML to handle bound variables in data structures: Preliminary report. In *Proceedings of the Logical Frameworks BRA Workshop*, 1990. 248

11. R. Milner. *Communicating and Mobile Systems: the π-Calculus*. Cambridge University Press, 1999. 240

12. R. Milner, M. Tofte, R. Harper, and D. MacQueen. *The Definition of Standard ML (Revised)*. MIT Press, 1997. 232, 242, 247

13. J. C. Mitchell and G. D. Plotkin. Abstract types have existential types. *ACM Transactions on Programming Languages and Systems*, 10:470–502, 1988. 239

14. L. C. Paulson. *Isabelle: A Generic Theorem Prover*, volume 828 of *Lecture Notes in Computer Science*. Springer-Verlag, Berlin, 1994. 231

15. S. Peyton Jones and J. Hughes, editors. *Report on the Programming Language Haskell 98. A Non-strict Purely Functional Language*. February 1999. Available from <http:www.haskell.org>. 249

16. F. Pfenning and C. Elliott. Higher-order abstract syntax. In *Proc. ACM-SIGPLAN Conference on Programming Language Design and Implementation*, pages 199–208. ACM Press, 1988. 248

Author Index

Lecture Notes in Computer Science

For information about Vols. 1–1757
please contact your bookseller or Springer-Verlag